08 09 10

Cliff

Lighthouse

Tourist Association

rine Trees

Clinic

idential Area   Harbor

N

Osaka

Wakayama

Forbidden Zones

22nd

0 3 0 8 A M — ; a = 0 7
0 7 0 0 A M — ; J = 0 2
0 9 0 0 A M — ; F = 0 1
1 1 0 0 A M — ; H = 0 8
0 1 0 0 P M — ; J = 0 5
0 3 0 0 P M — ; H = 0 3
0 5 0 0 P M ; D = 0 8
0 7 0 0 P M — ; G = 0 1
0 9 0 0 P M — ; I = 0 3
1 1 0 0 P M — ; G = 0 9

23rd

0 1 0 0 A M — ; F = 0 7
0 3 0 0 A M — ; G = 0 3
0 5 0 0 A M — ; E = 0 4
0 7 0 0 A M — ; C = 0 8
0 9 0 0 A M — ; D = 0 2
1 1 0 0 A M — ; C = 0 3
0 1 0 0 P M — ; D = 0 7
0 3 0 0 P M — ; H = 0 4
0 5 0 0 P M — ; F = 0 9
0 7 0 0 P M — ; B = 0 9
0 9 0 0 P M — ; E = 1 0
1 1 0 0 P M — ; F = 0 4

Koushun Takami
Battle Royale

Translated from the Japanese by
Yuji Oniki

English translation © 2003 by Yuji Oniki/VIZ Media, LLC.
The BATTLE ROYALE logo is a trademark of VIZ Media, LLC.
All rights reserved
First published in Japan by Ota Shuppan in 1999
Editorial acknowledgement: Tomo Machiyama

First published in Great Britain in 2007 by
Gollancz
An imprint of the Orion Publishing Group
Orion House,
5 Upper St Martin's Lane,
London WC2H 9EA

10 9 8 7

A CIP catalogue record for this book
is available from the British Library

ISBN-13 978 0 57508 049 2

Book design: Izumi Evers

Printed and bound in the UK by
CPI Mackays, Chatham ME5 8TD

The Orion Publishing Group's policy is
to use papers that are natural, renewable
and recyclable products and made from wood
grown in sustainable forests. The logging and
manufacturing processes are expected to
conform to the environmental regulations
of the country of origin.

www.orionbooks.co.uk

I dedicate this to everyone I love.
Even though it might not be appreciated.

"A student is not a tangerine."
——Kinpachi Sakamoto, *Third Year Class B, Kinpachi Sensei*

"But tramps like us, baby we were born to run"
——Bruce Springsteen, "Born to Run"

"It's so hard to love"
——Motoharu Sano, "It's So Hard to Love"

"During all those last weeks I spent there, there was a peculiar evil feeling in the air——an atmosphere of suspicion, fear, uncertainty, and veiled hatred. You seemed to spend all your time holding whispered conversations in corners of cafés and wondering whether that person at the next table was a police spy.

"I do not know if I can bring home to you how deeply that action touched me. It sounds a small thing, but it was not. You have got to realize what was the feeling of the time——the horrible atmosphere of suspicion and hatred."

——George Orwell, *Homage to Catalonia*

Third Year Class B, Shiroiwa Junior High School Student List

MALES

1   Yoshio Akamatsu

2   Keita Iijima

3   Tatsumichi Oki

4   Toshinori Oda

5   Shogo Kawada

6   Kazuo Kiriyama

7   Yoshitoki Kuninobu

8   Yoji Kuramoto

9   Hiroshi Kuronaga

10   Ryuhei Sasagawa

11   Hiroki Sugimura

12   Yutaka Seto

13   Yuichiro Takiguchi

14   Sho Tsukioka

15   Shuya Nanahara

16   Kazushi Niida

17   Mitsuru Numai

18   Tadakatsu Hatagami

19   Shinji Mimura

20   Kyoichi Motobuchi

21   Kazuhiko Yamamoto

Females

Introduction

[A pro wrestling fan's rant in an alternate world]

What? Battle Royale? "What's Battle Royale?" Come on, don't tell me you don't know that!? Why bother coming to a pro wrestling match, huh? The name of a move? The name of a tournament? No, Battle Royale's a pro wrestling match. What? "Today?" Today, here, you mean? No, it's not today's program. It's only held in large arenas for big events. Look, there's Takako Inoue. O-oh, sorry. That's right Battle Royale. It's still held in the All Japan Pro Wrestling League. In a nutshell, let's see Battle Royale is—you know how your usual pro wrestling match is one on one or between paired up partners, well with Battle Royale, ten or twenty wrestlers all jump into the ring. And then you're free to attack anyone, one on one, or ten against one, it doesn't matter. It doesn't matter how many wrestlers pin someone down—what, you don't even know what a pin is? Once your back's on the mat, the count goes, one, two, three, you lose. It's no different from a normal match. Players can also forfeit, and occasionally someone'll get knocked out. Oh yeah, and there's the count out. You can also be disqualified by breaking the rules. Most wrestlers lose by falls in Battle Royale. Hey, go Takako, go! Go, go! O-oh, sorry sorry. In any case, the ones who fall lose, they have to leave the ring. Fewer and fewer players remain in the game. There're only two left in the end. One on one, a very serious match. One out of those two will eventually take a fall. Then there's only one player left in the ring, and he's the winner. He wins. He's given a huge trophy and prize money. Get it? Huh? What about players who've been friends? Well, at first, of course they help each other out. But in the end they have to fight each other. You have to follow the rules. Which also means you get to watch some rare matches. Like way back when the tag-team partners of Dynamite Kid and Davey Boy Smith were the remaining players. Same thing happened with tag-team partners Animal Warrior and Hawk Warrior. In that match though I don't remember which one, but the guy intentionally went for a count out letting his partner win, a display of camaraderie which was kind of a letdown. Oh, you can also team up with players who used to be your enemies.

But the moment you think you're teaming up to get rid of someone else, this sneaky *friend* can suddenly betray and beat you. Let's see, a Battle Royale I'd like to see now? Well given how many federations there are, I'd like to see a Battle Royale between the leaders of each federation. Keiji Mutoh, Shinya Hashimoto, Mitsuharu Misawa, Toshiaki Kawada, Nobuhiko Takada, Masakatsu Funaki, Akira Maeda, Great Sasuke, Hayabusa, Kenji Takano, also Genichiro Tenryu, Riki Choshu, Tatsumi Fujinami, and Kengo Kimura could still be in the running. It'd be fun to add Yoji Anjoh and Super Delfin. They might actually end up being the last two remaining players. For women's first of all, Takako, then Aja Kong, Manami Toyota, Kyoko Inoue, Yumiko Hotta, Akira Hokuto, Bull Nakano, of course Dynamite Kansai, and Cutey Suzuki and Hikari Fukuoka, Mayumi Ozaki, Shinobu Kandori, and Chigusa Nagayo and...what? How could you not know any of them? Did you really come here to watch pro wrestling? Oh, no no no no no, Takako, fight back ! Takako! All—right.

GOVERNMENT MEMO

Government Internal Memo 1997, No.
00387461 (Top Secret)

Dispatched by Central Authority
Secretariat Special Task Force Defense
Supervisor and Battle Experiment
Advisor of the Special Defense Army

To: Supervisor in Charge of No. 12
1997 Battle Experiment No. 68 Program
(May 20, 18:15)

We have confirmed evidence of an
intrusion into the central government
operations system. The intrusion was
undetected on the date of its occur-
rence, March 12. We are currently
investigating any additional evidence
of re-entry.

The suspect's possible identity, purpose and any possible information
leaks are also being investigated, but
because the suspect's computer skills
were highly advanced, we anticipate a
significant delay in producing the
suspect's profile.

The Central Authority Secretariat

Special Task Force Defense Supervisor
and the Battle Experiment Division of
the Special Defense Army were informed
that data from Program No. 68 may have
been corrupted, and as a result we
immediately considered the postpone-
ment of Program No. 12 for 1997.

However, because preparations for No.
12 are complete, and because there is
no indication that the above data has
been leaked into the civilian population, we have concluded the program
should proceed as scheduled. However,
we will be considering rescheduling
future programs following No. 12, as
well as implementing design changes in
"Guadalcanal."

As the supervisor in charge of executing the experiment, you, supervisor of
Program No. 12 are to proceed with
extreme caution.

Furthermore, this infiltration incident is classified top secret information and is to be treated as such.

PART I

START GAME

42 students remaining

O

As the bus entered the prefectural capital of Takamatsu, garden suburbs transformed into city streets of multicolored neon, headlights of oncoming cars, and checkered lights of office buildings. A group of well dressed men and women stood talking to each other in front of a streetside restaurant while they waited for a taxi. Tired, squatting youths smoked in the clean parking lot of a convenience store. A worker on his bicycle waited for the lights to change at the crossing. It was chilly for a May evening, so the man had put on his worn out jacket. Along with these other drifting impressions, the worker disappeared behind the bus window, swallowed by the low engine rumble. The digital display above the bus driver's head changed to 8:57.

Shuya Nanahara (Male Student No. 15, Third Year Class B, Shiroiwa Junior High School, Shiroiwa Town, Kagawa Prefecture) had been staring outside, leaning over Yoshitoki Kuninobu (Male Student No. 7), who had the window seat. As Yoshitoki dug through his bag, Shuya stared at his own right foot, which was sticking out in the aisle, and stretched out his Keds sneakers with his toes. It used to be that Keds weren't hard to find, but now they were extremely rare. The canvas of Shuya's shoes were torn on the right heel, and the stray threads stuck out like cat's whiskers. The shoe company was American, but the shoes themselves were made in Colombia. At present, 1997, the Republic of Greater East Asia hardly suffered from a shortage of goods. In fact it was rich with commodities, but imports were hard to come by lately. Well, it was only to be expected in a country with an official policy of isolationism. Besides, America—both the government and the textbooks called them "the American Imperialists"—was an enemy state.

From the back of the bus, Shuya watched his forty-one

classmates, who were illuminated by dull fluorescent lights fixed in dingy ceiling panels. They were all in the same class from last year. They were all still excited and chatting away, since hardly an hour had passed since their departure from their hometown of Shiroiwa. Spending the first night of a study trip on a bus seemed a little cheap. Worse yet, it felt like they were going on a forced march. But everyone would calm down once the bus crossed the Seto Bridge and got on the Sanyo Highway and headed towards their destination, the island of Kyushu.

The loud students at the front who were sitting around their teacher Mr. Hayashida were girls: Yukie Utsumi (Female Student No. 2), the class representative who looked good with braided hair; Haruka Tanizawa (Female Student No. 12), her volleyball teammate who was exceptionally tall, Izumi Kanai (Female Student No. 5), the preppy whose father was a town representative; Satomi Noda (Female Student No. 17), the model student who wore wire-rimmed glasses which suited her calm, intelligent face; and Chisato Matsui (Female Student No. 19), who was always quiet and withdrawn. They were the mainstream girls. You could call them "the neutrals." Girls tended to form cliques, but there weren't any particular groups that stuck out in Shiroiwa Junior High School's Third Year Class B, so categorizing them didn't seem right. If there was a group, it was the rebel or—to put it more bluntly—the *delinquent* group led by Mitsuko Souma (Female Student No. 11). Hirono Shimizu (Female Student No. 10) and Yoshimi Yahagi (Female Student No. 21) rounded out that bunch. Shuya couldn't see them from where he was sitting.

The seats right behind the driver were slightly raised, and popping up above them were the two heads of Kazuhiko Yamamoto (Male Student No. 21) and Sakura Ogawa (Female Student No. 4), the most intimate couple in the class. Maybe they were laughing, because their heads shook slightly. They were so insular, the most trivial thing could have been entertaining them.

Closer to Shuya, lying in the aisle, was a large school uniform. It belonged to Yoshio Akamatsu (Male Student No. 1). He was the biggest kid in the class, but he was the timid type, the kind of kid who'd always end up the target of pranks and insults. His big body was crouched over, and he was busy playing a handheld video game.

Also in the aisle were the jocks Tatsumichi Oki (Male Student No. 3, handball team), Kazushi Niida (Male Student No. 16, soccer team), and Tadakatsu Hatagami (Male Student No. 18). They were all sitting together. Shuya himself had played Little League baseball in elementary school and was known as a star shortstop. Actually he'd been friends with Tadakatsu, but they'd stopped hanging out. Partly this was because Shuya had stopped playing baseball, but it also had to do with the fact that Shuya had started playing electric guitar, which was considered an "unpatriotic" activity. Tadakatsu's mother was uptight about that sort of thing.

Yes, rock was outlawed in this country. (Of course there were loopholes. Shuya's electric guitar came with a government-approved sticker which read, "Decadent Music Is Strictly Prohibited." Decadent music was rock.)

Come to think of it, Shuya thought, I've changed my friends too.

He heard someone laugh quietly behind big Yoshio Akamatsu. It was one of Shuya's new friends, Shinji Mimura. Shinji had short hair and wore an intricately designed ring on his left ear. By the time Shuya and Shinji became classmates in their second year, Shuya had already heard of him. Shinji was known as "The Third Man"—the team's first-string shooting guard. His athletic skill was equal to

Shuya's, though Shinji would have said, "I'm better, bro." Together on the basketball court for the first time in their second-year class competition, they made for a deadly combo, so it was only natural they'd hit it off. There was a lot more to Shinji than sports, though. His grades in subjects other than math and English weren't great, but his breadth of real world knowledge was incredible, and his views were mature, way beyond his peers. He somehow had an answer for any question about overseas information that couldn't be obtained in this country. And he always knew the best thing to say when you were down, like, "You know it, I'm the man." But he was never arrogant. Instead he'd smile and crack a joke. He was never full of himself. Basically Shinji Mimura was a good guy.

Shinji appeared to be sitting next to his buddy from grade school, Yutaka Seto (Male Student No. 12), the class clown. Yutaka must have cracked another joke, because Shinji was laughing.

Hiroki Sugimura (Male Student No. 11) sat behind them. His tall, lanky body barely fit into the narrow seat. He was reading a paperback book. Hiroki was reserved and studied martial arts, so he projected toughness. He didn't hang out with the other guys much, but once you got to know him a little he turned out to be nice. He was just shy. Shuya got along with him. Was he reading that book of Chinese poetry he liked so much? (Chinese books in translation were fairly easy to obtain, not surprising considering the Republic claimed China as "part of our homeland.")

Shuya once came across a line in an American paperback novel he'd dug out from a used bookstore (he managed to get through it with a dictionary): *friends come and then they go.* Maybe that's how things were. Just as he and Tadakatsu were no longer friends, there might come a time when he wasn't friends with Shinji and Hiroki anymore.

Well, maybe not.

Shuya glanced at Yoshitoki Kuninobu, who was still digging through his bag. Shuya had made it this far with Yoshitoki Kuninobu. And that would never change. After all they were friends ever since they wet their beds at that Catholic institution with the bombastic name, "the Charity House"—where orphans or other children who, due to "circumstances," were no longer able to be with their parents. You could say they were almost cursed to be friends.

Maybe we should cover religion while we're at it. In fact this country, under a unique system of national socialism ruled over by an executive authority called "the Dictator" (Shinji Mimura once said with a grimace, "This is what they call 'successful fascism.' Where else in the world could you find something so sinister?"), had no national religion. The closest thing to religion was faith in the political system— but this wasn't paired up with any established religion. Religious practice therefore was permitted as long as it remained moderate and at the same time wasn't guaranteed. So it was only practiced in private by dedicated followers. Shuya himself never really had any religious inclinations, but it was thanks to this particular religion's institution that he managed to grow up relatively unscathed and normal. He thought he should appreciate that much. There were state orphanages, but apparently their accommodations and programs were poorly run, and from what he heard they served as training schools for Special Defense Forces soldiers.

Shuya turned around and looked back. The group of delinquents that included Ryuhei Sasagawa (Male Student No. 10) and Mitsuru Numai (Male Student No. 17) was sitting on the wide seat at the back of the bus. There was…Shuya couldn't see his face, but he could see between the seats the head with the oddly styled, slicked-back, long hair poking out by the right window. Though on its left side (well, it seemed Ryuhei Sasagawa had left two seats open in between) the others were talking and laughing over something dirty, the head remained absolutely still. Perhaps he'd fallen asleep. Or maybe like Shuya he was watching the city lights.

Shuya was completely baffled by the fact that this boy— Kazuo Kiriyama (Male Student No. 6)—would actually participate in a childish activity like a study trip.

Kiriyama was the leader of the thugs in their district, a group that included Ryuhei and Mitsuru. Kiriyama was by no means big. At best he was the same height as Shuya, but he could easily pin down high school students and even take on local yakuza. His reputation was legendary throughout the entire prefecture. And his father being the president of a leading corporation didn't hurt. (There were rumors though that he was an illegitimate child. Shuya wasn't interested, so he never bothered to find out more.) Of course that wouldn't have been enough. He had a handsome, intelligent face, and his voice wasn't particularly low, but there was something intimidating about it. He was the top student in Class B, and the only one who barely kept up with him was Kyoichi Motobuchi (Male Student No. 20), who studied so hard he didn't get much sleep. In sports Kazuo was better and more graceful than almost anyone else in the class. The only ones at Shiroiwa Junior High who could compete with him seriously were, yes, the former star shortstop, Shuya, and the current star shooting guard, Shinji Mimura. So in every respect Kazuo Kiriyama was perfect.

But then how could someone this perfect end up a leader of thugs? That was really none of Shuya's business. But if there was one thing Shuya could tell, it was a sense, almost tactile, that Kazuo was different. Shuya couldn't say exactly how. Kazuo never did anything bad in school. He'd never bully around someone like Yoshio Akamatsu the way Ryuhei

Sasagawa did. But there was something so…remote about him. Was that it? At least that's how it felt.

He was absent a lot. The idea of Kazuo "studying" was completely absurd. In every class Kiriyama remained quietly seated at his desk as if he were thinking of something that had nothing to do with class. Shuya thought, if the government didn't have the power to enforce compulsory education on us, he probably wouldn't come to school at all. On the other hand he might just show up on a whim. I don't know. In any case, Shuya thought, I expected Kazuo to skip something as trivial as a study trip, but then he promptly shows up. Was this on a whim too?

"Shuya."

Shuya was staring at the ceiling panel lights wondering about Kiriyama when a perky voice interrupted his thoughts. From the seat across the aisle, Noriko Nakagawa (Female Student No. 15) offered something wrapped in crisp cellophane. The bag sparkled like water under the white light, and it was filled with light-brown discs—cookies, probably. On top was a bow tied with a gold ribbon.

Noriko Nakagawa was another girl who was neutral like Yukie Utsumi's group. Other than her kind eyes, which were noticeably dark, she had a round, girlish face and shoulder-length hair. She was petite and playful. In short, she was an average girl. If there was something particular about her, it was probably the fact that she wrote the best compositions in literature class. (This was how Shuya got to know Noriko. Shuya would spend break periods writing lyrics for his songs in the margins of his notebooks, and Noriko would insist on reading them.) She usually hung with Yukie's group, but because she'd showed up late today, she had no other choice but to take an open seat.

Shuya half-extended his hand and raised his brow. For some reason Noriko became flustered and said, "They're leftovers from the ones my brother begged me to bake. They're best fresh, so I brought them for you and Mr. Nobu."

"Mr. Nobu" was Yoshitoki Kuninobu's nickname. Although he had bulging, friendly eyes, the nickname seemed appropriate for someone who could be, oddly enough, mature and wise. None of the girls called him by that name, but Noriko had no problem calling the boys by their nicknames, and the fact that this hardly offended any of them indicated how uniquely disarming she was. (Shuya had a sports-related nickname, the same name as a famous cigarette brand, but in the same way that Shinji was referred to as "The Third Man" no one called him by this to his face.) He'd already noticed this before, Shuya observed, but she's the only girl who calls me by my first name.

Yoshitoki, who'd been listening in on them, interrupted. "Really? For us? Thanks so much! If you made them, I bet they're delicious."

Yoshitoki snatched the bag from Shuya's hand, quickly untied the ribbon, and took out a cookie.

"Wow, these are awesome."

As Yoshitoki praised Noriko, Shuya grinned. Could he be more obvious? The moment Noriko sat next to Shuya he'd been repeatedly glancing over at her, sitting upright, completely nervous.

It was a month and a half ago during spring vacation. Shuya and Yoshitoki had gone fishing for black bass at the dam reservoir that provided the city its water supply. Yoshitoki confessed to Shuya, "Hey Shuya, I got a crush on someone."

"Huh. Who is it?"

"Nakagawa."

"You mean from our class?"

"Yeah."

"Which one? There are two Nakagawas. Yuka Nakagawa?"

"Hey, unlike you, I'm not into fat girls."

"What the...? So you're saying Kazumi is fat? She's just a little plump."

"Sorry. Anyway, well, uh yeah, it's Noriko."

"Huh. Well, she's nice."

"Isn't she though? Isn't she?"

"All right, all right."

Yes, Yoshitoki was totally obvious. But in spite of his behavior Noriko seemed oblivious to Yoshitoki's feelings for her. Maybe she was slow with stuff like this or something. It wasn't surprising, given her personality.

Shuya took a cookie from the bag still in Yoshitoki's hand and examined it. Then he looked over at Noriko.

"So they lose their flavor?"

"Uh huh," she nodded. Her eyes strained, oddly. "That's right."

"Which means you're sure they taste pretty good."

He might have learned this form of sarcasm from Shinji Mimura. Shuya often used it lately, to the dismay of other classmates, but Noriko just emitted a happy laugh and said, "I guess so."

"Come on," Yoshitoki interrupted again. "I told you they were good, didn't I, Noriko?"

Noriko smiled. "Thanks. You're so nice."

Yoshitoki all of a sudden froze up as if he'd jammed his finger into an electric outlet and turned mute. Staring silently into his lap, he proceeded to devour his cookie.

Shuya grinned and ate the rest of his cookie. The warm, sweet taste and smell spread through his mouth.

"These are good," Shuya said.

Noriko, who'd been observing him all this time, exclaimed, "Thank you!" He could be wrong, but somehow the tone of her voice was different than when she thanked Yoshitoki. Well, wait...true, she was staring at him while he was eating the cookie. Were they really leftovers from the batch she'd baked for her brother? Maybe she'd baked them for "someone else." Or maybe he was just plain wrong.

Then for some reason Shuya thought of Kazumi. She was a year ahead, and a fellow music club member until last year.

In the Republic of Greater East Asia, rock music was strictly prohibited in school club activities, but when their adviser Ms. Miyata was absent, music club members would play rock on their own. That was the kind of membership the club attracted in the first place anyway. Kazumi Shintani was the best female saxophone player. When it came to rock saxophone though, she was the best in the entire club. She was tall (almost the same height as Shuya, who stood 170 centimeters) and plump, but with her remarkably mature face and her hair bundled by her shoulders, she looked awesome with her alto saxophone. Shuya was thrilled by the sight. Then she taught Shuya how to play difficult guitar chords. (She said, "I played a little before I started playing the saxophone.") From that point on Shuya spent every spare minute he had practicing his guitar, and by his second year he was the best player in the club. It was all because he wanted Kazumi to hear him play.

Then one day, when the two of them happened to be alone in the music room after school, Shuya played and sang a version of "Summertime Blues" which impressed her. "That was so great, Shuya. That was so awesome." That day Shuya bought a can of beer for the first time in his life and celebrated with a private toast. It tasted great. But three days later when he asked her out, confessing, "Um, I really like you," she responded, "I'm sorry, I'm already going out with someone." She graduated and went to a high school with a music department, along with her "boyfriend."

Which reminded Shuya of his conversation with

Yoshitoki at the dam over spring break. After sharing his feelings for Noriko, Yoshitoki asked him, "Are you still hung up on Kazumi?" Shuya answered, "Yeah, I think I'll be hung up over her the rest of my life." Yoshitoki looked stumped. "But she has a boyfriend, right?" Throwing the silver lure with all his might as if throwing a ball in from the outfield, he answered, "That doesn't matter."

Shuya took the bag of cookies from Yoshitoki, who was still staring down into his lap. "Aren't you going to leave some for Noriko?"

"O-oh yeah, I'm sorry."

Shuya returned the bag to Noriko. "Sorry about that."

"That's all right. I don't mind. You guys should take them all."

"Really? But we shouldn't be the only ones."

Shuya took his first glance at the guy sitting next to Noriko. Wrapped in his school uniform, Shogo Kawada (Male Student No. 5) leaned against the window with his arms crossed and his eyes closed. He might have been asleep. His hair was cropped so short he looked like a monk. His slightly stubbled face reminded Shuya of a punk racketeer at a carnival. Wow, facial hair, everyone! Doesn't he look kind of old for a junior high school student?

Well, there was one thing he knew. Although Class B consisted of the same students as it did last year, Shogo Kawada had transferred last April from Kobe. And due to some circumstance, an injury or illness (he didn't look like the bedridden type so it must have been an injury), Kawada had to stay behind a year because he was unable to attend school for over six months. In other words he was one year older than Shuya and his classmates. Shuya himself never told anyone this, but that was what Shuya had heard.

In fact he hadn't heard good things about Shogo. There was a rumor that he'd been a notorious thug at his last school and that his hospitalization was a result of a fight. To support this rumor, his body was covered with scars. A long scar from what appeared to be a knife wound ran over his left brow, and when they changed in the gym lockers (this was besides the point, but Kawada's body was built like a middleweight boxer's), Shuya was shocked to find the same kind of scars covering his arms and back. There were two round scars next to each other on his left shoulder. They looked like gunshot wounds, but that was unbelievable.

Every time he heard these rumors about Shogo, someone would inevitably suggest, "He's probably going to end up fighting Kazuo." Right after Shogo transferred to their school that fool Ryuhei Sasagawa tried to intimidate Shogo. The exact details of what followed were only hearsay, but apparently Ryuhei turned pale, retreated, and went crying for help from Kazuo. Kazuo looked indifferent though, and only glanced at Ryuhei. He didn't even say a word to Shogo. So at least for the time being they'd managed to avoid a confrontation. Kazuo didn't seem interested in Shogo. Shogo didn't seem interested in Kazuo. As a result Class B remained peaceful. They lucked out.

Everybody avoided Shogo because of his age difference and the rumors. But Shuya didn't like judging people on rumors. Someone once said, if you could see for yourself then there'd be no need to lend an ear to what others said.

Shuya pointed his chin past Noriko toward Shogo.

"I wonder if he's sleeping."

"Hmm…" She glanced over at Shogo.

"I didn't want to wake him up."

"He doesn't look like the type who's into cookies anyway."

Noriko chuckled, and as Shuya was about to, they heard, "No thanks."

Shuya glanced back at Shogo.

The strong, low voice echoed in his head.

Although Shuya wasn't familiar with the voice it obviously

came from Shogo, who still kept his eyes closed, though he didn't seem asleep. Shuya all of a sudden realized he'd rarely ever heard Shogo's voice, even though Shogo had transferred to their school over a month ago.

Noriko glanced at Shogo and then looked at Shuya. Shuya shrugged in response and crammed another cookie into his mouth.

He continued chatting with Noriko and Yoshitoki for awhile but...

It was almost ten o'clock when Shuya noticed something strange.

Something weird was happening inside the bus. Yoshitoki, who was on his left, had suddenly fallen asleep and was softly breathing. Shinji Mimura's body was slouching into the aisle. Noriko Nakagawa was also asleep. No one seemed to be talking. Everyone seemed to be asleep. Well yeah, anyone excessively health-conscious might be going to bed now, but still, this was their long awaited trip. Wasn't it a bit early to fall asleep right after leaving? Why doesn't everyone sing or something? Doesn't this bus have one of those atrocious machines Shuya hated—karaoke?

Worst of all, Shuya himself was overcome with drowsiness. He looked around in a daze...then he couldn't even move his head, which felt heavy. He slouched against the seat. His eyes drifted through the narrow space to the rearview mirror at the center of the large windshield fading in the dark....He managed to make out the tiny image of the driver's upper body.

The driver's face was covered with what appeared to be a mask. A hoselike tube extended downward from the mask. Thin straps were wrapped around his head, strapped above and below his ears. What was that? Except for the hose extending downward, it resembled an airline emergency oxygen mask.

So we can't breathe inside this bus? Ladies and gentlemen, this bus will be making an emergency landing due to engine trouble. Like, please fasten your seat belts, wear your oxygen masks, and follow crew member's instructions? Yeah, right.

He heard a scratching sound on the right. Shuya had to struggle to catch a glimpse over there. His body felt so heavy. It was as if he were immersed in transparent jelly.

Shogo Kawada was standing up and struggling to pry open a window. But whether it was jammed shut from rust or a broken lock, the window refused to budge. Shogo slammed his left fist against the glass. He's trying to break the glass. Why all the fuss?

But the glass didn't break. The fist ready to strike the glass all of a sudden went limp and clumsily dropped. His body collapsed into the seat. Shuya thought he heard that low voice he'd only recently familiarized himself with faintly gasp, "Damn."

Almost immediately Shuya fell asleep too.

At approximately the same time, students' families in Shiroiwa were visited by men in black sedans. Alarmed by the late night visit, the parents must have been shocked when the visitors presented them with documents stamped with the government's official peach insignia.

In most cases the parents would silently nod as they thought of their children whom they most likely would never see again, but there were those who frantically protested, in which case they would be knocked out by an electroshock baton, or in the worst case, be pummeled by fresh bullets spat out from a submachine gun, one step ahead of their children in departing from this world.

By then the bus assigned to Shiroiwa Junior High School's Third Year Class B's study trip had long since branched off from the rows of other buses and taken a U-turn towards the city of Takamatsu. After returning to the city it wove its way through various roads before it finally stopped and quietly turned off its engine.

The man in his forties whose hair was peppered gray looked like a typical nice bus driver. Still wearing the oxygen mask that was digging into his slightly sagging chin, he turned towards the Class B students with a faint look of pity. But as soon as another man appeared under the window, his face stiffened. He gave the Republic's idiosyncratic salute. Then he pressed the switch to open the door. Shuya glanced outside as the masked men in battle gear came rushing in.

Under the moonlight, the bluish-white concrete pier gleamed like bone, and beyond the pier the ship that would transport "the players" was swaying sluggishly in the wide open black sea.

42 students remaining

I

For a moment Shuya thought he was in a familiar classroom.

It wasn't the usual Third Year Class B classroom of course, but there was a lectern, a worn out blackboard, and on the left, a tall stand with a large television. There were rows of desks and chairs made of plywood glued onto steel tubes. On Shuya's desk someone had carved anti-government graffiti into the corner with a pen: "the Dictator loves women in uniform." Then he noticed everyone at their desks, the boys clad in buttoned up school uniforms and the girls in their sailor suit school uniforms, all forty-one classmates who'd only moments ago (at least that's what it felt like) been riding the bus together. The only thing was—

either sprawled over their desks or slouched back in their seats—they were all completely asleep.

From beside the frosted window on the side of the hall (assuming this building had the same layout as his school), Shuya surveyed the rest of the room. He seemed to be the only one awake. In front of him to his left and towards the middle of the room was Yoshitoki Kuninobu. Behind him was Noriko Nakagawa, and beyond Yoshitoki was Shinji Mimura. They were all sprawled on their desks, sleeping deeply. Hiroki Sugimura surrendered his large body to his desk (that was when it finally dawned on Shuya that the seating assignment was identical to the one they had at Shiroiwa Junior High School) by the windows on the left side. That was also when he began to realize why the place felt odd. The windows beyond Hiroki's body appeared to be covered with some kind of black board. Steel sheets? They provided an icy reflection of the dull light from the rows of fluorescent lights hanging from the ceiling. The frosted glass windows on the side of the hall seemed to be draped in black. Maybe they were boarded up too. It was impossible to determine the time of day.

Shuya looked at his wristwatch. It read one o'clock. In the morning? In the afternoon? The date read "Thurs/22," which meant that, unless someone had tampered with his watch, either three or fifteen hours had passed since he had that strange attack of drowsiness. All right, let's just assume that's the case. Still...

Shuya looked at his classmates.

Something felt off. Of course the whole situation was strange. But there was something in particular that disturbed him.

Shuya immediately realized what it was. Face down on her desk, Noriko had above her collar a silver metal band wrapped snugly around her neck. Because of his buttoned up collar Yoshitoki Kuninobu's band was barely visible, but Shuya managed to see it. Shinji Mimura, Hiroki Sugimura, everyone had one on their necks.

Then the thought occurred to Shuya. He reached for his own neck with his right hand.

He felt something hard and cold. The same thing must have been wrapped around his neck.

Shuya tugged at it a little but the fit was so tight it refused to budge. The moment he became conscious of it, he felt like he was suffocating. Steel collars! Steel collars as if we're dogs, damn!

He fidgeted with it for a while with his fingers, but then gave up. He wondered instead...

What happened to the study trip? Shuya noticed his sports bag sitting by his feet on the floor. Last night he'd casually tossed his clothes, towel, school field trip notebook, and a bourbon flask into it. Everyone else also had their bags by their feet.

Suddenly a loud noise erupted from the front entrance, and the door slid open. Shuya looked up.

A man came in.

He was stocky but well built. His legs were extremely short, as if they served as a mere appendage to his torso. He wore light-beige slacks, a gray jacket, a red necktie, and black loafers. They all looked worn out. A peach-colored badge was pinned to the collar of his jacket, indicating his affiliation with the government. His cheeks were rosy. What stuck out most though was the man's hairstyle. He wore it down to his shoulders like a woman in her prime. It reminded Shuya of the grainy Xeroxed tape cover of a Joan Baez tape he'd bought on the black market.

The man stood at the lectern and surveyed the classroom. His eyes stopped at Shuya, who was the only one awake (assuming this wasn't a dream).

The two stared at each other for at least a full minute. But perhaps because the other students were waking up, with their nervous breathing gradually spreading through the entire classroom, the man looked away from Shuya. Their voices woke up other classmates from their deep slumber.

Shuya looked at the rest of the classroom. As they woke up their eyes remained out of focus. Everyone was clueless. His eyes met Yoshitoki Kuninobu's as his friend turned back. Shuya pointed at his collar, tilting his neck slightly. Yoshitoki immediately touched his neck. He looked shocked. He shook his head left and right and turned to the lectern. Noriko Nakagawa also looked at Shuya with a dazed look. Shuya could only shrug in response.

As soon as everyone seemed awake the man spoke up in a cheerful voice, "All right, everyone awake? I hope you all slept well!"

No one replied. Even the class clowns, Yutaka Seto and Yuka Nakagawa (Female Student No. 16), were speechless.

42 students remaining

2

Wearing a broad grin, the man with long hair continued behind the lectern, "All right, all right. Then I shall proceed with the introduction. First of all, I am your new instructor, Kinpatsu Sakamochi."

The man who introduced himself as Sakamochi turned towards the blackboard and wrote his name in large vertical letters with the chalk. "Kinpatsu Sakamochi"? Was this some kind of joke? Given the situation, maybe it was a pseudonym.

Suddenly the female class representative, Yukie Utsumi,

stood up and said, "I don't understand what's going on here." Everyone looked over at Yukie. With her long hair neatly braided into a pair of pony tails, she looked pretty wound up, but her voice remained assertive. Nonetheless, Yukie probably had to delude herself into believing they'd been through a traffic accident or some other event that caused them all to lose consciousness.

Yukie continued, "What's going on here? We were all in the middle of our study trip. Right, everyone?"

She turned around and looked at everyone, setting off an avalanche of cries:

"Where are we?"

"Did you fall asleep too?"

"What time is it anyway?"

"Was everyone asleep?"

"Damn, I don't have a watch."

"Do you remember getting off the bus, coming here?"

"Who the hell is he?"

"I don't remember a thing."

"This is terrible. What's going on? I'm scared."

After observing Sakamochi quietly listening to them, Shuya slowly surveyed the room. There were several others who remained silent.

The first one he noticed was sitting at an angle behind him in the back row in the middle. It was Kazuo Kiriyama. Beneath his slicked-back hair his calm eyes were staring at the man at the lectern. His look was so calm, it didn't even resemble a glare. He paid no attention to his circle of followers addressing him: Ryuhei Sasagawa, Mitsuru Numai, Hiroshi Kuronaga (Male Student No. 9), and Sho Tsukioka (Male Student No. 14).

Then there was Mitsuko Souma, sitting in the second row by the window. She was the one who looked jaded. Her seat was separated from the rest of her "group," which consisted of Hirono Shimizu and Yoshimi Yahagi. Of course none of the other girls, nor boys for that matter, would even attempt to talk to her. (On Shuya's left, Hirono and Yoshimi were speaking to each other.) Even though Mitsuko had the gorgeous looks of a pop idol, she always wore a strange, listless expression on her face. She stared at Sakamochi with her arms folded. (Hiroki Sugimura sat right behind her, talking to Tadakatsu Hatagami.)

Shogo Kawada sat at the second to last row by the window. He was also silently staring at Sakamochi. But he took out a piece of gum, then began chewing it, continuing to stare at the teacher as his jaw moved.

Shuya looked to the front of the class. Noriko Nakagawa was still staring back at him. Her dark eyes were trembling nervously. Shuya glanced over at Yoshitoki, who was sitting in front of her, but Yoshitoki was busy talking to Shinji Mimura. Shuya immediately glanced back at Noriko, tucked his chin in slightly, and nodded. It seemed to have a calming effect on her. Her eyes seemed to relax a little.

"All right, all right, please be quiet." Sakamochi clapped his hands together several times to get their attention. The clamor suddenly subsided. "Let me explain the situation. The reason why you're all here today then…"

Then he said: "…is to kill each other."

Now no one responded. Everyone remained frozen, like figures in a still photograph. But—Shuya noticed—Shogo continued chewing his gum. His expression hadn't changed. But Shuya thought he'd caught a glimpse of a faint grin flash across his face.

Sakamochi continued smiling and resumed, "Your class has been selected for this year's 'Program.' "

Someone shrieked.

42 students remaining

3

Every junior high school student in the Republic of Greater East Asia knew what the Program was. It was even covered in school textbooks from the fourth grade on. Here we will quote from the more detailed *Republic of Greater East Asia Compact Encyclopedia:*

"**Program** *n.* 1. A listing of the order of events and other information [...] 4. A battle simulation program conducted by our nation's ground defense forces, instituted for security reasons. Officially known as Battle Experiment No. 68 Program. The first program was held in 1947. Fifty third-year junior high school classes are selected annually (prior to 1950, 47 classes were selected) to conduct the Program for research purposes. Classmates in each class are forced to fight until one survivor is left. Results from this experiment, including the elapsed time, are entered as data. The final survivor of each class (the winner) is provided with a lifetime pension and a card autographed by The Great Dictator. In reaction to protests and agitation caused by extremists during the first year of its enactment, the 317th Great Dictator gave his famous 'April Speech.' "

The "April Speech" is required reading in the first year of junior high school. Here are some excerpts:

"My beloved comrades working for the Revolution and building our beloved nation. *[Two-minute interruption for the 317th Great Dictator due to applause and cheers]* Now then. *[One-minute interruption]* We still have shameless imperialists prowling our republic, attempting to sabotage it. They have exploited the people of other nations, nations that should have become our comrades, betraying them, brainwashing them, and turning them into pawns for their own imperialist tactics. *[unanimous cry of indignation]* And they would jump at the chance to invade the soil of our republic, the most advanced revolutionary state in the world, revealing its evil scheme to destroy our people. *[Angry shouts from the crowd]* Given this dire circumstance the No. 68 Program experiment is absolutely necessary for our nation. Of course, I grieve at the thought of thousands, tens of thousands of youths losing their lives at the ripe age of fifteen. But if their lives serve to protect our people's independence, can we not claim then that the flesh and blood they shed shall merge with our beautiful soil passed down to us by our gods and live with us in eternity? *[Applause, a surge of cheering. One minute interruption]* As you are all aware, our nation has no conscription system. The Army, Navy, and Air Special Defense Forces, all consist of patriotic souls, young volunteers every one of them, passionate fighters for the Revolution and the building of our nation. They are risking their lives every day and night at the frontlines. I would like you to consider the Program as a conscription system unique to this country. In order to protect our nation, etc..."

Enough already. (Right outside the train station the middle-aged Special Forces recruiter would approach potential candidates with the catch phrase, "How about we go get some pork rice?") Shuya first heard about the Program before becoming a fourth grader. It was when he finally got used to the Charity House, where he was brought by a friend of his parents after both of them died in a traffic accident. (All his relatives had refused to take him in. He heard it was because his parents had been involved in anti-government activities, but he never confirmed this story.) Shuya thought it was when he was five. He was watching television in the play room with Yoshitoki Kuninobu, who'd been at the Charity House before Shuya. His favorite robot anime show had just ended and the current superintendent of the institution, Ms. Ryoko Anno (the daughter of the former superintendent; at the time she was probably still a high school student, but everyone who worked there was called Mr., Mrs., or Ms.) switched the channel. Shuya was just gazing at the screen, but as soon as he saw the man in a stiff suit addressing him, he realized it was only that boring show called "The News," the program they showed on every channel at various times.

The man was reading from his script. Shuya couldn't remember exactly what he said but it was always the same and probably went something like this:

"We have received a report from the Special Defense Forces and the government that the Program in Kagawa Prefecture ended yesterday at 3:12 p.m. It has been three years since the last Program was conducted here. The subject class was Third Year E Class from Zentsuji No. 4 Junior High School. The undisclosed location was Shidakajima Island, four kilometers away from Tadotsu-cho. The winner emerged after 3 days, 7 hours, and 43 minutes. Furthermore, with the retrieval of the corpses and autopsies conducted today, the causes of deaths for all 38 students killed have been determined: 17 from gunshot wounds, 9 from knife or blade wounds, 5 from blunt weapons, and 3 choked to death...."

An image of what appeared to be "the winner," a girl clad in a tattered sailor suit uniform came on the screen. Pressed between two Special Defense Forces soldiers, she looked back at the camera, her face twitching. Under her long messy hair, some dark red substance stuck to her right temple. Shuya could still clearly recall how her twitching face occasionally formed what appeared to be, strangely enough, a smile.

He realized now that this was the first time he had seen an insane person. But at the time he had no idea what was wrong with her. He only felt inexplicably afraid, as if he'd seen a ghost.

Shuya believed he had asked, "What is this, Ms. Anno?" Ms. Anno only shook her head and replied, "Oh it's nothing." Ms. Anno turned away from Shuya slightly and whispered, "Poor girl." Yoshitoki Kuninobu had already stopped watching a while ago and was preoccupied with eating his tangerine.

As Shuya grew older, this same local report, given at the rate of once every two years at any time without any warning, felt more and more ominous. From a pool of all third-year junior high school students, fifty classes were issued an annual guaranteed death sentence. That was two thousand students if each class consisted of forty students, no, more accurately, that was 1,950 students killed. Worse yet, it wasn't simply a mass execution. The students had to kill each other, competing for the throne of survivor. It was the most terrifying version of musical chairs imaginable.

But...it was impossible to oppose the Program. It was impossible to protest anything the Republic of Greater East Asia did.

So Shuya decided to give in. That was how most of the third-year "reserves" from junior high school dealt with it, right? Okay, our special conscription system? The beautiful homeland of Vigorous Rice Plants? How many junior highs were there in the republic? The birth rate might be declining but your chances were still less than one in eight hundred. In Kagawa Prefecture that meant only one class every other year would be "chosen." Put bluntly, you were just as likely to die in a traffic accident. Given how Shuya never had the luck of the draw, he figured he wouldn't be chosen. Even in the local raffle he'd never win more than a box of tissues. So he'd never be chosen. So fuck off, man.

But then sometimes when he heard someone in class, particularly a girl in tears, saying something like, "My cousin was in the Program and...," that dark fear choked him up again. He was angry too. I mean, who had the right to terrify that poor girl?

But within a matter of days the same girl who'd been so gloomy would begin smiling. And Shuya's fear and anger would gradually wane and disappear too. But the vague distrust and powerlessness he felt towards the government nonetheless remained.

That's the way things went.

And when Shuya entered his third year in junior high school this year, he along with his other classmates assumed they would be safe. Actually they really had no choice but to assume this.

Until now.

"That can't be."

A chair fell as someone stood up. The voice was shrill enough to make Shuya glance over at the desk behind Hiroki Sugimura. It was Kyoichi Motobuchi, who was the male class representative. His face was beyond pale. It had turned gray, providing a surreal contrast to his silver framed glasses, resembling one of those silkscreen prints by Andy Warhol illustrated in their art textbooks as "the decadent art of American imperialists."

Some of his classmates might have been hoping that Kyoichi would provide some adequate rational form of protest. Kill the friends you were hanging out with yesterday? It was impossible. Someone's making a mistake here. Hey rep, can you take care of this one for us?

But Kyoichi completely let them down.

"M-my father is a director of environmental affairs in the prefectural government. How could the class I'm in be selected for th-the Program?..."

Due to his shaking, his tense voice sounded even more wound up than usual.

The man who called himself Sakamochi grinned and shook his head, his long hair swinging in the air. "Let's see. You're Kyoichi Motobuchi, right?

"You must know what equality means. Listen up. All people are born equal. Your father's job in the prefectural government doesn't entitle you to special privileges. You are no different. Listen up, everybody. You all have your own distinct personal backgrounds. Of course some of you come from rich families, some from poor families. But circumstances beyond your control like that shouldn't determine who you are. You must all realize what you're worth on your own. So Kyoichi, let's not delude ourselves that you're somehow special—because you're not!"

Sakamochi bawled this out so suddenly, Kyoichi fell back into this seat. Sakamochi glared at Kyoichi for a while, but then his smile returned.

"Your class will be mentioned in today's morning news. Of course because the Program must be conducted in secret, the details will remain undisclosed until the game ends. Now let's see, oh right, your parents have already been notified."

Everyone still seemed lost in a daze. Classmates slaughtering each other? Impossible.

"You still don't believe this is happening, do you?"

Sakamochi scratched his head with a troubled look. Then he turned to the entrance and called out, "I need you guys to come in!"

In response the door slid open and three men came rushing in. They were all wearing camouflage fatigues and combat boots and tucked under their arms steel helmets bearing the peach insignia. It was immediately obvious they were Special Defense Forces soldiers. They had assault rifles strapped over their shoulders, and Shuya could see automatic pistols holstered onto their belts. One of the soldiers was tall with strangely kinked hair, giving the impression of someone frivolous, the other was medium height, with a handsome, boyish-looking face, and the last one wore a slight grin, but was eclipsed by the charisma of the other two. They were carrying a large, thick nylon sack resembling a black sleeping bag. Various parts of the bag poked up as if it were stuffed with pineapples.

Sakamochi stood by the window and the three men placed the bag on the lectern. Both sides of the bag protruded over the lectern, particularly the side facing the window, and dangled down, perhaps because the contents inside were soft.

Sakamochi announced, "Let me introduce these men who will be assisting you for the Program. Mr. Tahara, Mr. Kondo, and Mr. Nomura. Now why don't you show them what's inside?"

The frivolous one, Tahara, approached the lectern from the side of the hall, placed his hand on the zipper, and pulled the bag open. Something drenched in red liquid...

"AIEEEEE!"

Before it was fully open, one of the girls in the front row screamed and was immediately followed by the others. As the desks and chairs made a clattering sound, other voices asked, "Whaaat?" and a soprano chorus swelled up.

Shuya held his breath.

He could see the body of the teacher in charge of Class B, Masao Hayashida, inside the half open bag. No, he was now their former teacher. Or in fact he was now the former Mr. Hayashida.

His flimsy blue-gray suit was drenched in blood. Only half of his large black glasses that earned him the nickname "Dragonfly" remained. What could you expect, only the left half of his head remained. Underneath the remaining lens the marblelike, crimson eyeball gazed absently at the ceiling. Gray jelly, what must have been his brains, clung to his remaining hair. As if relieved to be released, his left arm, still wearing a watch, poked out of the bag, dangling in front of the lectern. The ones sitting in front might have actually seen the second hand ticking away.

"All right, all right, all right, quiet now. Be quiet. Silence!"

Sakamochi clapped his hands, but the girls' shrieking wouldn't subside.

Suddenly, the boyish looking soldier named Kondo pulled out his pistol.

Shuya expected a warning shot into the ceiling, but the soldier instead grabbed the bag containing Hayashida with one of his hands, and dragged the bag down from the lectern. He snapped Hayashida's head up to his face. He looked like a hero in a sci-fi flick fighting a giant bagworm.

The soldier pumped two bullets into Mr. Hayashida's head. The rest of Hayashida's head flew apart. The high powered bullets tore apart his brains and bones which formed a bloody mist and splattered all over the faces and chests of the students in the front row.

The echoes from the gunfire subsided. There was hardly any trace of Hayashida's head.

The soldier tossed Hayashida's body to the side of the lectern. No one was screaming.

42 students remaining

4

Most of the standing students timidly returned to their seats. The uncharismatic soldier on the far side dragged the bag containing Hayashida's body to the corner of the classroom, then joined the other two standing by the lectern. Sakamochi returned to his position behind the lectern.

Once again the room turned silent, but that silence was soon broken by the sound of someone groaning in the back, followed by the damp splash of vomit splattering against the floor. Shuya could smell it.

"Listen up everyone. As you can see, Mr. Hayashida vehemently opposed your class' assignment to the Program," Sakamochi said, scratching his hair. "Well, it was all so sudden, we do feel bad about it, but..."

The room grew silent again. Everyone now knew. This was real. It was no mistake, nor was it a prank. They were going to be forced to kill each other.

Shuya desperately tried to think clearly. The unreal situation had put him in a daze. His mind was spinning from the horrible corpse of Hayashida and the role it played in this horror show.

They had to escape. But how?...That's right...first he'd meet with Yoshitoki...Shinji and Hiroki...but how was the Program actually conducted? The details were never publicized. Students were given weapons to kill each other. That much was known. But could they talk to each other? How did the government monitor the game?

"I...I..." Shuya's thoughts were interrupted. He looked up and opened his eyes.

Yoshitoki Kuninobu half rose and gazed at Sakamochi, unsure, it seemed, whether he should continue. He looked as if his words were beyond his control. Shuya's body tensed up. Don't provoke them, Yoshitoki!

"Yeeees? What is it? You can ask me anything."

Sakamochi offered a friendly smile, and like a puppet Yoshitoki continued, "I...don't have parents. So who did you contact?"

"Ah ha," Sakamochi nodded. "I remember there was someone from one of the welfare institutions. So you must be Shuya Nanahara? Let's see, according to the school report you were the one with dangerous ideas. So…"

"I'm Shuya," Shuya interrupted, raising his voice. Sakamochi glanced at Shuya and then back at Yoshitoki. Still in a daze, Yoshitoki glanced back at Shuya.

"Oh, that's right. I'm so sorry. There was one more. So you must be Yoshitoki Kuninobu. Well, I contacted the superintendent of the institution where you were both raised. That's right…she was very pretty," Sakamochi said and grinned. While his smile appeared to be cheerful, there was something disturbing about it.

Shuya's face tensed up. "What the hell did you do to Ms. Anno?"

"Well, like Mr. Hayashida, she was very uncooperative. They both didn't accept your assignment, so in order to silence her, well, I had to…," Sakamochi continued calmly, "…rape her. Oh, don't worry. It's not like she's dead."

Shuya flushed red with anger and leaped up, but before he could say anything, Yoshitoki said, "I'll kill you!"

Yoshitoki was standing up. His expression had changed, though. He'd always been so friendly to everyone. No matter what happened, it was impossible to imagine him getting angry. His expression now was something he saved for those rare times he was truly enraged. No one else in class might have ever seen him like this, but Shuya had seen him this upset twice. The first time was when they were fourth graders and a car ran over the Charity House's pet dog, Eddie, right in front of the gate. Frantically, Yoshitoki chased after the fleeing car. The second time was only a year ago, when a man had been using the school's debt as leverage to come on to Ms. Anno. After she managed to pay back the money, and thereby rejected his advances, the man cursed her out right in front of them, as if he wanted all the Charity House's residents to hear him. If Shuya hadn't stopped Yoshitoki, the man would have lost his front teeth, though

Yoshitoki would have also been severely injured. Yoshitoki was extremely kind, and even when he was insulted or picked on he usually laughed it off. But when someone he truly loved was hurt, his response was extreme. This was something Shuya admired about Yoshitoki.

"I'll kill you, you bastard!" Yoshitoki continued, screaming, "I'll kill you and dump you into a pile of shit!"

"Hmm." Sakamochi looked amused. "Are you serious, Yoshitoki? You know one must be responsible for the things one says."

"Give me a break! I'm going to kill you! Don't you forget it!"

"Stop it, Yoshitoki! Stop it!"

Yoshitoki paid no attention to Shuya's screaming.

Sakamochi spoke in a strange, kind voice, as if to appease Yoshitoki.

"Look, Yoshitoki. What you're doing right now is voicing your opposition to the government."

"I'll kill you!" Yoshitoki didn't stop. "I'll kill you I'll kill you I'll kill you!"

Shuya could no longer contain himself and right when he was about to scream again, Sakamochi shook his head and waved his hand at the three Special Defense Forces soldiers standing by the lectern.

They resembled a chorus group, like the Four Freshmen. The men in fatigues, Tahara, Kondo, and Nomura, all lifted their right hands in a dramatic, emotionally charged pose. But their hands were holding guns. Now the chorus would have been something like, "Baby please, baby please, spend this night with me—"

Shuya saw Yoshitoki's bulging eyes open even wider.

The three automatic pistols exploded all at once. Just as he was stepping out into the aisle, Yoshitoki's body shook as if dancing the boogaloo.

It happened so quickly that Noriko Nakagawa, who sat

right behind Yoshitoki, along with the rest of the class, didn't even have time to duck.

The gunshot sounds hadn't even died down before Yoshitoki slowly tipped over to the right and crashed in between his desk and Izumi Kanai's on the right. Izumi shrieked.

The threesome stood with their right hands extended. Thin smoke from each of their barrels simultaneously trailed upward. Shuya then saw in between the legs of the desk the familiar face turned towards him. The bulging eyes remained open, fixed on a point on the floor. A bright puddle of blood began oozing out onto the floor. Yoshitoki's right shoulder began twitching down to his fingers.

Yoshitoki!

Shuya stood up to run to him, but Noriko Nakagawa, who was sitting closer, was quicker. "Yoshitoki!" she screamed and crouched down beside him.

Now Tahara, the frivolous one, aimed his gun at Noriko and pulled the trigger. Noriko tumbled forward as if she were swept off her feet and collapsed on top of Yoshitoki, who continued to twitch.

Tahara immediately pointed his gun at Shuya. Shuya's mind was racing now but his body was frozen. Only his eyes moved. He saw the blood spurting out of Noriko's calf.

Sakamochi said to Noriko, "You will not leave your desk without my permission." Then he looked over at Shuya, saying, "The same applies to you, Shuya. Now sit down."

Shuya did his best to take his eyes away from Noriko's bloody leg and Yoshitoki underneath her. He looked Sakamochi directly in the eye. His neck muscles had tensed up from the shock of the scene.

"What the hell is going on here!?" Tahara still pointed his gun at his forehead. Shuya remained still, bursting out, "What the hell are you doing!? We have to get some help for Yoshitoki…and Noriko…."

Sakamochi grimaced and shook his head. Then he repeated, "Forget about it and sit down. You too, Noriko."

Noriko, completely pale from looking at Yoshitoki lying underneath her, slowly looked up at Sakamochi. She seemed overwhelmed with anger more than she was with the pain she must have been suffering from. She raised her eyes and glared back at Sakamochi. "Please get some help." She spoke each word deliberately. "For Yoshitoki."

Yoshitoki's right arm continued to twitch. But while they watched over him the twitching subsided. It was evident his injury would be fatal unless he was treated immediately.

Sakamochi sighed deeply, then addressed the frivolous one, "Then Mr. Tahara, will you please take care of this."

Before they could figure out what he meant, Tahara pointed his gun downward and pulled the trigger. BLAMM. Yoshitoki Kuninobu's head bounced up once, then something from his head splashed onto Noriko's face.

Dumbstruck, Noriko's mouth hung open. Her face was covered with a dark red substance.

Shuya realized his mouth was hanging open too.

Although part of his head had been blown away, Yoshitoki's eyes still remained focused on the same part of the floor. He was no longer twitching, though. He was motionless.

"See?" Sakamochi said. "He was already dying. Now then, please return to your seats."

"Oh…" Noriko looked down at Yoshitoki's deformed head. "…my…"

Shuya was also stunned. His eyes were glued to Yoshitoki's face, lying between the legs of the desk. His thoughts were completely paralyzed, as if his own brains had been blown to bits. Memories of Yoshitoki flashed through his dazed mind. The little adventures they took, camping or walking down the river, a rainy day spent playing an old board game, mimicking "Jake and Elwood," the heroes who, like themselves, were orphans in the American movie *The Blues Brothers* (amazingly, it was a dubbed version, although the voice actors were horrible), which had become a blackmarket hit, and then just recently, Yoshitoki's face when he said, "Hey Shuya, I got a crush on someone." And then...

"Are you two deaf?" Sakamochi repeated. Yes, Shuya was deaf to his words. He just stared at Yoshitoki.

Noriko was no different. If they hadn't moved, they would have followed in Yoshitoki Kuninobu's footsteps. Right beside Sakamochi, Tahara pointed his gun at Noriko, while the other two pointed theirs at Shuya.

But it was thanks to a calm, in fact light-hearted voice calling out, "M-m-m-mister Sakamochi," that Shuya was brought back to his senses, at least enough to gaze numbly at the caller.

Beyond Yoshitoki's empty seat, Shinji Mimura had his hand raised. Noriko slowly looked at him too.

"Hm? Let's see. You must be Shinji Mimura. What is it?"

Shinji put his hand down and spoke, "Noriko looks injured. I was wondering if I could help her get back to her seat."

Despite the extremity of their situation, Shinji spoke in the usual voice of The Third Man.

Sakamochi raised his brow slightly, but then nodded.

"All right, go ahead. I really want to get things moving."

Shinji nodded, stood up, and walked towards Noriko. As he approached her, he took out a neatly folded handkerchief out of his pocket and leaned between Yoshitoki's corpse and Noriko. He first wiped Noriko's face, which was covered with Yoshitoki's blood. Noriko hardly reacted. Then he said, "Stand up, Noriko," and put his hand under Noriko's right arm to help her get up.

Then, with his back facing Sakamochi, Shinji looked at Shuya, who remained half-standing. Under his sharp, well defined brows, his eyes which always had a mildly amused look were now dead serious. He raised his right brow and moved his chin, shaking his head slightly. His left hand pushed down, as if he were making a pressing motion. Shuya didn't understand this signal. Shinji made the same move again.

Although he was still dazed, Shuya finally understood that Shinji was telling him to calm down. He looked back at Shinji...and slowly eased his way back into his seat.

Shinji nodded. After returning Noriko to her seat, he turned around and returned to his seat.

Noriko sat down. Blood poured out of the wound in her right leg dangling from her seat. Her white socks and sneakers were soaked in red, as if she were wearing Santa Claus boots, but only on her right foot.

Noriko was coming to her senses a little too. She seemed to be making a gesture to thank Shinji. But as if he could see out the back of his head Shinji shrugged his shoulders to stop her. Noriko withdrew and saw once again Yoshitoki's body lying below her right hand. She stared at him without a word but her eyes seemed to be brimming with tears.

Shuya also looked again at the corpse, his view partly obscured by the desks. Yes, it was a corpse. There was no doubt about it. It was hard to comprehend, but Yoshitoki had become a corpse, the corpse of someone with whom he had shared ten years of his life.

As he looked at Yoshitoki's gaping eyes, Shuya's anger became more pronounced and clear, like a throbbing pulse. The anger rushed through his entire body so powerfully that it almost made him shake. His feelings, which had been muted by the initial shock, were beginning to surface. Shuya turned and bared his teeth towards Sakamochi.

Sakamochi looked amused by Shuya. Shuya would never forgive him for this. He was going to kill the bastard.

Shuya had been on the verge of blowing up the

way Yoshitoki did. But then…

Shinji Mimura had intervened at the crucial moment, telling him to calm down….Shuya immediately recalled how he got the signal from him only moments ago. That's right…of course if he blew up now he would end up like Yoshitoki. And more importantly…now the girl whom Yoshitoki adored so much was severely injured. If he were to die now…what would happen to Noriko Nakagawa?

Shuya tried his best to tear his eyes away from Sakamochi. He looked down at his desktop. He felt wretched, as if his heart were being crushed from anger and sadness that had no outlet.

Sakamochi quietly laughed. He looked away from Shuya.

Shuya clenched both of his fists tightly under the desk in order to calm down his body which was shaking uncontrollably. He clenched them tighter and tighter. It was no easy feat to control his emotions though, with Yoshitoki's corpse lying right in front of him.

This was incomprehensible. How could it be? How could you lose someone…someone so close?

Yoshitoki has always been with me. It doesn't matter how trivial our experiences were. What about the time we played in the river, and I saved him from drowning? Or when we got our kicks collecting tons of grasshoppers, stuffing them into a small box, and how they died as a result? We both felt really bad about that. Or when we fought for that dog Eddie's attention? Or when we pulled a prank in school and ended up hiding in the faculty room attic? We almost got caught, but after we managed to escape, we had a good laugh….Yoshitoki and I were always together. It was a fact. He was with me.

So how could he be…gone now?

Shinji raised his hand again, "I have another question, Mr. Sakamochi."

"You again? What is it?"

"Noriko is injured. I understand we will be participating in the Program, but doesn't this make the game unfair?"

Sakamochi looked amused.

"Well, perhaps, yes. So what is it?"

"Which means she should be treated, which means the Program should be postponed until her recovery, no?"

Shuya had barely managed to hold back his anger, so he was amazed by the contrast in Shinji Mimura's calm conduct. It was a bit strange that Shuya could actually afford to be impressed. Yes, Shinji Mimura was a lot calmer than Shuya. Shinji was right. If Shinji's request was granted, that might buy them some extra time. Then they might be able to escape.

Sakamochi's face contorted into laughter.

"That's a very interesting suggestion, Shinji."

Sakamochi instead offered an alternative solution, "Then shall we kill Noriko Nakagawa now, and make the game equal?"

Noriko herself along with the rest of class suddenly froze up again. Shuya could see Shinji's back underneath his school uniform stiffen as he immediately responded, "I take it back, I take it back. Come on, I was just kidding."

Sakamochi burst out laughing again at Shinji's humorous tone. Tahara, whose right hand had been on his holster, quickly returned it to the strap of his rifle hanging off his shoulder.

Sakamochi clapped his hands again.

"All right then, listen up. First of all, each and every one of you differ according to your intelligence, physical dexterity, etc., etc. We're born unequal. So we will not treat Noriko Nakagawa—over there!! No whispering!" Sakamochi suddenly yelled. He threw a white object where Fumiyo Fujiyoshi (Female Student No. 18) was in the process of whispering something to the female class representative Yukie Utsumi, who was sitting next to her. Shuya wondered whether it was chalk for a moment, but of course that was absurd, given the circumstances.

The object made the thumping sound of a nail being pounded into a coffin. A thin knife was planted in the middle of Fumiyo Fujiyoshi's wide, fair-skinned forehead.

Yukie stared at the sight, her eyes open wide. A stranger sight though was Fumiyo herself raising her eyes, struggling to locate the knife planted in her forehead. Her head arched back in this attempt.

Then she collapsed to the side. As she fell, her left temple hit the corner of Yukie's desk and nudged it.

Now there was no room for doubt. Who could survive a knife planted in one's forehead?

No one moved. No one spoke a word. Yukie took a deep breath and stared down at Fumiyo. Noriko was also gazing at her. Shinji Mimura kept his lips pursed as he looked at Fumiyo collapsed between the desks just like Yoshitoki.

His throat dry, Shuya held his breath and thought, "He did that on a whim! A whim! Damn it! Our lives are totally at the mercy of this asshole Sakamochi!"

"Oops, I did it. I'm so sorry. The instructor killing someone, that's against the rules, huh?" Sakamochi closed his eyes and scratched his head. But his face became serious again and he said, "I need your undivided attention. Impulsive actions are strictly prohibited. That means whispering will not be permitted. It's hard on me but if you whisper, I'll toss another knife at you!"

Shuya clenched his teeth. He told himself to be patient and repeated this over and over to himself while two classmates were sprawled dead on the floor.

Still, he was drawn to Yoshitoki's face and couldn't help but look at him. He felt he was about to cry.

40 students remaining

5

"Allow me to explain the rules."

Sakamochi returned to his cheerful voice. The classroom began to reek of Yoshitoki Kuninobu's fresh blood, an odor entirely different than that of the dried blood of their instructor, "Dragonfly" Hayashida. Shuya couldn't see Fumiyo Fujiyoshi's face from his seat, but it seemed like there was very little blood coming out of her.

"I think you all know how this works. The rules are simple. All you have to do is kill each other. There are no violations. And," Sakamochi wore a wide grin, "the last remaining survivor can go home. You even get a nice card autographed by the Dictator. Isn't that wonderful?"

In his mind, Shuya spat to his side.

"Now you may think this is a horrible game. But in life the unexpected is bound to happen. You must at all times maintain self-control in order to respond properly to accidents. Consider this an exercise then. Also, men and women will be treated equally. There will be no handicaps for either side. I do have good news for the girls, though. According to Program statistics, 49% of past winning survivors have been girls. The motto here is, 'I'm just like the others and the others are like me.' There is nothing to be afraid of."

Sakamochi made a signal. The camouflaged trio went into the hall and began to haul in the large, black, nylon day packs. The packs formed a pile right beside the body bag of Mr. Hayashida. Some of them were lopsided, as if they might contain a pole-shaped object inside trying to poke out.

"We will have you leave one by one. Each one of you will take one of these bags prior to departure. Each pack contains food, water, and a weapon. Let's see, as I said, every one of you differs according to ability. So these weapons will add another random element. Well, that sounds complicated. In other words, it will make the game all the more unpredictable. You will each end up with a randomly selected weapon. As you leave in order, you will take the pack on top of the pile. Each pack also contains a map of the island, a compass, and a watch. Are there any of you who don't have watches? You all do? Oh, I forgot to mention this, but we are on an island with an approximate circumference of six kilometers. It's never been used for the Program. We had the residents evacuate the island. So there is absolutely no one else here. So…"

Sakamochi faced the blackboard and grabbed a piece of chalk. He drew a rough diamond shape next to where he had written his name, "Kinpatsu Sakamochi." On the top-right he drew an arrow pointing upward and the letter "N." He wrote an "X" inside the diamond, right of its center. With the chalk still pressed against the blackboard, he turned towards the students.

"All right then. We're in the school on this island. This is a diagram of the island, so this indicates the school. Got that?" Sakamochi tapped the symbol with his chalk. "I'm going to be staying here. I'll be overlooking your efforts."

Sakamochi then drew four spindle shapes scattered to the north, south, east, and west sides of the diamond.

"These are ships. They are there to kill anyone attempting to escape by sea."

Then he drew parallel vertical and horizontal lines over the island. The diamond shape indicating the island resembled a warped grill now. Starting from the top-left, Sakamochi wrote markers in each grid, "A=1," "A=2,"…in order. The next row read, "B=1," "B=2," etc.

"This is just a simplified diagram. The map inside your packs will look something like this." Sakamochi placed his chalk down and clapped his hands to clear off the dust.

"Once you leave the premises, you are free to go anywhere. However, announcements will be made across the entire island at the hours of twelve and six, in the morning and at night. That's four a day. I'll be referring to this map when I announce the location of zones that will be forbidden after a certain time. You must examine your maps closely and check your compasses against them. If you are in a forbidden zone you must clear out of the area as soon as possible. Because..."

Sakamochi put his hands on the lectern and looked at everyone.

"...of the collars around your necks."

Until he had made this remark, several students had failed to notice the collars. They touched their necks and looked shocked.

"That device is the result of the latest technology developed by our Republic. It is 100% waterproof, anti-shock, and uh-uh, no, no, it can't come off. It won't come off. If you try to pry it loose...," Sakamochi took a small breath, "...it will explode."

Several students who had been fingering their collars immediately released their hands.

Sakamochi grinned. "The collar monitors your pulse in order to verify signs of life and transmits this information to the mainframe at this school. It also pinpoints your exact position on the island for us. Now, let's return to the map."

Sakamochi swung his right arm back and pointed to the map on the blackboard.

"This same computer will also randomly select forbidden zones. And if there are any students left in the zone after the designated time—of course dead students won't matter—the computer will automatically detect anyone alive and immediately send a signal to his or her collar. Then..."

Shuya knew what he would say.

"That collar will explode."

He was right.

Sakamochi paused for a moment to examine everyone. Then he continued, "Why would we do this? Because if everyone huddled up together in one spot, the game wouldn't proceed. So we will make you move. Simultaneously, the area you can move around in will shrink. Got that?"

Sakamochi called it a game. No wonder. It was fucking outrageous. No one said a word but everyone appeared to understand the rules.

"All right, so that means hiding in a building will do you no good. Even if you hide in some hole you dug in the ground the transmission will reach you. Oh and by the way, you are free to hide in any building but you won't be able to use the phone. You won't be able to contact your parents. You have to fight on your own alone. But that's how the game of life is anyway. Now I did say that the game will begin without any forbidden zones, but there is one exception: this school. Twenty minutes after your departure this school will become a forbidden zone. So please first get out of this area. Let's see, you must be two hundred meters away. Got that? Now, in my announcements I will also read off the names of those who have died in the past six hours. Each announcement will be made regularly at six-hour intervals, but I'll also be contacting the last remaining survivor by announcement as well. Oh…and one more thing. There is a time limit. Listen up. A time limit. A lot of people die in the Program, but if no one dies within twenty-four hours then your time's expired, and it won't matter how many students are left…."

Shuya knew what he would say.

"The computer will detonate the collars of the remaining students. There will be no winner."

Again he was right.

Sakamochi stopped speaking. The entire classroom had become silent. The room was still reeking with the heavy stench of Yoshitoki Kuninobu's blood. Everyone remained in their collective daze. They were scared, but this situation, where they were about to be thrown into a killing game, seemed beyond their comprehension.

As if responding to their general state of mind, Sakamochi clapped his hands. "Well, I've covered all the tedious details. Now I have something more important to tell you. A piece of advice. Some of you might be thinking that murdering your classmates is impossible. But don't forget there are others willing to do it."

Shuya wanted to scream, you're full of it! But with the Fumiyo-Fujiyoshi-executed-for-whispering incident only moments in the past he could only stay put.

Everybody remained silent, but something had suddenly changed and Shuya knew it.

Everyone was looking around, glancing at the others' pale faces. Whenever anyone's gaze met, their eyes would nervously turn toward Sakamochi. It only happened within a matter of seconds, but their expressions were exactly the same: they were tense and suspicious, wondering who was already ready to take part. Only a few, like Shinji Mimura, remained calm.

Shuya clenched his teeth again. You're falling into their trap! Think about it, we're a group. There's no way we can kill each other!

"All right then, I need to make sure you get my point. You'll find some paper and pencils in your desks."

Everyone timidly took out their paper and pencils. Shuya had no choice but to follow his instructions.

"Now then, I want you to write this down. To memorize something, it's best to write it down. Write this. 'We will kill each other.' Write it three times."

Shuya heard the pencils scribbling against the paper. Noriko too held her pencil, looking morose. While Shuya wrote out this insane motto, he glanced at Yoshitoki's body, which remained lying between the desks. He recalled Yoshitoki's warm smile.

Sakamochi continued, "Okay then. 'If I don't kill, I will be killed.' Write this down three times too."

Shuya also glanced over at Fumiyo Fujiyoshi. Her white fingers poking out of the cuffs of her sailor suit uniform gently formed a bowl. She was the nurse's aide. She was quiet but very caring.

Then he looked up at Sakamochi.

Fucking bastard, I'll stab you in the chest with this pencil!

40 students remaining

6

"Now then, let's see, every two minutes one of you will be leaving the classroom. Once you go through this door and turn right down the hall you'll find the school exit. You are to leave immediately. Anyone loitering in the hall will be immediately shot. Now, who do we start with? According to the Program rules, once we determine the first person, the rest of the order will correspond to your classroom seating assignments. Male, female, male, female, got it? Once we reach the last seat number, we start over from the first number. So..."

At this point, Shuya recalled that Noriko's seating number was 15. It was the same as his. Which meant that he and Noriko could leave almost simultaneously (unless she was chosen first, which meant he would be the last one to leave).

But…could Noriko walk?

Sakamochi took out an envelope from his inner coat pocket.

"The first student is selected by lottery. Hold on a second…"

From his pocket Sakamochi produced a pink-ribboned pair of scissors and ceremoniously cut open the end of the envelope.

That was when Kazuo Kiriyama spoke up. Like Shinji Mimura, he also sounded calm. But his voice sounded cold with a harsh ring. "I was wondering when the game begins."

Everyone looked back to the last row, where Kiriyama was sitting. (Shogo Kawada was the only who didn't turn. He just continued to chew his gum.)

Sakamochi gestured with his hand, "As soon as you leave here. So you all might want to hide out to cook up your own strategies…since it's night right now."

Kazuo Kiriyama didn't respond. Shuya finally confirmed it was midnight, or 1 a.m.—no, it was already near 1:30 a.m.

After cutting open the envelope Sakamochi pulled out from it a white sheet of paper, and he unfolded it. His mouth formed an "O" and he remarked, "What a coincidence! It's student No. 1. Yoshio Akamatsu."

Hearing the announcement, Yoshio Akamatsu, who sat at the front row of the column near the windows (steel plates), looked shaken. He was 180 centimeters tall, weighing 90 kilograms, so he was large, but he couldn't even catch a fly ball, nor could he run a full lap around the track. Yoshio was always bumbling through gym class. Now his lips were pale blue.

"Hurry up, Yoshio Akamatsu," Sakamochi said. Yoshio held the bag he'd packed for the study trip and staggered to his feet. He made his way forward and received his day pack from the camouflaged trio, who now held their rifles at their waists. He stood at the open door and faced the darkness. He looked back at everyone with a terrified face, but then a moment later he vanished beyond the door. Two or three footsteps turned into the pounding sound of his running, which then faded away. It sounded like he fell once but then it sounded like he dashed off again.

In the quiet room several students took a deep, restrained breath.

"Now we will wait two minutes. Then the next one will be Female Student No. 1, Mizuho Inada—"

This routine continued ruthlessly on and on like this.

But there was something Shuya noticed when Female Student No. 4 Sakura Ogawa got up to leave. Sakura sat two seats behind Shuya, in the very last row. As she made her way to the exit, she touched the desk of her boyfriend Kazuhiko Yamamoto and left a piece of paper behind for him. She might have dashed off a message on that sheet of paper on which they'd been instructed to write, "We will kill each other."

Shuya might have been the only one who saw this. At the very least Sakamochi didn't seem to notice. Kazuhiko snatched the scrap of paper and clenched it tightly under his desk. Shuya felt a wave of relief. They weren't all consumed by this insanity yet. The bonds of love had yet to be severed.

But…what was her message? Shuya wondered as she left the classroom. Maybe—he glanced at the map Sakamochi had scrawled on the blackboard—she'd designated one of the areas for a meeting? But that map on the blackboard was too crude, and there was no guarantee at all it'd correspond to the maps they were given. Maybe she indicated a general direction or distance. Besides, the fact that they wanted to secretly meet only meant they didn't trust anyone else and they were certain others would try to kill them. Which in the end meant they were falling into Sakamochi's trap.

Shuya thought, I have no idea what lies beyond this room but I should at the very least be able to wait outside and talk to the students after me. None of Sakamochi's rules prohibit me from doing this. Everyone might be panicking from suspicion, but if we can just get together and discuss the situation then I'm sure we can come up with a plan. Plus, Noriko was the one who came immediately after him (could she walk though?). Shinji Mimura also came after him. Hiroki Sugimura would leave before him though....

Shuya considered passing a note to Hiroki but his seat was too far. Besides, if he tried anything he could end up like Fumiyo Fujiyoshi.

Hiroki Sugimura was up next. His eyes met Shuya's briefly right before he exited the room's sliding door...but that was all. In his mind, Shuya sighed deeply. He could only hope Hiroki had the same idea and would be waiting outside. If he could talk the others into waiting too...

In front and behind him, the quiet ones, Shogo Kawada, Kazuo Kiriyama, and Mitsuko Souma, left one by one.

Chewing his gum, Shogo exited with an indifferent look on his face, completely ignoring Sakamochi and the camouflaged trio. Kiriyama and Souma left the same way.

That's right. When Sakamochi said, "There are others willing to do it," the rest of the class must have immediately suspected these three students. Because they were "delinquents." They might not think twice about killing the others in order to survive....

But Shuya doubted Kazuo Kiriyama would. Kazuo had his own gang. On top of that, his gang was a lot tighter than your typical group of buddies. Hiroshi Kuronaga, Ryuhei Sasagawa, Sho Tsukioka, and Mitsuru Numai. The rules of this game turned everyone else into your enemy, but the five of them killing each other was unimaginable. Besides— Shuya made a careful note of this—when he left, his boys looked disturbingly calm. That's right, Kazuo probably passed around a note to the others. He's probably planning an escape for the five of them. Kazuo was more than capable of out-maneuvering the government. Of course, this also meant that Kazuo wouldn't trust anyone besides his gang.

Mitsuko Souma had a similar kind of group. Her seat was too far from the others, Hirono Shimizu and Yoshimi Yahagi, for her to be able to pass them notes. But…Mitsuko Souma was a girl. There was no way she would play this game.

Shogo Kawada was the only one who troubled Shuya. Shogo Kawada had no group. In fact he didn't even have a single friend. Ever since he transferred to their school, he hardly spoke to anyone in the class. On top of that, there was something elusive about Shogo. Even if he ignored the rumors, there were those wounds covering his entire body…

Could it be that…Shogo might be the only one willing to participate in this game? It was certainly possible.

But Shuya knew the moment he turned suspicious he was giving into the government, so he immediately dismissed the thought…though he had trouble dismissing the thought entirely.

Time passed.

Many of the girls were crying as they left.

Although it felt incredibly short, an hour must have passed according to his calculations (of course with Yoshitoki Kuninobu the elapsed time was reduced by two minutes). Female Student No. 14 Mayumi Tendo vanished into the hall, and Sakamochi called out, "Male Student No. 15, Shuya Nanahara."

Shuya grabbed his bag and stood up. He thought, I did all I could before leaving the classroom.

Instead of heading directly to the exit, he took the aisle on his left. Noriko turned around and watched Shuya approaching her.

Sakamochi raised his voice, "Shuya," and his knife.

"Wrong direction."

Shuya stopped. The three soldiers had their rifles cocked. His throat stiffened. Then he said nervously, "Yoshitoki Kuninobu was my friend. The least I could do is close his eyes. According to the Great Dictator's education policy, we're supposed to respect the dead."

Sakamochi hesitated for a moment, but then he grinned and put his knife down.

"You're so caring, Shuya. All right then."

Shuya took a small breath, then stepped forward. He stopped in front of Noriko's desk, where Yoshitoki's corpse was lying.

Although he'd demanded the right to close his friend's eyes, he couldn't help but freeze up.

Now that he was up close he saw, courtesy of the frivolous one, thin, red flesh and something white in Yoshitoki's blood-stained short hair. He realized it was bone. Thanks to the bullets wedged inside his head, Yoshitoki's big eyes bulged out even further. He looked stupefied with the upturned eyes of a starving refugee waiting to be fed. Pink, slimy liquid consisting of blood and saliva dripped out of his mouth, which opened slightly. Dark blood poured out of his nostrils. It flowed down his chin and into the pool of blood pouring out of his chest. It was horrible.

Shuya placed his bag near him and leaned over. He lifted Yoshitoki's body, which was lying down face first. As Shuya lifted him, blood came pouring out of the chest of his blackened school uniform, which was torn in three places, and splashed onto the floor. His lanky body felt incredibly light. Was it because all that blood had been drained out of him?

Holding Yoshitoki's light body, Shuya's head cooled down. More than sadness or fear, it was anger that overwhelmed him.

Yoshitoki...I'm going to avenge your death. I swear to you that I will.

There wasn't much time. He wiped the blood off Yoshitoki's face with the palm of his hand, then gently closed his eyes. He laid his body down and clasped his hands on his chest.

Then as he pretended to fumble over picking up his bag, he leaned over to Noriko as close as he could and quickly whispered, "Can you walk?"

That was enough to provoke the camouflaged trio to reach for their rifles, but Shuya managed to get a nod from Noriko. Shuya turned to Sakamochi and the trio, clenched his fist for Noriko to see, and pointed his thumb to the exit to indicate; I'll be waiting. I'll be waiting outside.

Shuya didn't look back at Noriko, but out of the corner of his eye he looked beyond Yoshitoki's desk, where Shinji Mimura stared ahead, faintly smiling with his arms folded. He might have seen Shuya's signal. Shuya felt all the more relieved. It was Shinji. If Shinji's on our side, we can escape, no prob

But...Shinji Mimura may have been more aware of their situation than Shuya was. He might have been saying with that grin, "Well, this may be adios amigos, Shuya." The thought didn't occur to Shuya at the time though.

He continued to walk. He took a moment to think before he received his black day pack, and he did the same as he approached Fumiyo Fujiyoshi's corpse, shutting his eyes. He wanted to remove the knife from her forehead, but decided against it.

When he stepped out of the classroom, he felt a pang of regret, wishing he had removed it for her.

40 students remaining

7

The hall was unlit. Only the light from the classroom shone on the floor planks. The windows on the side of the hall were also sealed with sheets of black steel. They provided protection against attacks from rebellious students like Shuya who might decide to escape the game. Of course, as soon as they were off, this area would already be forbidden.

He looked to his right. There was another room, then another, both identical to the room he'd just exited. And then at the end of the dark hall there was what looked like a double-door exit. At the end of the hall there was another room on the left.

Was it the school's faculty room? The door was open and the lights were on. Shuya looked beyond the door, where a legion of Special Defense Forces soldiers were sitting on steel folding chairs behind a wide desk. Twenty or thirty? No, there were as many soldiers as there were students.

In fact, Shuya was hoping that if his day pack came equipped with a gun (it was possible—along with "knife wound" and "choking," "gunshot wound" was listed as a cause of death in the Program reports), or if some of the others waiting for him were equipped with guns, then they could use them against Sakamochi and his men before everyone departed, in other words, before the school became a forbidden zone. But this hope was immediately extinguished. The three men with Sakamochi weren't the only soldiers accompanying him. Of course, that wasn't at all surprising.

One of the soldiers tilted his head and glanced up from the mug in his hand at Shuya. Like the faces of the trio in the classroom, his also lacked any expression.

Shuya took to his heels and hurried to the exit. He rushed impatiently. So now...now the only thing they could do was unite. But…maybe there were soldiers stationed outside to prevent them from waiting for each other? Still…

Shuya quickly ran through the dark corridor and went through the double doors. He descended several porch stairs.

Under the moon, an empty athletic field the size of three tennis courts spread out beyond the building. There were woods beyond the field. To his left was a small mountain. His field of vision expanded on the right. A pitch-black darkness spread out—the sea. Small points of light twinkled beyond the ocean. It must be the mainland. The Program officially took place within the prefecture of the selected junior high school. Sometimes the location was a mountain surrounded by high-voltage fences, or abandoned prison houses that hadn't yet been demolished, but for Kagawa Prefecture the Program was usually held on an island. According to the local news reports he'd seen (of course, in each case the location would only be announced after the game was over), every game in Kagawa took place on an island. This time was no exception. Sakamochi didn't mention the name of the island, but once Shuya checked its shape on the map he might be able to tell. Or maybe a building would reveal the name of the island.

The soft breeze blew in. He could smell the sea. It was cold for a May evening but it wasn't unbearable. He'd have to be careful when he slept not to tire himself from exposure.

But first…

There was no one. There weren't any soldiers, but Shuya was disappointed to find none of his classmates there. As Sakamochi had anticipated, everyone was hiding out. Even Hiroki Sugimura wasn't there. Only the soft breeze mixed in with the smell of the sea came drifting through the athletic field.

Damn it. Shuya grimaced. If we scatter like this, we'll fall into the government's trap. It might be all right if you were forming groups with your friends. Sakura Ogawa and Kazuhiko Yamamoto might be meeting somewhere, likewise Kazuo Kiriyama's gang. But anyone hiding alone would eventually have to confront someone....Who knew what would result from that kind of chaos? Wasn't chaos essential to the progress of the game?

That's right. Well at least I'm going to wait here for the others. First I have to wait for Noriko.

Shuya glanced back at the dark interior of the school building. They were told anyone loitering in the hall would be immediately shot, but the soldiers in the room at the end of the corridor didn't pay any particular attention to Shuya. They weren't exactly chatting up a storm. They just sat around, unarmed.

Shuya licked his lips and decided it was best for him to move away from the door. He looked outside again.

That's when he noticed it.

He didn't see it last time because he was too preoccupied with the overall view, but this time he saw something that looked like a garbage bag lying at his feet.

Shuya wondered whether it was someone's day pack, dropped by accident, but then his eyes widened.

It wasn't a garbage bag, nor was it someone's day pack. There was hair growing out of one end. Human hair.

It was a human being. Wearing a sailor suit school uniform. The body was in a V-shape, lying on its side, face down. The single pony tail tied with a wide ribbon looked familiar. No wonder. He'd just seen her off only three minutes ago. The stiff body belonged to Female Student No. 14, Mayumi Tendo.

Right beside her lobster-shaped braided hair, a dull, silver, twenty-centimeter stick poked out of the back of her uniform, diagonally, like a transistor radio antenna. There were four tiny flaps resembling a fighter plane's tail at the end of the stick.

What the...hell was this?

What he should have done was immediately seek cover. Instead Shuya stood there, stunned.

He recalled Sakamochi's reply to Kiriyama, who asked when the game began: "As soon as you leave here."

It was unbelievable—who could have done this? Did someone return to kill Mayumi Tendo just as she left the school?

Shuya stopped speculating and cautiously crouched down and checked the premises.

For some reason...there was no sign of the attacker. No arrows had flown at him when he'd been standing in a daze. Why? Satisfied with killing only Mayumi Tendo, did the assailant leave the premises? Or...was this some engineered "provocation"? Did the soldiers at the end of the hall kill her to convince everyone that some of their classmates were already willing to play the game? But if that were the case...

All of sudden Shuya realized Mayumi Tendo might still be alive. She might be unconscious from the shock of her wound. In any case, he should look at her.

If he hadn't realized something odd and restrained himself from taking a step forward a split-second later, Shuya would have dropped out of the game early. In other words...

A silver object whizzed right by Shuya's eyes. Yes—it came directly down, from above. Another antenna was planted in the ground.

Shuya shuddered. If he hadn't been standing at the exit, waiting for Noriko, he would have been immediately shot down. The assailant was on top of the building.

Shuya clenched his teeth, snatched up the arrow, and ran to his left. He moved impulsively but in an erratic way that eluded the assailant. He turned around and looked up. Under the dim moonlit sky, a large, dark shadow loomed above the gabled roof of the single-story school building.

Could that be…not Shogo…

He had no time to think. The shadow pointed its weapon at him.

Just to surprise him Shuya threw the arrow at the shadow. But thanks to Shuya's gifts as a star shortstop, the arrow flew at incredible speed and traced a fine arc right at the shadow. The shadow groaned, held its face, hunched over, and then began to sway. Then it fell.

Shuya stepped back and watched the shadow fall from a height of at least three meters and land with a thud on the ground. The object in the assailant's hand fell with a metallic crash.

Light leaked through the building exit. The large shadow was lying face down, wearing a school uniform. It was Yoshio Akamatsu. He was motionless now, perhaps because he was unconscious. A hybrid between a bow and rifle—were they called bow guns?—was lying by his hand. The day pack that had fallen by Yoshio's feet was half open. Shuya saw a stack of silver arrows inside.

Shuya felt a sudden chill. It was true. He was participating! Yoshio Akamatsu was in on this game. Yoshio had taken his weapon, returned here, and killed Mayumi Tendo!

Someone was coming from behind.

Shuya turned around. It was Noriko, who'd taken the situation in as she held her breath in surprise. Shuya's eyes went from Noriko's face to Mayumi Tendo—he ran over to Mayumi and touched her neck to check her pulse. She was dead. There was no doubt.

His brain felt like a fuse fizzling out. Others might be in the same state of mind as Yoshio. And one of them might just suddenly return this time, perhaps with a gun.

Shuya had no choice but to change his attitude toward the game now. So this was it. When Sakamochi said, "As soon as you leave here," this was what he'd meant.

Shuya stood up and ran to Noriko. He took her by the hand.

"We're running! Do your best, you have to run!"

Shuya began running, half-dragging Noriko, whose leg was injured. Which way though?

He couldn't afford to deliberate over his decisions. He headed towards the grove. First they'd hide in the grove, then they could, no—he dismissed the thought. Given Noriko's condition, they were defenseless against any attack. Staying near the area was too dangerous.

Waiting in front of the building for the others was completely out of the question. He rushed Noriko, and they entered the grove. Tall trees mixed in with short trees, and the ground was covered with fern.

Shuya turned to yell some warning to the remaining eleven students coming out (in their class of twenty-one pairs of boys and girls, there should have been twelve students following Shuya's and Noriko's seat numbers, but Fumiyo Fujiyoshi had to be counted out), but he gave up on the idea. Shuya reached the somewhat forced conclusion that they probably weren't as foolish as he was, so they'd flee the moment they emerged from the building anyway, especially once they saw Mayumi Tendo's corpse. For a moment he thought of Shinji Mimura—but he gave up on this idea too. Once again he forced himself into believing that there had to be some other strategy, another way for them to meet up. In any case, they had to leave.

Holding Noriko Nakagawa tightly, he haphazardly led their way into the grove. A bird cried out, "kaw kaw," and ruffled its wings as it flew away. He couldn't see it, but it didn't matter. He had no time to observe it anyway.

39 students remaining

8

Yoshio Akamatsu regained consciousness almost immediately, but because he'd been knocked out cold by the blow to his head he felt as if he were coming out of a deep slumber.

He first noticed how his head was throbbing. He felt out of it. What was it? Was it from playing video games yesterday way past midnight?...which meant that yesterday was Saturday, or was it Sunday?...then today must be Monday which means I have to be in school...but what time could it be...it's still dark, maybe...I can sleep a little more....

As he sat up, the sky and earth rotating ninety degrees, an empty field unexpectedly spread out in front of him. There was a mountain beyond the field, shaped like a bow, darker than the night sky.

All of a sudden, everything came back. Sakamochi, Mr. Hayashida's corpse, Yoshio's departure, discovering the bow gun in his day pack once he found some shelter in a small shack, his returning here, observing Takako Chigusa (Female Student No. 13) whose face was a little severe but beautiful, looking tense now as the track team's best runner dashed away at full speed, him struggling up the thin steel ladder by the side of the building in order to reach the roof. Then how, due to the trouble he had loading his bow gun with an arrow, Sho Tsukioka (Male No. 14) also managed to escape his reach. And then...

He turned around and saw the girl in the sailor suit uniform lying there.

It didn't exactly come as a surprise to Yoshio. What he felt now in conjunction with his memory wasn't guilt over killing one of his classmates so much as it was fear. It might have resembled a gigantic billboard sign standing in the middle of a wasteland inside his mind. On the sign were letters in blood that read, "I'm going to kill you!" In the background all his classmates held weapons like axes and pistols, attacking Yoshio, who stood in front of the sign as if it were a 3D movie.

Of course killing your classmates was wrong. And besides once the game time had expired they were all going to die anyway so it might have been absurd to fight at all. But that was just too rational. The fact was that Yoshio simply did not want to die. He was petrified by any of his classmates who'd bare their teeth at him. Just think about it, you're surrounded by a swarm of assassins.

And so his choice to reduce "the enemy" as efficiently as possible wasn't motivated by rational thoughts but instead from a deeper, primal fear of death. There was no need to discern your allies from your enemies. Everyone had to be an enemy. After all when Ryuhei Sasagawa used to pick on him, everyone looked the other way.

Yoshio scrambled to his feet. First, Shuya Nanahara, who'd been in front of him. Where did he go?... The bow gun. I have to get the bow gun. Where did it?...

Yoshio felt a blow against his neck as if he were struck by a club.

He fell forward with thud. His body twisted into the shape of a V, and his face scraped against the moist soil. The skin of his forehead and cheeks peeled away, but this no longer mattered to him. He was already dead by the time he had fallen.

The same kind of silver arrow which he had shot Mayumi Tendo with was now planted in the back of his neck.

38 students remaining

9

Kazushi Niida (Male Student No. 16) emerged from the building two minutes after Noriko Nakagawa. He stood at the exit for a while, shaking. The bow gun lying next to Yoshio Akamatsu's body was still loaded with an arrow. Although Kazushi had picked it up, he had no intention of shooting Yoshio. But the moment Yoshio stood up, he reflexively pulled the trigger.

Kazushi did his best to overcome his panic. That's right, the first thing was to get out of here. That was the priority. What he should have done in the first place was ignore Yoshio Akamatsu and Mayumi Tendo completely and run away. Given the circumstances, he had no other choice but to kill Yoshio. Yoshio Akamatsu had obviously killed Mayumi Tendo. So Kazushi hadn't done anything wrong.

Kazushi was very good at making excuses. Once he thought like this, the numbness in his head began to wane.

As he lowered the bow gun, he automatically grabbed Yoshio's day pack, which was loaded with arrows. Right before he moved on though, he stopped and picked up Mayumi Tendo's day pack too. Then he hurried off.

38 students remaining

10

Had they been running for ten minutes now? With his arm still wrapped around Noriko, he signaled they should be still, and they both stopped. Under the hazy moonlight shining through the branches overhead, Noriko looked up at him. Their heavy breathing echoed like a giant wall of sound, but Shuya tried his best to listen beyond the wall for other sounds in the area enveloped in darkness.

No one seemed to be chasing them. They were too short of breath to sigh, but they could relax a little now.

As he dropped his bags, a sharp pain ran through his right shoulder. He was in poor shape. An electric guitar was heavier than a bat, but it wasn't something you swung around. After putting the bags down, he placed his hands on his thighs and tried to rest.

Shuya urged Noriko to sit in the dark grove. After he checked again for any other suspicious sounds, he sat down next to her. The thick grass underneath them made a crunching sound.

He felt as if they'd covered a good distance, but given how they'd been zigzagging, and how they'd lost all sense of direction climbing the mountain, they might have only been a few hundred meters away from the school. At least the light leaking out of the building was no longer visible. This might have just been due to the thickness of the grove or the gentle slopes, though. Anyway it felt safer deep inside the dark grove. His decision was impulsive, but he was certain it was safer than the wide open seaside.

Shuya looked over at Noriko and whispered, "Are you all right?"

Noriko murmured, "Yes." She nodded slightly.

Shuya felt the urge to stay here for a while, but that wasn't an option. First he opened up the day pack. He dug into it, groping around, and found an object that felt like a bottle of water.

Shuya pulled it out. The sheath felt like leather and a leather grip poked out of it. It was an army knife. Sakamochi said that the day pack was equipped with a weapon. Was this it? He searched the bag a little more, but nothing else inside resembled a weapon. Only a bag that seemed to contain bread and a flashlight.

He unfastened the sheath and removed the knife. The blade was approximately fifteen centimeters long, and after checking it he returned it to the sheath and tucked it under his school uniform belt. He unfastened the lowest button on his uniform to make the grip immediately accessible.

Shuya grabbed Noriko's day pack and opened the zipper. He knew he wasn't supposed to go through a girl's things, but Noriko didn't pack this bag.

He found something strange. It was a curved stick approximately forty centimeters long. It had the texture of smooth, hard wood. Was this what they called a boomerang? A weapon used for fighting and hunting in primitive tribes. An aboriginal village hunting hero might be able to knock down an ailing, sluggish kangaroo with this thing, but what use could it possibly have for them? Shuya sighed and returned it to Noriko's day pack.

They finally stopped heaving like drown victims gasping for air.

"You want some water?" Shuya asked.

Noriko nodded and said, "Just a little."

Shuya took out the plastic bottle from his day pack, broke the seal of the twist-off top, and sniffed the contents. He spilled some on his hand and licked it cautiously. Then after taking a sip, making sure he had no abnormal reaction, he handed it over to Noriko. Noriko took the bottle and only swallowed a small mouthful. She probably knew that water was precious. Each bottle only contained approximately one liter, and they'd only have two. Sakamochi said they had no access to telephones, but what about the water system?

"Let me take a look at your leg."

Noriko nodded to Shuya's request and stretched out her right leg, which had been tucked in under her skirt. Shuya took out the flashlight from his day pack. He cupped it carefully with the palm of his hand to prevent its light from leaking out and pointed it at her leg wound.

The wound was on the outer calf. A section of flesh approximately four centimeters long and one centimeter deep had been scraped off. A thin stream of blood still flowed out of the ends of the pinkish flesh wound. It looked like she needed stitches.

Shuya quickly turned off his flashlight and grabbed his sports bag instead of his day pack. He grabbed the bourbon flask and two clean bandannas he'd packed for the trip. He uncapped the flask.

"This is going to hurt."

"I'll be okay," Noriko said, but once Shuya tilted the flask and poured the bourbon to disinfect her wound, she let out a small hiss. Shuya pressed one folded bandanna onto her wound. He opened up the other one, folded it, then began wrapping it around her leg tightly like a bandage. This would stop the bleeding for now.

After wrapping her leg, he pulled at both ends of the bandage tightly, tied them together, and mumbled, "Damn…"

Noriko whispered, "You mean Nobu?"

"Yoshitoki, Yoshio. Everyone and everything. I'm not into this. I am so not into this."

As he moved his hands Shuya glanced at Noriko. Then he looked down and finished tying his knot. Noriko thanked him and tucked her leg in.

"So Yoshio was the one who killed…," her voice was trembling, "…Mayumi?"

"That's right. He was above the exit door. I threw the arrow at him and he fell."

Now that he thought about it, Shuya suddenly realized he hadn't taken care of Yoshio. He'd instinctively assumed Yoshio would remain unconscious for a while, but for all he knew Yoshio might have woken up immediately afterwards.

Which meant he might have taken his bow gun, climbed up on the roof, and continued his slaughter.

Was I being too naïve again? Should I have just killed him over there?

With this thought Shuya checked his watch under the moonlight. The old, domestically manufactured Hattori Hanzo limited-edition diver's watch (along with most of his belongings, it had been donated to Shuya through the orphanage) read 2:40. Everyone might have left by now. At most there were only two or three students left, regardless of Yoshio Akamatsu's state. Shinji Mimura had already…Shuya was nearly certain Shinji could easily escape Yoshio.…By now he'd already left too.

Shuya shook his head. Now he felt foolish believing they could unite against their situation.

"I never thought someone like him would actually try to kill everyone else to survive. I understand the rules, but I didn't think anyone would actually participate."

"You might be wrong about that though," Noriko said.

"Huh?" Shuya looked into Noriko's face, too dark to discern under the moonlight.

Noriko continued, "You know how Yoshio was always timid. I think he was scared. That must've been it. I mean you have no idea who might turn against you. He might have been convinced everyone was coming after him. I think he was really scared. And that if he didn't do anything he would end up being…killed.…"

Shuya sat down against the nearest tree trunk and stretched his legs out.

The ones who were terrified might try to kill each other.…The same idea had occurred to Shuya, but he had also thought the ones who were scared would basically hide out. But if they were terrified out of their wits, they might actually take their own initiative.

"I get it."

"Yes," Noriko nodded. "It's still horrible that he started killing indiscriminately."

They remained silent for a while. Then Shuya came up with an idea. "Hey, you think if he'd seen the two of us together he wouldn't have attacked us? Wouldn't it prove we're not playing the game?"

"Well yes, maybe."

Shuya started thinking. If as Noriko said Yoshio had just been overwhelmed by paranoia...

That moment back there was when he first realized someone was willing to play. That was why he fled. But maybe that was wrong. How could they possibly kill each other? It was outrageous. Then should he have waited for the others, leaving aside what he should have done with Yoshio?

Either way, it was too late now. Everyone would be gone by now even if they went back. Besides, did Yoshio do that simply out of fear?

He was getting confused.

"Hey, Noriko."

Noriko lifted her face.

"What do you think? I fled from the school grounds the moment I realized there might be others like Yoshio. But...if he really did it out fear...in other words, do you really think any of us would actually participate? What I mean is that...I'm thinking of gathering everyone together to escape from this game. What do you think?"

"Everyone?"

Noriko fell silent and tucked her knees under her skirt. Then she said, "Maybe I'm not as generous."

"Huh?"

"I couldn't handle some of them. I could trust my friends...." Noriko mentioned the name of their class representative, Yukie Utsumi. Shuya knew Yukie since elementary school.

"Like Yukie. But I don't think I could trust the other girls. There's no way I could be with them. Don't you think? I have no idea what was going through Yoshio's mind, but I'm afraid of everyone else too. I mean…I just realized I don't know a thing about everyone else. I don't know what they're really like. I mean…you can't see into someone's mind."

I don't know a thing about everyone else.

She was right, Shuya thought. What do I know about this group that I spend the day with at school? He suddenly felt like there was an enemy out there.

Noriko continued, "So I-I'd be suspicious. Unless it was someone I really trusted, I'd be suspicious of them. I'd be afraid they might want to kill me."

Shuya sighed. The game was horrible. But it also seemed flawless. In the end, it was a bad idea to invite everyone indiscriminately to form a group unless you were certain about them. What if—let's just say what if—they betrayed you? It wasn't just his life but Noriko's too he'd be endangering. Yes—it was only natural the others before him had immediately fled the premises. That was more realistic.

…

"Hold on a sec," Shuya said. Noriko glanced up at Shuya. "Then that means us being together won't necessarily prove we're harmless. The others might suspect that I plan on killing you eventually."

Noriko nodded. "Yes, I'll be suspected too, just like you. A classmate might avoid us once they see us together, but I also think anyone we invite will turn away. I mean it would depend on each person."

Shuya held his breath. "It would be scary."

"Yes, it's really scary."

So the ones who fled from the school premises might have been right. But what mattered to him was protecting Noriko

Nakagawa, the girl Yoshitoki adored. Maybe he should have been content with the fact that at the very least Noriko Nakagawa was safe by his side now. He had done the safest thing. But...

"But," he said, "at the very least I wanted Shinji to join us. I think he'd come up with a really good plan. You'd be okay with Shinji, right?"

Noriko nodded and said, "Of course." Given the amount of time she spoke with Shuya at school, she had many occasions to talk to Shinji Mimura....Besides...

Shuya recalled how Shinji had helped her up and how he'd signaled him to calm down. He realized now that if Shinji hadn't done those things, he and Noriko would have remained dazed and been shot down like Yoshitoki.

As if she were thinking along the same lines that led to the inevitable, she looked down and quietly said, "So Nobu's gone."

"Yeah," Shuya answered quietly, as if it were a bizarre fact, "I guess so."

Then they fell silent again. They could reminisce but now was not the time. Besides, Shuya couldn't bring himself to take a stroll down memory lane over Yoshitoki. It was too heavy.

"I wonder what we should do."

Noriko stiffened her mouth and nodded without a word.

"I wonder if there might be a way to gather the ones we trust together."

"That's..." Noriko considered it, then became silent once again. It was true—there was no way. At least for now.

Shuya sighed deeply once again.

He looked up and saw through the twigs the gray night sky dimly glowing under the moonlight. So this was what it meant to be in a "no-win situation." If they simply wanted everyone to join, all they had to do was walk around and shout. But that would be an open invitation to get themselves killed by any of their opponents. Of course he hoped there weren't any opponents but...in the end, he had to admit he was scared too.

The thought led to an idea, though. Shuya turned to her and asked, "But you're not afraid of me?"

"What?"

"Didn't you wonder whether I'd try to kill you?"

Under the moonlight, he couldn't see well, but Noriko's eyes seemed to widen a little. "You would never do something so horrible."

Shuya thought a little more. Then he said, "But you can't know what someone's thinking. You said yourself."

"No," Noriko shook her head. "I just know that you would never do that."

Shuya looked at her face directly. He probably looked dazed. "You can...tell?"

"Yes...I can. I..." She hesitated, but then continued, "I've been watching you for so long now." She might have delivered these words more stiffly in a normal situation, or at least one that was a little more romantic.

That was how Shuya recalled the anonymous love letter he'd received written on light blue stationary. Someone had put it inside his desk one day in April. This wasn't the first love letter the former star shortstop and current self-proclaimed (sometimes by others as well) rock and roll star of Shiroiwa Junior High had received, but it made enough of an impression on Shuya for him to hold onto it. There was a poetic quality to the letter that touched him.

It read, "Even if it's a lie, even if it's a dream, please turn to me. Your smile on a certain day isn't a lie, it's not a dream. But having it turn to me might be my lie, my dream. But the day you call my name, it won't be a lie, it won't be a dream." And then, "It's never been a lie, it's never been a dream that I love you."

Was Noriko the one who sent that letter? He remembered observing how the writing resembled hers, and how the poetic style seemed similar too....So then...

Shuya thought of asking her about the letter, but decided not to. This wasn't the right time. Besides, he had no right to bring it up. After all he was so hung up over another girl, Kazumi Shintani, who would never, to take the phrase from that love letter, "turn to him," other girls and that love letter were of little concern to him in comparison. The most important thing now for him was to protect "the girl Yoshitoki Kuninobu adored," not to find out "who had a crush on him."

Then he recalled the bashful look Yoshitoki gave him when they had that talk. "Hey Shuya, I got a crush on someone."

Noriko asked him, "What about you, Shuya? Aren't you afraid of me? No, wait, why then did you help me?"

"Well..." Shuya thought of telling her about Yoshitoki. Come on, my best friend had a crush on you. So if I'm going to help anyone, it's got to be you, no matter what. I mean, really, come on.

He decided against this too. They were better off discussing this later, hopefully when they could take the time to, assuming that is, there would be any time later.

"You were injured. I couldn't just leave you alone. And besides, I trust you. I'll be damned if I didn't trust someone cute as you."

Noriko broke into a slight grin. Shuya did his best to return the smile. They were in a horrible situation, but he felt slight relief in forming a smile.

Shuya said, "In any case, we're lucky. At least we're together."

Noriko nodded. "Yes."

But...what were they supposed to do now?

Shuya began packing his bag. If they were going to rest in order to come up with a strategy, they needed to find a place that offered visibility. Again, they had no idea what the others were up to. At the very least they had to be extremely cautious. That was what it meant to be realistic in the face of horrific circumstances.

He kept the map, compass, and flashlight by his side. This was the world's worst orienteering game.

"Can you still walk?"

"I'm all right."

"Then let's move on a little more. We have to find a place to rest."

38 students remaining

II

Mitsuru Numai (Male Student No. 17) proceeded cautiously between the grove and the narrow moonlit beach that was approximately ten meters wide. He was carrying his issued day pack and his own bag on his shoulder. He held a small automatic pistol in his right hand. (It was a Walther PPK 9mm. Compared to the other weapons that had been issued in this game, this one ranked high. Along with most of the guns used in this program, this mass-produced model was imported cheaply from Third World countries that had remained neutral towards both the nations of the Republic of Greater East Asia and the American Empire and its allies.) Mitsuru was familiar with a model-gun version of the pistol, so he didn't need the accompanying manual. He even knew there was no need to cock the pistol before pulling the trigger. It came with a cartridge of ammunition which he'd since loaded into the gun.

The gun in his hand made him feel somewhat secure, but he held something even more important in his left hand, the supplied compass. It was the same cheap tin model Shuya had, but it did the job. Forty minutes prior to his departure from the classroom, his great leader, Kazuo Kiriyama (Male Student No. 6) had passed him this note: "If we're really on an island, then I'll be waiting at the southern tip."

Of course...everyone was an enemy in this game. That was the fundamental rule. But the bond in the "Kiriyama Family" was absolute. It didn't matter that they were labeled thugs. They were thick as thieves.

Furthermore, the bond between Mitsuru Numai and Kazuo Kiriyama was special. Because...in a way it was Mitsuru who made Kazuo Kiriyama into what he was now. If there was one thing he knew, that the other more square students like Shuya Nanahara didn't, it was the fact that as far as Mitsuru knew, Kazuo Kiriyama, at least until junior high, was no "delinquent."

Mitsuru's memory of his first encounter with Kazuo Kiriyama was so vivid it remained unforgettable.

Mitsuru had been a bully ever since elementary school. But he was never needlessly cruel. Brought up in a generic family, he wasn't particularly bright, nor did he display any other gifts. Fighting was the best way he could prove himself. "Strength" was the only standard he had, and he never fell short of it.

So it was only inevitable, on his first day in junior high, he'd do his best to discourage any competitors coming from other elementary schools in his district. Of course, judging from the strength of kids he'd encountered in the local hang-outs, he knew the kids from the other elementary schools hardly presented a threat. Not everyone might have heard of him, though. There should be only one king—

that was the best way to maintain order. Of course he wouldn't have thought to put it this way, but he knew this was what was going on.

As expected, there were two or three competitors. It all happened after the entrance ceremony and class introduction, after school, when he was in the process of taking care of the last one.

In the deserted hall by the art classroom, Mitsuru grabbed the kid by the lapels and shoved him against the wall. The kid was already bruised above the eye. His eyes were brimming with tears. It was a cinch. It'd only taken two punches.

"Got it? So you don't mess around with me."

The kid nodded his head frantically. He was probably just begging to be released, but Mitsuru wanted verbal confirmation.

"I'm asking you! Did you get that!?"

He thrust the kid's body up with his left arm. "Answer me. Am I the baddest guy in his school? Am I?"

Mitsuru became irritated because his opponent wasn't responding. He lifted him up higher, when he suddenly felt *those* eyes on him.

He let go of the kid and turned around. The kid fell to the floor and scrambled away, but there was no way Mitsuru could go after him now anyway.

He was surrounded by four guys much taller than him. The badges on their worn out collars indicated they were third-year students. You could immediately tell what they were. They were just like him.

"Hey, kid," the pimply faced one who had a creepy grin said. "You shouldn't pick on the weak."

Another one with orange-tinted hair down to his shoulders pursed his abnormally thick lips and continued, "You've been naughty." His "faggoty" voice made the four of them crack up, laughing, "HEEEE," as if they were all insane.

"We'll have to teach you a lesson."

"Yes, we must."

Then they screeched again, "Hee hee!"

Mitsuru tried a surprise kick at the pimply faced one in front of him, but he was immediately tripped by the one on his left.

As soon as he fell back, the pimply one kicked him in the face, knocking out his front teeth. The back of his head pounded against the wall that he'd been busy using on his classmate. He felt dizzy. Something hot oozed down the back of his head. Mitsuru tried to get up on all fours, but then the one on his right kicked him in the stomach. Mitsuru groaned and puked. One of them said, "What a fucking mess."

Damn, he thought. Bastards…fucking cowards…I could take on any of them if it was just one on one….

But there was nothing he could do now. After all, he'd been the one who deliberately chose a deserted place to intimidate his classmate. There wasn't a chance a teacher would appear.

They pressed his right wrist against the floor. One of them carefully pried Mitsuru's index finger back and tucked it under his leather shoe. For the first time in his life Mitsuru experienced real fear.

No…this can't be.

It was. The sole of the shoe came down as Mitsuru's finger made a horrible cracking sound. Mitsuru shrieked. He'd never been in such pain. They kept laughing, "Hee hee hee!"

Mitsuru thought. These bastards…they're insane…they're not at all like me…they're crazy….

They were preparing his middle finger.

"S-stop…"

Without an ounce of pride left, Mitsuru begged for mercy, but they ignored his pleas. The same cracking noise came. Mitsuru's middle finger was ruined now. Mitsuru screamed again.

"Let's have one more then."

That's when it happened.

The door to the art classroom suddenly slid open.

"Can you guys keep it down?" The voice was quiet, though.

For a moment Mitsuru wondered if it was a teacher. But a teacher would have intervened a lot sooner, and besides, a request to keep it down would have been strange.

With his back still pressed to the floor Mitsuru glanced over at the door.

He wasn't too big, but he was incredibly good looking. He was holding a paint brush.

He'd seen him at the class introduction. He was one of Mitsuru's classmates. His family seemed to have recently moved here. No one knew who he was, but since he was quiet and appeared obedient Mitsuru didn't pay much attention to him. Given how his looks were so refined, he probably came from a nice family. Someone like him would do his best to avoid fights, so he was nothing to worry about.

But what was he doing in the art classroom? Probably painting, but wasn't that a little strange on the first day of school?

The pimply guy went up to the boy. "Who the fuck are you?" He stood in front of the boy. "Who the fuck are you? First year? What the fuck are you doing here? Huh? What was that you said?"

He knocked the paint brush out of the boy's hand, and the dark blue paint from the brush splattered against the floor.

The boy slowly looked up at the pimply guy.

The rest needed little explanation. The small boy beat up the four third-year students. (They were all lying on the floor, completely paralyzed.)

The boy approached Mitsuru. After looking him over he only said, "You should have your hand examined at a hospital." Then he went back inside the classroom.

Mitsuru gazed at the four bodies lying on the floor. He was completely stunned by something so completely unprecedented. He felt in awe of the boy, like a rookie boxer doomed to mediocrity upon suddenly encountering a world champion. Mitsuru saw genius.

From that point on Mitsuru served that boy—Kazuo Kiriyama. He had no need to acknowledge it. Kazuo Kiriyama had beaten up four guys at once when Mitsuru could have only taken them on one on one. There should only be one king, and those who weren't should serve under him. He reached this conclusion a long time ago. The idea probably came from his favorite boys' manga magazine.

Kazuo Kiriyama was a mystery.

When Mitsuru asked how he managed to learn how to fight so viciously, he'd only respond, "I just learned." Kazuo would only ignore any further attempts to find out more. Mitsuru would then try to coax more out of him by suggesting he must have had a reputation in elementary school, but Kazuo only denied it. Then maybe he'd been a champion in karate or something? Kazuo denied this too. Another odd point, Mitsuru learned later, was the fact that Kazuo had broken into the art classroom to paint the day they met. When Mitsuru asked why he did that, Kazuo only replied, "I just felt like it." This was how Kazuo's strange persona contributed to Mitsuru's attraction to him. (Furthermore, the quality of the painting depicting a view from the classroom of the empty courtyard far exceeded the first-year junior high level, but Mitsuru never got to see this painting, because Kazuo had tossed it into the trash after completing it.)

Mitsuru showed Kazuo around. The small town,

including the cafe where his friends hung out, the place he stashed stolen goods, the shady dealer who provided illegal goods. Mitsuru's talents were in fighting, but he did his best to show him every place he knew. Kazuo always appeared calm. He came along maybe out of curiosity. Eventually he took on upper class students besides the ones he'd beaten up, bullies from other schools, or sometimes high school students.

Without exception Kazuo had them instantly writhing on the ground. Mitsuru was crazy about Kazuo. It was perhaps no different from the joy a trainer feels in training a champion boxer.

Kazuo wasn't only strong, though. He was extremely smart. Quite simply, he excelled at everything. When they broke into the liquor store's warehouse, it was Kazuo who came up with the brilliant plan. Kazuo saved Mitsuru from numerous jams he got himself into. (Since he got involved with Kazuo, he never got arrested by the police.) Furthermore, his father was supposedly the president of a leading corporation in the prefecture—no, the entire region of Chugoku and Shikoku. He was fearless. Mitsuru believed some people were destined for greatness. He thought, this guy is going to be someone so extraordinary I can't even imagine what he'll become.

Mitsuru made him the leader of his gang, which continued to stir up trouble. Mitsuru only wondered once whether it was right to get Kazuo involved. Kazuo strictly prohibited (he never said so, but that was the vibe he gave off) Mitsuru and the others from visiting his house (in fact it was a mansion), so Mitsuru had no way of telling whether Kazuo's parents were aware of their son's activities. He was concerned his gang might be a bad influence on Kazuo, who was so obviously well bred. After thinking about it a lot, Mitsuru finally shared his concerns with Kazuo.

But Kazuo only said, "I don't care. This is fun too." Mitsuru decided it was all right then.

And so, he and Kazuo had been through a lot together. The king and his loyal advisor.

Even though they were now in an extreme situation, this was why, while killing other classmates was possible, it was out of the question when it came to the members of the Kiriyama Family. After all, Kazuo himself had passed them notes. Mitsuru was certain Kazuo had already planned out a strategy to deal with this situation. He'd outwit Sakamochi, and then escape. If he really wanted to, Kazuo Kiriyama could take on the entire government, no prob.

These were Mitsuru's thoughts as he left the school and walked approximately twenty-five minutes southward. He saw only one person the whole time. The figure who vanished into the residential area southeast of the school was probably Yoji Kuramoto (Male Student No. 8). That made Mitsuru nervous, of course. He'd already encountered the corpses of Mayumi Tendo and Yoshio Akamatsu lying outside the school when he left. The game was well on its way.

Mitsuru's priority was to get to the place assigned by Kazuo as soon as possible. The others were irrelevant. What mattered was how his group would escape from here.

As he moved south, Mitsuru became increasingly tense as any shelter he could hide behind grew sparse. Underneath his school uniform, his entire body was drenched in cold sweat. Sweat oozed out of his short, permed hair and dripped down his forehead.

A little bit further ahead the coast curved right and left, and somewhere in the middle of this curve a rugged reef extended eastward from the hill and sank into the ocean like a buried dinosaur only revealing its back. The reef was much taller than Mitsuru, blocking his vision beyond it. Glancing at the sea, he saw islands and other small lights that indicated a larger piece of land beyond the dark, vast, horizontal expanse of water. This had to be an island in the Seto Inland Sea. That much was certain.

Once he surveyed the area, Mitsuru crossed the border between beach and woods. Exposing himself under moonlight, he walked toward the reef. He clung to the steep rock and began climbing. The rock was cold and smooth and with his right hand holding a gun and his bags strapped around his shoulders it wasn't an easy climb. After the climb, he found the reef was approximately three meters wide, and the beach spread out beyond the rocks. As he prepared to climb down the other side of the reef, a voice all of a sudden addressed him: "Mitsuru." Mitsuru almost jumped. He turned around and raised his pistol.

He sighed with relief. Then he lowered his gun.

Kazuo Kiriyama was in the shadow of a bulging boulder. He was sitting on a protruding rock. "Boss..." Mitsuru said with relief.

But...

Mitsuru noticed three lumps lying at Kazuo's feet.

His eyes squinted in the dark...but then they immediately widened.

The lumps were humans.

The one facing up, glaring at the sky, was Ryuhei Sasagawa (Male Student No. 10). The one lying on his side, scrunched up, was Hiroshi Kuronaga (Male Student No. 9). It was undoubtedly them, the other members of the Kiriyama Family. The third one was wearing a sailor suit uniform, and because she was face down it was hard to tell, but she looked like Izumi Kanai (Female Student No. 5). And...there was a puddle under their bodies. It looked black, but Mitsuru knew of course what it was. If the sun were shining on them now, the color of this puddle would have been identical to the color of the national flag of the Republic of Greater East Asia—crimson red.

Completely confused, Mitsuru began to shiver. What was...what was this?...

"This is the southern tip." Under his slicked-back hair, the perpetually calm eyes of Kazuo looked up at Mitsuru. He wore his coat over his shoulders like a boxer draped in his robe after a fight.

"Wh-wh-wh-what—" Mitsuru's trembling jaw made his voice shake. "What's going on here—"

"You mean this?" Kazuo nudged Ryuhei Sasagawa's body with the tip of his plain (but nice) straight-tip leather shoe. Ryuhei's right elbow, which had been resting on his chest, traced an arc and splashed into the puddle. His pinkie and ring finger disappeared into the puddle.

"They all tried to kill me. Kuronaga and Sasagawa ...both. So I...killed them."

That can't be...

Mitsuru couldn't believe it. Hiroshi Kuronaga was a nobody who tagged along with the group, so he was all the more loyal to Kazuo. Ryuhei Sasagawa was more arrogant, always putting up a front (sometimes it got to be a hassle to stop him from picking on Yoshio Akamatsu), but Ryuhei had been extremely grateful ever since Kazuo pulled some strings to stop the cops from arresting his younger brother for stealing. These two would have never betrayed Kazuo....

Mitsuru caught a whiff in the air. It was blood. The smell of blood. The odor was far more intense than the smell of Yoshitoki Kuninobu's blood back in the classroom. The difference was in the quantity. There was enough blood splashed around here to fill a bathtub.

Crushed by the smell, Mitsuru's trembling chin dropped. Come to think of it...it was impossible to know what someone's true thoughts were. Maybe Hiroshi and Ryuhei were so afraid of being killed that they went nuts. In other words, they just couldn't deal with the pressure. They showed up here at the assigned location, but they tried to ambush Kazuo.

But...Mitsuru's eyes were glued to the other corpse. Izumi Kanai, who was lying face down, was a cute, petite girl. She was the daughter of a town official (of course in this kind of ultra-centralized, bureaucratized society, being a town official or council person was just an honorary post without any influence), and although she wasn't in the same league as Kazuo she probably came from one of the five richest families in town. She wasn't stuck up at all, though, and Mitsuru thought she was kind of cute. Of course, given how different their backgrounds were, he wasn't stupid enough to get hung up over her.

And now she was—

Mitsuru somehow managed to say something. "S-so boss, Izumi...how about..."

Kazuo's calm, cold eyes stared at him. Intimidated by the look he gave him, Mitsuru searched for an answer on his own. "So I-Izumi tried to kill you...too?"

Kazuo nodded.

"She just happened to be here."

Mitsuru hesitated, but then forced himself to believe what he said. Well, maybe it was possible. I mean, that's what the boss said. He spat out, "I-I'm all right. I would never think of killing my boss. Th-this game is bullshit. We're going to take on Sakamochi and those bastards from the Special Defense Forces, right? I'm totally up for it—"

Of course they couldn't approach the school now, because it was a forbidden zone. That's what Sakamochi said. But knowing Kazuo, Mitsuru was sure Kazuo had already come up with a plan.

He stopped speaking. He noticed Kazuo was shaking his

head. Mitsuru moved his tongue, which had now turned gooey, and continued, "Then we're escaping? All right then, we'll find a boat—"

Kazuo said, "Listen." Mitsuru stopped again.

Kazuo went on, "I'm fine either way."

Although Mitsuru clearly heard him, he kept on blinking. He didn't understand what Kazuo meant. He tried to read Kazuo's thoughts from the expression in his eyes, but they just calmly shone in the shadow over his face.

"Wh-what do you mean, you're fine either way?"

Kazuo lifted and pointed his chin at the night sky, as if he were stretching out his neck. The moon shone brightly and cast a gloomy shadow on Kazuo's well-defined face. He kept this pose and said, "I sometimes lose track of what's right and wrong."

Mitsuru was even more confused. That was when an entirely different thought occurred to him. Something was missing.

And then he realized what it was.

The Kiriyama Family consisted of Mitsuru, and Ryuhei and Hiroshi, whose bodies were lying there, plus Sho Tsukioka, who was missing. He'd left before Mitsuru. So then why...

Of course Sho Tsukioka might have lost his way. Or he might have been killed by someone else. But...Mitsuru felt the truth was more ominous than that.

Kazuo went on, "Like now. I just don't know." The sight of Kazuo going on like this seemed, strangely enough, sad.

"Anyway." Kazuo looked back at Mitsuru. Then, as if he were following a musical score that had suddenly switched to *allegro*, he began speaking rapidly, as if it were beyond his control.

"I came here. Izumi was here. Izumi tried to escape. I held her back."

Mitsuru held his breath.

"That's when I tossed a coin. If it came up heads I'd take on Sakamochi and—"

Mitsuru finally understood, before Kazuo finished talking. No...it can't be...

He didn't want to believe it. It was unbelievable. Kazuo was the king and he was his loyal advisor. It was supposed to be about absolute, eternal loyalty and service. That's right—even Kazuo's hairstyle. Right around the time Mitsuru's broken fingers healed up, he'd been the one who insisted on it to Kazuo. "It looks good. You look so bad, boss." Kazuo kept the hairstyle after that. It was a silly little detail, but for Mitsuru it symbolized how close they were.

But...Mitsuru finally realized, maybe it was too much of a hassle for Kazuo to change his hairstyle. He might have been too preoccupied with other stuff to fuss over his hair. Then there were other things he realized. Mitsuru had firmly believed his relationship with Kazuo centered around a sacred team spirit, when in fact Kazuo might have just been in it for kicks or just "just"—that's right, just an experience, just an experience to be had, no feelings attached to it whatsoever. Kazuo himself had once said, "This is fun too."

All of a sudden the one thing that had disturbed Mitsuru from early on returned with full force. Mitsuru thought it wasn't such a big deal, so he'd done his best to ignore it all this time: Kazuo Kiriyama never smiled.

Mitsuru's next thought might have been touching on the truth: and it always seemed like a lot was going on in his head. Which was probably the case. But maybe there's something incredibly dark going on in Kazuo's mind, something so dark it's beyond my imagination? Maybe it isn't even something dark, maybe it's just an absence, a kind of black hole—

And maybe Sho Tsukioka had already sensed this about Kazuo.

Mitsuru had no more time to think. He was completely

focused on his index finger (that's right, one of the fingers broken that fateful day) on the trigger of the Walther PPK in his right hand.

A sea breeze blew in, mixed in with the odor rising from the puddle of blood. The waves kept crashing in.

The Walther PPK in Mitsuru's hand quivered slightly— but the school coat draped over Kazuo's back was already moving by then.

There was a mildly pleasant rattling sound. Sure, it was different, but something about the pulse of 950 bullets ignited every minute resembled the tapping of an old manual typewriter you'd find in an antique store. Izumi Kanai, Ryuhei Sasagawa, and Hiroshi Kuronaga were all stabbed, so these were the first gunshots to echo through the island since the game began.

Mitsuru was still standing. He couldn't see under his school uniform very clearly, but there were four finger-sized holes running from his chest down to his stomach. His back for some reason had two large can-sized holes. His right hand holding the Walther PPK was trembling by his waist. His eyes were staring up towards the North Star. But given how bright the moon was tonight, the star probably wasn't visible.

Kazuo held a crude lump of metal resembling a tin dessert box with a handle. It was an Ingram M10 submachine gun. He said, "If the coin came up tails, I decided I'd take part in the game."

As if he'd been anticipating these words, Mitsuru crashed forward. As he fell, his head hit the rock and bounced back up five centimeters only once.

Kazuo Kiriyama sat still for a while. Then he got up and approached Mitsuru Numai's corpse. He gently touched the bullet ridden body with his left hand, as if checking for something.

This was no emotional response. He didn't feel anything,

no guilt, no grief, no pity—not a single emotion.

He simply wanted to know how a human body reacted after it was shot. No, he merely thought, "It might not be such a bad idea to know."

He removed his hand and touched his left temple—to be more accurate, a little further behind his temple. Any stranger would have thought he was merely straightening out his hair.

But that wasn't it. He did it because of a strange feeling he had—not pain, not an itch, but something elusive and infrequent, occurring only several times a year, when he'd reflexively touch the spot which, along with the feeling, became quite familiar to Kazuo.

Kazuo's "parents" had provided him with a special education. But in spite of learning what there was to know about the world at such a young age, Kazuo himself had no idea what caused this feeling. It was inevitable. Any trace of the damage had almost completely disappeared by the time he was old enough to recognize himself in the mirror. In other words, he knew nothing: the fact that he'd almost died from a freak accident which caused the damage when he was still inside his mother's womb, of course, the fact that his mother was killed by the accident, the conversation his father and a highly reputed doctor had concerning the splinter digging into his skull right before his birth, the fact that neither his father nor the doctor who boasted the operation was a success knew that the splinter had gouged out a cluster of very fine nerve cells. Every one of these facts were from another time. The doctor died from liver failure, the father, or more accurately, "his real father," also died from complications. So there was no one left to share these facts with Kazuo.

One thing was absolutely certain—it was a given for Kazuo. Although he might not have particularly realized it, or more appropriately, perhaps because he was incapable of coming to such a realization, this was what it came down to: he, Kazuo Kiriyama, felt no emotion, no guilt, no sorrow, no pity, towards the four corpses, including Mitsuru's—and that ever since the day he was dropped into this world the way he was, he had never once felt a single emotion.

34 students remaining

12

On the northern side of the island, opposite from where Kazuo and the others were, a steep cliff hung over the sea. It was over twenty meters high. On the cliff was a small field with a crown of wild grass. The waves crashed against the cliff and exploded into mist that drifted into the mild wind.

Sakura Ogawa (Female Student No. 4) and Kazuhiko Yamamoto (Male Student No. 21) sat together at the edge of this cliff. Their legs hung over the edge. Sakura's right hand gently held Kazuhiko's left hand.

Their day packs and bags, along with their compasses, were scattered around them. Just as Kazuo had assigned the others to meet at the southern tip of the island, Sakura had scribbled "at the northern tip" on the piece of paper (right beside "We shall kill each other") she passed on to Kazuhiko. At least they were lucky enough to meet somewhere that didn't coincide with Kazuo's meeting place. Despite their circumstances, they were lucky enough to spend some time alone. There was a Colt .357 Magnum tucked into Kazuhiko's belt, but he already knew he wouldn't be using it.

"It's quiet," Sakura murmured. Beneath her hair, which was cut short for a girl, her pretty profile, beginning with her wide forehead, seemed to be forming a smile. She was tall, so she looked slim, and as always, she sat up straight. Kazuhiko had only recently arrived. As they hugged each other, her body trembled slightly like a wounded little bird.

"Yeah, it is," Kazuhiko said. Aside from the bridge of his nose, which was slightly wide, he was good looking. He turned away from her to look at the view. The dark sea spread out under the moonlight, the black outlines of the islands scattered, and beyond them there was land. The lights were shining brightly on the islands and what appeared to be the Honshu mainland in the distance. It was a little before 3:30 a.m. In between those lights floating in the dark most people were sleeping peacefully. Or maybe there were kids like him studying late into the night for their high school entrance exams. It didn't look terribly far, but it was a world beyond their reach now.

Kazuhiko confirmed the existence of the small black dot approximately two hundred meters out at sea. It appeared to be one of the ships "there to kill anyone attempting to escape by sea" that Sakamochi had mentioned. Although the Seto Inland Sea was always busy with boat traffic, even at night, not a single ship passed by to send out its lights. The government prohibited all traffic here.

It was chilling. Kazuhiko peeled his eyes off the black dot. He'd seen the corpses of Mayumi Tendo and Yoshio Akamatsu when he left the school. He also heard the sound of gunshots in the distance before he arrived here. The game had begun, and it would continue until the end. He and Sakura had already observed this, and this too no longer seemed to matter anymore.

"Thank you so much for this." Sakura was looking at the tiny bouquet of flowers in her left hand. On his way over here Kazuhiko had found several clover-like flowers which he then bundled together. At the top of the long, thin stems, the small petals were bunched together like a cheerleader's pom poms. They weren't the most impressive set of flowers, but this was all he could find.

Kazuhiko did his best to smile. "Oh, you're very welcome."

Sakura looked down at the small bouquet, then finally said, "So we'll never be able to go home together. We won't be able spend time together walking around town, eating ice cream, and doing anything else anymore."

"Well…"

Sakura interrupted Kazuhiko. "It's futile to resist. I should know. I heard my father was against the government, and then one day…"

Kazuhiko could tell from her hand that she was trembling.

"The police came and killed my father. No warrant, nothing. They just came in without a word and shot him dead. I can still remember it clearly. We were in the kitchen. I was still small. I was sitting at the table. My mother held me tight. Then I grew up and ate my meals at the same table."

Sakura turned to Kazuhiko

"It's no use resisting."

It was the first time she had ever told him about the incident, even though they'd been going out for two years. The first time they slept together, just a month ago at her house, she hadn't mentioned it.

Kazuhiko felt there must be something else to say, but all he could muster up struck him as incredibly trite. "Wow, that must have been hard."

But Sakura broke into a smile. "You're so kind, Kazuhiko. You're so kind. That's what I like about you."

"I like you too. I love you so much."

If he weren't so inarticulate, Kazuhiko could have said so much more. How much her expressions, her words, her gentle manner, and untainted pure soul meant to him.

How important, in short, her existence was to him. But he wasn't able to put it in words. He was only a third-year student in junior high, and worse yet, composition was one of his worst subjects.

"Well." Sakura closed her eyes and took in a deep breath, as if a little relieved. Then she breathed out. "I really wanted to make sure I saw you."

Then she went on. "Horrible things are going to happen. No—according to what you said, they've already begun. Just yesterday we were all friends—and now we're going to kill each other." Putting this thought into words, she trembled again. Again Kazuhiko could tell from her hand.

Sakura gave him a weary smile that betrayed fear along with the terrible irony of the fate awaiting them. "I couldn't take that."

Of course not. Sakura was kind. Kazuhiko didn't know anyone else kinder.

"Besides…," Sakura spoke again, "we can't go back together. Even if by some miracle one of us could go back, we still wouldn't be together. Even if…even if I were to survive…I couldn't bear being without you. So…"

Sakura stopped. Kazuhiko understood what she was getting at. So I'm going to kill myself here. Before anyone gets me. Right in front of you.

Instead of finishing what she had to say, she said, "But you have to live."

Kazuhiko smiled grimly, then squeezed her hand tightly and shook his head. "No way. I'm with you. Even if I were to survive, I couldn't stand being without you. Don't leave me alone."

Tears came streaming out of Sakura's eyes which were fixed on Kazuhiko's eyes.

Sakura turned away from Kazuhiko. Wiping her eyes with her left hand that was holding the bouquet of clovers, all of a sudden she blurted out, "Did you see the final episode of *Tonight, at the Same Place*, which airs every Thursday night at nine?"

Kazuhiko nodded. It was a TV drama broadcast by the national DBS network. It was a superfluous love story produced by the Republic of Greater East Asia Television Network, but it was quite good, topping TV ratings for the last several years.

"Yeah, I saw it. You wanted me to watch it."

"Yes, I did. So what I was thinking…"

As she spoke, Kazuhiko thought, this is exactly how we'd always talk. It was always about something really ordinary and meaningless, but there was something so blissful about these conversations they had. Sakura wants us to stay the way we've always been.

The thought suddenly made Kazuhiko want to cry.

"Well, I was all right about the two main characters ending up together. That's how it's supposed to be. But I don't know about Miki's friend Mizue, the one played by Anna Kitagawa. How could Mizue have given up on the guy she loved? I know I would have gone after him."

Kazuhiko grinned. "I knew you'd say that."

Sakura laughed bashfully. "I can't hide anything from you." Then she said happily, "I still remember when we became classmates in junior high. You were tall and good looking, sure, but the thing that really got me was how I thought, 'This guy would understand me, he would understand me down to the core of my heart.' "

"I don't know how to say this very well but," Kazuhiko twisted his tongue a little and thought for a moment, then continued, "I think I felt the same way."

He said it well.

Then he leaned over a little, towards Sakura. With his left hand still clutching her right hand, he wrapped his other hand around her shoulder.

They hugged in this position and exchanged kisses. Was it just a few seconds? Was it a minute? Or was it eternity?

In any case, the kiss ended. They heard a rustling sound. They sensed someone in the bushes behind them. That was their signal: all aboard. The train is departing, so you better get on board.

They had nothing left to say. They could have fought against the intruder. He could have taken his gun and aimed it at the person behind them. But she wouldn't want that. What she wanted was to leave this world quietly before they got sucked into this horrible massacre. Nothing was more important to him than her. There was no room for compromise. If this was what her trembling soul wanted, then he would follow her. Had he been more eloquent he might have described his feelings as something like, "I'm going to die for her honor."

Their two bodies danced in the air beyond the cliff, the black sea in the background, their hands still clasped together.

Yukie Utsumi (Female Student No. 2) poked her head out from the bushes a little. She held her breath and watched them. She had no intention whatsoever of harming anyone, so she had no idea that the noise she made signaled their departure. She was simply stunned by the sight of the No. 1 couple in class vanishing beyond the grassy cliff. The sound of waves quietly brushing up against the sheer rock face continued and the small clovers Sakura dropped remained lying on the grass.

Even when Haruka Tanizawa (Female Student No. 12) approached her from behind and asked her, "What's wrong, Yukie?" Yukie just stood there trembling.

32 students remaining

13

Megumi Eto (Female Student No. 3) sat in the dark, hugging her knees while her small body shook violently. She was inside a house slightly removed from the island's most populated area on the eastern shore. The lights might have worked, but Megumi didn't dare try them. The moonlight coming through the window didn't reach under the worn out kitchen table she was hiding under. It was almost pitch black, so she couldn't check her watch, but two hours had probably passed since she sat down here. It was probably almost 4 a.m. Was it one hour since she heard that distant, faint sound that sounded like firecrackers? No, Megumi didn't even want to think about what that really was.

She raised her face and saw, silhouetted against the moonlight, the cupboard and kettle right above the sink. She was aware the government probably relocated the island's residents to some temporary housing units, but the remaining traces of someone's life in this house was unnatural and creepy. It reminded her of the ghost story she'd heard as a child, about the ship *Marie Celeste* whose entire crew suddenly vanished into thin air, leaving behind their meals and possessions in mid-use. She became even more terrified.

Immediately after her departure she had no idea where she was headed. Next thing she knew she was in the middle of this residential area. The first thought that occurred to her was that there weren't too many students out yet. She was the sixth to leave the school. Five were already out…but only five. There were fifty or sixty houses in this area, so the chances of encountering one of them were close to nil. And as long as she locked the door and kept the place to herself…then she would be safe at least until she had to move. The collar that would explode if she remained in one of the forbidden zones was oppressive, but there was nothing she could do about it. Sakamochi had warned that, "If you try to pry it loose, it will explode." In any case, the important thing was to make sure she could hear Sakamochi's announcement of the time and location of each forbidden zone.

So Megumi had tried to enter a house, but the first one was locked. So was the second one. She went to the backyard of the third one and broke the sash window with a rock she found on the ground. It made such a huge sound, she ducked under the veranda. No one seemed to be in the area, though. She entered. There was no use locking the sash now. She had to laboriously close the storm door. Once it was shut, the inside turned pitch black, and she felt as if she'd wandered into a haunted house. She managed to pull out her flashlight though and searched the house. She took two fishing poles and used them to jam the storm door shut.

And now she was under the kitchen table. Killing each other was out of the question. But what if...just what if this area (checking the map, she found the whole area was almost completely inside sector H=8) never turned into a forbidden zone, then she might end up surviving.

But...Megumi continued shaking as she continued to think. That was terrible. Of course...according to the rules of the game, everyone was your enemy so you couldn't trust anyone. That's why she was shaking right now...but, but even if the game ended and she turned out to be the sole survivor, then that would also mean everyone else had died: her friends (like Mizuho Inada and Kaori Minami), as well as Shuya Nanahara, who made her heart flutter every time she thought of him.

Megumi pulled her knees in and thought of Shuya in the dark. What she really loved about him was his voice. That slight rasp that was neither too high nor too low. He apparently loved censored music called "rock," so he always looked really unhappy in music class when they had to sing songs praising the government and the Dictator, but he sang incredibly. The sound from his guitar when he played improvised passages was superb. Its unfamiliar rhythm made you want to dance. And yet there was also something graceful about the sound, not unlike the sound of bells chiming in a beautiful church. And then there was his longish permed hair (Shuya once said, "I'm imitating Bruce Springsteen," but Megumi had no idea what he was talking about), not to mention his slightly drowsy looking, kind eyes with double eyelids. Also he moved so gracefully since he'd been a star Little League player ever since elementary school.

Her shaking subsided a little when she thought of Shuya's face and voice. Oh, if only Shuya Nanahara were with me right now, it would be so wonderful....

So then...so then why didn't she ever tell Shuya how she felt about him? By love letter? Or by sending someone to bring him, so she could confess to him directly? Or by phone? Now she'd never get the chance.

That's when it occurred to her.

The phone.

That's right. Sakamochi said we wouldn't be able to use phones in the houses. But...

Megumi grabbed her nylon bag, which was lying next to her supplied day pack. She pulled open the zipper and shoved aside her clothes and personal effects.

She touched a hard square object and grabbed it.

It was a cell phone. Her mother bought it for her for this trip in case something (well, this wasn't just *something*) happened during her trip. It was true she'd been envious of the other one or two classmates who owned one, and there was something thrilling about the feeling of having your own private link, but Megumi also thought her parents were being overprotective, and that her mother was neurotic. She wondered, "Why would a junior high school kid need this?" when she put the shiny phone into her bag. She'd completely forgotten about it until this very moment.

Megumi flipped open the phone with her trembling hands.

The phone automatically switched from receive mode to send mode and the small LCD panel and dial buttons lit up with a green glow. Her knees under her skirt and bags were now visible. But more importantly, there, without a doubt, was the antenna and air wave symbols lighting up on the display panel, indicating it was ready for a phone call!

"Oh…God…"

Megumi frantically pressed the dial buttons, the numbers for her home in Shiroiwa-cho. 0, 8, 7, 9, 2…

After a moment of silence, the phone on the other end began to ring in her ear, and her chest filled with hope.

One, two, three rings. Please answer it. Dad, Mom. I might be calling at an unreasonable hour, but you must be aware your daughter is in an emergency situation. Hurry…

The ringing was interrupted by a voice answering, "Hello."

"Oh Dad!" In her cramped position Megumi closed her eyes. She thought she would go crazy from relief. I'm going to be saved. Saved! "Dad, it's me! Megumi! Oh Dad! Please help me! Please, save me from here!" She shouted into the phone in a frenzy, but she came to herself because there was no response. Something…was wrong. What…why won't Dad…no, this was…

Finally, the voice at the other end spoke, "I'm not your dad, Megumi. This is Sakamochi. I told you the phones wouldn't work, Megumi."

Megumi shrieked and tossed the phone to the floor. Then she hurriedly slammed the "End" button.

Her heart thumped frantically. Once again Megumi was overcome with despair. Oh, no...so it failed...so I am going to die here...I'm going to die....

But then Megumi's heart leaped.

...it was a shattering sound.

The sound of broken glass.

Megumi turned towards the origin of the sound. It came from the sitting room which she had checked to make sure it was locked. Someone was coming. Someone. Why, though? Of all the houses here, why this one?

Megumi panicked and closed the cell phone panel, which had been still glowing green. She put it in her pocket, took the weapon from her day pack, and pulled the double-bladed diver's knife from its plastic sheath. She gripped it tightly. She had to escape as quickly as possible.

But her body was frozen and she couldn't move. Megumi slowed her breathing. Please, please, please God, make sure they can't hear my pounding heart.

She heard the sound of a window opening, then closing, then the sound of careful, quiet footsteps. They seemed to be moving around the house, but then they headed directly towards the kitchen and Megumi. Megumi's heart pounded even louder.

A thin ray of light shot through the kitchen. The ray glided over the kettle and cupboard above the sink.

Someone sighed with relief and said to herself, "Good, there's no one here."

The footsteps entered the kitchen. As soon as Megumi heard the voice, though, Megumi was aghast. Any minuscule hope that she could work something out in case the intruder turned out to be a friend had been completely shattered. Because...it was the voice of *her*, Mitsuko Souma (Female Student No. 11), the meanest girl in the entire school. Even though she had the cutest, most angelic face, a single glance from her was enough to intimidate any teacher.

Mitsuko Souma was more frightening to Megumi than any of the ill-reputed boys, Kazuo Kiriyama and Shogo Kawada. It might have been because, like Megumi, Mitsuko Souma was a girl, and also, yes of course, because Megumi herself had been harassed by Hirono Shimizu, who was in Mitsuko's gang, when they first became classmates in second-year. If they were in the same hall, Hirono would trip her or slash her skirt with a razor. Lately, maybe because she'd simply lost interest in Megumi, Hirono had stopped harassing her. (She was still disappointed though when she learned that her third-year class was to be the same as her second-year class.) Mitsuko herself didn't pick on Megumi, but Mitsuko was someone even Hirono couldn't defy.

That's right...Mitsuko Souma would relish killing someone like her.

Megumi's body began trembling again. Oh...please no, don't shake...if she hears me...Megumi wrapped her body tightly with her arms to keep her arms from shaking.

From beneath the table Megumi could see Mitsuko's hand holding a flashlight and the belt of her skirt glowing behind it. She heard the sound of Mitsuko rifling through the drawers of the sink.

Please hurry...hurry up and get out of here. If you could at least just get out of this room...that's right, then I could go to the bathroom. I could lock it from inside and escape through the window. Please hurry...

BRRRRIING. The electronic signal rang, and Megumi felt her heart leap out of her mouth.

Mitsuko Souma also seemed to quiver, slightly. The beam from her flashlight suddenly disappeared along with the belt. She seemed to be approaching the corner of the room.

Megumi realized the sound was coming from her pocket.

She frantically pulled out the cellular. Her mind went blank and she automatically flipped it open and randomly pressed the buttons.

A voice leaked out, "Hey, it's Sakamochi again. I just wanted to remind you, Megumi, to turn off your cell phone. Otherwise, if I call you like this, everyone will know where you are, right? So…"

Megumi's fingers found the "End" button, cutting off Sakamochi's voice.

The suffocating silence continued for a while. Then she heard Mitsuko's voice, "Megumi?" She asked, "Megumi? Is that you?"

Mitsuko seemed to be in the corner of the dark kitchen. Megumi carefully placed her cell phone on the floor. The only thing in her hands now was her knife. Her hands were shaking even more, and the knife felt like a fish wiggling loose, but she gripped it as tight as she could.

Mitsuko was taller than Megumi, but she couldn't have been much stronger. Mitsuko's weapon—could it possibly be a gun?—no, then Mitsuko would have aimed it over here and fired. If Mitsuko didn't have a gun—then Megumi might have a chance. That's right, she had to kill. If she didn't kill, Mitsuko would surely kill her.

She had to kill.

There was a clicking sound, and once again the flashlight beam appeared. It lit up the bottom of the table, and Megumi squinted for an instant. Now was the time—all she had to do was get up, run toward the source of the light with her knife out.

But Megumi's intentions were about to be abruptly undermined by an unexpected turn of events.

The flashlight beam fell on a lower spot, and Mitsuko Souma sank down on the floor into the light, staring at Megumi. Tears were streaming down Mitsuko's cheeks.

"I'm so glad…," her trembling lips finally parted, and she managed to say in a feeble voice, "I'm…I'm…I'm so scared…."

Mitsuko's voice was half shrieking. She thrust both of her hands forward as if seeking Megumi's protection. Her hands were empty.

Then she continued, "I can trust you, right? I can trust you. You wouldn't think of killing me, would you? You'll stay with me, won't you?"

Megumi was stunned. This was Mitsuko Souma crying. She's asking for my help….

Oh…as the shaking in her body subsided, Megumi felt an indescribable emotion well up inside her.

That's right. So that's how it was. It didn't matter how bad her reputation was, Mitsuko Souma was just another third-year junior high school student like her. Even Mitsuko Souma couldn't take part in something as horrible as killing other classmates. She was just lonely and scared out of her wits.

And…oh, how terrible, I'd actually considered it. I thought of killing her.

I'm so…I'm so horrible.

Megumi burst into tears, overwhelmed by self-loathing along with the security that she now felt she was no longer alone, she was with someone.

The knife slipped through Megumi's hands. She crawled on the floor, emerged from under the table, and held Mitsuko's offered hands. As if a dam inside her were bursting, she blurted out, "Mitsuko! Mitsuko!"

She knew she was shaking this time from a different kind of emotion. It didn't matter. She was…she was…

"It's all right. I'll stay with you. We'll stay together."

"Uh-huh." Mitsuko scrunched up her tear-stained face and squeezed Megumi's hands in return, nodding and repeating, "Uh-huh, uh-huh."

Megumi held Mitsuko like this on the kitchen floor. She felt the warmth of Mitsuko's body and she felt all the more guilty as her arms felt Mitsuko's body trembling helplessly.

I-I was really thinking of doing something horrible...so horrible...I was actually trying to kill this girl....

"Hey...," Megumi began to blurt out, "I-I..."

"Hm?" Mitsuko lifted her teary eyes up to Megumi.

Megumi pursed her lips tightly to stifle a shriek and shook her head. "I-I'm so ashamed of myself. For a moment, I was trying to kill you. I thought of killing you. Because I was...I was so scared."

Mitsuko's eyes widened when she heard this—but she didn't get upset. All she did was slightly nod her face which had been scrunched up from crying hysterically. Then she offered a warm smile. "That's okay. Really. Don't get too upset. It's only to be expected. In this awful situation. Really, don't get upset. Okay? Just stay with me, please?"

After Mitsuko said this, she gently held Megumi's face with her left hand and pressed her left cheek against Megumi's cheek. Megumi could feel Mitsuko's tears.

Oh. Megumi thought, I was so wrong about her. It turned out Mitsuko Souma was an incredibly kind girl. She managed to forgive someone who tried to kill her with such a kind response, "It's okay." Didn't our teacher, Mr. Hayashida, who's already been killed, warn us how wrong it is to judge people just by their reputations?

With these thoughts, Megumi felt something well up inside her again. She held Mitsuko's body even more tightly. That was all she could do for now. I'm so sorry, I'm so sorry, I am such a horrible person, I am really—

The slashing sound Megumi heard sounded like a lemon being cut.

It was a nice sound. The knife must have been really sharp

and the lemon fresh, the way they are on television cooking shows, as in, "Today, we'll be cooking lemon salmon."

It took her a few seconds to realize what had occurred.

Megumi saw Mitsuko's right hand. On the left side under her chin. Her hand held a gently curved, banana-shaped blade that reflected dully against the flashlight beam. It was a sickle—the kind used to harvest rice. And now its tip was stuck in Megumi's throat....

Her left hand clutching the back of Megumi's head, Mitsuko dug the sickle in further. It made another crunching noise.

Megumi's throat began to burn, but it didn't last very long. She couldn't say a word and lost consciousness as her chest warmed over with blood. She expired, unable to form any idea of what it meant exactly to have a blade stuck in her throat. Betrayed in the arms of Mitsuko, she died without any thoughts concerning Shuya Nanahara or her family.

Mitsuko let go of Megumi, who collapsed onto the floor right beside her.

Mitsuko quickly turned off her flashlight and stood up. She wiped away the annoying tears (which she could produce any time. It was in fact one of her special talents). Holding the sickle in her right hand up to the moonlight, she whipped the blood off onto the floor. The blood drops made a splattering sound against the floor.

Not bad for starters, Mitsuko thought. She was hoping for a knife that was easier to use, but it turned out a sickle wasn't so bad. She hadn't been careful enough though in entering a house that might already be occupied. From now on I'll have to be more careful....

Looking down at Megumi's corpse, she spoke slowly and quietly, "I'm sorry. I was also trying to kill you."

31 students remaining

PART 2

MIDDLE STAGE

31 students remaining

14

Their first night broke into a bright dawn.

Shuya Nanahara looked up and watched the blue sky gradually turning white through the thicket. The branches and leaves of oak, camellia, some kind of cherry, and other kinds of trees wove an intricate net around them and hid them.

Shuya realized several things as he reexamined the map. The island was roughly diamond shaped. The hills rose upward on the south and north end of the island. They were now located at the south side of the northern mountain, near the slope on its west side. According to the map coordinates, the location seemed to be in sector C=4. Along with contour lines, the map was detailed, including the residential area and other houses (indicated by light blue dots), various buildings (there wasn't much besides symbols indicating a medical clinic, a fire station, and a lighthouse—and then a town hall, a fishermen's coop, that was about it), and roads small and large, allowing him to check where each area was according to the positions of land formations, roads, and scattered houses.

At night he'd already confirmed as soon as they were higher up the hill that the map faithfully represented this island. Silhouettes of islands, large and small, were scattered across the black sea—and as Sakamochi had said, there was (almost exactly west of the island) the silhouette of what appeared to be a guard ship with its lights turned off.

Immediately west of where Shuya and Noriko were, the grove ended abruptly and was replaced by a steep slope. There was a small field below, and beyond it the slope continued on toward the ocean. There was a small shack with a raised floor in the middle of the field that they had passed through last night. Seeing the worn out wooden Shinto archway ten meters away from the shack, Shuya assumed it was a shrine (which was also marked on the map).

The front door was open, and there was no one inside.

Just as he had with the other houses, Shuya decided against hiding in this shrine. There might be others doing the same thing…and given how there was only one entrance, they'd be trapped the moment they were found.

Shuya settled on a place surrounded by shrubbery relatively near the sea, where they could lie down and rest. Higher up the hill the shrubbery seemed thicker, but he thought that would also attract others, and in case they met someone who turned out to be an enemy, he thought they were better off somewhere not too steep, where it was hard to run. After all Noriko's leg was injured.

Shuya sat down against a tree, which was approximately ten centimeters wide. Noriko sat immediately to his left. She leaned against the tree, her injured right leg limply stretched out. They were completely exhausted by now. Noriko slowly closed her eyes.

Shuya discussed their course of action with Noriko, but they couldn't come up with much.

He first thought of finding a boat to escape from the island. But he immediately realized how futile that'd be. There was a guard ship out at sea and furthermore—

Shuya slowly reached for his neck and touched the cold surface of "that thing." He'd gotten used to the sensation, but it felt heavy, as if it were their inescapable fate itself, choking out their existence.

Yes—that collar.

Once a special signal is transmitted from the school, the bomb inside the collar explodes. According to rules this would happen to anyone caught in a forbidden zone, but of course the same would apply to anyone attempting to escape by sea. In fact these collars rendered those guard ships unnecessary. Even if they managed to find a boat, it was impossible for them to escape as long as these collars were on their necks.

Then—the only way out was for them to attack Sakamochi at the school and disable the collar locks. But even with that, the G=7 sector where the school was located had become a forbidden zone since the game started, so it was impossible to approach it. Besides, their locations were constantly being monitored.

He continued to think this through while the area was lit up by morning. It would be dangerous for them to move in the sunlight. He thought they should wait again for nightfall.

But here again there was another problem, the time limit. "If no one dies within twenty-four hours." The last time Shuya saw someone die was when he left the school, which was over three hours ago. If everyone remained alive, in a little more than twenty hours everyone would be dead. Even if they made an attempt to escape, by nightfall it might be too late to get their act together. Ironically, more classmates dying would buy them more time to survive. Shuya tried to shake this thought off.

They were trapped.

Shuya kept on wishing, if only they could meet up with Shinji Mimura. With his wide range of knowledge and accompanying broad expertise to apply it, a guy like Shinji could come up with a solution to their situation.

He also kept on regretting not taking the risk of waiting for Shinji after Yoshio Akamatsu's attack. *Did I really do the right thing? Would I have been attacked as an enemy there? Maybe Yoshio Akamatsu had been the only exception.*

No...that wasn't necessarily true. There might be a lot more "enemies." It was impossible to determine who your enemy was in the first place. *Who was still normal and who wasn't anymore? But—maybe we're the ones who aren't being normal anymore? Maybe we're insane?*

He felt like he was going crazy.

In the end we have no choice but to sit here and see

what'll happen. But will we come up with a solution? If that doesn't work, we can wait until night to look for Shinji Mimura—but will we even be able to do that? Even though the island was small, with a diameter of six kilometers, finding someone under these conditions wouldn't be easy. Besides, will we even have enough time between nightfall and the "expiration time"?

Furthermore—let's assume by some stroke of luck (what an expression) we end up hooking up with Shinji, or it's just the two of us, and we somehow manage to escape , we would be considered fugitives. Unless we emigrate somewhere, we'll spend the rest of our lives as fugitives. And then one day we'll end up being assassinated by a government agent in some abandoned alley, leaving our bodies for the fat mice that come out and nibble at our fingers—

In the end...you might be better off going crazy.

Shuya thought of Yoshitoki Kuninobu. He was shaken by Yoshitoki's death, but maybe Yoshitoki was better off insofar as he didn't have to experience this insanity. This situation that seemed absolutely hopeless.

We might be better off committing suicide. Would Noriko agree to killing ourselves?

Shuya glanced over at her and for the first time closely observed Noriko's profile in the peaceful, dawning light.

She had well defined eyebrows, eyelashes soft against her closed eyes, a cute nose with its flat tip, and full lips. She was a very cute girl. He could see why Yoshitoki had a crush on her.

Now there was sand stuck to her face, and her hair hanging slightly past her shoulders was frayed. And—of course the collar. The gaudy silver collar wrapped around her neck as if she were a slave from ancient times.

This damn game was taking away all her attractive qualities.

Shuya then suddenly felt a surge of incredible anger. And with it, he came to his senses.

We won't lose. We'll survive. Not only that, we'll fight back. It won't be some lame-ass counter-punch. They come with a straight right punch, and I'll wail back at them with a baseball bat.

Noriko opened her eyes. Their eyes met and they stared at each other. Then Noriko quietly said, "What's wrong?"

"Nothing...well, I was thinking."

Shuya was embarrassed, because he'd been staring at Noriko, and she'd caught him doing this, so he just blurted out, "I know this sounds weird, but I just hope you're not thinking of committing suicide."

Noriko looked down, her face ambiguous, forming what might have been a smile. Then she said, "No way...although..."

"Although what?"

Noriko thought for a moment. Then she continued, "I might want to commit suicide if we were the only ones left. Then at least you would be..."

Astonished, Shuya shook his head. He shook it frantically. He had mentioned the idea randomly. He didn't expect her to respond like this.

"Don't be absurd. Don't you even think of it. Look, you and me, we're together to the very end. No matter what. All right?"

Noriko smiled a little, offered her right hand, and touched Shuya's left hand. "Thanks," she said.

"Look, we're going to make it. Don't even think of dying."

Noriko smiled a little again. Then she said, "You haven't given up then, Shuya?"

Shuya nodded with some force. "Of course not."

Noriko nodded and said, "I've always thought this, but you've always had this positive force."

"Positive force?"

Noriko smiled. "I don't know how to say this but you have this positive attitude about living. Like right now you're totally determined to live. And…" She still had a faint smile on her face as she looked directly at him. "That's what I really like about you."

Shuya felt a tinge of embarrassment and replied, "That's because I'm an idiot."

Then he said, "Even if we could escape, you know, I mean it wouldn't matter to me, because I don't have any parents. But, you…you won't be able to see your mother or your father—or your brother. Would you be all right with that?"

Noriko smiled a little again. "I can deal with that—I made up my mind ever since…this game began." She paused, then added, "What about you?"

"What do you mean?"

Noriko continued, "You won't be able to see her anymore…."

Shuya hesitated. It was true, Noriko knew a lot about Shuya. As Noriko herself said, "I've been watching you for so long now."

He'd be lying if he said it didn't matter. He'd been so into Kazumi Shintani—all this time. The thought of never seeing her again was—

But Shuya shook his head, "It's not a big deal."

He thought of adding, "It was just a one-way crush anyway," but he was interrupted by the sudden blare of Sakamochi's voice ringing through the air.

31 students remaining

15

"Good morning everyone."

It was Sakamochi's voice. The speakers were impossible to locate, but his voice came through loud and clear, aside from some metallic distortion. The speakers were probably installed not only in the school but also all over the island.

"This is your instructor Sakamochi. It is now 6 a.m. How are you all doing?"

Before he could grimace, Shuya's jaw dropped, astonished by Sakamochi's cheerful tone.

"Well then, I will now announce the names of your dead friends. First, Yoshio Akamatsu."

Shuya's cheeks stiffened. Yes, it was another death, but the announcement of Yoshio's name also meant more to Shuya.

Yoshio Akamatsu wasn't dead at that moment. Then—was he killed in an attempt to kill someone else? Or, no, did he remain unconscious, lying there...and then blown to bits by this nice collar we're wearing because the school was now a "forbidden zone"?

Regardless, the fact that Shuya had knocked him out didn't make him feel very good.

This line of thought immediately evaporated though, with the announcement of other names of the dead.

"Next, No. 9 Hiroshi Kuronaga, No. 10 Ryuhei Sasagawa, No. 17 Mitsuru Numai, No. 21 Kazuhiko Yamamoto. And then, let's see, the girls. No. 3 Megumi Eto, No. 4 Sakura Ogawa, No. 5 Izumi Kanai, No. 14 Mayumi Tendo."

This list of names meant that their chances of survival were slightly increased, but this thought didn't even occur to Shuya. He felt dizzy. The faces of his dead classmates drifted through his head and disappeared. They were all killed, which meant that there were killers out there. That's right, unless some of them had committed suicide.

"It" was continuing. The game was undeniably in progress. A long funeral procession, a crowd of people wearing black. A man in a black suit with a somber know-it-all face addressed them, "Oh, Shuya Nanahara and Noriko Nakagawa? You two, that's right, you're a little early. But you did just pass by your own graves right here. We carved in the number you two share, No. 15. Don't worry, we're offering a special bonus."

"Good going everyone. I'm very impressed. Now then, the forbidden zones. I will announce their areas and times. Take out your maps and mark them."

Still shocked by the number of dead classmates and angered by Sakamochi's tone of voice, Shuya nonetheless reluctantly pulled out his map.

"First, an hour from now. At seven. 7 a.m. in sector J=2. Get out of J=2 by 7 a.m. Got that?"

J=2 was slightly to the west of the southern tip of the island.

"Next, in three hours, F-1 at 9 a.m."

F=1 was on the west shore of the island, but it was a remote area in the south.

"Next, five hours later. H=8 at 11 a.m."

Most of the residential area on the eastern shore was in H=8.

"That's all for now. Now then, I want you all to do your best today—"

Shuya and Noriko's location wasn't in Sakamochi's forbidden zones. Sakamochi claimed the zones were randomly selected. In any case, they'd made the right move avoiding the residential area. But their location could be included in the next announcement.

"Sakura and…" As Noriko spoke, Shuya turned to her. "Sakura and Kazuhiko's names were mentioned."

"Yeah…" Shuya moaned deep down in his throat. "I wonder if…they killed themselves."

Noriko looked down at her feet. "I don't know. But they must have been together, knowing those two, until the very end. They somehow managed to meet each other."

Shuya had seen Sakura pass a note to Kazuhiko. He and Noriko were only making hopeful observations, though. For all they knew, the two might have been killed separately, in separate places by insane classmates.

Dismissing the image of her slipping the note to him as their hands touched, Shuya pulled out his student list from his pocket. It came with the map in the day pack. It was in bad taste, but he had to mark the information down. He took out his pen, and then as he was about to cross out the names—he decided not to. It was just too…it was just too awful.

Instead he entered a small check mark by the names. He also included Yoshitoki Kuninobu and Fumiyo Fujiyoshi. Shuya felt like he was turning into the man in the black suit from the vision he just had. "Let's see, you, and also you. And you. What's your coffin size? It's a tight fit, but we can offer our popular No. 8 model to you at a specially reduced price."

Enough. In any case, three out of four of Kazuo Kiriyama's gang are dead. Hiroshi Kuronaga, Ryuhei Sasagawa, and Mitsuru Numai. The only ones who weren't mentioned were Sho Tsukioka—nicknamed "Zuki." He was a little weird. And Kazuo Kiriyama himself.

He recalled Mitsuru Numai's smug face when Kazuo Kiriyama left the classroom. Shuya had assumed Kazuo would organize his gang and attempt an escape. So what did these results mean? Maybe, even though they'd agreed to meet somewhere, they turned suspicious and turned against each other? Then Sho Tsukioka and Kazuo managed to escape—would that mean Sho Tsukioka and Kazuo were still together? No, something completely different might have happened. Shuya had no idea.

Then he recalled the faint sound of guns going off. He'd

only heard it once. If that had been gunfire—then which one of these ten did it kill?

His thoughts were interrupted all of a sudden by a rustling sound. Noriko's face stiffened. Shuya immediately stuck the pen and list into his pocket.

Shuya listened closely. The sound continued. In fact—it was approaching them.

He whispered to Noriko, "Be quiet."

Shuya grabbed his day pack. They had to be able to move at any moment, so he'd put everything he needed in it. He left some of his clothes in his sports bag, but it wasn't a big deal to toss it. Noriko had also packed her bags the same way.

He hoisted the two day packs on his left shoulder. He offered Noriko his hands to help her up. They waited in a crouched position.

Shuya pulled out his knife. His right hand held it in a reverse grip. I might know how to use a guitar pick, he thought, but I don't know a thing about how to use *this*.

The rustling became increasingly louder. It was probably only a few meters away.

He was overwhelmed by the same tension he felt outside the school. He held Noriko's shoulder with his left hand and pulled her back. He stood up and stepped back. The sooner the better. As soon as possible!

They made their way through the bushes and came out onto a foot trail. It winded up the hill. Trees loomed above them, branches bunched together, and the sky was blue.

Still holding Noriko, Shuya treaded backwards with her for several meters along the trail. The rustling sound continued in the bushes they'd just left. The sound grew and then—

Shuya's eyes widened.

A white cat jumped out of the bushes and landed on the

trail. It was scraggly, and its hair was frayed, but in any case, that's what it was—a cat.

Shuya and Noriko looked at each other. "It's a cat," she said and broke into a smile. Shuya also grinned. Then the cat turned to them as if it had finally noticed them.

It stared at them for a while and then ran up to them.

Shuya returned his knife into the sheath while Noriko crouched, cautiously bent her injured leg, and offered her hands to the cat. The cat jumped into her hands and nuzzled her feet. Noriko slipped her hands under the cat's front feet and hugged it towards her.

"Poor kitty. Look how thin it is." Noriko said as she pursed her lips towards the cat as if to kiss it. The cat responded enthusiastically, purring, meow.

"It must be a domestic cat. It's so friendly."

"I don't know."

The government had relocated all the residents of this island for the sake of this game. (Because the Program was a secret operation until it was over, they must not have been informed.) As Noriko said, maybe this cat had been owned by someone here and abandoned after its owner left. There weren't any houses in the area, so did it get lost in the hills? Shuya wondered as he casually looked away from Noriko. He turned...

...in shock.

There was someone wearing a school coat ten meters away, standing on the trail as if his feet were glued to it. Although he was of medium height, like Shuya, he had a solid build from his training on the handball team. His skin was tanned, and he had a buzz cut. His hair stood up at the front. It was Tatsumichi Oki (Male Student No. 3).

31 students remaining

16

Noriko followed Shuya's eyes and turned around. Her face suddenly grew tense. That's right…what was going on with Tatsumichi? Was he an enemy or not?

Tatsumichi Oki stood there, staring at them. Shuya felt his field of vision grow narrow from the tension—the way it might in a speeding car—but in the corner of his eye he could still make out the large hatchet in Tatsumichi's right hand.

Shuya reflexively raised his hand to the knife tucked in his belt.

That set it off. Tatsumichi's hand, the one holding the hatchet, twitched, and then he began running towards them.

Shuya shoved Noriko, who was still holding the cat, into the bushes.

Tatsumichi was already right in front of him.

Shuya quickly lifted up his day pack. The hatchet went right into it, splitting it open so its contents spilled to the ground. Water sprayed out of the bag from the broken water bottle. The blade reached Shuya's arm. A searing pain ran under his skin.

He tossed down the torn day pack and leaped back to gain some distance. Tatsumichi's face was so wound up the whites of his eyes formed circles around his pupils.

Shuya couldn't believe it. Yes, they were in a dire situation, and Shuya had been for a moment suspicious too, but how could he?…How could that cheerful, nice guy, Tatsumichi, do such a thing?

Tatsumichi quickly glanced over to where Noriko was, in the bushes. Following his gaze, Shuya looked over at Noriko too. Noriko's face and lips froze at Tatsumichi's glance. The cat had already gone off elsewhere.

Suddenly Tatsumichi turned to Shuya and swung his hatchet sideways.

Shuya met the blow with the knife he'd pulled out from his belt. Unfortunately it was still inside its leather sheath, but in any case, there was a locking sound. He managed to stop the blow about five centimeters away from his cheek. Shuya could see the blue ripple on the hatchet blade, probably formed when it had been forged.

Before Tatsumichi could swing back, Shuya tossed his knife out and grabbed Tatsumichi's right arm, which was holding the hatchet. But Tatsumichi forced a swing, which although slow managed to hit the right side of Shuya's head. Some of the slightly wavy long hair above his right ear fell, and a sharp tear ran through his earlobe. It didn't hurt much. A silly, inappropriate thought crossed his mind: well, it's no big deal, Shinji had his pierced, after all.

Tatsumichi switched the hatchet from his right hand to his left but before he could swing at Shuya again, Shuya swept his left leg under Tatsumichi's feet. Tatsumichi's legs swayed, all right now, fall!

But he managed to stay up, teetered, and then spun around. He fell on top of Shuya. Shuya moved back into the shrubbery. The sound of crushed branches surrounded them.

Shuya continued moving back. Forced by Tatsumichi's awesome strength, he was now practically running backwards. Noriko's face was vanishing from his sight. In this unreal situation, another absurd thought crossed his mind. He recalled Little League practice. Shuya Nanahara, backwards-running champion, yeah!

Then his feet felt funny.

He suddenly recalled how there was a steep slope towards the field with the shrine.

I'm falling!

The two of them tumbled down the slope covered with shrubbery. The clear early morning sky and greenery spun around and around. But he still managed to hold onto Tatsumichi's wrist.

He felt as if they'd fallen from a great height, but it was probably only ten meters or so. Their bodies crashed with a loud thump, and they were still. The area was bathed in sunlight. They'd fallen into the field.

Shuya was crushed under Tatsumichi. He had to get up before Tatsumichi could!

But that was when Shuya felt something strange. Although Tatsumichi had come at him with the force of an air compressor, the strength in his arms had completely gone. They'd gone limp.

His face under the lower part of Tatsumichi's chest, Shuya saw why, as he looked up.

Right above him, the hatchet was lodged into Tatsumichi's face. Half of the blade stuck out from his face like the top layer of chocolate on a Christmas cake. The hatchet had landed on his forehead, neatly split open the left eyeball (a gooey liquid leaked out with his blood), and a pale blue light reflected off the blade inside his mouth.

Tatsumichi still held onto the hatchet, but Shuya was the one holding his wrists. Shuya felt a horrible sensation running at the speed of light from Tatsumichi's face to his wrists.

As if tracing the course of this sensation, blood slid down the blade, flowing from Tatsumichi onto Shuya's hands holding Tatsumichi's wrists. Shuya let out a low groan, released his hands, and got out from underneath Tatsumichi's body. Tatsumichi's body rolled over, face up, his horrific dead face thrust into the morning light.

Huffing and puffing, Shuya felt a numb urge to vomit.

The incomparable horror of Tatsumichi's face wasn't a trivial matter, but for Shuya something even more important concerned himself. Yes. He had killed someone. Worse yet, a fellow classmate.

It was no use convincing himself it was an accident. After

all—he had done everything he could to deflect the blade, and therefore direct it towards Tatsumichi by twisting Tatsumichi's wrists as far back as possible.

He felt incredibly nauseous.

But Shuya gulped and held back the urge to vomit. He lifted his head and looked up at the slope he'd just tumbled down.

He couldn't see beyond the shrubbery covering the slope. He'd left Noriko alone. That's right, the important thing now was to protect Noriko. He had no time to puke. He had to hurry back to Noriko, Shuya told himself as if these thoughts would calm him down. He stood up and stared down at Tatsumichi's face and the hatchet for a while.

He hesitated but then pursed his lips together and pried Tatsumichi's fingers loose from the handle of the hatchet that split his face. He couldn't just leave Tatsumichi like this. Of course he couldn't bury him—but Tatsumichi's hatchet face was just too much. He couldn't bear it. He grabbed the handle and tried to pull the hatchet out of Tatsumichi's face.

Tatsumichi's face was stuck to it though as it came up with the hatchet. The hatchet was lodged in so deeply, it was stuck.

Shuya took a deep breath. Oh God.

Then he thought about it. No. What's this about God? Ms. Anno was a devoted Christian but no thanks to her faith in God she ended up getting raped by Sakamochi. Ah, praise the Lord.

Shuya felt another surge of anger.

He clenched his teeth and knelt beside Tatsumichi's head and put his trembling left hand on his classmate's forehead. With his right hand he pulled on the hatchet, which made a horrible spurting sound as blood sprayed out of Tatsumichi's face, and the hatchet came loose.

He felt as if he were in a nightmare. Cracked in the

middle, Tatsumichi's head was now asymmetrical. It looked too unreal. It looked like a plastic fake. Shuya realized for the first time in his life how malleable and fragile the human body was.

He gave up trying to close Tatsumichi's eyes. His left eyeball and eyelid was split, the eyelid shriveled and swollen so badly it couldn't be shut. His right eye was probably manageable, but who'd want a winking corpse? It was in bad taste given the circumstances.

He felt sick again.

But he stood up again and turned around. To get back to Noriko he'd have to take the long way around up the foot trail.

Shuya's eyes opened wide **again** though now because...

...there was a boy wearing glasses and a school coat in the middle of the field—the male class representative, Kyoichi Motobuchi.

And this representative was holding a pistol.

30 students remaining

17

Behind his silver-framed glasses, the class representative's eyes met Shuya's. His hair that was always so neatly parted at a 7:3 ratio was now a complete mess. The lenses of his glasses looked smudged, and the eyes behind them were bloodshot and wide open the way Tatsumichi's eyes were. His face was incredibly pale, as it was inside the classroom, once again resembling a Warhol print. It didn't look human anymore.

As the gun flinched, Shuya twisted his body and ducked backwards. With an explosive pop, the gun set off a small flame. Something hot grazed the top of his head. Of course he might have just imagined it. Anyway, the bullet missed him.

Still on his back, Shuya didn't have time to think. He just tried to retreat. The tall grass made a rustling sound under his back.

He was too close. He couldn't escape. Kyoichi Motobuchi was only several meters away from Shuya, aiming directly at his chest.

Shuya's face grew as stiff as a plaster sculpture. More than protecting Noriko, more than anything, it was real fear that caught him now, welling up inside. The next tiny lead bullet that gun spits out will kill me...kill...me!

"Stop it!" Another voice yelled.

Kyoichi suddenly turned in a diagonal direction. Shuya also followed Kyoichi's glance—

A large figure stood in the shade of the shrine. Buzzed hair, no, the head was practically bald, the prominent scars above his brows, the tough face of a thug. It was Shogo Kawada (Male Student No. 5). He held a pump-action shotgun (a sawed-off Remington M31).

Without any warning Kyoichi shot at Shogo. Shuya saw Shogo quickly duck. As he heard the explosion from the shotgun that Shogo held in his kneeling position, sparks flew from the muzzle like a flame thrower, and the next moment Kyoichi's right arm was gone. Bloody mist shot into the air. Kyoichi gazed blankly at the half-sleeve of his school uniform. The rest of his sleeve, from his elbow to the hand that was holding the gun, was now lying on the grass. Shogo quickly pumped the shotgun and loaded the next shot. A red plastic shell flew out to the side after spitting out its pellets.

"AIEEEE!"

Kyoichi screamed like an animal as he suddenly realized what had happened. Shuya thought he would fall to his knees.

But he didn't. The representative instead ran for his arm. He pried the gun loose from his right hand with his left hand. Like a one-man baton relay. Great. Shuya once again felt like he was watching a bad horror flick. Or better yet, reading a bad horror novel.

Damn, this was bad.

"Stop it!" Shogo shouted, but Kyoichi refused and pointed his gun at Shogo.

Shogo shot again. Kyoichi's body bent over into a triangle shape, with his waist pointing out like a long jumper, but blown backwards. He landed feet first, and as if in time-lapse photography the next moment he was falling on the ground face up. He sank into the overgrown grass and remained still.

Shuya scrambled to his feet.

He could see Kyoichi's body between the blades of grass. There was a gaping hole in the stomach of the school coat, and the contents inside looked like a trash bin in a sausage factory.

Shogo hardly paid any attention to the corpse and quickly approached Shuya with his shotgun. He pumped the shotgun again and ejected the empty shell.

Shuya was overwhelmed by the quick succession of events and the horrific deaths of Tatsumichi and Kyoichi, but he managed to say between heavy breaths, "Hold on, I'm—"

Shogo stopped behind Kyoichi's body and said, "Don't move. Drop your weapon." Shuya finally realized he was still holding the hatchet.

He did as he was told. The blood-drenched hatchet fell to the ground with a thud.

That was when Noriko appeared, standing where the trail nose dived. Dragging her leg, she had made her way through the thicket, following Tatsumichi and Shuya after they tumbled down the slope. (Shuya then realized that less than a minute had elapsed since his confrontation with Tatsumichi Oki.) She'd turned pale from the gunfire, but now she was holding her breath at the sight of the sprawled out corpses of Tatsumichi and Kyoichi while Shogo and Shuya faced each other.

Shogo immediately noticed Noriko and pointed his shotgun at her. Noriko's body stiffened. "Stop it!" Shuya shouted. "Noriko is with me! We don't want to fight at all!"

Shogo turned slowly to Shuya. He had a strange, blank look.

Shuya shouted at Noriko, "Noriko! Shogo saved me. Shogo isn't an enemy!"

Shogo looked at Noriko and then returned his gaze to Shuya. Then he lowered the muzzle.

After remaining frozen for a while, Noriko raised her hand to indicate her hands were empty, then nearly slid down the steep trail. She staggered, dragging her right leg, and as she drew herself up next to Shuya they both looked at Shogo.

Shogo stared back at them as if they were a pair of Armadillo twins. Shuya noticed that the stubble on his cheek and chin had grown a little.

"First, let me explain," Shogo finally said, "I had no choice but to shoot Kyoichi. You understand?"

Looking over at Kyoichi's body, Shuya considered Shogo's words and realized that maybe, maybe the representative had totally lost control. He might have seen me beat Tatsumichi Oki and gotten the wrong impression. Noriko wasn't around so it would have been natural.

As Shogo said, Shuya had no right to fault Shogo for his actions. If Shogo didn't kill Kyoichi, then Kyoichi would have killed Shuya. After all—he had also killed someone. Tatsumichi Oki.

He looked back at Shogo.

"Yeah, I know. Thanks. You saved me."

Shogo shrugged. "I was just trying to stop Kyoichi, but I guess I ended up doing that as well."

Adrenaline was still rushing through his body, but Shuya

managed to blurt out, "I'm so glad. I'm so relieved we've met someone else who's normal."

In fact Shuya was surprised. Back in the classroom he thought if anyone was going to play the game it'd be Shogo. But not only was he not playing along, he'd managed to save Shuya's life.

Shogo stared at them for a while, as if he were thinking through something. Then he said, "So you two are together?"

Shuya raised his brow. "That's what I said."

Then Shogo asked, "Why are you two together?"

Shuya and Noriko looked at each other. Then they looked at Shogo. Shuya was in the middle of saying, "What do you mean...," but then stopped as Noriko asked the same question, but she stopped in mid-sentence too, realizing Shuya was asking the same thing. Shuya and Noriko looked at each other again. Shuya thought Noriko was giving him the green light to speak first, but then as soon as he began speaking, his words overlapped with hers, "That's because..." Once again Shuya and Noriko exchanged glances. They ended up facing Shogo without saying a word.

A quick grin ran across Shogo's face. If he was smiling, it was the first time Shuya had ever seen him smile.

Shogo said, "All right, all right. In any case, we have to hide out. We don't want to be standing out here in the open."

29 students remaining

18

Yuko Sakaki (Female Student No. 9) was wading through the thicket. It was dangerous for her to run so recklessly, but she had to escape. That was her priority.

She played back the scene she had just witnessed in her

head. The incident she saw from the bushes. Tatsumichi Oki's head split wide open. Shuya Nanahara yanking out the hatchet from his head.

She was horrified. Shuya Nanahara had killed Tatsumichi Oki. He did it flawlessly.

Until Shuya pulled out the hatchet from Tatsumichi's head, Yuko was so transfixed she couldn't take her eyes off the scene. But as soon as she saw the red on the hatchet, fear took over. She grabbed her day pack and held her mouth shut because it would have shrieked on its own. Tears welled up in her eyes.

The sound of gunfire followed behind her, but she could hardly hear it given the state she was in.

29 students remaining

19

After Shuya and Noriko returned to the thicket where they'd settled last night and picked up their bags, Shogo remarked their view was no good here. Shuya thought he'd been thorough choosing this location, but Shogo seemed abnormally adept in this environment, so they did as he said and moved towards the mountain. The dirty cat was gone.

"Hold on. I'm going to find Kyoichi's and Tatsumichi's bags."

Shogo left them in the nearby shrubs. Noriko sat down to rest, and Shuya sat next to her. He was holding the revolver (Smith & Wesson .38 Chief's Special) Shogo had given him after retrieving it from Kyoichi's body. It made him feel uncomfortable, and he didn't want to carry it— he'd seen that grotesque one-man baton hand off—but he managed to hold it.

"Shuya, here."

She held out a pink band-aid. She must have found it in the day pack Tatsumichi Oki's hatchet had torn through. Shuya touched his right ear with his left hand. The bleeding seemed to have stopped, but he felt a stinging pain.

"Hold still." Noriko drew near him and opened the band-aid seal.

As she carefully wrapped it around his earlobe, she said, "I wonder why so many of us came here. Five students, if we include Shogo and us."

Shuya looked back at Noriko. The thought didn't even occur to him thanks to all those action scenes, but she was right.

He shook his head.

"I don't know. We came here to get as far away as possible, right? We avoided climbing the hill and avoided the shore, where there's too much visibility. Maybe we were all thinking the same thing and ended up at the same place, thinking we'd be safe here, including the representative—and Tatsumichi."

The moment he mentioned Tatsumichi, he felt a nauseous pain in his stomach again. His face split down the middle, left and right out of alignment like a peanut. And this corpse was lying right nearby. Ladies and gentlemen, the magnificent Peanut Man....

Along with the nausea, Shuya's thoughts which had been numbed by the adrenaline rush of fighting finally grew clearer and the sensation of numbness finally subsided. He was coming back to his senses.

"Shuya. You're pale. Are you okay?" Noriko asked, but Shuya couldn't respond. A shiver ran through his body, and he began to tremble. His body shook as if it were vibrating. His teeth chattered uncontrollably as if dancing a crazy tap dance.

"What's wrong?" Noriko put her hand on his shoulder.

Shuya answered, his teeth still chattering, "I'm scared."

Shuya twisted his neck to the left and looked at Noriko. She glanced back at him with a look of concern.

"I'm scared. I'm scared shitless. I just killed someone."

Noriko looked into Shuya's eyes for a while, then she cautiously moved her injured right leg and sat diagonally in front of Shuya with her knees bent. Then she gently opened her arms and wrapped them around Shuya's shoulders. Her cheek touched his trembling cheeks. He felt her warmth, and his nostrils which had been overwhelmed with the smell of blood could detect a slight whiff of something like cologne or shampoo.

Shuya was surprised, but he was grateful for the comforting warmth and smell and sat still, hugging his knees.

It reminded him of the time his mother hugged him as a child before she died. As he looked at the collar of Noriko's sailor suit, he had a fleeting image of his mother. She spoke clearly, always so full of energy. Even as a child he thought she was a stylish mother. Her face, oh man, looked a lot like Kazumi Shintani's. She was always exchanging smiles with his father who, with his mustache, didn't seem like your typical salaryman. (Wrapped in her arms, he would hear her say, "Your father works in law and helps people in trouble. It's a very important job in this country.") Some day I'm going to marry someone like my mom and then I'll be smiling all the time the way Mom and Dad are. Their smiles made him feel that way.

The trembling gradually subsided and disappeared.

"Are you all right?" Noriko asked.

"I think so. Thanks."

Noriko slowly let him go.

After a while, Shuya said, "You smell nice."

Noriko smiled bashfully. "Oh God, I didn't take a bath yesterday."

"No, you really do smell nice."

A smile flashed across Noriko's face again, when the bushes rustled. Shuya shielded her with his left arm and held the Smith & Wesson.

"Don't shoot. It's me."

Parting the thick bushes, Shogo entered. Shuya lowered the gun.

Shogo carried two day packs along with the shotgun slung over his shoulder on a sling. He took out a small cardboard box and tossed it over to Shuya.

He caught it in mid-air and opened it. The golden bottoms of bullets in neat rows. Five bullets were missing like cavities.

"Bullets for your gun. Load it," Shogo said, then put his shotgun by his side and pulled at some worn out fishing wire. He pulled at one end tightly and Shuya saw how the wire went straight into the deep end of the bushes. Shogo then took out a small knife from his pocket and snapped the blade out of its handle. Shogo's supplied weapon was a shotgun, so, Shuya figured, the knife he must have brought on his own.

Shogo made a notch with the knife into a nearby tree trunk no thicker than a can of Coke. Then he fit the taught wire snugly into the notch and cut off the excess. He tied the remaining wire around the tree trunk in the same manner.

"What are you doing?" Shuya asked.

"This?" Shogo put away his knife and answered, "You might call it a primitive alarm system. We're at the center. The wire runs around us in a circle with a twenty meter radius. The wire's doubled. The moment it catches someone, this will be pulled and fall from the tree. Don't worry, the intruder won't even notice. It'll provide us with a warning."

"Where did you find that wire?"

Shogo tilted his head slightly.

"There was a little general supply store. I wanted to get my hands on some things, so that was my first destination. That's where I found it."

Shuya looked astonished. Of course. No matter how small this island was there had to be at least one supply store. But the thought never even crossed his mind. Of course it wouldn't have been possible for him to wander around given how he had to look after Noriko.

Shogo sat down where he could face both Shuya and Noriko. He began sorting through a day pack that belonged either to Tatsumichi or Kyoichi. Taking out a bottle of water and some bread rolls, he said, "How about some breakfast?"

Still hugging his knees, Shuya shook his head. He had no appetite whatsoever.

"What's wrong? You feel nauseous from killing Tatsumichi?"

Shogo examined Shuya's face and said casually, "Don't let it get to you. Let's say each person kills one person. The game's like a tournament. It's forty-two, no, forty students, so if you kill five or six, then you'll be the winner. Four or five more, that's all you'll need."

Shuya knew he was joking, but no, it was all the more offensive because he was joking. He glared at Shogo.

Sensing Shuya's anger, Shogo drew back.

"Sorry man, I was just kidding."

Shuya asked in a hostile tone, "So you don't feel nauseous? Or did you already kill someone before Kyoichi?"

Shogo merely shrugged.

"Well, this time, it was my first."

It was a strange way to put it, Shuya thought, but he had no idea what was so odd about it. He felt confused. If Shogo was the rumored delinquent he was said to be then he might be bold in a way Shuya could never be.

Shuya shook his head and changed the subject. "You know, there's something I don't get."

Shogo raised his brow. The ugly scar above his left brow moved with it. "What's that?"

"The representative...Kyoichi..."

"Hey." Shogo pointed his chin up at him to cut him off. "I thought you understood. I didn't have any choice. Are you saying I should have let him kill me? I'm not Jesus Christ, okay? Besides, I can't be resurrected, although I've never tried it out...."

"No, that's not what I meant."

As Shuya continued, he wondered whether Shogo was kidding again. Was Shogo Kawada the joking type?

"I think the reason Kyoichi tried to shoot me was that he saw me kill...Tatsumichi up close. I killed Tatsumichi. And that was because he attacked me—"

Shogo gave a light nod.

"So it was only natural that Kyoichi would try to kill me."

"That's true. Maybe. But even so I—"

"No," Shuya interrupted Shogo. "Forget about that. What I mean is that Tatsumichi...Tatsumichi came after me even though I didn't do a thing. And besides, I was with Noriko. Why did he have to attack us?"

Shogo shrugged and put his water bottle and bread by his feet.

"Tatsumichi was up for it. That's all. What's to understand?"

"No, well...theoretically, yes, but...I just don't get it. How Tatsumichi could—"

Shogo cut off Shuya's hesitant words, "There's no need to understand."

"Huh?"

Shogo's lips twisted slightly as if grinning, then he went on, "I'm only a transfer student, so I don't know much about you and your classmates. But what do you know about Tatsumichi? Maybe there's someone really ill in his family, so he felt he had to survive. Or maybe he was just being selfish. Or maybe he went insane from fear and lost his capacity for reason. Or there's even this possibility: you were with her. He might have thought you teamed up with her. How can he tell whether he's invited? You and her might have decided he's a threat. Or if you were actually playing the game, then you could use this same excuse to kill him. Hey, did you provoke him at all?"

"No…" Shuya stopped, recalling how he'd reflexively touched his knife when he faced Tatsumichi. Shuya himself had also been afraid. He'd been afraid of Tatsumichi.

"Was there something?"

"I touched my knife." He looked at Shogo. "But that's not enough to—"

Shogo shook his head. "Oh yeah it is, Shuya. Tatsumichi might have thought, I have to beat you, since you're holding a weapon. Everyone's fuse in this game is pretty short."

He said, as if to conclude the topic, "But in the end Tatsumichi was up for it. That's the best way to understand it. Look, there's no need to understand. What it comes down to is this. Once your opponent attacks you with a weapon, you don't hesitate. Otherwise you'll die. You can't afford to think about it. The first thing you do is anticipate your opponent. You shouldn't trust people too much in this game."

Shuya took a deep breath. Did Tatsumichi really want to kill me? Then again, as Shogo said, it might be pointless to think too much about it.

…

Shuya looked up at Shogo again.

"That's right."

"What?"

"That's what I forgot to ask."

"So what is it? Come on."

Shuya continued, "Why are you here with us?"

Shogo raised his eyebrows. He licked his lips.

"Good point. I might be against you too."

"That's not what I mean." Shuya shook his head. "You saved me. No, you also risked your life trying to stop Kyoichi. I'm not suspecting you."

"Well, you got it wrong, Shuya. You don't seem to understand this game yet."

"…what do you mean?"

Shogo continued, "In order to survive, being in a group gives you an advantage this game."

Shuya considered this, then nodded. He was right. You could take turns being on the lookout, and you were stronger in case of an attack.

"So?"

"Think about it." Shogo nudged the shotgun resting on his knees with his hand. "Do you think I was risking much to stop Kyoichi? Do you think ordering him to stop would have actually stopped him? Maybe I was already planning on killing Kyoichi. Did I really have to kill him? Kyoichi never struck me as the type who'd attract a group, but maybe I ordered him to stop just to put on an act for you guys to join me. Wouldn't it be in my best interests to join you guys and then kill you off later?"

Shuya stared at Shogo's face, surprised by this series of clear and logical explanations. It was true Shogo was a year older than them. But he talked like an adult—a wise, mature adult. In this sense he resembled Shinji Mimura.

Shuya shook his head.

"There'll be no end to it if I start getting suspicious. You're not against us." He glanced over at Noriko "That's what I think."

"Me too." Noriko nodded. "If we can't trust anyone we'll lose."

"That's a noble thought, girl," Shogo nodded. "If that's the way you want it. I'm just telling you that you got to be careful in this game." Then he asked, "So what is it?"

Shuya all of a sudden remembered he was the one with the questions. "That's right. You. Why do you trust us? Teaming up with you doesn't necessarily rule out that one or both of us is against you. You said so yourself. You have no reason to trust us."

"I see," Shogo responded, as if amused. "An applied question. You're getting the hang of it, Shuya."

"Come on, I want an answer."

Shuya waved his hand still holding the revolver. Shogo drew back as if to warn him it was dangerous.

"Well?" Shuya insisted. Shogo raised his brow again. Then he revealed that faint smile on his face. He looked up at the branches looming above them and then looked back at Shuya and Noriko. He looked serious.

"First of all—"

Shuya saw something intense run across Shogo's calm eyes. He didn't know what it meant but it was intense.

"I have my reasons. I have a problem with the rules. No, the game itself."

Shogo stopped for a moment and then continued, "You're absolutely right, but...you see, I'm embarrassed to admit this, but I've always based my decisions on my conscience. So—"

Shogo grabbed the barrel of his shotgun standing between his knees as if it were a cane and looked at them. A bird was chirping deep in the woods. Shogo looked solemn. Shuya listened nervously.

"You two make a nice couple. That's what I thought when I saw you this morning, and I still think so now."

Shuya stared at him, his mouth agape.

Couple?

Noriko spoke first. Her cheeks were bright red. "You have it all wrong. We're not. I'm not—"

Shogo looked at Shuya and Noriko and grinned. Then he broke out laughing. It was an unexpected, friendly laugh. He continued chuckling.

"That's why I trust you. Besides, you just said so yourselves. There's no end once you start getting suspicious. Isn't that enough?"

Shuya finally grinned. Then he said sincerely, "Thanks. I'm so glad you trust us."

Shogo continued smiling, "Oh no, the honor's mine."

"I knew you were an individualist the day you transferred to our school."

"Easy with the fancy terminology. Sorry but I was born with these looks. I can't help it if I don't look friendly."

Noriko gave him a warm smile and said, "I'm so glad. Now we have one more on our side."

Responding to Noriko, Shogo rubbed his finger against the stubble under his nose and made an unexpected gesture. He turned to Shuya and offered his right hand. "I'm glad too…now that I'm not alone."

Shuya squeezed his hand. Shogo's palms were thick. In keeping with his appearance, it felt like the hand of a fully mature man.

Shogo stretched, passed Shuya, and offered his hand to Noriko. "You too."

Noriko squeezed his hand.

Then he looked down at Noriko's leg wrapped in bandannas and remarked, "I'd forgotten about this. Show me your leg wound first, then we'll talk about our plans."

29 students remaining

20

The sunlight reflecting off the opaque window with the detailed patterns began to turn white. As sunlight came directly through the top of the window into the building where Yumiko Kusaka (Female Student No. 7) was sitting against a wall, she squinted her eyes. She was remembering the trite phrase repeated in the sermons given by the local priest of the Halo Church which her parents and she (before her name was even registered) attended, "The sun will come every day, blessing every one of us with joy."

Oh yeah, I am so blessed to be part of such a wonderful game, ha ha ha.

Yumiko lightly shook her short, boyish hair with a sarcastic smile. She looked over at Yukiko Kitano (Female Student No. 6), who was sitting near her, also against the wall. Yukiko remained in a daze, staring at the wooden floor bathed in light. Even though it had the bombastic name "Okishima Island Tourist Association" the building resembled a plain town council hall. Down by the lower entrance, there was an office desk, a chair, and a rusty file cabinet. The desk had a phone (she'd tried using it, but of course, as Sakamochi had warned, there was no dial tone). Inside the file cabinet they only found some unattractive tourist flyers.

Yumiko and Yukiko had been friends ever since nursery school. At nursery school they were in separate classes and lived in different neighborhoods too. They met thanks, once again, to the Halo Church where their parents took them. When they met it was Yumiko's third visit, but for Yukiko it seemed like it was her first, and she looked intimidated by everything there including the gong ringing with every chant and the general atmosphere of the heavily decorated church. So Yumiko approached the quiet girl left alone by her who were preoccupied with some other task and said, "Don't you think this is all so stupid?"

The girl looked a little shocked, but then…she smiled. They were friends ever since.

Although their names sounded similar, they were very different from each other. Yumiko was energetic and got labeled a tomboy. Even now (although the chances of that "now" returning were very, very low) she batted fourth on the softball team. Yukiko was domestic and baked cakes for Yumiko. Yumiko was now fifteen centimeters taller than Yukiko. Yukiko often said she envied Yumiko's height and her well defined face, but Yumiko was in fact more envious of Yukiko for her petite body and round cheeks. That's right, they were totally different, but they were still best friends. That didn't change.

Fortunately (well, that's putting it harshly), the death of Yoshitoki Kuninobu (Male Student No. 7) before his scheduled departure enabled their own departures to be only two minutes apart from each other. After Yumiko left the classroom, she hid behind a pole and waited for Yukiko, whose face had turned white. They left together (twenty minutes later Yoshio Akamatsu returned to begin killing, but they were unaware of this) and headed north far beyond the residential area, following the road on the eastern shore. A little ways up the northern mountain they found a single building standing alone on a hill. They locked themselves inside here.

…over four hours had passed since then. They were exhausted from the extreme tension and remained sitting next to each other as time flew by.

Yumiko looked away from Yukiko and along with her stared at the floor.

Even though she was in a daze, she continued to think. What in the world were they supposed to do now?

Sakamochi's announcement was audible even inside this building. Aside from Yoshitoki Kuninobu and Fumiyo Fujiyoshi, nine classmates were already dead. Aside from Sakura Ogawa and Kazuhiko Yamamoto...the others couldn't have been suicides. Someone was killing someone else. Right now someone might have been dying. In fact she thought she'd heard gunfire right after the 6 a.m. announcement.

How could you kill your classmates? Of course those were the rules, but she couldn't believe there could be people who'd actually follow them. But...

But if someone tried to kill her...if she could assume that much, then she would probably fight back. Yes.

If so, then...

Yumiko looked at the megaphone lying in the corner of the room. Could she use that? If she could...

Wasn't there something she could do? She was simply afraid of doing it, though. Not just of doing it. Because while she couldn't believe anyone was playing the game, she also couldn't rid herself of this overwhelming fear. That's what made her seek shelter here with Yukiko. What if...what if someone really did...

But—

She recalled something from when she was in elementary school, the face of her best friend. It wasn't Yukiko. The friend was crying. For some reason, the only clothes she could remember on her friend was her pink sneakers.

"Yumi," Yukiko said and interrupted Yumiko's thoughts. She faced Yukiko.

"Let's eat our bread rolls. We won't come up with any good ideas if we don't eat." Yukiko provided a kind smile. It felt slightly forced, but it was still her usual smile.

"Okay?" Yukiko repeated and Yumiko returned her smile and nodded.

"All right."

They took out their bread rolls and water from their day packs. Yumiko looked at the two cans inside. The cans were a greenish silver, and at the top a cigar-sized stick stuck out, attached to a lever and a metal ring approximately three centimeters in diameter. She assumed it was a "hand grenade." (Yukiko's "weapon" was a set of darts. It must have been some kind of joke. It even came with a wooden target board.)

After she finished half of her roll and took a sip of her water, Yumiko said, "You feel a little better now, Yukiko?"

As Yukiko chewed on her bread, her round eyes grew wider.

"You've been shaking all this time."

"Oh." Yukiko broke into a smile. "I think I'm fine now. I mean with you by my side."

Yumiko smiled and nodded. She wondered whether she should bring up "what they should do" while they ate...but decided against it. She just wasn't feeling confident enough about her idea. It could be extremely dangerous. To go through with it wouldn't only endanger herself but Yukiko as well. But on the other hand, it was this kind of danger that was forcing everyone to panic over the deadline. What was the right thing to do?—Yumiko just wasn't sure yet.

They remained quiet for a while. Then Yukiko all of a sudden said, "Hey, Yumiko."

"Hm? What?"

"You might think this sounds stupid but..." Yukiko lightly bit on her small but full lips.

"What is it?"

Yukiko hesitated but then finally let it out, "Did you have a crush on anyone in our class?"

Yumiko's eyes suddenly grew wide.

Wow. This was exactly the kind of topic you discussed at night when you're on a study trip. After going through the rituals of playing cards, pillow fighting, and checking out the inn, late at night you could bitch about your teachers, or talk about the future, but none of those were in the same league as this topic. It was *the* holy topic. And of course she'd expected to have this kind of conversation during their study trip, until they'd fallen asleep on the bus.

"You mean, a guy?"

"Yes."

Yukiko's downcast eyes bashfully looked over at Yumiko.

"Hmm." Yumiko hesitated a little but then replied honestly, "Yes, I did."

"I see." Yukiko looked down at the knees of her pleated skirt and said, "I'm sorry I never told you, but I like...Shuya."

Yumiko nodded without saying a word. She already had a hunch.

In her mind Yumiko pulled out her file on Shuya Nanahara. He was 171 centimeters tall, weighed 58 kilograms, his eyesight was 1.2 in the right eye, 1.5 in the left, and although he was thin he was muscular. In elementary school he was a Little League shortstop and batted first, but he quit and now preferred playing music. He was an excellent singer and guitarist. Because of his status as the team's best player during his Little League days, combined with the fact that the first kanji character to his last name meant "seven," he had the baseball nickname of "Wild Seven," just like the cigarette brand. His blood type was B, and he was born, just as the first character of his first name indicated, in the fall. He lost his parents when he was young, and now he lived in a Catholic orphanage called the Charity House. He was best friends with Yoshitoki Kuninobu (oh God and now he was dead) who also lived in the Charity House....His strongest subjects were in the humanities, literature, and English, so he was a decent student. He had a unique face, his lips were slightly curved, but his double eyelids were sharply defined and kind looking, so he wasn't bad looking at all. His hair was slightly wavy and long, covering his neck and touching his shoulders.

That's right. Yumiko's file on Shuya Nanahara was filled to bursting (she was pretty confident hers was more thorough than Yukiko's). One of the more important subjects in the file was his height. Because, she thought, if Shuya didn't grow any taller then she wouldn't be able to wear high heels with him, because that would make her taller than him if they walked together.

But now that she was sure about Yukiko, she wouldn't be able to share these thoughts with her.

"Huh." Yumiko tried to look as calm as possible. "Really?"

"Yes."

"Hm."

Yukiko looked down. Then she made the point she'd wanted to make all along, "I really want to see him. I wonder what he's doing."

As she sat with her hands glued to her thighs, she burst into tears.

Yumiko gently touched Yukiko on the shoulder. "Don't worry. Knowing Shuya, no matter what happens—" Realizing though that this might have sounded funny, she immediately added, nervously, "You know how athletic he is, plus he seems really gutsy. I mean I don't really know but..."

Yukiko wiped away her tears and nodded, "Uh huh." Then as if she felt better, she asked, "So who do you like, Yumiko?"

Yumiko could only look up at the ceiling and force a moan, "Hmm," as she thought it through. She was in trouble. Maybe I'll just randomly pick someone just to avoid the issue.

Tatsumichi Oki was a star player on the handball team. Even though his face was kind of coarse he seemed like a nice guy. Everyone called Shinji Mimura a genius basketball player, and he knew so much. He even had a "following" of girls who were into him. (They weren't from their class, maybe because his general reputation among the Class B girls was that he was a playboy.) Mitsuru Numai acted like he was a badass, but he didn't really seem so bad. He was kind to girls (oh God but he's dead too now). Hiroki Sugimura seemed to have a brooding quality that was kind of cool. Some girls were afraid of him because he practiced martial arts, but to Yumiko that was attractive. But he was close to Takako Chigusa. Takako would get on my back if she ever found out, she can be so harsh. But she's a good girl. Come to think of it, everyone was, both boys and girls.

...

I'm back to the same question. Should I not trust them?

"So who is it?" Yukiko asked again.

Yumiko faced Yukiko again.

She hesitated again—but then she decided to let it out. At the very least, she should bring it up. After all, Yumiko was the ideal companion she could share her thoughts with.

"Can I ask you something?"

Yukiko tilted her head, puzzled.

Yumiko folded her arms to concentrate. Then she asked, "Do you really think there are people who want to kill others...in our class?"

Yukiko knit her brows slightly.

"Well...I mean the fact is that...they di—" As she pronounced the word "died" her voice trembled. "...died. All of them. It was announced this morning. Nine students have already been killed since our departure. They couldn't have all been suicides....Besides, didn't we just hear gunfire a little while ago?"

Yumiko tilted her head as she looked at Yukiko. She spread out her hands. She noticed for the first time that her left cuff was slightly torn.

"Now look. You see how terrified we are here. The two of us, right?"

"Uh huh."

"And I think the others are in the same state. Everyone must be terrified. Don't you think so?"

Yukiko seemed to mull over her point. Then she said, "Yes, maybe. I've been so preoccupied with my own fear, that thought didn't even occur to me."

Yumiko nodded once and continued, "And because we were lucky enough to end up together it's probably nowhere near as bad as being alone, which I'm sure would be absolutely terrifying."

"Yeah, you're right."

"And what would happen if you encountered someone in that state of fear, Yukiko?"

"I'd run away."

"What if you couldn't?"

Yukiko seemed to consider the situation carefully. Then she spoke slowly, "I-I-I just might fight. If I had something I might throw it...or if I had something like a gun I might, I just might shoot it....Of course, I'd try to talk. But if it happened quickly and I didn't have any choice..."

Yumiko nodded.

"Exactly. That's why I think no one here really wants to kill anyone. I think it's because we're so terrified we become deluded that everyone else is out to kill us and so we resort to fighting. And in that state even if no one attacked, we might even end up attacking others on our own." She interrupted herself, unfolded her arms, put her hands on the floor, and continued, "I think everyone's just terrified."

Yukiko pursed her small, full lips together. After a while, she looked down at the floor and said in a halting voice, "I don't know. I just can't trust some of them, like Mitsuko

Souma's gang…and Kazuo Kiriyama's—"

Yumiko forced a smile and moved her sitting position by shifting her legs under her pleated skirt. "I'll tell you what I think, Yukiko."

"Hm."

"We're going to die the way things are going. Time limit? If no one dies in the next twenty-four hours? Even if we survive that long, we'll still end up getting killed."

Yukiko nodded. She looked scared again. "That's…that's true."

"So the only thing we can do is have everyone cooperate to find some way out of here, right?"

"Well…yes but—"

"I have to tell you something…." Yumiko interrupted Yukiko and then tilted her head slightly.

"I once had a horrible experience because I didn't trust someone. I was in elementary school."

Yukiko stared at Yumiko "What happened?"

Yumiko glanced up at the ceiling. She recalled the face of her friend crying. And the pink sneakers.

Yukiko looked back at Yumiko.

"Do you remember the Egg Cats? They were such a big fad. Everybody loved them."

"Yeah, they were character figures. I had a celluloid board with them on it."

"And I had an Egg Cats tri-tip ballpoint pen. The limited edition. I mean it seems like such a silly thing now, but at the time I absolutely adored it."

"Uh huh."

"Well, it disappeared…." Yumiko looked down. "I suspected my friend of stealing it. She wanted it so badly. On top of that, I realized it was gone after first period gym class and she'd excused herself from gym because she wasn't feeling well and returned to our classroom. And, this is really awful, she didn't have a father and her mother worked at a bar, so she didn't have a good reputation."

Yukiko nodded slowly. "Uh huh."

"I bombarded her with questions, but she said she didn't know. And I even told the teacher about it. Our teacher, come to think of it, the teacher must have been biased too. The teacher told her to tell the truth. But she just cried and said she knew nothing about it."

Yumiko looked back at Yukiko.

"When I came home, I found the pen on my desk."

Yukiko remained silent and continued listening.

"I apologized to her. She said it was all right. But it just turned out all awkward and she ended up—I think her mother ended up remarrying—transferring schools and that was it. We were such good friends, as close as you and me. But in the end I wasn't able to trust her."

Yumiko shrugged and then continued.

"So ever since that incident I've been doing my best to trust people. I want to trust people. If I can't then everything falls apart. This is different from what the folks at that stupid Halo Church preach. This is my belief. I hope you understand."

"I do."

"So let's consider this situation now. Well yeah, Mitsuko Souma does seem dangerous. That's her reputation. But I doubt she's so bad she'd actually get off on killing people. She can't be that bad. No one in our class could be that bad. Don't you think?"

Several moments later Yukiko nodded and replied, "Yes."

"So...," Yumiko continued, "...if we could just contact everyone appropriately then the fighting would stop. Then we could figure out together how to deal with the circumstances. No, even if we couldn't do anything, at the very least we could avoid killing each other. Don't you think?"

"Yes..."

Yukiko nodded, but she sounded hesitant. A little worn out from talking, Yumiko took a deep breath and shifted her legs again.

"In any case, that's my opinion. Now let me hear yours. If you're against it, then I won't do it."

Yukiko looked down at the floor in contemplation.

After two full minutes she mumbled, "Remember how you once told me that I'm always too worried about other people's opinions?"

"Hm?...Did I say that?"

Yumiko examined Yukiko's face. Yukiko looked up and their eyes met.

Yukiko smiled gently. "I think you're absolutely right. That's my opinion."

Yumiko smiled back at her and said, "Thanks." She felt grateful towards Yukiko for seriously considering the idea on her own before sharing her thoughts. And now it seemed that her response confirmed the validity of her idea.

That's right. We have to do this. I don't want to die without putting up a fight. If there's a chance then let's go for it. That's right. Just as I said to Yukiko, I want to trust people. Let's try it.

Then Yukiko asked, "But how are we going to do this? How can we contact everyone?"

Yumiko pointed at the megaphone lying in the corner of the room. "We have to figure out how to use that."

Yukiko gave several small nods and looked up at the ceiling. Then she uttered, "If all goes well, I'll be able to see Shuya."

Yumiko nodded. "Yes, I'm sure we will," she said hopefully this time.

29 students remaining

21

"All right."

Shogo tossed the needle and thread onto the day pack beside him and said to Shuya, "I need the whiskey again."

Noriko's bent right leg rested on its side. The wound on her calf was sewn up with coarse cotton thread. Shogo had managed to stitch it up. Of course they had no anesthetic, but Noriko managed not to cry during the ten-minute operation.

Shuya offered the flask to Shogo. Next to them was a small rock pit. The empty can rested on top of the charcoal, and the water inside was boiling. (Shogo had explained how he'd found the charcoal along with the needle and thread at the supply store.) He disinfected the needle and thread with the boiling water, but applying it directly to her wound was out of the question. Shogo had already soaked her wound with whiskey before he began stitching. He was going to disinfect again. Noriko, who'd managed to relax a little, now grimaced again.

Shuya looked at his watch. Because of the time it took to boil the water, it was already past 8 a.m.

"Okay," Shogo said as he pressed the disinfected bandanna on her wound. Then he quickly wrapped another bandanna around Noriko's leg. "We're done."

He added with a note of concern, "I hope the wound hasn't been infected."

Noriko tucked in her leg and showed her gratitude to Shogo, "Thank you. That was impressive."

"Well, I'm good at playing doctor," Shogo said as he took out a Wild Seven cigarette from his pocket, put it between his lips, and lit it with a disposable lighter. Did he get those from the store, or did he bring them along for the trip? Like

Buster and hi-night, they were a popular brand.

Shuya gazed at the package, illustrated with silhouettes of motorcycle riders. He had no idea what they were referring to. The cigarettes piqued his curiosity, because Shuya's baseball nickname was the same as this cigarette brand. The name came naturally. Shuya was the star player of his Little League team. He was a great clutch hitter with men in scoring position, and once he was on base, and no one else could get any hits, he could create his own scoring opportunities by stealing a base (he held the impressive record of stealing home three times in one season). When the bases were loaded, and their pitcher was in a pinch, he'd make the play to get them out of the jam, and if the pitcher was too tired, he'd switch from shortstop to pitcher. "Wild Card Nana (Seven)" hara. That's right.

In his second year of junior high he became classmates with the star shooting guard of the basketball team, Shinji Mimura. Shinji's nickname was "The Third Man," which he got during his first year when he sat on the bench as the second backup guard. But with five minutes left and their team trailing by twenty in the district finals, this third man came onto the court and single-handedly brought his team to victory. Ever since then Shinji was a fixture in the starting lineup, and Shiroiwa Junior High turned into one of the prefecture's top-ranked basketball teams. But because of that game, and because of the kanji character of "three" in his last name, the "Third Man" name stuck.

For this year's class games, the girls as a joke made a pair of uniforms stitched with the numbers 7 and 3. Shuya and Shinji wore these uniforms during the games. It felt like a remote world. Shuya wondered again where Shinji was. Shinji would have been a big help.

As if the thought suddenly occurred to him, Shogo searched his pockets and pulled out a small leather pouch.

He took out a sheet of white pills wrapped in aluminum foil and plastic and gave it to Noriko.

"Pain relievers. You should take some."

Noriko blinked. But then she took the pills.

Shuya said to Shogo, "Hey…"

"What?" Shogo slowly blew smoke out his mouth and looked at Shuya. "Don't stare at me. It's not that uncommon to see a junior high kid smoking. Anyway I'm old enough to be in high school. And you're the one who brought your own supply of whiskey."

So high school students are allowed to smoke? Well, that wasn't his point anyway. Shuya shook his head, "That's not what I meant. Did you find those pills at the store too?"

Shogo shrugged. "Well yeah. It wasn't exactly merchandise. I took it out of the first aid kit behind the cash register. It's not a big deal. Just some aspirin called Gomez. What an obnoxious name for aspirin, huh? Anyway it'll stop the pain."

Shuya pursed his lips. Well, he might be telling the truth, but… "I don't get how you can be so well prepared. And where'd you learn to stitch up a wound?"

Shogo's mouth broke into a wide grin. He shrugged and replied, "My dad was a doctor."

"What?"

"He ran a small dump, a clinic in the slums of Kobe. I've seen him sew people up ever since I was a kid. In fact I was a pretty good nurse. I even did some work myself. My dad couldn't even afford to hire a nurse."

Shuya was speechless. Was he telling the truth?

Shogo held up the cigarette between his fingers, as if to cut off Shuya's response. "It's true. Just think about it and you'll see how important medicine is in these circumstances."

Shuya kept quiet for a moment, but then recalled

something else that puzzled him.

"Oh yeah…"

"What?"

"You mind if I ask—"

"Skip the formalities, Shuya. We're in this together."

Shuya shrugged once and then rephrased what he had to say. "Back on the bus, you were trying to open the window. You must have realized there was sleeping gas."

Hearing this, Noriko gave Shogo a puzzled look.

This time Shogo shrugged.

"So you saw me? You should have lent me a hand."

"I couldn't. How did you know what was going on, though? I mean there was no smell or anything—"

"Oh yeah there was," Shogo replied and rubbed his half finished cigarette into the ground. "It was faint, but if you've smelled it once you'd recognize it."

"How did you recognize it?" This time Noriko asked.

"My uncle actually worked at a state chemical lab and—"

"Come on," Shuya interrupted him.

Shogo grimaced and said, "If I have to, I'll explain it later. As far as I'm concerned I blew it big time. I should've noticed sooner. And I certainly didn't expect this to happen…but we should be focused on the present. Do you have any plans?"

If I have to, I'll explain later? That statement bothered Shuya, but Shogo was right. Their priority was to come up with a plan for their escape. He put his questions on hold and said, "We're planning on escaping."

Shogo lit another cigarette and nodded. Then as if suddenly remembering what he had to do, he tossed dirt onto the charcoal inside the rock pit. Shuya heard the sound of Noriko swallowing a pill with water.

Shuya continued. "How hard do you think it'll be?"

Shogo shook his head. "The question is whether it's possible at all. My answer would be 'extremely remote.'

So what then?"

"Well even if we escaped..." Shuya lifted his hand up to his neck, to the object that was wrapped around Shogo's and Noriko's necks as well. "...we'd be immediately discovered because of these collars."

"Yep."

"And we can't get near that school."

Sakamochi had said that "twenty minutes after your departure this school will become a forbidden zone." Bastard.

"True."

"But maybe there's a way to lure him out here? Then we take Sakamochi hostage. That's how we get them to disable the collars."

Shogo raised his brow. "And?"

Shuya licked his lips and continued, "Before doing that we locate a ship and escape by taking Sakamochi with us." Even as he was saying it, Shuya knew his plan was hopeless. He hadn't even figured out how they were going to lure Sakamochi out from the school. No, you couldn't even call it a plan, just an "idea."

"That's it?" Shogo asked. Shuya could only nod.

Shogo once again puffed on his cigarette. Then he said, "First of all, there aren't any ships."

Shuya bit his lip. "You never know."

Shogo briefly smiled and blew out more smoke. "I told you how I went to that supply store by the harbor. There weren't any boats. Not one. Not even damaged ones left on the shore. Every single boat's been taken away. I mean, they were absurdly thorough."

"Then...the guard ship will do. As long as we can hold Sakamochi hostage."

"That's impossible, Shuya," Shogo interrupted him. "You saw how many Special Defense Forces soldiers they had.

Besides..." Shogo pointed to the silver collar around his neck. "They should be able to send the command to ignite these at any time regardless of what zone we're in. Anytime, anywhere. The odds are stacked against us. Even if we managed to capture Sakamochi, I'm sure as far as the government's concerned, he's expendable."

Shuya fell silent again.

"Do you have any other ideas?" Shogo asked him.

Shuya shook his head. "No. What about you, Noriko?"

Noriko also shook her head. But she had something else to say.

"That's why I suggested we gather as many people as we can, even if they're only the ones we trust, to come up with a plan together. I thought if we met together as a group we might come up with a good idea...."

That's right, Shuya thought. That's what I forgot to say.

Shogo only raised his scarred left brow. "And who are the ones you trust?"

Shuya replied enthusiastically, "There's Shinji Mimura. Then there's Hiroki Sugimura. Let's see, as far as the girls go, there's our class representative, Yukie Utsumi. Shinji is really amazing. He knows a lot. He knows so many different things. He's good with machines too. He'd come up with something."

Shogo rubbed his stubbly chin with his left hand as he stared at Shuya. Then he said, "Shinji, huh..."

Shuya looked surprised. "What's wrong?"

"Well...," Shogo seemed hesitant but continued, "I saw Shinji...."

"What!? Where!?" Shuya raised his voice. He exchanged looks with Noriko. "Where? Where did you see him?"

Shogo pointed his chin to the east. "It was at night. West of the school. He seemed to be searching for something inside a house....He had a gun, and I think he noticed me."

"Why didn't you call out to him?" Shuya raised his voice scornfully. Shogo gave Shuya a puzzled look.

"What do you mean?"

"Well, come on, he helped Noriko get back to her seat in the classroom. You saw that? Besides—"

Shogo predicted the rest, "He tried to have the game postponed for Noriko's injury, right? So that there'd be a chance for everyone to escape?"

Exactly. Shuya nodded.

Shogo shook his head. "You expect me to trust him on account of those acts? No way. Besides, he might have been trying to con everyone into believing he was a trustworthy guy. It'd suit him fine if he planned on getting rid of everyone later."

"That's ridiculous!" Shuya raised his voice. "How cynical can you get? He's not that kind of guy. He's—"

Shogo silently extended both of his palms forward and Shuya fell silent. He was right. Raising your voice was not a good idea. In fact it was a very bad idea.

Then Shogo said, "Cut me some slack. I don't know Shinji. Like I said before, the rule is to suspect, not trust, everyone in this game. And you have to be all the more suspicious of someone who's smart. Besides, even if I invited him to join me, he probably would've refused."

Shuya was about to say something, but then exhaled and decided against it. Shogo had a point. In fact, it was odd how Shogo could trust him and Noriko at all. Shogo did say though that it was because they made "a nice couple."

"Well then...," Shuya continued, "we should at least go where you saw Shinji. We can definitely trust him. I guarantee it. He'd come up with a good idea. He's—" But once again he was interrupted.

Shogo shook his head and said, "If Shinji is so smart then do you think he'd stay where I saw him?"

He was right.

Shuya sighed. It was a very long, deep sigh.

"Hey...," Noriko spoke up, "Shogo, I was wondering if there was any way we can contact others like Shinji."

Shogo shook loose another cigarette and shook his head. "I doubt it. If we were trying to reach a general, unspecified number of people, well maybe, but contacting a particular party or person would be difficult."

They fell silent for a while. Shuya stared at Shogo, who had his cigarette stuck between his lips. The tip of the Wild Seven crackled and grew shorter.

"Then...," Shuya said, nearly speechless, "there's nothing we can do."

Shogo responded flatly, "Oh but there is."

"What?"

"I have a plan."

Shuya stared again at Shogo's face wrapped in a cloud of smoke. Then he suddenly became excited and asked, "What do you mean? Is there a way out?"

Shogo looked over at Shuya and Noriko. Then he looked up at the sky in contemplation, his cigarette still dangling from his lips. His right hand touched the smooth surface of the collar around his neck, as if it annoyed him. The smoke slowly drifted by.

Shogo said, "There might be a way." Then he continued, "On one condition, though."

"What's that?"

Shogo shook his head slightly and then brought his cigarette closer to his lips. "We have to be the only survivors."

Shuya knit his brows. He didn't understand. "What do you...mean?"

"It should be obvious." Shogo looked back at them. "Meaning the three of us have to be the only ones alive. The others would have to be dead."

"But…" Noriko immediately raised her voice. "That's too much! So we're just looking after ourselves?"

Shogo held his cigarette held between his fingers over his crossed legs and raised his brow, "Shuya's escape plan would amount to the same thing, though."

"No," Shuya intervened. "That's not what Noriko's saying. She's asking you whether our survival comes at the cost of everyone else. Right, Noriko? That would just be…horrible."

"Hold on guy." Shogo waved his hand. He crushed his cigarette against the ground. "I'm not against our group expanding, as long as we can trust them. But whether we find others or not, everyone besides the ones in our group will have to die."

"If that's the case," Shuya said enthusiastically, "We could inform everyone. If you have the most reliable plan then no one will oppose it. Then everyone would be saved? Right?"

Shogo pursed his lips in response to Shuya. Then he asked in a slightly irritated tone, "What if we're attacked before we even manage to get a word in?"

Shuya took a deep breath.

"Unless you're actively out to kill people, then, relatively speaking that is, the smartest way to survive would be to stay put and hide. That's the reason why," Shogo pointed to his collar, "the government is using this to force us to move. That's one of the basic tenets of this game. Don't forget that. You move around aimlessly, and you're a walking target for someone lurking in the shadows. With Noriko injured like this, we're prime targets."

He was right.

"Besides, when you insist everyone has to be saved, that only means we might not get killed here. But what if we end up as fugitives? We'll be chased by the government, and the probability that we'll get killed in the end is extremely high. I doubt anyone would submit to a plan like that. Don't forget. You don't know who your enemies are in this game. Blindly accepting everyone could ruin everything for you."

"But no one's…"

"That bad? Can you really say that, Shuya?" Shogo's eyes grew stern. "It'd be wonderful if everyone in this class were good. But if we're going to be realistic, we have to be careful. Think about it, you yourself were attacked by Yoshio Akamatsu and Tatsumichi Oki."

Shuya had told Shogo about Yoshio's assault when Shogo was stitching Noriko's leg. Shogo was absolutely right. He had no idea what Yoshio Akamatsu was thinking. He might have been trying to kill Shuya.

Shuya sighed. His shoulders drooped down as he feebly mumbled, "Then…then we're going to let most of our classmates, the good ones, just die. That's what this means, right?"

Shogo moved his chin up and down slightly, nodding. "It's not easy, but yes. I don't know if it's going to be most of the class, though."

They fell silent for a while. Shogo lit another cigarette. He smoked too much. And he was a minor.

Then Noriko said, "Hey wait." Shuya looked back at Noriko. "You said we might escape if everyone else dies, but we could also run out of time, if no one dies for twenty-four hours…."

"Yeah," Shogo nodded. "That's correct."

"In that case, I guess your plan wouldn't work."

"That's right. But I highly doubt that'll happen. Besides, if everyone can really get along and agree to my plan then they're totally welcome. But I doubt that'll happen. So there's really no need to worry about it. Apparently only 0.5% of the national Programs have ended due to time expiration."

Shuya blurted out, " 'Apparently'? How would you know?"

"Hold on." Shogo again made a pushing gesture with his hands to stop Shuya. "We have more urgent matters at hand. You haven't asked me what my plan is."

Shuya fell silent. Then he asked, "What is it?"

Shogo shrugged. Through the corner of his mouth, which was still holding the cigarette, he curtly replied, "I can't tell you."

Shuya knit his brows. "What?"

"Not yet."

"Why?"

"I just can't."

"What do you mean, 'not yet'? Then when do you plan on telling us?"

"I suppose when it's just the three of us left. Let me just tell you one thing, though. My plan won't work if anyone tries to intervene. So my plan can't start until we're the only ones left."

Shuya fell silent again. He stared at Shogo, who continued smoking, but then Shuya heard a voice whispering something inside his head. It was faint, but he could hear it.

As if he could hear this voice, Shogo grinned.

"I know what you're thinking, Shuya. There might be something else going on here. I might be joining you just as a means for my own survival. In fact, I might not have a plan at all. Once we're down to three, I might kill you two and win the game. That would work out nicely for me, right?"

Shuya was slightly intimidated. "That's not…"

"No?"

Shuya held his tongue and glanced over at Noriko. Noriko remained silent, staring at Shogo.

Shuya looked back at Shogo.

"That's not it. It's just that—" Shuya stopped all of a sudden.

It was someone's voice. It was very distant, but he could tell it was electronically distorted. A voice calling, "Hey, everyone—"

29 students remaining

22

The voice continued. "Listen up, everyone—" It was a girl's voice.

Noriko said, "It's Yumiko." She was referring to Yumiko Kusaka (Female Student No. 7). She was a tall, energetic girl who batted fourth on the girls' softball team.

"I'm going to go check this out." Shogo's face stiffened. He took his shotgun and stood up. He began walking east into the thicket towards the voice.

"We'll go with you."

They weren't done talking, but Shuya tucked his Smith & Wesson in front and offered his shoulder to help Noriko up. Shogo glanced back at them, but said nothing and began walking.

Once they reached the end of the thicket, Shogo stood still. Shuya and Noriko too stopped walking.

With his back towards them, Shogo exclaimed, "Why they're..."

Shuya walked up right behind Shogo, and like Shogo he and Noriko poked their heads out of the thicket.

It was a mountain peak. There was a viewing platform between the trees scattered on the peak. It was probably five or six hundred meters away from the foot of the mountain, where they were. But they could still see it clearly. The platform was a crude construction, resembling a shack with a missing wall. There were two figures standing under its roof. Shuya's eyes widened.

The voice reached them. "Everyone. Stop fighting and come here—"

Shuya saw an object held in front of the taller figure's face—it was probably Yumiko's. Was it a megaphone? The one cops use to address criminals cooped up inside buildings under siege? It felt slightly absurd ("Put down your weapons and come out with your hands up"), but he could see how her voice could reach not only them but the rest of the island.

"And the other one?" Shuya whispered.

Noriko replied, "It's Yukiko. Yukiko Kitano. They're really close."

"This is really bad," Shogo said with a grimace. "They'll get themselves killed totally exposed like that."

Shuya bit his lower lip. Basically Yumiko Kusaka and Yukiko Kitano were attempting to convince everyone they should stop fighting. They were doing what Shuya had considered but gave up on after he was attacked by Yoshio Akamatsu. They firmly believed no one really want to play the game. They chose that spot to be as visible as possible. Or maybe they were already near that location.

"I'm sure no one wants to fight like this. So let's get together here—"

Shuya hesitated. He needed more time to process the situation—plus the conversation they were having hadn't been resolved. What if—it was unlikely—but what if Shogo was against them?

In the end Shuya spoke to Shogo, "Can you look after Noriko, Shogo?"

Shogo turned around. "What are you going to do?"

"I'm going over there."

Shogo knit his brows and said, "What are you, stupid?"

His putdown angered Shuya, but he simply answered, "What do you mean? They're risking their lives doing this. They have no intention to play the game. They really don't. So they can join us. Besides, you just said they were endangering themselves."

"That's not what I meant." Shogo bared his teeth. It was an odd thing to notice, but they looked remarkably healthy. "I just told you. It's best to stay put in this game. How far do you think that spot is from here? You have no idea who you'll encounter on the way."

"I know that!" Shuya shot back.

"No, you don't get it. Everyone knows about those two now. If anyone attacks them, then the enemy's going to wait for others offering themselves up like you. With more targets—"

What gave Shuya the creeps wasn't so much Shogo's warning but his calm tone of voice.

"Please—everyone come here. We're alone here—we're not fighting!"

Shuya slid his shoulder loose from Noriko's right arm.

"I'm going."

He gripped the Smith & Wesson and walked out of the bushes, but Shogo tugged on Shuya's left arm.

"Stop it!"

"Why!?" Shuya's voice grew louder. "You want me to just sit back and watch them get killed?" He raised his voice uncontrollably and blurted out, "Or is my leaving going to decrease your chances of survival? Is that it? Is that what's going on? Are you our enemy?"

"Shuya, stop it…" Noriko moaned, but Shuya wasn't finished—then he saw how calm Shogo looked even as he still held onto his arm.

Although they hardly resembled each other, Shogo's

composure reminded Shuya of the former superintendent of the Charity House, Ms. Anno's elderly father. After his parents died when he was still a kid, this man, who was the only authority figure and guardian he knew, sat down with him. He also wore the same kind of expression.

Shogo said, "It's none of my business if you want to die, but if you go now and don't return, then you'll drastically decrease Noriko's chances of survival. Have you forgotten that?"

Shuya took a deep breath. Once again Shogo was right.

"But—"

Shogo calmly continued, "I'm sure you must know this, Shuya...but loving someone always requires you to not love others. If you care about Noriko, don't go."

"But..." Shuya felt like crying. "So what are you suggesting? We just let them get killed?"

"I didn't say that."

Shogo released Shuya and turned towards the peak where Yumiko continued her shouting. He held his shotgun.

"We'll be decreasing our chances of survival slightly. Only slightly." Shogo pointed the shotgun into the air and pulled the trigger. The gunpowder blast was ear-shattering. Shuya thought his eardrums had been blown out for a moment. The sound reverberated against the side of the mountain. Shogo's left hand pumped the shotgun, ejecting the spent cartridge. He followed with another shot. The sound rippled through the air.

I get it.... The gunfire will scare off Yumiko Kusaka and Yukiko Kitano, forcing them to stop and go hide instead.

Yumiko's voice, amplified by the megaphone, stopped. It felt as if Yumiko and Yukiko were looking down where they were. But we're hidden by the bushes, so they probably can't tell who we are.

"Come on! Shoot some more!"

Shuya was riled up, but Shogo refused, "No. Someone

might have already figured out our location with those two shots. Any more could be fatal for us."

Shuya considered it. Then he tried to point his Smith & Wesson into the air.

Shogo once again tugged at his arm.

"Stop it! How many times do I have to tell you?"

"But—"

"We can only hope they've hidden themselves now."

Shuya looked over at the peak. Then he heard it again. Once again, Yumiko Kusaka's voice shouted, "Stop it! I know none of us want to fight—"

Shuya shook off Shogo's grip. He couldn't take it anymore. He wanted them to hide somewhere safe no matter what. He had his fingers on the trigger of the Smith & Wesson when—

All of a sudden they heard a distant, rattling sound like that of rapid typewriter tapping. Then Yumiko's shriek, "Urgh—" reached them. Of course her cry was also amplified by the megaphone. After a moment's pause, "AIEEE—" a scream that sounded like it came from Yukiko Kitano. This too reached them courtesy of the cheap megaphone. Under the platform roof on the mountain peak, a tall figure appeared to collapse and Yukiko's screaming continued, "Yumiko!" followed by a loud thud, the sound of the megaphone hitting the ground. Shuya heard the rattling sound again but this time it was much quieter. Shuya realized the megaphone had also been picking up this sound as well. Once the megaphone was broken, the sound was drastically reduced. And now the figure of Yukiko also collapsed into the shadows of the short trees, disappearing along with Yumiko from their sight.

Shuya and Noriko's faces turned white.

29 students remaining

23

Yukiko Kitano was crawling on the concrete floor of the viewing platform towards Yumiko Kusaka. Her stomach was burning, and she felt paralyzed, but somehow she managed to crawl towards her. Yukiko left a trail of red on the concrete, which was now a canvas of violent brushstrokes.

"Yumiko!" Yukiko let out a shriek that tore through her stomach, but she didn't care. Her best friend had fallen and was now motionless. That was what mattered to her now.

Yumiko had fallen forward, facing Yukiko, but her eyes were closed. A gooey red pond began to ooze out from under her body.

Once Yukiko reached Yumiko, she struggled to lift her forward. Then she shook her by the shoulders.

"Yumiko! Yumiko!"

As she shouted, a red mist sprayed into Yumiko's face, but Yukiko didn't even realize it was coming from her mouth.

Yumiko slowly opened her eyes and gasped, "Yukiko…"

"Yumiko! Wake up!"

Yumiko grimaced. Then she finally managed to utter, "I'm so sorry, Yukiko. I was stupid…you should…hurry…and escape."

"No!" Yukiko cried and shook her head. "We have to go together! Come on!"

Yukiko frantically looked around. There was no trace of the assailant. They were probably shot at from a distance.

"Hurry!"

She tried to raise Yumiko's body, but it was impossible. She immediately realized she could barely support her own body. The pain was much worse now, attacking her stomach as she shrieked and fell forward again. She still managed to face Yumiko.

Yumiko's face was right in front of her eyes. Her glazed

eyes stared at Yukiko. She asked in a feeble voice, "You can't move, Yukiko?"

"Nope," Yukiko did her best to form a smile. "I guess not."

"I'm so sorry," Yumiko quietly apologized again.

"That's all right. We...we did what we had to...right? Yumiko?"

Now she could tell Yumiko was about to cry. Although Yukiko thought she wasn't seriously injured, she was now beginning to rapidly fade. Her eyelids grew heavy.

"Yukiko?"

Yukiko was brought back by Yumiko's voice.

"Whaaat?"

"There's something I didn't tell you when we were talking."

"?"

Yumiko smiled a little. "I also had a crush on Shuya."

For a moment Yukiko didn't understand what Yumiko was talking about. She couldn't tell whether this was because it was so unexpected or because she was fading.

Finally though Yumiko's words knocked at the door of Yukiko's heart and entered. So...that's how it was.

Then as her mind sank into the mist, Yukiko remembered a scene. She and Yumiko had gone shopping together. It was a cheap ¥3,000 bargain-sale item, but they'd found a pair of beautiful earrings, and although they hardly ever shared the same tastes—they ended up fussing over who really deserved these earrings. Finally they agreed to split the cost so that both of them would end up with one earring each. That was the first time they actually bought jewelry. And now, as always, that earring was tucked away in the drawer of her desk at home located near the border between Shiroiwa and the neighboring town.

For some reason, Yukiko felt incredibly content. It

was strange, given how she was dying.

"Really..." Yukiko said. "Really..."

Yumiko again smiled faintly. Yukiko opened her mouth just once more. She could say one last thing. That's right, she wasn't sure about religion, but if the Halo Church had ever offered her something beautiful it was Yumiko. We met at the church, and we've been together ever since.

"Yumi...ko. I'm so happy that we've been..."

As Yukiko was about to say "friends," Yumiko's head shook with the sound of a bang. A red hole formed in her right temple—and now Yumiko merely gawked at her. The faraway look she had might have been unintentionally appropriate given their location, the viewing platform.

Yukiko opened her mouth in shock and horror when she heard another pop, this time accompanied by a blow to her head. It was the last sensation she ever felt.

Kazuo Kiriyama (Male Student No. 6) remained crouched so no one outside the platform could see him. He lowered the Walther PPK that had belonged to Mitsuru Numai and picked up the girls' day packs.

27 students remaining

24

After the two shots were fired, Shuya and Noriko remained frozen. Above them, a hawk cried.

After checking the premises, Shogo turned back and said to them, "It's over. Let's go back."

As Shuya held up Noriko by her arm, he looked at Shogo standing above them. His lips trembled uncontrollably.

"What do you mean, 'It's over'? You could be a little more considerate."

Shogo shrugged his shoulders.

"Look, this is the way I talk. I'm not good at expressing myself. In any case, now you see, right? Some of our classmates are really up to the task. And let me just add that this wasn't something Sakamochi and his crew cooked up. They don't want to die either, so they're cooped up in that school."

Shuya still wanted to say something back, but he managed to restrain himself and began walking, holding Noriko's arm.

As they walked, Noriko said in a hoarse voice, "It's so terrible....How awful can it get?"

Once they reached their location Shogo said, "We have to get ready, just in case. We're going to move about a hundred meters."

"I thought you said it was best to stay put—"

Shogo puckered his lips and shook his head. "You saw what happened. Whoever it was, that bastard is merciless. On top of that, he has a machine gun. He probably figured out where we are. If he does, then we're better off moving away from here." He added, "Just a little. We'll move over just a little."

27 students remaining

25

Yutaka Seto (Male Student No. 12) was running frantically down the slope. He was on his hands and knees, so he was actually crawling through the bushes. His size-S black school coat covering his small body had nearly turned white from dirt. His large eyes had a childish innocence to them, but right now the class clown's face was contorted with fear.

After he'd left the school building and up until a few

moments ago, Yutaka Seto had been hiding out in the bushes near the northern peak, in other words approximately fifty meters below from where Yumiko Kusaka and Yukiko Kitano were calling to everyone with their megaphone.

Although he was at an angle from them, Yutaka could see them clearly. He kept on hesitating, deliberating over what he should do, but finally right when he decided to join them, he heard the sound of distant gunfire. He thought he could see the two look in the opposite direction from him. Then as he hesitated over whether he should go check it out, within a matter of ten or twenty seconds he heard the sound of rapid-typewriter-rattling gunfire and Yumiko Kusaka's amplified shriek. He saw her fall. Then Yukiko Kitano was also shot down.

They were probably still alive at that point. But Yutaka just could not bring himself to come out and rescue them. After all—he was a born jokester, fighting was just not his thing, and on top of that, his supplied weapon turned out to be a fork, the normal kind you would use to eat spaghetti. Then he heard a gun being fired twice, somewhere beyond his sight. He knew then that the assailant had finished off Yumiko and Yukiko.

The moment he realized this he took his bags and slid down the side of the mountain. I'm the next target! I know it! After all I'm the nearest one!

All of a sudden Yutaka realized he had created a cloud of dust all around him. Oh no! No! This sucks! This blows more than your mama! Hey, now's not the time to come up with stupid jokes!

Yutaka then changed his approach, keeping his palms (his right hand held the fork, so it was clenched) and shoe soles on the ground to make sure his body wouldn't slide down the slope. He felt the skin of his hands scraping away, but he didn't care. Damn, if someone saw me now they'd think it was funny. Ladies and gentlemen, the Human Beetle.

After moving forward like this for several minutes Yutaka finally stopped. Slowly he turned around. Through the trees he could make out the summit where Yumiko Kusaka and Yukiko Kitano had been killed, but it seemed far. Everything was still. He strained his ears. There was no sound.

Did I escape? Am I safe now?

As if answering his own question, something dug into his shoulder.

Yutaka froze up with fear and shrieked, "Aieee!"

"You fool!" Someone hissed as the grip on his shoulder relaxed and instead a clammy hand covered Yutaka's mouth. But Yutaka was completely oblivious to this voice, utterly convinced he was caught by the killer, and swung the fork in his hand in a fit of fear.

The fork made a clacking sound and stopped there....For some reason, nothing happened. Yutaka nervously opened his eyes.

The figure in front of him was wearing a school coat. He'd blocked the fork with his large automatic pistol (Beretta M92F). He held the gun in his left hand. Given their respective positions, and the fact that he had his right hand over Yutaka's mouth, Yutaka's fork would have stabbed him pretty deep if he were right handed. But this guy was left handed. And there was only one left handed guy in Class B.

"That was dangerous, Yutaka."

The front of his wet-looking hair was styled with gel. His eyebrows rose at a sharp angle, and beneath them were his piercing but humorous eyes. Finally there was the earring in his left ear. It was Yutaka's best friend, "The Third Man," Shinji Mimura (Male Student No. 19), grinning at him and gently removing his hand from his mouth. Stupefied, Yutaka lowered his fork. Then he finally yelled out, "Shinji! It's you Shinji!"

"You idiot!" Shinji Mimura hissed at Yutaka, and once again shut Yutaka's mouth while he shouted from relief. Then he let go and said, "This way. Don't say a word. Just follow me," and walked ahead of him into the low bushes.

As Yutaka followed him, dazed, he gradually saw how he had descended from the top of the mountain to the more level area below. Within a matter of minutes he'd covered a good distance.

Yutaka then glanced at Shinji Mimura's back. But then he was suddenly overwhelmed by a horrible idea and felt weak in the knees.

Maybe Yumiko Kusaka and Yukiko Kitano were killed by...Shinji? Then the killer chasing Yutaka would be him! But then why hasn't he killed me yet? I mean, come on, I always thought of him as my best friend, and Shinji knows that. If we're together, Shinji could, for instance, have me keep watch and help him increase his chances of survival. Then, when we're the last two left, Shinji could kill me. Wow, what a great idea! If this was a video game, that's what I'd do.

You jerk! What are you thinking!?

Yutaka shook off the thought. Shinji didn't have a machine gun—and nothing else could have made that sound. He was certain he didn't have one, and besides, most of all, this was Shinji. He was his best friend. He would never kill those girls off like that, as if they were flies.

"What's wrong, Yutaka?" Shinji turned around and whispered. "Hurry up."

Once again Yutaka followed Shinji in a daze.

Shinji continued to walk carefully. Once they covered a distance of approximately fifty meters he stopped. With his gun in his right hand, he pointed down toward his feet. "You have to step over this here," he warned Yutaka. Yutaka narrowed his eyes and noticed a thin, dull piece of thread stretched tightly between the trees.

"Is this…"

"It's not a trap," Shinji said after stepping over the thread. "There's an empty can tied to it over there. Once it's tugged, we can hear it fall."

Yutaka nodded, eyes opened wide. Shinji had been hiding out. And this was a kind of tripwire alarm. Impressive. The Third Man was more than just a star athlete.

Yutaka stepped over the thread.

They reached a thicket twenty meters away. Shinji stopped walking. He said to Yutaka, "Let's sit down."

Yutaka sat down, facing Shinji. He realized he was still holding his fork. He put it on the ground when all of a sudden he felt a stinging pain from his left palm and right fist. The skin had peeled off, revealing red flesh on his knuckles.

Seeing this, Shinji put down his gun and pulled out what appeared to be a day pack from a nearby bush. He took out his water bottle and towel, doused one end with water, and said, "Give me your hands, Yutaka." Yutaka held them out, and Shinji wiped them thoroughly, but gently. Then he tore the dry part of the towel into thin shreds and wrapped them around Yutaka's hands.

Yutaka said, "Thank you." Then he asked, "So you've been hiding here?"

"Yeah," Shinji smiled and nodded. "I caught a glimpse of you from here moving around in the bushes. You were pretty far away, but I could tell it was you. So even though it was a little risky, I went in your direction."

Yutaka choked up. Shinji risked his life for my sake.

"It's dangerous if you don't move carefully."

"Uh huh." Yutaka was about to cry.

"Thanks so much, Shinji."

"I'm glad…." Shinji exhaled. "Even if I die, I

wanted to make sure I got to see you."

Now Yutaka's eyes were watering. He held his tears back though and changed the subject, "I was...right near Yumiko and Yukiko. I-I wasn't able to help them."

"Yeah," Shinji nodded. "I saw that too—that's how I found you. Don't let it get you down. I wasn't able to do anything for them either."

Yutaka nodded. Recalling how Yumiko Kusaka and Yukiko Kitano were killed only moments ago, he trembled.

27 students remaining

26

They ended up moving approximately one hundred meters southwest of their previous position. By the time Shogo was done tying the wire around the bushes again, it was already 9 a.m. The sun was high in the sky, and the air smelled like a forest in May. The sea, which was visible as they moved through the trees, glistened a brilliant blue. Islands were scattered across the Seto Inland Sea. If they were hiking...this would have been a prime spot.

But they weren't. Every single boat that passed by circled around the island at a great distance, tiny as dots, and the nearest one was the gray guard ship in charge of the western region. Even that ship was pretty far, but you could see the machine gun installed at its head.

After Shogo was done setting the wire, he took a deep breath and sat down in front of Shuya and Noriko. Once again he placed his shotgun between his feet.

"What's wrong? You're both so quiet now," Shogo asked.

Shuya looked up at Shogo. He hesitated—and then asked,

"What made them do that?"

Shogo lifted his brows. "You mean Yumiko and Yukiko?"

Shuya nodded. After hesitating, he said, "I mean it should have been obvious. They could have anticipated that. I mean, according to the rules of this game…," he sighed, "we're supposed to kill each other."

Shogo put another cigarette between his lips and lit it with his disposable lighter. "They seemed close. Weren't they in some religious group?"

Shuya nodded. They were very normal girls, but there was always something that separated them from the other girls, like Noriko and the neutral faction that included Yukie Utsumi and her friends. He thought it was because of their religion. "They were part of some Shinto religious group called the Halo Church. They have a church located on the Yodo River bank, off the state highway when you're heading south."

Shogo exhaled and suggested, "Maybe that was part of it. You know, 'Love thy neighbor.' "

"No, I don't think so," Noriko said. "They weren't—especially Yumiko—very committed. They said they didn't really get it, that it was just a social thing."

Shogo mumbled, "I see," and looked down. Then he continued, "Well, the good aren't always saved, and this game is no exception. It can be the irresponsible ones that end up making it. But I respect anyone who stands by their conscience, even at the risk of failing and being rejected by everyone." He stared back at them. "They tried to believe in their classmates. They must have believed, if we could all get together, then we might end up being saved. We should commend them for that. We couldn't do that."

Shuya took a deep breath. Then he agreed, "Yeah." After a while, Shuya looked up at Shogo again. "I don't think…you're an enemy. So I want to trust you."

Noriko joined in, "Me too. I don't think you're a bad person."

Shogo shook his head and grinned. "I have to tell you, I have no talent cheating girls."

Shuya grinned back. Then he said, "So why won't you tell us? No, if you can't tell us how we're escaping, that's fine. But why not? Is it in case we meet up with other people and tell them too much? Is it because the others can't be trusted? Or that you can't trust them?"

"Hold off on the interrogation. I'm not that smart."

"I don't believe you."

Shogo rested his elbows against his knees, held his chin, and looked to his side in contemplation. Then he looked back at them. "Shuya. You're right. I don't want the others to find out about my plan, and even if you two didn't tell them, I wouldn't want the others to even know that you two knew what it was. So I can't tell you."

After Shuya thought about it, he exchanged glances with Noriko and nodded. "Okay then, I understand. We'll trust you. But—"

"Something else bugs you?"

Shuya shook his head. "It just seems like there's no way out of this situation. So I'm—"

"Perplexed?"

Shuya nodded.

Shogo blew out some smoke and rubbed his cigarette into the ground. He ran his hand through his short hair and said, "Nothing is perfect. Most things have flaws."

"Flaws?"

"Yeah, a weak spot. I'm going to aim for that weak spot."

Shuya didn't understand. He squinted his eyes.

Shogo continued, "I know this game better than you two do."

"How's that?" Noriko asked.

"Don't stare at me with those big eyes, girl. I'm shy."

Noriko gave a blank stare and then smiled a little, asking again, "How?"

Finally Shogo said, "Do you know what happens to the survivor of this game?"

Shuya and Noriko looked at each other and shook their heads. That's right, there was one survivor in the Program. After you manage to make it through this absurd game, the Special Defense Forces soldiers shove you in front of the news cameras so they can have an image of the victor ("Smile. You must smile."). But they had no idea what happened to the survivor after that.

Shogo looked at Shuya and Noriko and continued, "The winner's forced to transfer to another school where he or she is ordered not to mention the game and is instructed instead to lead a normal life. That's all."

Shuya felt his chest well up inside and his face froze. He stared at Shogo and realized that Noriko was holding her breath.

Shogo said, "I was a student in Third Year Class C, Second District, Kobe, Hyogo Prefecture." He added, "I survived the Program held in Hyogo Prefecture last year."

27 students remaining

27

Shogo's face softened as he continued, "They even gave me a card autographed by the Dictator. What an honor that was. It looked like some kid scribbled on it, though I can't remember the details, since I tossed it into recycling."

In sharp contrast to Shogo's cheery voice, Shuya took a deep breath. It was true any third-year junior high school student could get thrown into the Program, but…how could you end up in it twice? Of course if he didn't have to stay back, it would never have happened, but even so the chances were as slim as winning the lottery. But now it all made sense how Shogo was so familiar with the game, how he noticed the sleeping gas, and of course, the scars all over his body…but if it was true—it was completely outrageous!

"That's…," Shuya said, "that's outrageous."

Shogo shrugged. "The game was in July, but because I suffered heavy injuries, I was hospitalized for a long time. It gave me time though to study a bunch of things including stuff about this country—but only while lying in bed. The nurses and staff were really generous and brought me books from the library. I guess the hospital was my school. In any case, that was how I ended up repeating third year all over again. But…"

Shogo looked at them.

"…I have to say, even I didn't expect I'd be in this game again."

That's right. Shuya recalled their recent—actually it was already three hours ago—conversation. When Shuya asked, "Did you already kill someone before Kyoichi?" and Shogo had answered, "Well, this time, it was my first."

Noriko then asked, "So those who've been selected…" She rephrased the question, perhaps thinking that it sounded too much like winning a sweepstakes prize, "So the ones who've been in it already aren't exempt?"

Shogo grinned. "I suppose not, since I'm here. From what we're told, classes are chosen randomly by computer, right? My experience gives me the upper hand, but I guess the computer doesn't exclude me. So here's another case of perverted equality."

Shogo cupped his hands around the lighter and lit another cigarette.

"Now you understand how I detected the gas odor. Not to mention…," he pointed at the scar above his left brow, "this scar."

"How could they?" Noriko said as if she were about to cry. "It's too awful."

"Come on, Noriko." Shogo broke into a smile. "Now I get the chance to save you guys."

Shuya offered his hand to Shogo.

"What's this? I can't read your palm."

Shuya smiled and shook his head. Then he said, "I'm sorry I suspected you. A handshake. We're sticking together till the very end."

Shogo replied, "All right." He gripped Shuya's hand and shook it. Noriko smiled in relief.

27 students remaining

28

Kinpatsu Sakamochi (supervisor) was sitting at his faculty desk, rummaging through some scattered documents. To the north and south of him, a Special Defense Forces soldier stood by steel-plated windows equipped with gun ports. The lights inside stayed on because the building let hardly any sunlight in. Five or six soldiers were sitting at a desk facing Sakamochi, staring at a row of desktop computer monitors. Another three soldiers were wearing headphones connected to another machine that wasn't a computer. On the west wall was a large generator powering the lights, computers and other equipment. The generator's low hum filled up the room over the sound insulation. The other soldiers were taking a break in the room the students had been in.

"Now then, Yumiko Kusaka died at 8:42 a.m. and, uh

huh, Yukiko Kitano, she also died at forty-two minutes after the hour." He combed his long hair back behind his ears. "Ahh—I'm so busy!"

The old black phone on the desk rang, and with his pen still in hand, Sakamochi distractedly picked up the receiver.

"Yes, this is Okishima Island School, Third Year Class B, Shiroiwa Junior High School Program Headquarters," Sakamochi answered haphazardly, when all of a sudden he stood up straight, cradling the receiver with both hands.

"Yes sir. This is Sakamochi, Superintendent. I appreciate all you've recently done for us. Yes sir. My second kid just turned two. Yes, and the wife's getting bigger by the day with the third. Oh, no. Well, we just want to contribute to our nation, joining the fight against its dwindling youth population. And how can I help you, sir?"

Sakamochi listened for a while, and then smiled, "Ah ha. My oh my. So you've got your money on Shogo Kawada? I'm betting on Kazuo Kiriyama. I have my money on him. Well, yes, Shogo Kawada is serious competition. He has experience, which is almost unheard of. Of course he's still alive. And how are you, sir? My, that's impressive. Excuse me? The current status? I believe you have access to it on the monitor. The central government's top secret website—oh, you're not good with computers? Uh, well sir, then yes, if you could just hold on a moment, sir."

Sakamochi put down his receiver for a moment and then called on a tough looking soldier sitting in front of the monitors, "Hey, Kato. Is Kawada still with those two?"

The solider named Kato tapped silently on his keyboard and curtly replied, "He is."

The radar in the students' collars enabled them to plot out each student's location on a map on the monitor. Sakamochi was about to frown at Kato's gruff attitude, but then realized how Kato was only one of the many problem students he'd had ever since he was a junior high school teacher, so it was nothing new. He picked up the receiver.

"Sorry to keep you waiting, sir. Let's see. Shogo Kawada is proceeding with two other students. That's Shuya Nanahara and Noriko Nakagawa. Let's see. Well, they're actually talking about escaping together. Would you like to hear our recording of their conversations? Oh yes, sir. Hmm, I'm not sure if he is sincere. I mean it's hard to say, but I'd say it's a bluff. Probably. I mean it's impossible to escape. Oh, and yes, hold on, one moment, sir. Documents, documents. Yes, Shogo Kawada, right? He didn't appear to have been the controversial type at his previous school. No anti-government actions or statements. Yes. His father died during the previous game. Looks like his father got drunk and provoked the government...but apparently Kawada himself said, 'Good riddance. He was a bastard anyway.' Hmmm, they probably didn't get along. Maybe his father insisted on some compensation. Yessir. If that's so, then he's better off with those two than fighting alone. Shuya Nanahara is an excellent athlete, so he'll be useful. Although Noriko Nakagawa is injured. Yes, our Tahara shot her. Yes, of course. They totally trust Shogo Kawada. Helping an injured girl, I mean, how brilliant. His conversation has been most impressive."

Offering a subservient smile, Sakamochi raised his brow in response to his caller. He combed back the hair over his right ear with his free right hand.

"Whaaat?" he replied. "That can't be. I mean that occurred in March. I did receive the report. But if that's true, then right now...yessir. The central government officials are always prone to exaggeration. Besides, these are junior high school kids. Then they would have known we were listening in on them. Right now there are no signs that any of these students know this. Yessir. So…yes, yes, yessir. Very well then. Oh no, please, I couldn't possibly accept…well, if you must insist then, thank you very much, sir. Yes, yes. Well then, goodbye."

Sakamochi took a deep breath and hung up the phone. He held up his pen again and exclaimed, "I'm so busy!" He combed back his hair and began to write frantically on his documents, as if he were clinging to them.

27 students remaining

29

When Shinji first found Yutaka Seto, he seemed on edge from the shock of witnessing the deaths of Yumiko Kusaka and Yukiko Kitano, but after a while he seemed to calm down. In a spot beyond the thick branches, where the warm sunlight poured in, Shinji Mimura was listening closely again. There didn't seem to be anyone else around. Only the sound of a little bird chirping. Whoever killed Yumiko and Yukiko didn't seem to have noticed Yutaka and Shinji. Still, he had to be careful.

"Relax when you have to. But also be on your toes when you have to. The point is, make no errors of judgment."

His uncle had told him this. He was the one who taught him everything. Starting with basketball, he was the man most responsible for the education of the boy known as The Third Man. His uncle had also taught him computer basics. When his uncle showed him how to access foreign internet connections, he warned Shinji, you can never be too careful. And now was one of those times he had to be on his toes. That much was certain.

"Hey, Shinji." Shinji looked back at Yutaka. Yutaka was

leaning against a tree, hugging his knees, staring between them. "Come to think of it, I should have been waiting for you in front of the school. Then we could have been together from the start." He looked up at Shinji. "But I was too scared...."

Shinji crossed his arms with his Beretta in his left hand.

"I don't know about that. That might have been dangerous."

That's right, Shinji realized, Yutaka probably didn't know that Mayumi Tendo and Yoshio Akamatsu were killed in front of the school. Besides—

That was when he realized Yutaka was crying. His eyes were filled with tears which began to flow down his cheeks, tracing two thin, white lines down his dirty face.

"What's wrong?" Shinji asked kindly.

"I..." Yutaka lifted his wounded fist and wiped his eyes with a strip from the towel Shinji had wrapped around his hand. "I'm so pathetic. I-I'm a fool and a coward—" He stopped and then said as if spitting up something stuck in his throat, "I wasn't able to save her."

Shinji lifted his brow and glanced at his friend. This was something he didn't bring up, but since Yutaka did...

Shinji said slowly, "You mean Izumi Kanai."

Yutaka nodded, still hunched over.

Shinji remembered being in Yutaka's room when Yutaka told him, with a mix of pride and embarrassment, "I like Izumi Kanai." And Izumi Kanai ended up being one of the first to die. They were informed of her death by the 6 a.m. announcement. He had no idea where she died. He only knew she died somewhere on the island.

"There wasn't...anything you could do, though," Shinji said, "Izumi left before you did."

"But I..." Yutaka continued, his head still hunched over. "I couldn't even find Izumi...I was so scared...I thought, no, it couldn't happen to her, she's all right...I tried convincing myself. Then at six o'clock she was already..."

Shinji listened without saying a word. He heard the chirping again up in the treetops. There might have been another bird. The chirping overlapped, as if the birds were talking to each other.

Suddenly Yutaka looked up at Shinji. "I made up my mind," he said.

"About?"

His eyes still wet, he directly looked at Shinji. "Revenge. I'm gonna kill that bastard Sakamochi and the rest of the fucking government."

Shinji was surprised. He stared at Yutaka.

Of course he was also totally pissed off at this game and the government that ran it. He didn't really know Shuya Nanahara's best friend Yoshitoki Kuninobu very well—he was a little too laid back for Shinji—but he was a nice guy. And the government brutally murdered him. Then Fumiyo Fujiyoshi, and now as Yutaka said, Izumi Kanai, and then others like Yumiko Kusaka and Yukiko Kitano, killed right before their eyes, and then more classmates. But—

"But...you might as well be committing suicide."

"I don't care if I die. What else can I do for Izumi now?" Yutaka stopped and looked at Shinji. "Is it ridiculous for a wimp like me to be saying this?"

"No..." Shinji paused a bit and then shook his head. "Not at all, Yutaka."

Shinji stared back at Yutaka and then looked up at the cluster of branches above them. He wasn't surprised by Yutaka's sudden emotional outburst, though it wasn't part of with his clownish persona. Here was another side of Yutaka. That's why they'd been friends for so long. But—

"I don't care if I die. What else can I do for Izumi now?"

I wonder what it's like to feel that way about a girl, Shinji

195

wondered as he stared at the olive-colored layer of tree leaves shining brilliantly in the direct sunlight. He had dated girls and slept with three in fact (not bad for a junior high kid, huh?), but he'd never felt that way about a girl the way Yutaka did.

Maybe it had something to do with his parents not getting along. His father saw another woman. (Apparently he was an excellent bureaucrat, but though it might have been presumptuous for his kid to be saying this, he was a vile man. It was unbelievable he could be the brother of Shinji's uncle, who radiated brilliance.) His mother couldn't hold anything against his father, and so whether it was flower arrangement or a women's group, she went from one hobby to another, lost in her own world. They had normal conversations. They did what was necessary. But they didn't trust each other, and they didn't help each other. Their mutual disgust accumulated as they grew older.... Well maybe that was what most parents were like.

Meanwhile...ever since Shinji Mimura became his school's star basketball player, he got popular with the girls— so going out with them was easy. Kissing them was easy. Then after a while sleeping with them was easy too. But...he never fell in love with anyone.

Regrettably he had no opportunity to bring this up with his uncle who always had the right answer for everything. It only concerned him recently, and it was already two years since his uncle's death.

The earring on Shinji's left ear came from him. His uncle always had it with him. He told Shinji, "The woman I loved wore this. She died a long time ago though." It was one of Shinji's prized possessions. After his uncle's death, he took it as a keepsake without anyone's permission. He could hear his uncle saying, "You'll end up becoming jaded at that rate. It's not a bad thing to love someone and be loved by someone.

Hurry up and find yourself a nice girl."

But he still never found someone he could really fall for.

He remembered how his precocious sister, Ikumi, who was three years younger than him, asked, "Do you want a romantic marriage or an arranged marriage?" and how he'd answered, "I may end up not getting married at all."

Ikumi. Shinji thought of his sister. I hope you fall in love with someone nice and have a good marriage. I might end up dying without knowing what it's like to be in love.

Shinji looked back at Yutaka. "Can I ask you something, Yutaka? I'll apologize in advance if it sounds offensive."

Yutaka looked blankly at him. "What is it?"

"What was so great about Izumi?"

Yutaka stared at Shinji and then his tear-drenched face broke into a smile. Maybe this would be his way of offering his bouquet of flowers to the dead.

"I don't know how to say it, but she was so pretty."

"Pretty?" Shinji repeated, then quickly added, "I mean, I'm not saying she wasn't."

Izumi Kanai, well, she wasn't a dog for sure, but as far as pretty girls went, there was Takako Chigusa (oh, I guess she's my type), Sakura Ogawa (well, she had Kazuhiko Yamamoto, and those two are gone), and Mitsuko Souma (well, she's out of the question, no matter how pretty she is).

Yutaka then smiled a little again and said, "When she looked drowsy and rested her cheeks on her hands, she was pretty."

And then he continued, "When she was watering flowers by the classroom window, the way she touched the leaves, she was pretty."

"When she dropped the baton at the annual field day and burst into tears afterwards, she was pretty."

"When she was hanging out during our breaks, listening to Yuka Nakagawa, holding her stomach as she burst out laughing, she was so pretty."

Ah.

As he listened to these observations, Shinji suddenly felt like he totally understood. Yutaka's observations didn't explain anything, but it felt right. Hey Uncle, I think I actually might begin to understand what this is all about.

When Yutaka was done speaking he looked at Shinji

Shinji looked at him kindly and tilted his head slightly. Then he grinned.

"I thought you'd become a comedian when you grew up but now I think you could be a poet."

Yutaka smiled too.

Then Shinji said, "Hey."

"What?"

"I don't know how to say this, but I think Izumi's really happy to know that someone loves her that much. She's probably crying right now up there in heaven."

Compared to Yutaka's poetic observations, his words sounded cheap, but he had to say it. But now Yutaka's eyes began to well up with tears again. The tears flowed down his cheeks again. They formed several white stripes on his cheeks.

"You think?" Yutaka replied, all choked up.

Shinji extended his right hand toward Yutaka's shoulder and gently shook it. "Of course." Shinji took in a breath and continued, "And as for your revenge, I'm in."

Still filled with tears, Yutaka's eyes opened wide. "Really?"

"Yep." Shinji nodded.

Yes, it was something he'd been wondering about. No, not the stuff about girls. He wondered about his future in this shitty Republic of Greater East Asia.

He'd brought this kind of thing up with Yutaka once before. Yutaka said something like, "I don't have a clue," and then added, "At the very least I'll probably become a comedian." Shinji had laughed at Yutaka's facetious reply. But it was a serious concern for him. Actually, it must have been serious for Yutaka too. It was just that Yutaka chose not to bring it up. What it came down to was, as he had once said to Shuya Nanahara, "This is what they call 'successful fascism.' Where else in the world could you find something so sinister?" This country was insane. Not just this stupid game, but anyone who showed even the slightest bit of resistance to the government was immediately discarded. The government couldn't care less even if you were innocent, and continued to cast an intimidating shadow over the lives of everyone who had no other choice but to obey its policies and who found consolation only in the small things that life had to offer. And even when their sources of happiness were taken away, well you just had to bow down and put up with it.

But Shinji began to believe this was wrong, no matter what. No, everyone must have been thinking what he was thinking. But no one would come out with it. Even Shuya Nanahara let off steam by listening to that illegally imported rock music—it never went beyond that though. Shinji began to think he should protest, even if it was dangerous. The more he learned about the world, the more he began to hold this conviction.

Then it happened, two years ago. His uncle's death. Officially it was reported as an accident. As they asked his family to claim his body, the police informed them he'd been electrocuted while working alone at night at his company's factory. But something had seemed wrong with his uncle for a while. His uncle seemed preoccupied, which was unusual for him—as usual, Shinji tapped on his uncle's computer, and then asked, "Is there something wrong?" His uncle was in the middle of replying, "One of my old mates..." but restrained himself and grew evasive,

"Oh no, it's really nothing."

Old mates.

His uncle hardly ever talked about the past. He'd always change the subject, and Shinji, realizing his uncle avoided talking about it, decided not to dig into his uncle's past anymore. (When he asked his father, who was his uncle's older brother, about it, he only replied that it was something Shinji didn't need to know.) Nevertheless, at the core of his wide range of knowledge that went beyond making legal and illegal distinctions, at the core of every explanation his uncle provided about the world or society, Shinji detected a profound disgust if not hatred towards their nation. And also...a shadow-like presence. Shinji had once told him, "You're so great." His uncle only grimaced and replied, "No, you're wrong. I'm not at all. You couldn't survive in this country if you really wanted to be good. I'd be dead if I were really a good person." That was what led Shinji to believe his uncle had fought against the government. But for some reason he stopped. That was what Shinji suspected.

That was also why Shinji was disturbed when he heard his uncle mention his "old mates." But this was his uncle, so he'd be fine, he assured himself and decided not to bombard him with questions.

But his concern turned out to be right on the mark. Shinji had suspected his uncle's "old mates," with whom he'd lost touch, had gotten back in contact him. And though his uncle had probably hesitated, he decided to take on an assignment. And as a result...something happened. It was true that the police in this country had the right to execute civilians without any trial, so usually it wouldn't matter whether they shot you in an alley or at work. But when the person involved was related to someone important, then it wasn't unlikely they'd conspire to kill you in the form of an "accident." Unfortunately, Shinji's father was a director at a well known firm (in other words, he was a first-class worker according to the Republic's employment ranking system—with the exception of a top-level government bureaucrat, it was the highest rank), and what was even more upsetting was that if this were true, then that worthless father of his had assisted, however indirectly, the government in "taking care of" his uncle like that.

It couldn't have been accidental. His uncle would never die from electrocution. That was just too lame!

The original owner of his earring was probably linked to that part of his uncle's past. Outraged over his uncle's murder, Shinji swore he'd never bow down to this country.

Of course he knew that his uncle's statement, "You couldn't survive if you really wanted to be good," was also a warning, which turned out to be true in the case of his uncle's own death. After all you've taught me, Shinji thought, I'm going to figure out how to do what you gave up on a long time ago. I...want to be good. That's what I learned from you after all.

But he had no clear ideas and he hadn't really taken any action. He had heard of anti-government groups but he had no idea how to contact them. Besides, his uncle told him, "It's best not to trust groups and movements. They're not very reliable." He also thought he was a little too young. And above all he was scared.

But now even if he were lucky enough to escape this stupid game he'd become a fugitive. Then—he came to the ironic conclusion—didn't that mean he could do as he pleased? Whether he did it in a group or on his own wouldn't matter. What mattered was that he could give all he had against this government now—this determination welled up inside him.

And now, after talking to Yutaka, he was absolutely certain of it.

Leaving aside this complicated stuff for the moment though, he decided to share his honest feelings on the other topic with Yutaka.

"I really envy you for being in love with someone like that. So if you're going for it, I'm on your side."

Yutaka's lips began to tremble. "Damn, really? You really will?"

"Yeah, I will." Shinji touched Yutaka's shoulder and added, "But our first priority is to escape. Killing that bastard Sakamochi wouldn't even put a dent in the government. If we're going to go for it, we have to aim as high as we can, right?"

Yutaka nodded. Then he wiped his eyes.

Shinji asked him, "Did you see anyone other than Yukiko and Yumiko?"

His eyes red from rubbing, Yutaka looked at Shinji and shook his head, "Nope. I...ran out of the school...and kept on running....Did you see anyone, Shinji?"

Shinji nodded. "When I first left—you probably don't know this but—Mayumi and Yoshio were killed in front of the school."

Yutaka's eyes opened wide. "Really?"

"Yeah. Mayumi was probably killed right as she was leaving."

"...and Yoshio?"

Shinji answered with his arms folded, "I think Yoshio was the one who killed Mayumi."

Yutaka's face stiffened again. "...really?"

"Yeah. Why else would Yoshio, the first one out, be there? Yoshio came back. Then, hiding in the shadows, he probably shot Mayumi....Since they both had arrows in their bodies, he must have tried to get rid of the next one...but instead his weapon— probably a bow gun, given those arrows—must have been taken by someone else, who then shot him.

That's the most likely scenario."

"Who was the next one though?..."

"Shuya."

Yutaka's eyes widened again. "Shuya? Shuya killed Yoshio?"

Shinji shook his head. "I don't know. The only thing we know is that Yoshio wasn't able to kill Shuya. So it was probably Shuya. But maybe Shuya just knocked Yoshio out. He's got a soft spot after all. And then Yoshio might have been killed by someone who came out later." Shinji thought about it and added, "Besides, Shuya must have left with Noriko Nakagawa. He might not have had time to finish off Yoshio."

"Noriko? That's right, Noriko was shot. And you..."

"Yeah," Shinji grinned wryly. "Getting the game delayed would have helped. I knew it was impossible but it was worth trying. Noriko came after Shuya. Shuya gave a clear signal to Noriko before he left. I could tell because I was near him."

Yutaka nodded. "That's right. Noriko got shot so Shuya..."

"And given what happened to Yoshitoki..."

Yutaka nodded several times. He completely understood. "I get it....Nobu had a crush on Noriko, right? So Shuya had to take care of Noriko."

"Yeah. Well, even if that wasn't the case, given Shuya's personality, he'd probably planned on gathering everyone who came out after him. But after Yoshio's attack it was out of the question. Noriko was injured too. So he probably just took off with Noriko as his only partner."

Yutaka nodded again. Then he looked down. "I wonder where Shuya is. We'd be so strong if Shuya and you were together."

Shinji raised his brow. Yutaka might have been

recalling their powerful combinations when they were paired up in class games. It was true, Shinji also thought, Shuya Nanahara would be a great partner. It wasn't just his athletic talent. Just like Shinji, Shuya was daring and fearless, with the ability to respond under pressure. He was one of the few classmates he could rely on in this situation. An honest guy like him (and as far as Shinji was concerned a little too spacey) could never kill his classmates.

Shinji placed his right on Yutaka's shoulder. Yutaka lifted his face. "I'm just glad I'm with you. I'm so glad we're together."

Yutaka was once again on the verge of bursting into tears. Shinji gave him a reassuring smile. Yutaka held back his tears and smiled.

Shinji continued, "Enough about the dead. I noticed something. You know how the woods are right in front of the school athletic field?"

"Yeah."

"There was someone there. A group of students."

"…really?"

"Yeah. I think they were waiting for someone. Of course, there were only five students left after me. Kyoichi Motobuchi, Kazuhiko Yamamoto, Chisato Matsui, Kaori Minami, and Yoshimi Yahagi. Anyway, they didn't make any attempts to call out to me. It was a group, so I doubt they would have been hostile right off, but I didn't have any particular reason to seek them out and join them, either. You just said you should have waited…but under the circumstances that would have been impossible. The fact is that Yoshio probably came back and killed Mayumi. I was thinking that if someone came back there and found that group in the woods they'd be finished. Of course, they might have been armed. Anyway, I booked out of there."

Shinji stopped. After moistening his lips with the tip of his tongue, he went on, "I also saw two other students."

Yutaka's eyes opened wide again. "Really?"

Shinji nodded. "I moved around a lot last night. And…one of them was a girl. You know she has that weird hair that stands up…so I think it was Hirono. While I was checking out the foot of the mountain, I saw her moving beyond those bushes."

"You didn't call out to her?"

Shinji shrugged. "I don't know. I guess I'm prejudiced against her. I just don't trust Mitsuko's friends."

Yutaka nodded.

"The other one I saw was Shogo Kawada."

Yutaka opened his mouth as if to say, wow. He exclaimed, "Shogo-san, huh." Just like his classmates Yutaka politely referred to Shogo as "Shogo-san." "He's a little intimidating so…"

"Yeah, well, that's why I avoided him. But…" Shinji glanced up at the sky. Then he looked back at Yutaka. "He seemed to notice me. I'd just left a house where I was searching for some stuff. He was there, around the house, but he immediately took cover in the path between the fields. I think he was carrying a shotgun. I hid behind the door…I think he was checking me out for a while. But then he disappeared. He didn't try to attack me at all."

Yutaka responded, "Huh. Then that means he's not an enemy."

Shinji shook his head. "Not necessarily. He might have seen my gun and decided he was better off not attacking me. In any case, I decided not to follow him."

"I see…." Yutaka nodded, but then looked up as if he'd realized something. "I know I haven't seen anyone, but I could've sworn I heard another gun go off before Yumiko and Yukiko were shot."

Shinji nodded. "I heard it too."

"It wasn't a machine gun. Do you think it was aimed at them too?"

"No," Shinji shook his head. "I don't think so. I think whoever fired it did it to stop them. It was so obvious what they were doing was risky. The shooter wanted to scare them with the gunfire so they'd run and hide."

Yutaka leaned forward excitedly, "Then...then that shooter isn't an enemy."

"Yeah well, we don't have any way to hook up. Even though I have a rough idea where the gunshot came from....The shooter's probably already on the move since the machine gun shooter knows where he is too."

Disappointed, Yutaka drew back. They fell silent while Shinji continued thinking, his arms folded. Shinji wanted to know if Yutaka had seen anyone they could trust. He thought they could hook up with a classmate if he or she hadn't moved, but come to think of it, he'd trust anyone Yutaka would trust, so if Yutaka had seen others who were trustworthy Yutaka would have been with them by now. But Yutaka was alone. So the question was pointless.

But...in any case, who could he trust? Shuya...and then maybe Hiroki Sugimura? The rest were...girls. He could probably trust the class representative, Yukie Utsumi, and her friends...but he didn't have a good reputation with the girls in his class, probably because he slept around. Ah well. Hey Uncle, I should have found a steady girlfriend, huh?

But how lucky was he to hook up with Yutaka? He could absolutely trust him.

Yutaka asked him, "Hey Shinji. You said you

were looking for something."

Shinji nodded. "I did."

"What was it? What were you looking for? A weapon? I was too scared. It never even crossed my mind."

Shinji looked down at his watch. It should be done by now. An hour had elapsed since the machine began its password search.

Shinji got up and tucked his gun in front. "Yutaka, can you move over?" Yutaka moved away from the tree he was leaning against. Beyond it, there were bushes spreading out over the ground, forming a thicket.

Shinji walked over there and stuck his arms into the bushes. Carefully he pulled out the accessories and cables together.

Yutaka looked astonished.

Shinji had pulled out a car battery (the power source), a partially disassembled cell phone, and a laptop computer. They were all connected by a patch of red and white cables.

The liquid crystal monitor display had been left on, with the computer screen display turned off.

Which meant…Shinji puckered his lips and whistled quietly, pressing down on the space bar. The computer, conserving its energy in sleep mode, turned on with the sound of its hard drive spinning and the grayscale display lighting up on the screen.

After searching for the final line in the tiny window on the screen, Shinji's eyes twinkled mischievously. "Geez. Just a switch of vowels. Too simple for me to guess on my own," he said.

"Hey, Shinji, is this—" Yutaka finally blurted out in amazement. Shinji closed and opened his fists as he always did before tapping away on the keyboard. Then he grinned at Yutaka.

"It's a Macintosh PowerBook 150. I didn't expect to find such a good machine on this lousy island."

27 students remaining

30

Yoshimi Yahagi (Female Student No. 21) waited until her watch read 10 a.m. and then cautiously looked out the rear entrance of the house. It was on the southern end of the residential area of the island, so it was far from the house where Megumi Eto was killed, but Yoshimi had no idea Megumi had died there anyway. She just heard her name in this morning's announcement.

She was more preoccupied with the forbidden zone announced this morning. At 11 a.m. all collars in sector H=8, which included the houses here, would explode. The computer would not respond to pleas for it to wait.

The rear entrance faced a narrow alley that ran between the houses. Yoshimi held the heavy automatic pistol (Colt Government Model .45) with both hands, pulling back the tight hammer with her right thumb. She quickly checked the premises. There was no one in the alley in either direction.

Even though as a member of Mitsuko Souma's gang she was considered a "delinquent," her round face had a childish quality. Right now though, it was breaking out in a cold sweat. It was only an hour or two ago that she saw from the second floor window Yumiko Kusaka and Yukiko Kitano calling on everyone to join them. Then the rattling machine gun. No doubt about it. The killing was continuing. Not everyone was hiding out like she was. There were others willingly killing their classmates. And it was impossible to know where they might show up.

She stepped out and cautiously tiptoed to her right with her back pinned up against the wall of the house where she had been hiding. She turned south at the corner and saw a field extend up a gentle slope. The mild slope was covered with patches of green and headed up to the southern mountain. The houses there weren't as crowded together as they were here. She decided it was best for her to reach the southern mountain. Then she'd be safe for the time being.

Yoshimi shouldered her day pack, checked around again, then ran out to the small thicket by the field.

She reached it in a matter of seconds. Holding her gun with both hands, she pointed it left and right, but no one was there.

Yoshimi was already panting after that brief excursion. She had further to go, though, to get out of sector H=8. She actually might be beyond the border, but it wasn't as if there was a white line running on the ground. It was best to err on the side of caution. Otherwise she'd go nuts. There were blue dots on the map indicating houses and the group of houses where she was was cluttered up with so many dots she had no idea exactly where she was. The sector border was at the edge of this clutter.

Yoshimi felt like crying. If…if she wasn't in Mitsuko Souma's gang then she'd have probably found someone, yes, some nice girl she could trust, and joined up with her. But no one trusted her. Well, she'd done some bad things with Mitsuko Souma and Hirono Shimizu. Stealing from, even at times terrorizing her classmates. No one would believe her even if she insisted she meant no harm. They might attack her on sight.

Before she hid in the house last night she saw another girl heading in the opposite direction. She was leaving the residential area. Was it Kayoko Kotohiki (Female Student No. 8)? Maybe she'd first hid in the residential area but then decided against it and moved on. (Her decision proved a good one, since the area became the game's first forbidden zone.) It was a perfect opportunity to contact someone, given the timing and proximity, but Yoshimi just couldn't bring herself to do it.

And what about Mitsuko Souma and Hirono Shimizu? It was true they were bad…but they were her friends after all. If she could find them…would they trust her? And…could she trust them? No…she probably couldn't.

Overwhelmed by despair, she thought of a certain boy's face again. It was the same face she'd been thinking of ever since the game began. The one who said he didn't care she was with Mitsuko Souma, he still liked her. He kissed her gently on the bed and kindly warned her, "Stay out of trouble." The boy who made her believe she could actually change.

When she left the school building…she thought he might be waiting for her. But of course there was no one there. Of course there wouldn't be. There were the corpses of Mayumi Tendo and Yoshio Akamatsu lying on the ground, though. Chances were if you stuck around you'd end up like them. (She had no idea where their killer had gone.)

Where could he possibly be right now? Or…or was it too late…

She felt her chest tighten. Her eyes filled with tears.

She wiped her eyes with the sleeve of her sailor suit and moved through the thicket towards its edge. She had to move a little further ahead.

Still holding the gun, she looked for her next source of shelter. Now there were several tall trees bunched together on her right with dense, tall weeds all over.

She ran across the field again. Her face was scratched by a

small branch as she slid into the edge of the thicket. She got up slowly and looked around. She couldn't see completely through the thick green shrubbery, but no one was in sight.

Yoshimi still kept low as she crept forward in the thicket. It was all right, it was all right, no one was in the area.

She reached the edge of the thicket. Now the greenery of the southern mountain was right in front of her. Large and small trees and also a dense grove of what looked like bamboo. It looked like there were plenty of places to hide there. All right...all right...then I just have to get there....

Suddenly, she heard a rustling sound behind her. Her heart leaped.

Yoshimi lowered herself, holding the Colt .45 in her hands, and slowly turned around. The hair on the back of her neck was standing straight up.

She caught a glimpse of a black school coat moving between the trees approximately ten meters away. Her eyes opened wide with fear. Someone was over there. Someone!

She clenched her teeth to contain her fear and lowered her head. Her heart was pounding.

She heard another rustling sound.

There wasn't anyone in the thicket just a moment ago. Someone had come here after her. Why? Was this person after her?

Yoshimi turned pale.

No, not necessarily. The student might just be on the move like her. That's right. If she'd been noticed, he or she would have come right after her. She hadn't been noticed yet. Then...then it was best to let him pass. Don't move. Just don't move.

There was the rustling sound again. The person was moving again. Crouching, Yoshimi could see between the dense leaves the figure moving through the woods. Revealing its profile, it moved from Yoshimi's right to her left. Oh yes!

He's not headed towards me....

As she sighed though, she suddenly did a double take.

The figure was too far into the trees to see. The rustling sound gradually became distant.

She couldn't be wrong. Was she just hallucinating out of panic? No, that couldn't be.

Yoshimi stood up, hunched over, and proceeded to follow the sound. Moving several meters ahead, she looked toward the source of sound in the shade of the dense leaves. In her narrow field of vision she was able to make out the school coat.

Yoshimi put both of her hands on her chest. Had it not been for the gun she held in her hands, she would have looked like she was praying.

But Yoshimi was praying, no doubt. If there were a god who could bring about such a miraculous turn of events, then she was thanking it. She held no particular religious beliefs, but it didn't matter which god it was. She was grateful. *Oh God thank you! I love you!*

Yoshimi blurted out as she stood up, "Yoji!"

Yoji Kuramoto (Male Student No. 8) trembled for a moment, but then turned around slowly. His face had a Latin look. His thick-lashed eyes opened wide and then returned to their normal size. For a split second his face seemed to turn blank, but she was convinced it was just her mind playing tricks on her. The face then formed a smile. The smile of the boy who loved her more than anyone else.

"Yoshimi—"

"Yoji!"

Holding her day pack and Colt .45 in her right hand, Yoshimi ran toward Yoji. Her eyes filled with tears.

Yoji held Yoshimi in his arms, gently, but also with reassurance in the tiny space of the thicket.

Then without saying a word Yoji kissed her on the lips.

He kissed her eyelids. The tip of her nose too. It was how Yoji always kissed her. It might not have been appropriate, given the circumstances, but she was ecstatic.

After kissing her he looked into her eyes and said, "So you were safe. I was worried about you."

Remaining in each other's arms, Yoshimi responded, "Me too, me too." Tears came rolling out of the corners of her eyes and down her cheeks.

When Yoji left the classroom before her, he took a glance at Yoshimi, who was on the verge of crying as she watched him leave. She had left too, and dawn came. And she had been terrified every single moment until now. But now she was with someone she thought she'd never see alive again.

"I-it's a miracle," Yoji said, somewhat belatedly, as if he were in shock.

"It really is. I can't believe it. I thought we'd never see each other again. In this...horrible..."

Yoji gently brushed his hands through Yoshimi's hair while she cried. "It's going to be all right now. We'll stay together no matter what happens."

Yoji's words sounded reassuring and tears came gushing out from her eyes. The rules only allowed one survivor, but I get to be with the one I love most. There was something about a time limit, but we'll just stay together until time runs out. If someone attacks us, Yoji will protect us. Oh God tell me I'm not dreaming.

Yoshimi remembered everything that happened between them since she met Yoji in their second year, when they ended up classmates. That special autumn day, when they bumped into each other on the street and decided to go to a movie together, then Christmas, then the strawberry shortcake they ordered and split at the cafe, that night's kiss, New Year's, dressing up in a long-sleeved kimono for the first temple visit (the sacred lot she drew was only "fair luck," while his was "very good luck," and he gave her his), and the unforgettable Saturday, January 18th, the night she spent at Yoji's house.

"Where have you been?" Yoshimi asked.

Yoji pointed to the group of houses. "In a house over there. But you know this collar...if I stay there, it's supposed to explode. So..."

Yoji looked serious, but Yoshimi thought it was funny. They were right near each other! She'd been wondering ever since the game began where could he be, only to find out he was right nearby....

"What's up?"

"I was hiding in one of those houses too. We were probably right next door to each other."

They laughed. Yoshimi realized how wonderful it was to share a laugh with someone you loved. It might be considered trivial, but no, it was essential. And now it was hers once again.

Yoji slowly let go of Yoshimi. His eyes suddenly fell on her right hand. Realizing she was still holding the gun, she burst out, "Ha ha ha. I forgot...."

Yoji also smiled. "Nice weapon. Look what I ended up with."

He showed her what he'd been holding. She hadn't noticed it at all. On closer look, she saw that it was a dagger, the kind you might see in an antique store. The strip of thread wrapped around the grip was worn out, the oval-shaped guard had turned greenish blue, and as Yoji revealed by pulling the dagger out of its sheath, the blade was spotted with rust. Yoji returned the blade to its sheath and tucked it in his belt.

"Hey, let me check that out," Yoji said.

She offered the gun to him. "You hold onto it. I doubt I can do much with it...."

Yoji nodded and took the Colt .45. He held the grip and checked the safety. He pulled the slide, revealing the first bullet in the chamber. The hammer was still cocked.

"You have bullets for this?"

The gun's cartridge was fully loaded. Yoshimi nodded, took the box of bullets out of her day pack, and handed it over to him. Yoji took it with one hand, opening it up with his thumb to check the contents. Then he tucked it into his uniform pocket.

All of a sudden…Yoshimi couldn't believe her eyes. She was completely clueless as to what was going on—as if she were watching some baffling magic trick—as she looked at Yoji's hands.

Yoji was pointing the Colt .45 at her.

"Yoji?…"

After repeating his name, she saw how Yoji had become a different person.

His face was contorted. The thick-lashed eyes, the large hooked nose, his wide lips, each part of his face looked the same as before, but she'd never seen this expression with its twisted mouth, revealing its teeth.

The contorted mouth spat out these words, "Go away. Get out of here!"

Yoshimi didn't understand what he meant.

Yoji sounded irritated. "I said get away from me!"

Still in a daze, her lips quivered, "Why?"

As if fed up with her, Yoji cried out, "You expect me to be with a bitch like you!? Get out of here, bitch!"

Something inside of Yoshimi began to crumble, first slowly, then quickly.

"Why?" Yoshimi's voice trembled. "Did I…did I do something wrong?"

The gun was still aimed at her. Yoji spat to his side.

"Give me a break. Even I know you're a slut. I know

you've been arrested by the cops....On top of that you slept with a guy old enough to be your dad. I know that too! You expect me to trust a bitch like you!?"

Yoshimi's jaw dropped as she stared at Yoji's face.

It was...true. She'd been arrested several times for stealing, and the police had taken her in once for blackmailing a high school student. And then there was...prostitution. A while ago Yoshimi had slept with some middle-aged men Mitsuko Souma had introduced her to. The money was good, she wasn't the only one doing it, and at that time of her life she was getting so fed up with everything. So wearing makeup she'd never worn, acting like an adult, and being with men who seemed in their own way generous didn't seem like a bad thing. Yoshimi assumed Yoji had known all this about her.

Ever since she started dating Yoji that autumn day, she had put an end to all of that. Of course she continued being friends with Mitsuko Souma and Hirono Shimizu. It wasn't like she was suddenly a star pupil, but she did stop prostituting herself, and she did her best to keep herself out of trouble. And she'd believed Yoji forgave her and loved her anyway.

...that's what I believed all along.

A tear rolled down Yoshimi's cheek.

"I-I stopped doing that." Different tears began streaming down her cheeks. "I wanted to be...I wanted to be good to you, Yoji."

Yoji stared at Yoshimi as if her words had completely shaken him up.

But then his expression returned.

"You liar! Stop pretending to cry!"

Yoshimi stared at Yoji with her wet eyes. Words came tumbling out, "Then...then why did you go out with me?"

Yoji immediately replied, "Come on, I thought a slut like

you'd be easy! Get out of here! Bitch!"

Suddenly prompted by some force, Yoshimi ran towards Yoji. It might have been because she couldn't bear listening to Yoji anymore, or maybe it was because she couldn't deal with the fact that Yoji was pointing a gun at her. "Stop it! Please stop it!" she cried and tried to grab the gun from his hand.

Yoji quickly dodged her and shoved her. The day pack slid off her shoulder down to her left hand, and Yoshimi fell back on the grass.

Yoji pinned Yoshimi down.

"What the hell are you doing!? Bitch! You tried to kill me! I'll kill you, bitch!"

Yoji pointed his gun at her while Yoshimi frantically grabbed his right wrist with both her hands. Yoji immediately shifted the gun from his right hand to his left. Yoji's hand moved slowly downward. To her forehead! Yoshimi felt her heart pounding.

Yoshimi stuck out her hands and cried in desperation.

"Yoji! Please! Please stop it, Yoji!"

Yoji said nothing. His bloodshot eyes glared down at her. His arm came down methodically, like a machine. Five more centimeters…four…three…the bullet could now brush her hair. Two more centimeters, and…

Though she was torn up with sadness and fear, a thought suddenly occurred to her.

She understood everything now. She didn't want to, but it turned out the person she adored was only an illusion. Still…

Still, it was a wonderful illusion. With Yoji, she thought she could start over. It was Yoji who gave her that illusion. Without Yoji she would never have believed it could happen.

Oh, that time we ate ice cream at the only burger joint in Shiroiwa…she had ice cream on her nose and Yoji said, "You are so cute." Even now she believed he'd been sincere.

I loved you.

Yoshimi suddenly relaxed her arms. Yoji cocked the gun and placed it against her forehead. His finger was ready to pull the trigger.

Yoshimi stared back at Yoji and quietly said, "Thank you, Yoji. I was so happy being with you."

Yoji's eyes opened wide and remained frozen, as if he'd suddenly realized something important.

"Go ahead...shoot me."

Yoshimi smiled warmly and closed her eyes.

Pointing the gun at her, Yoji began to tremble.

Yoshimi waited for the burning bullet to pierce her head, but the gun wouldn't fire.

Instead she heard his hoarse voice, "Yoshimi..."

Yoshimi slowly opened her eyes again.

They met Yoji's. Through the thin film of her tears, she saw how his eyes were now those of her beloved Yoji. They were even filled with remorse and self-reproach.

Ah—

So he understands—Yoji—is it true?

TUNK! It was a pleasant but somewhat strange, damp sound.

Simultaneously, Yoji's right finger pulled the trigger. But it was on accident, the result of his finger's reflex. The gunshot exploded like a firecracker and made her shriek, but the muzzle had already been pointed away from her, and the bullet lodged into the patch of grass above her head. A tiny cloud of dirt rose in the air.

Yoji's lifeless body fell on top of Yoshimi. He remained motionless.

As she tried to pry herself loose, she saw someone smile over the shoulders of Yoji's black school coat. It was her old partner in crime, Mitsuko Souma.

Yoshimi had no idea what was going on. She only knew that the smile on this angelic, adorable, beautiful face absolutely terrified her.

Mitsuko asked Yoshimi if she was all right as she grabbed her hand and pulled her out from under Yoji's body.

Yoshimi staggered to her feet in the bushes and looked down. An extremely sharp sickle (a sickle! as one of the more urban girls in Shiroiwa, Yoshimi had never seen one before) was planted in the back of Yoji's head.

Leaving aside the sickle for now, Mitsuko immediately went for the Colt .45 in Yoji's right hand. His muscles had tightened, so she had to pry each stiff finger loose. The gun was finally in her hands, and she grinned.

Yoshimi looked down at Yoji's lifeless body, trembling. She was trembling violently. Uncontrollably. In one flourish she had just lost someone incredibly important to her. It was like the sensation she had when a precious glass ornament she had as a child accidentally fell and shattered on the floor. But…this was far more precious.

Yoshimi came to her senses and looked at Mitsuko (of course she had been looking at her all this time, but she was too incapacitated to process this visual information), who proceeded to wrestle with the sickle to dislodge it from the back of Yoji's head. She gripped the handle with both hands and tried shaking it loose, swinging Yoji's head along with it.

"No!…"

Yoshimi screamed and shoved Mitsuko aside. Mitsuko fell back onto the grass, exposing her well formed legs, from the hem of her pleated skirt up to her thighs.

Yoshimi shielded Yoji's body. The sickle was still planted in his skull. Her tears fell onto his body. The sickle was telling her: shaking me won't revive me, don't shake me, there's a sickle stuck in me, man, that hurts.

Her chest tightened with waves of remorse. She felt as if she were drowning, as if the world were coming to an end.

She thought of the cause behind all of this, and her tear-stained eyes glared fiercely at Mitsuko. If looks could kill, her glare would have. Yoshimi couldn't care less now what kind of game this was or who her enemies and allies were. That's right. If anyone was her worst enemy, it was Mitsuko Souma, who'd killed her love.

"Why'd you kill him!?"

The words sounded empty to Yoshimi. She felt as if she had become a hollow bag in a human shape. But the words came pouring out. The human body could do strange things.

"Why! Why'd you kill him!? It's horrible! It's just too awful! You're evil! Why'd you have to kill him!? Why!?"

Mitsuko contorted her mouth in an expression of dissatisfaction. "You were about to get killed. I saved you."

"No! I got Yoji to understand me! You're so evil! I'll kill you! I'll kill you! Yoji understood me!"

Mitsuko shook her head and shrugged, pointing the .45 at her. Yoshimi's eyes opened wide.

And so Yoshimi heard the dry pop one more time. Her forehead felt as if it were being crushed by a car. That was all.

Yoshimi Yahagi fell onto the corpse of her beloved Yoji Kuramoto and remained motionless. The .45 caliber bullet had demolished the back of her head. But her mouth remained open as if she were screaming and blood came flowing out from its side. It soaked Yoji's school coat, oozing out into a dark patch.

Mitsuko lowered the smoking Colt .45 and shrugged again. She'd planned on using Yoshimi to shield her from bullets.

She leaned over and whispered into the ear of Yoshimi's half-destroyed head, "I'm sure he understood." There was a strange topping of gray jelly brains and blood on her earlobe. "I killed him because it looked like he wasn't going to kill you after all."

Then, once again, she proceeded to pry loose the sickle from Yoji's head.

25 students remaining

31

The faint sound reached Shuya and the others. Shuya looked up. Then they heard it again. They waited, but that was it. They only heard the rustling sound of treetops deep inside the thicket shaking in the wind.

Shuya looked at Shogo, who was sitting next to him.

"Was that a gunshot?"

"That was a gunshot."

"Then someone's already..." Noriko began to speak, but Shogo shook his head and responded, "We don't know for sure."

They had all remained silent for several minutes, but the gunfire prompted discussion.

Shogo spoke up, "Look, as long as you trust me, it's cool but...like I said before, we have to survive till the very end. So I just want to make sure." Shogo looked over at Shuya. "Are you willing to be merciless against the enemy, Shuya?"

Shuya swallowed deeply. "You mean the government?"

"Including them, yeah." Shogo continued, "As well as your other classmates, if and when they attack us."

Shuya nodded slightly and then answered, "If that's what it comes down to, I will." His voice sounded feeble, though.

"Even if the classmate was female?"

Shuya's lips tightened as he looked back at Shogo. He looked down again. "If I have to I will."

"All right then. As long as we're on common ground." Shogo nodded and grabbed the shotgun resting on his crossed legs. Then he added, "Someone else will finish you off if you get too hung up on every person you kill."

Shuya was about to say something but hesitated. He decided it was best not ask, but couldn't stop himself from blurting out, "So you were merciless a year ago?"

Shogo shrugged. "I killed. You want to hear the details? How many guys I killed? How many girls I killed until I won?"

Noriko crossed her arms over her chest and brought in her elbows.

"No...forget it." Shuya shook his head. "That's pointless."

They fell silent again. Then Shogo said, as if offering an explanation, "I had no choice. Some of them lost their minds...and then some were willingly killing as many as they could....Most of my friends died pretty quickly, and I didn't have any time to hook up with anyone. And I-I just couldn't offer myself up and get killed by someone." He paused and added, "I also had something I had to do, so I couldn't die."

Shuya lifted his face. "What's that?"

"Come on, it's so obvious." Shogo smiled a little, but his eyes glimmered fiercely all of a sudden. "I was going to tear up this fucked up country, this country that tosses us into this fucked up game."

Watching Shogo's lips tremble in anger, Shuya thought, he's just like me. He wants to bring down these assholes in charge of this game, these assholes who won't think twice about making us play this fucked up game of musical chairs, this game of mutual fear and loathing. He wants to send them to hell just like me.

Or maybe...Shogo mentioned in passing he'd lost his friends early on, but I bet he lost someone equally important as Yoshitoki was to me.

Shuya thought of asking him about this, but didn't.

Instead he asked, "You said you'd done a lot of studying...so that was for this purpose?"

Shogo nodded, "That's right. I would have done something against this country eventually."

"Like what?"

Shogo only grimaced. "I wonder." He shook his head. "It's not so easy bringing down a system that's already built up. But I would have done something. Well no, I'm still going to. That's why I have to survive this time too."

Shuya looked down at the revolver and looked up. Another question had occurred to him.

"Can you tell me something?"

"What?"

"What's the purpose of this game? How could this serve any useful purpose?"

Shogo's eyes widened...but then he looked down and began to chuckle. He found it funny. Then he finally said, "There is no purpose."

Noriko raised her voice. "But they insist it has some military purpose."

Shogo kept on smiling and shook his head. "That's just crazy nonsense. Of course this whole country's insane, so maybe it's completely rational."

Shuya felt a rush of anger once again as he spoke, "Then how could this go on for so long?"

"That's easy. Because there's no one speaking out against it. That's why it's still going on."

Seeing how Shuya and Noriko were at a loss for words, Shogo added, "Look, this country's run by a bunch of idiot bureaucrats. In fact you have to be an idiot to be a bureaucrat. My guess is that when this lovely game was first proposed—some crazy military strategist probably came up with it—there was no opposition. You don't want to stir things up by questioning the specialists. And it's terribly difficult to end something that's already been established. You interfere, and you're out of a job. No, worse yet, you might be sent to a forced labor camp for ideological deviation. Even if everyone were against it, no one could say it out loud. That's why nothing changes. There are a lot of screwed up things in this country but they all boil down to the same thing—fascism."

Shogo looked at Noriko and Shuya. He added, "You two, and the same applies to me, we can't say anything. Even if you think something's wrong, your life is too precious to risk it by protesting, right?"

Shuya couldn't say anything back. His hot flash of anger all of a sudden went cold.

"It's shameful," Noriko said.

Shuya looked at Noriko. Noriko looked down sadly. He agreed. He felt the same way.

"Did you know there was a country called the South Korean People's Republic?" Shogo asked. Shuya looked at Shogo, who was staring at a pink azalea flower on a tree branch right in front of them.

It seemed irrelevant, but Shuya answered anyway, "Yeah, it was the southern half of the current Democratic Nation of the Korean Peninsula, right?"

You could learn about what was known as the South Korean People's Republic and the Democratic Nation of the Korean Peninsula—and the civil strife between the two Korean nations immediately west of the Republic of Greater East Asia's inland sea—in a textbook: "Although our relations with SKPR were cordial, due to conspiracies concocted by the imperialists of the United States and the DNKP, the SKPR was annexed by the DNKP." (Of course, following this explanation, the summary would continue, "Our nation must immediately oust the Korean Peninsula imperialists and annex this country not only for the freedom and democracy of the Korean people, but in order to progress towards our goal in attaining the co-existence of Greater East Asia peoples."

"That's right," Shogo nodded. "That country was just like ours. An oppressive government and dictator, ideological propaganda, isolationism, and information control. And support for snitching. It failed though after forty years. But the Republic of Greater East Asia is doing quite well. Why do you think that is?"

Shuya thought about it. He hadn't really given it much thought, but the textbooks explained South Korea's defeat as "a cunning conspiracy instigated by the imperialists including the American imperialists" (The vocabulary employed in these textbook explanations was beyond junior high level.) But then why was the current Greater East Asia still prosperous? Of course the SKPR was geographically located right next to the DNKP but...

He shook his head. "I don't know."

Shogo looked at Shuya and nodded. "First of all, it's a question of balance."

"Balance?"

"That's right. While the SKPR was totalitarian—of course, this country is essentially totalitarian. But it employs a subtle, well, this just might have been a fortunate result, but it skillfully managed to leave little bits of freedom intact. By providing this kind of candy, they can proclaim, 'Of course, every citizen has the right to freedom. However, freedom must be controlled for the sake of the public good.' The claim actually sounds legit, huh?"

Shuya and Noriko silently waited for Shogo to continue.

"That was how the country became this way. Seventy-five years ago."

Noriko interrupted him, "Seventy-five years ago?" Hugging her knees under her pleated skirt, Noriko tilted her head with a puzzled look on her face.

Noriko then looked over at Shuya. Shuya nodded and then looked back at Shogo. "I heard something about how the history they teach us is a big lie and that the current Dictator is hardly the 325th Dictator. In fact, he's only supposed to be the twelfth one, right?"

Shinji Mimura had told him this. Noriko wouldn't know. It would never be taught at school and most adults kept their mouths shut about it (maybe they didn't even know), and even Shuya was appalled when he first heard it from Shinji. After all, this meant that before the appearance of the First Dictator less than eighty years ago—in other words, before the Great Revolution—the name of the country and system of government had been totally different. (Shinji had claimed, "Apparently, it was a feudal society. People wore these psychedelic hair styles called chonmage, and there was a caste system. But to be blunt, it was better than what we have today.")

Shuya glanced at Noriko's surprised face, but when he heard Shogo's next statement, "Well, even that might not be true," he raised his brow.

"What do you mean?"

Shogo smiled and said, "There is no Dictator. He doesn't exist. He's just made up. That's what I heard."

"What?"

"That can't be...," Noriko said hoarsely, "but we see him on the news...and on New Year's he makes an appearance in front of everyone at his palace...."

"Right." Shogo grinned. "But who is this 'everyone at the palace'? Have you ever met someone who was actually there? What if they were actors too, just like the Dictator?"

Shuya considered the possibility....It made him nauseous. Nothing but lies, there was no truth. Everything felt uncertain.

"Is that really true?" he asked despondently.

"I don't know. It's just something I heard. But it seems likely to me."

"Where did you get that information? By computer on that thing called the Net?"

Shuya thought of Shinji Mimura when he asked him this, but Shogo only grinned again.

"Unfortunately, I'm no good with computers, but there are ways to find out if you want to. It seems likely, because that would allow the government to have no supreme authority. That way everyone at the center of the government would be equal. They would have equal freedom. Which means that their responsibilities are also equal. There would be no inequality. There'd be no objections. The only thing is that there has to be some subtle trick going on....The whole charade has to be kept secret from the general public. The leader figure just has to play a charismatic role."

Shogo took a deep breath and continued, "Anyway, that's neither here nor there. To get back to what I was saying, the country implemented this system, and it just kept on successfully evolving. What I mean by 'success' is that it succeeded as an industrialized nation. Even though the country stuck to isolationism, it traded with other countries that remained neutral, not only to us but to America as well, and imported raw materials from them and sold products to them. The products sold well. Of course they would. Their quality is really high. Serious competition against the U.S. The only things this country lags behind in are space technology and computers. But the high quality comes as a result of the individual's subservience to the group and an oppressive government. Still..." he stopped. He shook his head and continued, "I have a feeling that once we've reached this level of success even the people themselves are afraid of changing the system. With this kind of success, and this high standard of living, they won't be willing to make a few sacrifices, even if there may be a few little problems. And overthrowing the government would be out of the question."

Shogo looked over at Shuya again and gave him a sarcastic smile. "And one of the 'few little problems'? This wonderful game. Of course the students and their families might have been dealt a bad hand, but they're a small minority. Even the families eventually let it go. Sorrow passes with time."

Shogo's winding explanation finally returned to this stupid game, the pride of the Republic of Greater East Asia. Perhaps it was Shuya's grim frown that made Shogo ask, "What's up?"

Shuya replied, "I feel like puking." He finally began to understand exactly what Shinji Mimura meant when he said, "This is what they call 'successful fascism.' Where else in the world could you find something so sinister?" Shinji must have known and understood long ago everything Shuya had just learned.

"Ha! Wait till you hear this one. It'll make you sick." Shogo almost looked as if he were relishing this as he continued, "I think that the fundamental difference between the SKPR and this country is ethnic."

"Ethnic?"

Shogo nodded. "Yeah. In other words, I think that this system is tailor-made to fit the people of this country. In other words, their subservience to superiors. Blind submission. Dependence on others and group mentality. Conservatism and passive acceptance. Once they're taught something's supposedly a noble cause by serving the public good, they can reassure themselves they've done something good, even if it means snitching. It's pathetic. There's no room for pride, and you can forget about being rational. They can't think for themselves. Anything complicated enough sends their heads reeling. Makes me want to puke."

He was exactly right. It was completely revolting. Shuya felt his stomach turn.

That was when Noriko interrupted Shogo, "I don't agree at all."

Shuya and Shogo looked at Noriko. The way she was hugging her knees and hunched over, Shuya thought she was tired out. But she looked at both of them and spoke clearly, "I didn't know about this. This is the first time I've ever heard any of this. But if what you just said is really true, and if everybody were really informed, I don't think they would sit still.…It's because no one knows about this that we've ended up in this situation. You say we've always been like this, but I refuse to believe that. I'm not saying we're especially noble, but I think we're just as capable as any other people on this planet of thinking responsibly."

Shogo responded with a surprisingly kind and gentle smile. "I like what you just said."

Shuya meanwhile all of a sudden saw Noriko in a different light. She didn't really stick out in class, nor was she so outspoken she'd express her opinions the way she had just done now. It was odd, but ever since this game began he was seeing another side of Noriko. And maybe—it might only mean Shuya had been totally ignorant—Yoshitoki had perceived this side of her long ago.

Anyway it was a much more admirable response than his knee-jerk "It makes me want to puke." Once again she was absolutely right. No matter what, this was their country, the place where they were born and grew up (although he wasn't so sure how much more growing up was left for them). The U.S., a.k.a. the American Empire, might liberate this country some time in the future, but the fact was that this was their deal. They shouldn't, and in the end they couldn't, rely on others.

Shuya looked over at Shogo and asked him, "Hey Shogo. Do you think we can change this country?"

Much to Shuya's disappointment Shogo shook his head. He thought that, given his pledge to "tear up this fucked up country," he would reply affirmatively, that they would change it.

Shuya said somewhat clumsily, "But you just said you'd tear up this country."

Shogo lit a cigarette, which he hadn't done in a while, and then folded his arms. "I'll tell you what I think." He unfolded his arms, removed the cigarette from his lips, and exhaled a cloud of smoke. "I think history comes in waves."

Shuya didn't understand, but before he could ask what he meant, Shogo continued, "At some point in time, when the situation is ripe, this country will change. I don't know whether it will happen in the form of a war or a revolution. And I have no idea when the time will come. For all I know it may never happen."

Shogo took another drag and then exhaled. "In any case, right now I don't think it's possible. Just like I said, this country is insane, but it's also well run. Extremely well run." Shogo pointed at them, the cigarette between his fingers. "Now here we have a rotten nation. If you can't stand it, then the wisest thing to do would be to abandon it and go somewhere else. There are ways to escape this country. Then you can avoid the stench. You might get homesick once in a while, but life outside would be grand...but I'm not doing that."

Shuya rubbed his hand against his thigh. He was hoping Shogo's statement would correspond with his thoughts: I want to do something here because in the end this is my country. Didn't Bob Marley sing, "Get up, stand up...you can't fool all the people all the time"?

But Shogo's response fell short of this expectation.

"I'm doing this for myself. I want revenge...even if it's for my self-satisfaction...I want to strike against this country.

That's all. I really doubt it'll actually lead to change in this country in the long run."

Shuya took a short breath...then uttered, "This sounds hopeless."

"It is hopeless," Shogo replied.

25 students remaining

32

When they heard the two distant shots, Yutaka cringed. Shinji stopped typing on the keyboard.

"Hey—"

Shinji nodded. "Another gunshot."

He quickly returned to his computer, though. It seemed harsh, but he couldn't afford to be concerned with others.

Yutaka looked down at Shinji's fingers. He was holding the Beretta. Shinji had handed it to his towel-bandaged hand and requested he keep watch.

"Hey, Shinji. What are you trying to find on that laptop? Won't you tell me now?" After Shinji had booted up the communications software and dialed up with the cellular phone, he kept typing away at that keyboard, only occasionally exclaiming "Bingo! Bingo! Bingo!" or "Oh damn, oh yeah, right," without giving Yutaka a single explanation.

"Hold on a sec. I'm almost there."

Shinji was typing again. At the center of the gray screen, English sentences interspersed with "%" and "#" characters streamed by. Shinji seemed to be responding to them.

"All right."

Shinji stopped typing after the requested data began to download. The basic operation was Unix, but he'd set up a separate graphics window to indicate the download status in Mac format. Shinji stretched his arms over his head. Now he'd just have to wait for the download to be completed (of course once it was he'd have to rewrite the log entry to erase all traces of his operation). Then he had to come up with a strategy based on the data he received. He'd either have to rewrite the data or come up with his own program to deceive his opponents. The latter would be a hassle, but he probably wouldn't need more than half a day to do the job.

"Shinji, tell me what's going on," Yutaka insisted.

Shinji smiled, moved back from the laptop, and leaned against the tree again. He had to admit, this was exciting. He took a deep breath to calm himself down. It was only natural, though. Although he wasn't sure when he told Yutaka, "It's a PowerBook 150," now he was now certain—they were going to win.

He spoke slowly, "I've been trying to figure out how to escape."

Yutaka nodded.

"And so..." Shinji pointed to his neck. He himself couldn't see it, but he assumed Yutaka could see the silver collar wrapped around his neck, the same one Yutaka had on his neck. "The first thing I wanted was to get rid of this. This is giving our positions away to that bastard Sakamochi. For example, the fact that we're together. Thanks to this device, even if we try to escape, they'll locate us, or worse yet, they can just send a signal to blow up the collars and kill us. So I needed to figure out how to get rid of this collar."

Shinji opened up his hand. Then he shrugged. "But I gave up. You can't pry it loose without knowing how it's built. Sakamochi said it would explode if you took it apart, and I doubt he was bluffing. The outer casing must be loaded with a fuse wire for the device. It's probably set to ignite once you cut it. It's too dangerous to cross that bridge. I thought of inserting a metal plate inside the band, but it would be too thin to protect my neck from being blown to bits."

Yutaka nodded again.

"That's how I came up with the idea of controlling the school computer that's tracking us and controlling the ignition signal. Get it?"

It was of course his uncle who'd taught him the basics of computer programming, but ever since his death Shinji was as passionate about improving his skills on his uncle's computer as he was about basketball. As a result he became extremely adept. He learned how to tap into an international line that was strictly prohibited by the government and obtain even higher levels of computer skills and new information on the entire world through the *real* internet. (What the nation called "the internet" was really a joke, a closed net referred to as "Greater East Asia Net.") While he might not be executed for these actions, they were illegal enough to send him away for a two-year stint at a juvenile prison for ideological offenses. That was how he acquired the skill to escape detection. Of course he never told anyone about it, but he'd shown some websites to Yutaka (mostly pornographic ones, come on, gimme a break). In short, Shinji was good at computer hacking.

"I looked for a personal computer. I already had a cell. I guess you're allowed to keep your stuff in this stupid game. I should have brought my notes, but I can't complain, since I found this laptop. Now all I needed was electricity. I yanked that battery out of a car. I had to adjust the voltage, but that was pretty easy."

As Shinji explained, Yutaka finally began to grasp how the PowerBook and cell phone functioned together. But then a thought suddenly occurred to him and he said, "Hey, but didn't Sakamochi say we couldn't use phones? So cell phones are an exception?"

Shinji shook his head. "No, they won't work. I tried the number for the weather report and Sakamochi's voice chimed in, 'A beautiful day at the Shiroiwa Junior High Program Headquarters.' I was so pissed I immediately hung up. So they're controlling the nearest cellular transmitter. My guess is none of the phone companies will work here."

"Then…"

Shinji lifted his finger, interrupting Yutaka. "Think about it. Their communication system has to reach beyond this island. I mean, their computers must be linked to the central government's for security purposes. Then how would they do that? It's simple. They've selectively employed numbers for military purposes from the cellular phone lines."

"So that means…"

Shinji interrupted Yutaka again and grinned. "But even if that were the case, I thought…they must have at least made some minimal effort to protect themselves from anyone at the telephone company tampering with their lines."

Shinji reached out for the cell phone on the ground. Then he said, "I didn't tell you, but my cell is a custom model. It has two types of ROM memory for phone numbers and passwords. You can't tell looking at it, but you can switch the other one on by turning this screw ninety degrees. And this other number is something I came up with just for fun to make free calls…." He let go of his phone and continued, "It's the cellular number used by phone company technicians to test phone lines."

"Then…that means…"

Shinji winked. "That's right. Bingo! The rest is simple. It was a bit of a pain to hook up the phone modem to the cellular. It's not like they came with tools. But I managed to do it. So that's how I got my line. Then I accessed my computer at home. I can't hack with your average communications software, so I downloaded my special tools—like codebreaking software. Then I went for the prefectural government's site. The central government's operations must have high quality security systems, but I figured the prefectural government's systems would be easy to break into. My hunch turned out to be right. Even though this game is directly managed by the central government, it must have some contact with the government branch of the prefecture where the game's taking place. I was right about that too. There were a lot of unfamiliar addresses in their communications log files. Going through e-mails I found one to the superintendent, notifying him of the game's commencement. I broke into the sender's website, in other words, the temporary server for the school building on this island. It took some work, but as I poked around as much as I could without getting caught, I found an operation backup file they'd completely spaced out on. So I took that. In other words, I found a strange code that seemed important. I've been having the Mac break the code before I hooked up with you. So that's what I was up to."

Shinji reached out for the PowerBook as it continued to download data, opened up another memo file, and showed the immense 24-point display. Yutaka took a look. "Kinpati Sakamocho."

"Sakamocho?..."

"Yeah. I think it's Spanish. So the password was a bit complex due to this silly change in vowels. That's what the password for this system is. That's how I got free access. I was checking out as much as I could. I completely downloaded the entire data contents of the school's computer. I'm going to alter the data, go back into that system, and disable these collars. By making the school premises a forbidden zone, they think they're totally safe against us, but now we'll be able to attack them by surprise. We'll have a chance. And once we control the school, we should be able to help out the others. Even if that's not possible, we can falsify the data to claim we're dead and then escape this island for good."

With this brief but intense summary, Shinji took a deep breath and grinned. "What do you think?"

Yutaka looked astonished. "It's amazing."

Tickled by his friend's response, Shinji smiled. Thanks, Yutaka. It's always nice to be admired for your talents.

"Shinji…," Yutaka asked, still looking astonished.

Shinji raised his brow. "What is it? You have a question?"

"No." Yutaka shook his head. "I-I was just wondering."

"What is it?"

Yutaka looked down and stared down at the Beretta in his hand. Then he looked up. "I was wondering why you're friends with someone like me."

Shinji had no idea what Yutaka was talking about. His mouth hung open. Then he asked, "What are you talking about?"

Yutaka looked down again. Then he said, "It's just that…I mean you're so awesome. I can see how you'd be friends with someone like Shuya. Shuya's as athletic as you are, and he's a great guitar player. But…but I'm nothing. So…I was just wondering why you're friends with me."

Shinji stared at Yutaka, who kept looking down. Then he began to speak, "That's ridiculous, Yutaka."

Hearing Shinji's gentle voice, Yutaka looked up.

Shinji continued, "I am who I am. And you're you. Even if I'm pretty good at basketball or computers, or popular with the girls, that's doesn't make me a better person. You can make people laugh and you're kind. When you're serious, you're a lot more sincere than I am. Like with girls. I'm not resorting to that cheap cliché about everyone having something to offer, but I am saying there are a lot of things I admire about you." He shrugged and then smiled. "I like you. We've always been buddies. You're an important friend. My best friend."

He saw Yutaka's eyes brimming with tears again. Then, just as before, he said, "Damn, thanks, Shinji. Thanks so much." Then he wiped away his tears and laughed, "But if you stick around with a crybaby like me you'll end up drowning before we escape."

Shinji started to laugh but then—he heard a ring.

He knit his brows and sat up. It was the Macintosh's standard warning sound.

Shinji knelt in front of the PowerBook and stared at the screen.

His eyes opened wide. A message informed him the line had been disconnected and the download aborted.

"Why?"

Shinji moaned. He began typing rapidly on the keyboard, but he couldn't save the connection. He quit the Unix communications software and began working on dialing up the modem with another communication application.

A message appeared, reading, "The number you have dialed is no longer in service." He received the same message no matter how many times he tried. The connection between the modem and phone appeared to be fine. Just to make sure though, he disconnected the phone from the modem and pressed the digits on the phone directly. He tried the weather report once again.

The cell phone had no signal at all now. Which meant…no, the battery was still fully charged….

That can't be….Holding the cell phone, Shinji gaped at the PowerBook screen, which was no longer operating. His hacking was undetectable. That's why it was called hacking. And Shinji had the technique.

"Shinji? What's wrong, Shinji?"

Yutaka called out to him, but Shinji remained speechless.

25 students remaining

33

After the star icon appeared at the edge of the small liquid crystal screen, Hiroki Sugimura (Male Student No. 11) kept close watch. It was the same icon as the one in the center of the screen that had been there ever since he'd turned on this handheld device.

He was in the residential area on the island's eastern shore. It was going to become a forbidden zone soon. He'd been carefully but quickly moving between the houses, and finally he saw a change in the device. He'd found the device in his day pack. It looked like one of those mobile data terminals salarymen use. The change was the first response the device gave ever since he turned it on at 6 a.m., after he went through the manual. His priority was to sweep the soon-to-be forbidden zones, but the device responded in none of those areas—sector J=2 on the south shore, sector F=1 in the west—and from there he moved here to sector H=8.

Technically speaking, it wasn't really a weapon. But right now, depending on how he used it, it could prove more useful than any weapon. He wasn't sure whether he was actually using it properly, though.

Hiroki gripped his stick again with his other hand. (It came off a mop he found inside a shack at the north end of the residential area. If he wanted to he could have taken a large blade, but this was more useful for him, since he'd been studying martial arts ever since he was in elementary school.) He proceeded to move diagonally away from the wood-sided wall he'd been pressed up against. He had a large frame, over 180 cm tall, but he moved dexterously as he pinned himself against the wall of the next house. The star icon was approaching the similar icon in the center.

He remembered the manual explaining the display system and turned his head. It was this house…inside this house.

Hiroki put the device in his pocket and moved around to the house's backyard.

There was a family garden in the small yard with tomato stalks up to his waist, yams planted in the ground, and green onions. Next to them pansies and chrysanthemums in different colors were in bloom. In front of the garden was a child's tricycle. Its chrome handlebars sparkled in the noontime light.

The veranda's storm doors were shut. Opening them might make a big noise. Hiroki circled over to the right.

There was a window. It was broken. He was certain now. There was someone inside. And if he'd read the radar's manual right then he or she was still there.

Since this area would soon be in a forbidden zone, no one should be here now. So most likely it was a corpse inside. But…he had to know for sure.

Hiroki slowly lifted his face to the window and looked in. It was a guest room with tatami floormats.

He slid the window open. It made no sound. He grabbed the window frame and swiftly leaped up like a cat and entered the house.

The room had an alcove. At the center was a low table and a large TV in the corner by the window on Hiroki's side. There was nothing else. Hiroki tiptoed out of the room.

In the hall he smelled something odd, as if he'd caught a whiff of rusty metal.

He quickly moved down the hall. The smell became stronger.

It came from the kitchen. From inside the shadow of a column, Hiroki peeped in.

He saw a pair of white sneakers and a pair of socks on the floor beyond the table. He could see the legs up to their calves.

Hiroki's eyes opened wide. He ran over to the table.

A girl in a sailor suit was lying face down. Her face looked away from Hiroki. She was small with short hair, and under her face a puddle of blood formed on the floor. There was a lot, but the surface was already congealing into a dark red.

She was definitely dead. The question was—

Small body. Short hair.

She looked like one of the two girls he was looking for. They were both equally important to him. She resembled one of them. He couldn't remember whether she was wearing sneakers like these, though.

Hiroki put aside his stick and day pack and knelt down beside the corpse. He touched the girl's shoulder with his trembling hand. After a moment's hesitation, he clenched his teeth and turned the body over. The shiny red blood that hadn't congealed yet gave off a strong odor.

It was a horrible sight. There was a deep gash in her thin throat right above the neck band (which was what in fact led him here). The wound gaped open like a hole, perhaps due to her blood being completely depleted. It resembled an infant's mouth, still without teeth. The blood had flowed down from the wound, sullying the silver collar then down her chest. Her mouth, nose, and left cheek were all immersed in a pool of blood. He deduced, this must have occurred after she fell. Drops of blood had formed on the tips of her eyelashes above and below her glazed eyes. They had hardened as well.

It was Megumi Eto (Female Student No. 3).

It wasn't her.

While the horrific state of the corpse had shocked him, he was still relieved. He closed his eyes for a while and took a deep breath. Then he felt guilty for feeling relieved. He gently lifted Megumi's body, removed her from the pool of blood, and placed her face up. Rigor mortis was setting in, so she felt like a doll. After doing this he closed her eyes. After some thought he tried to fold her arms over her chest, but her body was too stiff now, so he finally gave up.

He grabbed his stick and day pack and stood up. After briefly looking over Megumi's body, he headed towards the guest room he had entered. It was almost 11 a.m.

25 students remaining

34

Time quietly passed. Shogo continued to smoke without uttering a word. Noriko kept quiet too. In the thicket little birds chirped away, and the branches above them rustled in the breeze, letting in a web of light that moved back and forth like a pendulum. You could hear the sound of ocean waves if you listened hard enough. Now that they were settled in the woods, it almost felt as if they were leading a peaceful life.

This partially came from the hope Shuya now had after talking to Shogo. They could escape. And if that was what they wanted, they were best off lying low and waiting. Despite Noriko's injuries, they were safe as long as they kept a close watch. After all, there were three of them, and two of them had guns.

But Shuya couldn't stop thinking about the distant gunshots they heard an hour ago.

Had someone else been killed? It could have meant...he didn't even want to consider it...but it could have been Shinji Mimura or Hiroki Sugimura. Even if it was neither of them, it could have been another innocent classmate. Shuya and Noriko might be saved thanks to Shogo, but the others were living in terror of being killed at any moment.

That was enough to disturb Shuya. Yes, yes, he'd already discussed it with Shogo. Shogo told him it was best to sit still.

He was absolutely right. He also said as long as Noriko was injured, they'd be prime targets. Again he was right. But…but was it right for them to sit back like this? Yumiko Kusaka and Yukiko Kitano kept their faith in the others even though they knew they didn't have a chance of escaping. On the other hand, with Shogo's help, he and Noriko had a good chance. But did that mean they shouldn't be risking their lives?

It was clear someone was a murderer—someone was "intentionally murdering" others. They'd witnessed Yumiko's and Yukiko's deaths. And there might be other murderers. In fact the students he'd confronted—Yoshio Akamatsu, Tatsumichi Oki, and Kyoichi Motobuchi—might have all been trying to kill him. He doubted anyone like that would voluntarily join them. No, someone like that would only join them just to betray and kill them when the time was right.

But shouldn't we at the very least be looking for others we can trust?

Even if we try though, there's no way to tell them apart from the others. If we tried to help everyone, an "enemy" would eventually sneak into our group, and that would mean certain death. Noriko and Shogo would get killed too.

Shuya let out a deep sigh. He racked his brains. No matter how many times he went over it, he came to the same conclusion. There was nothing they could do. He could only hope they'd somehow come across Shinji Mimura and Hiroki Sugimura. But what were the chances that would happen?

"Hey," Shogo said as he lit another cigarette. Shuya looked at him.

"Stop thinking too much. It's no use. Just concentrate on yourself and Noriko."

Shuya lifted his brow. "Are you psychic?"

"Sometimes. Especially when the weather's this nice." Shogo took another drag. Then, as if the thought had suddenly occurred to him, he added, "Is it true?"

"What?"

"What Sakamochi said about you. That you have dangerous ideas."

"Oh, that." Shuya looked down and nodded.

"What'd you do?" Shogo looked at him mischievously. Shuya returned the look.

There were two things he'd done. The first was how he quit the baseball team. That's right, when he entered junior high school, he joined both the baseball team and the music club, but he was turned off by the baseball team's military-style discipline and win-at-all-costs attitude. (It wasn't surprising. Baseball was the national pastime. It was the sport the nation endorsed for international tournaments. Unfortunately, baseball was also popular with the American imperialists, so if the national team lost to them in the Olympics, the Baseball Federation directors would all have to commit harakiri.) On top of that, the team's coach, Mr. Minato, would get on the case of players who weren't very good, even if they loved the game. So by the second week, Shuya was completely fed up and announced he was quitting in a four-letter diatribe against Mr. Minato and the Baseball Federation. And that was how the golden rookie of Shiroiwa Junior High School embarked on a different path towards becoming a different kind of star (according to him)—a rock 'n' roll star. At any rate, this incident didn't look so good on his school record. But Sakamochi was probably referring to the other thing....

"Nothing," Shuya replied. "Sakamochi was probably referring to my listening to rock. He was hassling me for being in the music club."

"Ah," Shogo nodded, wanting to know more. "You play guitar, right? Is that how you started listening to rock?"

"No. I heard rock, and that was how I started playing guitar. I was at the orphanage...."

Shuya recalled the middle-aged handyman who worked at the Charity House. He was upbeat and his thinning hair was slicked back, sticking up at the nape of his neck. ("It's called a duck's tail.") Now he was in a forced labor camp on Sakhalin Island. None of the kids at the orphanage, including Shuya and Yoshitoki, knew the details. When he said goodbye to them, he didn't offer an explanation and only said, "I'll be back, Shuya, Yoshitoki. For a while though, I'll be swinging a pickaxe and belting out 'Jailhouse Rock.' " Then he gave his old auto-winding wristwatch to Yoshitoki and Gibson electric guitar to Shuya. It was Shuya's first guitar. Was he doing all right now? He heard that workers at the forced labor camps often died from overwork and malnutrition.

"Someone gave me a tape. He also gave me his electric guitar."

"Hmm." Shogo nodded.

"Who do you like? Dylan? Lennon? Or Lou Reed?"

Shuya stared back at Shogo. He was taken aback. "I'm impressed."

It wasn't easy getting your hands on rock in the Republic of Greater East Asia. Foreign music was strictly monitored by an organization called the Popular Music Judiciary Committee, and any kind of music that remotely resembled rock would never make it through customs. It was treated like an illegal drug. (He'd even seen a poster in the prefectural civil office with the same red-circle-and-diagonal-line pattern placed over a photo of a sleazy-looking long-haired rocker. It read, "Stop Rock." Great.) Basically, the Republic didn't like the music's rhythms, not to mention the lyrics, which might agitate the people. Bob Marley was one of them, but an obvious example would be Lennon's lines, "You may say I'm a dreamer/But I'm not the only one/I hope some day you'll join us and the world will be as one." How could the nation not consider that a threat?

The only music you could find at record stores was domestic, mostly trite idol pop. The most extreme imported music Shuya came across was probably Frank Sinatra. (Although "My Way" might have been appropriate song for this country.)

For a while Shuya thought the handyman with the duck's tail hairdo was sent to the camps for this, so Shuya thought there was something scary about the tapes and guitar the man had left behind. Apparently he was wrong, though. Once he entered junior high, he found out there were plenty of others who were into rock and owned electric guitars. (Of course Kazumi Shintani was also a huge rock fan!) It was through this group he was able to get dubbed copies of "The Times They Are A-Changin' " and "Stand!"

But that was only within a close knit group. If there had been a survey of the number of students who'd never heard rock, over 90% would have said they hadn't. (Even those who had would say they hadn't, so the actual result would be 100%.) Given how broad Shogo's knowledge seemed to be, it wasn't that strange for him to be exposed to it, but Dylan and Lennon were pretty extreme artists.

"Don't look so freaked out," Shogo said. "I'm a city kid from Kobe. I'm not a bumpkin like you guys from Kagawa. I know something about rock."

Shuya broke into a slight grin. His guardedness lifted. Then he told Shogo, "My favorite's Springsteen. I like Van Morrison too, though."

" 'Born to Run' is great. I like Van Morrison's 'Whenever God Shines His Light.' "

Shuya gawked and then broke into a grin. "You know a lot!"

Shogo grinned back. "I told you. I'm a city kid."

Shuya noticed how Noriko stayed silent. He was worried

she might feel excluded.

"Noriko, did you say you've never listened to rock?"

Noriko gave him a smile and shook her head. "I've never really heard it. What's it like?"

Shuya smiled. "The lyrics are really something. I don't know how to describe it well, but it's music that really expresses people's problems. Of course, songs can be about love, but at times they can be about politics or society, or the way we live our lives, and life itself. Along with the words, the melody and beat help get the message across. Like Springsteen singing, 'Born to Run'…." Shuya recited the end of the song, "Together Wendy we can live with the sadness/I'll love you with all the madness in my soul/Someday girl I don't know when we're gonna get to that place where we really want to go/And we'll walk in the sun…"

He continued by singing the last line softly, "…*but tramps like us, baby we were born to run.*"

He said to Noriko, "We'll definitely listen to it some time."

Noriko opened her eyes and nodded. Under normal circumstances her face might have lit up, but she only responded with a weak smile. Shuya was too tired to notice though.

He told Shogo, "If everyone listened more to rock then this country would come crumbling down."

That's right…just like Noriko said, "It's because no one knows about this…" Shuya thought rock music revealed everything that was essential. That was why it was banned by the government.

Shogo rubbed his stubby Wild Seven cigarette into the ground. He lit another. Then he said, "Shuya."

"What?"

"Do you really think rock has that kind of power?"

Shuya nodded enthusiastically. "Of course it does."

Shogo stared at Shuya and looked away. "I don't know. It might just serve as an outlet for our frustrations, a convenient way to let off steam. It might be banned, but if you really want to listen to rock, you can. So it also serves as an outlet. That's what I mean. This country is very clever. Who knows, it might end up promoting rock and roll as a national resource."

Shuya felt as if he'd been dealt a blow. Rock was his religion, music sheets were the pages of his bible, Springsteen, Van Morrison, and his other heroes were the equivalent of the twelve disciples. Of course he was getting used to being shocked, what with his classmates dying around him, so relatively speaking, it wasn't that shocking.

Shuya calmed himself down and slowly replied, "I don't know about that."

Shogo nodded several times. "I do. In any case, it's not about being banned or promoted. That's not what rock's about. Anyone who wants to hear it should be able to when they want to. That's what it comes down to, right?"

Shuya thought about this. Then he said, "I never thought about it like that. But I see where you're coming from." Then he added, "Incredible. I didn't realize how perceptive you are."

Shogo shrugged.

They fell silent for a while.

Then Shuya said, "But…I still do believe rock is powerful. It's a positive force."

Which was what Noriko had said about Shuya.

Shogo unwrapped a new pack of cigarettes while he looked at Shuya. Shogo grinned. He lit the cigarette dangling from his mouth. Then he said, "To be honest, I agree with you."

Shuya smiled back at him.

"It's ironic that we're really in that situation though," Shogo observed.

Shuya was puzzled, "What do you mean?"

"The only thing we can do now is run, " Shogo replied. *"We were born to run."*

25 students remaining

35

Kaori Minami (Female Student No. 20) got up when she heard the faint rustling sound. It came from the grove at the foot of the hill to the north, slightly to the east of the island's central region. On the map it was designated sector F=8.

She held tightly onto her gun. The gun was a small SIG-Sauer P230 9mm Short automatic pistol. It felt large in Kaori's small hands.

Without knowing it, Kaori bit her lip. She'd been hearing the same sound over and over once the game began and up until now, while she hid herself here. And every time she was relieved to find out it was only caused by the wind or some small animal (a stray cat?). But that didn't stop her terror. She bit down and cut open her lip, which was now covered with cuts that had become scabs. This time…it might be an enemy. An enemy…that's right. One of her classmates would attack her. The images of the corpses of Yoshio Akamatsu and Mayumi Tendo vividly came to mind.

And when she'd left the school, she'd heard a voice coming from the woods in front of her. It was the voice of the school representative, Yukie Utsumi. Then she saw other figures with Yukie in the dark grove. Calling out from the dark, Yukie spoke in a hushed but clear voice, "Kaori! Come join us! It's just girls! You're safe with us!"

But…how could she? How could she trust anyone under these circumstances? If she stayed with them, she would have had to constantly watch her back. Kaori ran away from Utsumi's invitation and in the opposite direction…and now she was here. And now…was that the sound of an enemy approaching?

She waited for a while, holding the gun with both hands, but the sound disappeared.

She waited a little more. The sound was gone.

Kaori let out a sigh of relief. She got down on her knees and crouched down in the shrubs. The crooked leaves touching her cheeks annoyed her, so she changed her position. With the palm of her hands she kept on rubbing her face where the leaves had touched her. Her pimples had given her enough grief. She didn't want her face to swell up from some poison ivy. Even if she was going to die soon, she didn't want that.

She felt a chill run down her spine. Die? Am I going to do die? Am I really going to die?

The thought alone was enough to make her heart beat faster. She felt like she was going to have a seizure.

Am I going to die? Am I going to die? Like a crummy CD player unable to ignore a scratch on the disc the ringing words skipped over and over deep inside her head. Am I going to die?

Kaori snatched desperately at the brass locket she wore around her neck underneath her uniform. It popped open, and a bright, cheerful face with long hair smiled at Kaori.

As she concentrated on it, Kaori's pulse finally managed to slow down and return to its normal pace.

It was a photo of Junya Kenzaki of the pop group Flip Side. He was the most popular member with girls. This special locket was only available to fan club members. Kaori was proud to know she was the only student in her school who had one. (Of course most girls nowadays could care less. Besides, lockets were passé. But Kaori didn't think so.)

Oh…Junya. I'm all right, right? You'll protect me, right?

She thought Junya Kenzaki was telling her, "It's all right. Of course you're all right. Shall I sing your favorite song, 'Galaxy Magnum'?" Kaori's breathing calmed down a bit. Then she asked the photo:

"Say, Junya. Should I have joined Yukie? I wonder if that would have saved me? No, that can't be."

A tear came rolling down Kaori's cheeks.

How could this be happening? She wanted to see her mom. She wanted to see her dad. She wanted to see her sister and her kind grandma and grandpa. She wanted to take a bath, rub cream on her pimples, sit on the comfortable couch in the living room, and sip on a cup of cocoa while she watched a video of Flip Side's TV show. (Although she'd seen this episode many, many times already.)

"Junya, help me. Please…I feel like I'm going crazy."

The moment she actually heard her voice say this out loud, Kaori felt as if she were really going insane. It freaked her out. Nausea welled up to her chest. She was crying frantically now.

She suddenly heard a rustling sound behind her, and her body flinched. It was much louder than the previous sound.

Her eyes bleary with tears, she turned around.

A boy was looking at her through the shrubs. It was Hiroki Sugimura (Male Student No. 11). He'd snuck up behind her!

Kaori was completely terrified and too numb to think as she lifted the gun and pulled the trigger. Her wrists jerked back with the popping sound. A gold shell flew out, and the sun's rays reflected off it as it shone through the branches.

Hiroki had already disappeared deep inside the thicket.

The rustling continued and also disappeared.

Kaori was trembling. She was still holding the gun. Then she snatched her belongings and ran in the opposite direction. As she ran, her agitated mind raced with thoughts. She was sure Hiroki Sugimura was trying to kill her. Why else would he have snuck up behind her without saying anything? Hiroki Sugimura probably didn't have a gun. He saw that I did and ran away in a panic. If I hadn't noticed him—and shot at him—then Hiroki Sugimura would probably have stabbed my chest with a knife or something. A knife! I have to be careful. I have to shoot anyone I come across. No mercy. Otherwise, I'll end up getting killed...killed!

Oh no...I can't stand this anymore. I want to go home. Take a bath. Pimple cream. Cocoa! Video. Flip Side. Junya. No mercy. Shoot. Shoot! Cocoa. Junya. Cream! For my pimples! No mercy, Junya.

Tears came streaming down Kaori's cheeks. The lid on the locket on her chest remained open and Junya Kenzaki's cheerful face swung violently left and right, up and down.

No mercy. Junya. I'm going to be killed! Shoot. Mom. Sister! Dad. Shoot! Shoot! The new record release!

Kaori was losing her mind.

25 students remaining

36

"All right then, here's the body count."

Sakamochi's voice continued. It was the noon announcement.

New members on the waiting list for funerals were Tatsumichi Oki, Kyoichi Motobuchi, and of course Yukiko

Kitano and Yumiko Kusaka. The other ones were Yoji Kuramoto and Yoshimi Yahagi.

"I will announce the forbidden zones for this afternoon. Now, I want you to take notes. Get your notebooks out."

Once again, Shuya pulled out his map and pen from his pocket. Shogo also had his map out.

"At 1 p.m., J=5. At 3 p.m., H=3. At 5 p.m., D=8. Got that?"

J=5 was the southeast shore of the island. H=3 was near the top of the southern mountain. D=8 was the hilly area on the southeast side of the northern mountain peak. Their zone, C=3, wasn't announced. That meant they wouldn't have to move.

"It may be rough losing your friends, but cheer up. You're all so young, you've got so much ahead of you! Over and out."

With this series of happy-go-lucky platitudes, Sakamochi's announcement came to an end.

Shuya sighed. He put away the map and examined the student list, which was now ridden with check marks. "We're down to twenty-five students. Damn."

Shogo cupped his hand as he lit another cigarette. Then he said, "It's like I said. The numbers are steadily dwindling."

Shuya looked up at Shogo. He got Shogo's point. The more classmates that died the closer they were to escaping. But...

"That was uncalled for."

Shogo only shrugged. He shifted his eyes and then said, "Hey, I'm sorry."

Shuya wanted to say more, but he tore his eyes away from Shogo's face. He pulled in his knees and stared down between them. There were several tiny yellow flowers poking out from the grass, and an ant was crawling up one of the stems.

This was the issue. Shuya had felt like they'd become buddies when they talked about rock, but in the end there was still something about Shogo that bothered him. Was it simply that there was a cold side to Shogo?

He took in a small breath…and then thought of something else. Of the six deaths Sakamochi had announced, Yoji Kuramoto and Yoshimi Yahagi were the only ones Shuya didn't witness. He was pretty sure they were going out. Did that mean they were together? And the two gunshots they heard after 10 p.m…was that them? If so, who could have…

He remembered the sound of the machine gun slaughtering Yukiko Kitano and Yumiko Kusaka. Did the same person kill them too? Or…

"Shuya," Shogo said. He looked up. "You haven't had breakfast, right? This government-supplied bread sucks, but I found some coffee and strawberry jam at the supply store. Let's eat."

Shogo took out a jar and a slim can (200g) of canned coffee. The jar's label was illustrated with strawberries, and he could see the shiny, thick, red contents inside the glass. Shuya assumed Shogo was going to toss the coffee into a pot of boiling water on the fire. Shogo also pulled out a bag of plastic cups.

"You loaded up."

"Yep," Shogo nodded. Then he proceeded to pull out a long, thin box. "Look at this. An entire carton of Wild Sevens."

Shuya decided to cheer up. He smiled, nodding. He took out the bread in his day pack and offered one to Noriko.

"Noriko, we should eat."

Noriko looked up, still hugging her knees. "I'm…all right. I'm not hungry."

"What's wrong? Is your appetite…"

Shuya realized as she looked down again how pale her face had become. He'd suddenly realized how quiet she'd been.

"Noriko?"

Shuya approached her. Shogo observed them as he opened the lid of the coffee can.

"Noriko."

Shuya touched her on the shoulder. Noriko clenched her hands together. Her lips were tightly shut, forming a straight line across her pale face. Only now did Shuya finally realize that air was painfully hissing through her lips. She was having difficulty breathing. She closed her eyes, released her hands, put them on his arm, and leaned against him.

Her body temperature, which he sensed from her hands and through the shoulder area of the sailor suit, felt abnormally high, as if she were nursing a chick underneath her clothes. Shuya brushed off the hair on her forehead and felt her forehead.

It was incredibly hot. The cold sweat on her forehead drenched the palm of his hand.

Panicking, he turned to Shogo.

"She's got a fever! Shogo!"

"I'm…fine," Noriko said weakly.

Shogo put down the can of coffee and got up. He exchanged positions with Shuya and touched her forehead. He rubbed his chin and then held her wrist. He seemed to be taking her pulse as he checked his wristwatch.

"I'm sorry about this," he said as he put the fingers of his right hand to her lips and had her open her mouth. Then he pressed the skin under her eyes downward and looked under her lower eyelids.

"You must feel cold."

Narrowing her eyes, Noriko nodded, "Yeah…a little…"

"How is she?" Shuya asked nervously. He'd been

holding his breath.

"Just give me your coat," Shogo said as he removed his own school coat. Shuya quickly removed his too and gave it to Shogo. Shogo carefully wrapped the two coats around Noriko's body.

"Bread. I need the jam and water too," Shogo instructed, and Shuya swiftly snatched the bread and water he'd offered to Noriko as well as the jam left on top of Shogo's day pack. Shogo hastily dipped the bread into the jar, covering it with red jam. He offered it to Noriko.

"You have to eat this, Noriko."

"I know...but..."

"Just eat it. Even a little will help," Shogo's insisted. Noriko hesitantly took the bread and nibbled on the bread a couple times. She made an effort to swallow it. Then she returned the rest of the bread to Shogo.

"No more, huh?"

Noriko barely shook her head. Even shaking her head seemed to exhaust her.

Shogo wanted her to eat more, but then he set the bread aside and once again pulled out the small pouch of medicine from his pocket.

"It's cold medicine," he said and gave her a capsule that was different from the pain reliever he'd given her before. Noriko nodded. With Shogo's help she managed to swallow it down with water from the bottle. Water came streaming from her mouth, but Shogo gently wiped it away.

"Okay, now lie down."

Noriko nodded obediently and lay down on the grass, still wrapped up in the two coats.

"What's going on, Shogo? Is she gonna be right?" Shuya asked.

Shogo shook his head. "I don't know for sure yet. It may just be a fever. But she might be infected from the wound."

"What..."

With Noriko lying down, Shuya looked down at the bandanna bandage wrapped around her right calf.

"But...I thought we cleaned out her wound."

Shogo shook his head again. "She moved around the woods a lot after she was shot, right? She might have been infected before we treated her."

Shuya stared at Shogo for a while and then knelt down beside Noriko. He reached his hand out to Noriko's forehead.

"Noriko..."

Noriko opened her eyes. She smiled feebly.

"I'm all right...I'm just a little tired. Don't worry."

But her breathing hardly indicated she was all right.

Shuya looked over at Shogo again. He restrained himself from sounding overly agitated and said, "Shogo. We can't stay here. We have to move. We should at least find a house where she can get warm—"

Shogo cut him off, "Just hold on. Let's just wait and see for now." He tightly wrapped the makeshift blanket-coats around Noriko's body.

"But..."

"It's too dangerous for us to move. I told you."

Noriko faintly opened her eyes. She looked over at Shuya and said, "I'm so sorry...Shuya..." Then she said to Shogo, "I'm sorry," and closed her eyes.

Shuya's lips tightened as he looked down at Noriko's pale face.

25 students remaining

37

Takako Chigusa (Female Student No. 13) stuck her head out from under the shadow of a tree trunk. She was halfway up the eastern side of the island's southern mountain. According to the map she was somewhere near the border between H=4 and H=5. There was a grove full of trees that grew shorter as she headed up the mountain.

Takako gripped her weapon, an ice pick, and looked back.

The house she'd been hiding inside was obscured by trees and no longer visible. It was decrepit and overrun by tall grass and seemed like it'd been abandoned even before the island had been evacuated. She remembered something like a chicken shack was connected to the main building. Now she couldn't even see the rusty tin roof. How far had she come? Two hundred meters? One hundred meters? Takako was the girls' track team's best short-distance sprinter (she held the prefect's all-time second-place junior-high record for the 200-meter), so she had a good sense of running distances, but she wasn't sure now—mainly because of the hills and bushes, not to mention the tension she was feeling.

After eating awful bread and water for breakfast, Takako decided to wait until 1 p.m. to leave the house. She'd been hearing what sounded like gunshots ever since the game started and hid in a corner of the abandoned house, but now she thought staying cooped up like that wouldn't do any good. She had to join up with someone—at least a friend she could trust—and proceed.

Of course it was possible friends she trusted wouldn't trust her. But...

Takako was a beautiful girl. Her upward-curving eyes were a little fierce-looking, but they matched with her sharp chin, well formed mouth, and nicely defined nose, all of which gave her an "aristocratic" look. Her long hair was dyed with orange streaks, which might look odd at first, but with her jewelry—which included earrings, two in her left ear, one in her right, designer rings on the middle and ring fingers of her left hand, a total of five bracelets on her wrists, and a pendant made from a foreign coin—she managed to assert her own look that made her all the more attractive. Her teachers didn't really approve of her hair and gaudy jewelry, but she got good grades and because she was the track team's star sprinter, she never got directly criticized. Basically Takako was very proud. She wasn't going to be bound by the silly school rules that the other girls followed.

Whether it was—unfortunately enough—because of her beauty, or her pride, or whether it was because she was simply shy, Takako didn't have many close friends in her class. Her best friend was Kahoru Kitazawa, whom she'd known ever since elementary school, but she was in another class.

But...

But there was someone in her class whom Takako could trust. The student wasn't a girl, though. She'd known him since they were kids.

And with him in mind, she couldn't help being preoccupied by something.

When she left the school building Takako thought someone who'd left before her might come back. In that case, she'd have to leave with extreme caution. And it was best to leave the school by foiling the assailant's expectations.

When she came into the hall, she peeked outside through the exit door. There were woods in front of her, and a hill on the left. The area to her right was relatively open. The assailant, if there was one, would have to be hiding in the woods or in the hill.

Takako stayed down as she left the building and dashed to her right, staying close to the school building wall. The track star let her mighty legs cut loose. She didn't even have to think about it. She ran down the street through a cluster of houses and into a narrow alley. Then she ran toward the base of the southern mountain. All her energy was focused on getting away from the school and finding somewhere to hide.

But...

What if there had been someone in the woods or in the hill in front of the school who had no intention of attacking her? In other words...what if..."he," who'd left before her, had hid in the woods or the mountain, had been waiting for her? Maybe she'd lost her chance by running out of there at full speed?

No.

She didn't think so. What else could she have done? Anyone hanging around the school was jeopardizing his or her life. They had known each other since they were kids—it was nothing more than that. They had remained decent friends through all these years. She thought it was presumptuous of her to think that he—Hiroki Sugimura (Male Student No. 11)—would risk his life waiting for her.

The important thing was finding someone now. Finding Hiroki Sugimura would be ideal, but she knew that was too optimistic. She'd settle for the school representative Yukie Utsumi or some average girl. As long as she was careful not to get shot, she could calm them down....If they were calm already, that would be even better (although the thought of someone calm under these circumstances was a bit scary too). To find that someone...that was all she could do for now.

The one thing she knew not to do was to raise her voice. She had proof of that, now. From the abandoned house Takako had also seen Yumiko Kusaka and Yukiko Kitano die on top of the northern mountain.

So Takako decided to leave the abandoned shack where she was hiding and climb up to the peak of the southern mountain. Once she was there, she'd descend the slope by circling the mountain, checking for anyone hiding in the bushes. She could throw pebbles at the bushes just as she'd been doing ever since she left the shack. Once she figured out who it was she could decide whether or not to approach that person. At noon Sakamochi had announced that the area around the peak of the southern mountain would become a forbidden zone at 3 p.m., but as long as she didn't run into any problems she'd be able to completely survey the area before then. Also, if there was anyone in the area then he or she would have to be out of there by 3 p.m. She'd have a better chance locating someone on the move.

Takako checked her supplied wristwatch. It was 1:20 p.m. She usually wore bracelets so she never wore a watch, but she couldn't afford that luxury now. Then she touched her collar.

"If you try to pry it loose it will explode."

It was suffocating—not only the way it dug into her neck, but its mere presence. The chain of her pendant lightly tapped against the band.

Takako decided to ignore it and gripped her ice pick (what good was this weapon though?) with her left hand. With her right she grabbed some pebbles and tossed them out in front of her to her left and right.

They made a rustling sound in the grove.

She waited for a while. No response. She moved forward. She took a deep breath, ready to run up the open ground between the bushes.

Suddenly she heard a rustling sound. Someone's head popped out of the bushes, approximately ten meters to her left. She could see the back of his coat and the back of his head. Its hair was slightly disheveled but still smooth. His head turned left and right checking the area.

Takako froze. She was in trouble. It was a guy. Guys were trouble. She had no particular reason to think so, but she had a hunch anyone besides Hiroki Sugimura was trouble. And she could immediately tell this guy was not him.

Takako held her breath and slowly stepped back into the thicket behind her. She knew this would happen, but that didn't stop her from trembling.

Suddenly the boy turned around. Their eyes met. The face, which had an expression of utter astonishment, belonged to Kazushi Niida (Male Student No. 16).

Oh man, why did I have to bump into this jerk? What mattered now was that she was totally exposed and how dangerous that was. She turned around and started running back the way she came.

"Wait!"

She heard Kazushi's voice. The sound of him waded through the thicket, coming after her.

"Wait!" Now he was shouting. "Wait!"

Ugh—What an idiot—

Takako hesitated for a few moments and then stopped. She looked back. If Kazushi had a gun and wanted to shoot her he'd have done that by now. More troubling was his shouting. It endangered not only his life but hers. Just as it was moments ago there didn't seem to be anyone in the area.

Slowing down, Kazushi descended the slope.

Takako realized Kazushi held a rifle loaded with an arrow in his right hand. It wasn't pointed at Takako right now—but if it was, could she dodge it and run away? Should she have stopped?

No. Takako reassured herself, she'd done the right thing. Kazushi Niida was a forward on the soccer team. Top athletes like him were as fast if not faster than track runners. Even though Takako was a star track runner, he'd have eventually caught up with her.

Either way it was too late.

Kazushi stopped several meters away from her. He had wide shoulders and was relatively tall and well built. His smooth hair was long, which was the current fashion with soccer players, but now it was disheveled, as if he'd been playing in a close match that had gone into overtime. A smile emerged on his face, which was pretty good looking except for his bad teeth.

What does he want? Takako thought as he observed his face.

He might not have any harmful intentions. He might actually be thinking he finally found someone he could trust.

But Takako didn't have a very good impression of Kazushi Niida. To put it bluntly, she couldn't stand his kind of chumminess. She also couldn't stand his arrogance. They'd been classmates ever since their first year in junior high. (Hiroki became her classmate in second-year.) Without putting much effort into them, Kazushi was above average in grades and sports, but in spite of that—or maybe it had nothing to do with that—his immaturity really stuck out. He tried to impress others, and when he'd screw up he'd come up with some lame-ass excuse. Furthermore, and this was really stupid, but when they were first-year students, there were rumors that she and Kazushi were going out. (Junior high kids don't have anything better to do. Well, let them say what they want.) Every time the rumors got going again he'd go to her desk and touch her on the shoulder (how dare he) and tell her, "There's a rumor floating around about us." Takako would turn away and brush his hand off with the reply, "Oh, I'm so honored." She let it slide, scoffing at him on the inside ("Go away you little brat. You've got some nerve"), but now...she wasn't in the position to do the same thing.

Takako spoke cautiously. She had to get away from him as quickly as possible. That's what it came down to.

"Don't shout, you idiot!"

"I'm sorry," Kazushi answered. "But you were the one who took off."

Takako didn't mess around with her response. Get to the point, cut to the chase. Her best features. "The fact is, I don't want to be with you." She looked at Kazushi and managed to shrug her tense shoulders.

Kazushi's grimaced. "Why?"

Because you act like you're such a goody-goody, she thought.

"Look, we both know why. Okay, later," Takako said as she got ready to run. Still, she felt herself hesitating as her feet trembled.

She stopped.

Because out of the corner of her eye she saw the weapon in Kazushi's right hand pointed at her.

Takako slowly turned around, keeping a close eye on his fingers on the trigger of his bow gun.

"What's this?" she asked

She casually slid the day pack off her left shoulder and caught its strap. Would it be able to shield her from the force of the bow gun?

"I don't want to resort to this," Kazushi said. This was exactly what she couldn't stand about him. He was making excuses, but in fact he was trying to gain the upper hand. "So you better stay with me."

That pissed her off. But that was also when she noticed something. When she was hiding in the shack her uniform skirt got caught on a broken door. The tear resembled the slit up a Chinese dress, and now Kazushi was looking down at it. His eyes were strangely glazed over. It gave her the creeps.

Takako quickly moved her legs to cover them as much as possible. Then she said, "Give me a break. You expect me to join you with that stuck in my face?"

"So you promise not to run away?" Kazushi spoke in his usual arrogant voice. He didn't lower the bow gun.

Takako had to put up with him. "Just put that down."

"So you won't run?"

"Are you deaf?" Takako said sharply, and Kazushi reluctantly lowered his weapon.

Then he assumed a smug tone as he said, "I've always thought you were fine."

Takako raised her well defined, elegantly arched eyebrows.

She was exasperated. After threatening her life like this, he has the nerve to say I'm fine!

Kazushi's eyes fell on her legs again. He made no effort to be subtle, and his eyes were locked onto them now.

Takako lifted her chin slightly. "So?"

"So I won't kill you. Just stay with me."

Takako shrugged again. Any hesitation she might have had was now wiped out by anger. "I told you I don't want to," she spat out. "Later."

Takako turned to...no, this time she began moving backwards and staring back at Kazushi. Kazushi lifted his bow gun again. His face had the expression of a kid begging for a toy at a department store. Mom, I want it, I want it!...I see now.

Takako quietly said, "Stop this."

"Then...stay with me," Kazushi repeated. The way he tilted his head revealed how frantic he was trying to calm his nerves.

Takako repeated, "I told you, no."

Kazushi didn't lower the gun. They glared at each other.

Takako couldn't bear it anymore. "You know...what do you want? Say it. You're not killing me off. I tell you, I don't want to be with you, but you insist. I don't get it."

"I..." Kazushi stared at Takako with that leer in his eyes and said, "I'm saying I'll protect you. So...just stay with me. We're safer together, right?"

"You've gotta be joking. You have the nerve to threaten me like that and say you'll protect me? I can't trust you. Get it? Can I go now? I'm going."

Kazushi replied, "If you move I'll shoot you." He aimed the bow gun directly at her chest.

By openly threatening her like this Kazushi lost any chance he had of keeping to a civilized code of conduct (not that he had much of sense of that to begin with). He stood still and said, "You better obey me, girl. A woman obeys his man."

Takako was furious. Then he had the nerve to say, "You're a virgin, aren't you?" in a casual tone, as if he were only confirming her blood type (B).

Takako was at a loss for words.

"..."

What...did this asshole say?

"Am I wrong? Hiroki wouldn't have the guts to sleep with a girl."

Kazushi said this because probably he, along with many of her other classmates, had the mistaken assumption that she was going out with Hiroki Sugimura. She had two reasons to be especially annoyed, though. First of all, her relationship with Hiroki was none of their business. Second, Kazushi's making fun of Hiroki pissed her off.

Takako broke into a grin. She'd realized a long time ago how she could always grin when she was absolutely furious.

So she grinned like this at Kazushi and said, "What's it got to do with you?"

Kazushi might have misinterpreted Takako's grin. Kazushi grinned back. "So I'm right."

Still smiling, Takako glared back at him. Yes, in fact you are right. I might look a little flashy, but just as you said, I'm a virgin. An innocent 15-year-old girl. However...

It's none of your business, asshole!

Kazushi continued, "We're gonna die anyway. Don't you want to try it once before you die? I'd be a good partner."

Although Takako had never felt so angry in her life, she couldn't help but gawk back at him in amazement. Her mouth might have even hung open. His exasperating, outrageous behavior was bad enough, but now it was so out of control it was like he was from another world. Captain

Columbus, that is San Salvador Island. Okay, they're barbarians. Beware of the barbarians.

Takako looked down—and burst out in laughter. It was incredibly funny. This sitcom would have been a hit.

She lifted her face. She must have been glaring at Kazushi, but she'd still give him one last chance.

"This is my last offer. I don't want to be with you. Just put that down and leave me alone. Otherwise, I'll take it that you're going to kill me. All right?"

Kazushi didn't move his bow gun. Instead he raised it up to his shoulders and threatened her, "This is *my* last warning. You better obey me, Takako."

The fact that Takako felt a thrill at this exchange, which was in some ways the turning point of their encounter, may have been indicative of her personality. And from here on…she couldn't be held responsible for what would happen.

Takako took a step forward to put an end to this conversation with this asshole.

"I see. So you just want to rape me. Right? You think dying gives you the right to do anything?"

Kazushi glared back at her. "That's not what I said.…"

What's the difference? She laughed at him inside. Let me guess what you'll say next. I don't want to rape you, but you better take off your clothes?

Takako continued grinning as she calmly tilted her head. She said, "Right now, you might want to worry more about your life than about your lame-ass dick."

Kazushi's face suddenly flushed. His mouth twisted as he spouted off, "Shut up! You really want to get raped?"

Takako grinned and answered, "So the truth comes out."

"I told you to shut up!" Kazushi repeated. "I can kill you if I want, you know!"

He made her sick. She remembered how he tried to coax her into it just moments ago, saying, "I won't kill you."

Kazushi paused and then boasted, "I already killed Yoshio."

Takako was a little shocked, but she merely lifted her brow and remarked, "Huh." Even if it were true…given how he'd been hiding, he'd probably been terrified, then somehow bumped into Yoshio Akamatsu and ended up killing him by accident. After that, too scared of anyone stronger than him, he probably spent this whole time hiding. But knowing him, she knew that if he ended up surviving by hiding until he had one weaker final opponent, he'd say something like, "I have no choice" and kill him or her without hesitation.

"I was thinking," Kazushi continued, confirming Takako's suspicion. "I decided this is a game. So I'm not going to pull any punches."

Takako continued staring at Kazushi, still wearing that grin.

Ah ha. I understand now. So whether it was by consent or by raping me you were going to fuck me and then kill me. As long as you could survive by having everyone else including myself die? I see. Did you calculate how many times you could fuck me too?

Her spine tingled with disgust and fury.

"A game?" she repeated after him and then gave a big smile. "But aren't you ashamed doing this to a girl?"

Kazushi looked shocked, but then his face became sulky again. His cold eyes shone. "You want to die?"

"Go ahead, shoot me."

Kazushi hesitated. It was her chance. Takako threw the pebbles she'd cautiously taken out of her pocket at his face. As Kazushi covered his face to shield himself, she quickly turned around, dropped the day pack, and dashed back the way she came, all the while holding onto the ice pick.

She thought she could hear him curse behind her. With a good runner's sprint she'd covered fifteen meters when suddenly she felt a blow against her right leg and fell face forward. Her cheek got cut as it scraped against a tree root poking out of the ground. She was more upset over this wound on her face than she was over the sharp pain in her leg. That asshole cut my face!

Takako twisted her body around. A silver arrow pierced her skirt and was planted in the back of her right thigh. Blood dripped down her well toned leg muscles.

Kazushi caught up with her. Seeing her sitting there, he tossed aside the bow gun and took out a pair of short sticks chained together—nunchaku—from under his belt and held them in his right hand. The chain rattled (this weapon, by the way, had been in Mayumi Tendo's day pack, which Kazushi then took after killing Yoshio Akamatsu). (His own weapon for some bizarre reason was a plain shamisen banjo that was completely useless. Of course, this had nothing to do with Takako.)

Takako glanced at the bow gun on the ground and thought, you'll regret you put that down.

"It's your fault," Kazushi said, panting. "You provoked me."

Still seated, Takako glared up at Kazushi. The bastard was still making excuses. She couldn't believe she'd actually been classmates with this idiot for over two years.

"Wait," Takako said. As Kazushi knit his brows she got on her knees and twisted her right shoulder around, pulling out the arrow in one swift motion as she clenched her teeth. She could feel the flesh tear, followed by a gush of blood. Her skirt was torn again. So now her skirt had two slits.

She tossed the arrow aside and stood up, glaring at Kazushi. She was all right. The pain was incredible but she could take it. She shifted the ice pick over to her right hand.

"Don't do it," Kazushi said. "It's no use."

She tilted the ice pick sideways, pointing it at his chest.

"You said this was a game, right? Fine. I'll be your opponent. I won't lose against an asshole like you. I'll give everything I have to erase your existence. Got it? Do you understand? Or are you too stupid?"

But Kazushi still seemed at ease. He was probably thinking how she was a girl, and what's more, injured, so he couldn't lose against her.

"I'll say it again," she continued, "Don't even think of raping me after beating me to a pulp. Look, little kid, you should worry more about your life than your dick."

Kazushi's face contorted, and he raised the nunchucks up to his face.

Takako gripped her ice pick. The tension between them mounted.

He was probably fifteen centimeters taller, twenty kilograms heavier. Takako was probably the number one female athlete in her class but she had little chance of winning. On top of this, her right leg was pretty badly injured. But…she couldn't lose, no matter what.

Suddenly, Kazushi made a move. He came forward, swinging the nunchucks down!

Takako blocked them with her right arm. One of her two bracelets flew into the air (it was made by South American Indians, it was a favorite, damn). She felt a sting run up her arm up to the center of her skull. Despite the sting though, she thrust the ice pick upward. Kazushi grimaced as he stepped back, dodging it. Once again they were two meters apart.

Takako's left arm was stinging now. But she was all right, nothing was broken.

He resumed his attack. This time he swung the nunchucks with the motion of a backhand tennis swing.

Takako dodged them by crouching down. The nunchucks skimmed her long, streaked hair—several strands flew into the air. Takako quickly swung her ice pick at his right wrist. She felt it wound him slightly as Kazushi groaned a little and stepped back.

They were apart again. Kazushi's wrist, the hand holding the nunchucks, was red. But the cut didn't seem severe.

The wound on her right leg was throbbing. She could tell the entire leg below her thigh was covered with blood. She wouldn't last much longer like this. She also noticed a panting sound. It came from her lips.

Kazushi once again swung his nunchucks. She could see he was aiming at the left side of her head and her shoulder.

Takako stepped forward. She suddenly recalled something Hiroki, who was a martial arts expert, had taught her, "You can defeat your opponent by throwing his timing off. Sometimes, taking a bold step forward can be crucial."

The nunchucks hit her shoulder, but just as Hiroki had said, it was only the chain, which hardly hurt her. Takako leaped into his chest. Kazushi's face, his eyes wide open in dismay, was right in front of hers. She thrust the ice pick upward.

Kazushi shoved Takako away with his empty left hand. Takako lost her balance from her wounded right leg and fell forward.

Barely escaping her stab, Kazushi rubbed his unharmed chest with his left hand. "You're really something," he said.

Kazushi quickly swung his nunchucks down at Takako, who was slow getting up. This time he was aiming at her face!

Takako blocked the blow with her ice pick. Along with the metallic clang, the ice pick flew into the air and landed in the dirt. The only thing left in her hand now was intense pain.

Takako bit her lip. She glared at him as she stepped back.

Kazushi grinned and slowly came forward. Undoubtedly this guy was mentally disturbed. He had no qualms about beating a girl to death. In fact, he was enjoying it!

Kazushi swung his nunchucks again. She dodged them by bending back—but the nunchucks followed her instead. Perhaps he'd gotten used to them. This time Kazushi managed to extend his reach.

She felt a sharp thud against the left side of her head. She began to sway. A warm liquid came flowing out her left nostril.

She was on the verge of falling. Kazushi must have looked like he was sure he'd won.

Still swaying, Takako's pretty, sharply curved eyes squinted.

As she fell, she stretched out her long legs and with all her might kicked Kazushi's left knee from the right side. Kazushi let out a painful moan and fell on his left knee. His body floundered and rotated halfway on his knee. Now she saw his back.

Had she tried to take the ice pick, Takako might have lost. But that wasn't what she did.

She leaped onto Kazushi's back.

She clutched onto his head as if riding on his shoulders. Her weight forced him to fall forward.

If a thought occurred to her it was in choosing which fingers she should use. Her index and middle…no…the strongest combination would be her middle finger and thumb. And…Takako had always taken good care of her nails. No matter how many times her team coach Mr. Tada scolded her about them she refused to shorten her nails.

Hanging onto Kazushi, Takako grabbed hold of his hair and yanked his head back. She could tell where they were.

Kazushi must have suddenly realized her intentions. She saw him shut his eyes.

It was useless though. Takako's right middle finger and thumb tore through his eyelids and dug into his eye sockets.

"AIEEEEEEEEEEE!"

Kazushi screamed. He fell on his arms, got up on his knees,

dropped his nunchucks, and tried to brush off her hands. His body moved frantically as he tried to get rid of her.

Takako held tightly onto Kazushi and refused to let go. She pushed her fingers in further. Her thumb and middle finger dug in up to their second joints. As she dug in, she felt something pop and realized it was his eyeballs. She didn't expect eye sockets to be this small. Takako didn't hesitate to bend her sharp fingers inward. Blood and a semi-transparent slimy liquid came oozing down his cheeks like weird tears.

"ARRRRGH," Kazushi cried as he got up and swung his arms around frantically. He tried to pry her right hand loose from his head with both of his hands and pulled at Takako's hair.

Takako leaped off Kazushi, who ended up with what felt like several strands or even a bundle of hair. Well, she couldn't be worried about that now.

She looked for her ice pick and found it. She snatched it up.

Kazushi moaned and swung his arms at the (literally) unseen enemy. Then he fell back on his rear end. His eyes were open, but his eyes were completely immersed in a sea of red. He resembled an albino monkey now. Takako dragged her right leg and limped toward him. She lifted her wounded right leg and stomped down onto his unprotected crotch. The purple-striped white track sneaker was now red, soaked with Takako's own blood. Underneath its sole she felt a squashing sensation as if she were crushing a rodent. "URGH," Kazushi moaned. He held his crotch and turned on his side, balled up like a fetus. Now Takako began stepping on his throat with her left leg. She put her weight on it. Kazushi reached out, trying to move her foot, hitting it feebly, trying to free himself.

"Hel..." Kazushi uttered. It sounded like a tiny draft of

air because his throat had been crushed.

"Help…"

Yeah right, Takako thought. She could tell her mouth was breaking into a grin. She realized she wasn't angry anymore. She was actually enjoying this. She was sure about it. So what? She never claimed to be Pope John Paul II or the 14th Dalai Lama.

On her knees now, she thrust the ice pick into his mouth (she saw several cavity fillings). His arms which were struggling to pull at her leg suddenly froze. Takako pushed further. It sunk into his throat without much resistance. Kazushi's entire body, from his chest down to his toes, then went into convulsions as if swimming the submariner. Then it stopped. The albino eyes still remained open, surrounded by a spider's web pattern of gooey blood like running paint.

She felt a sudden surge of pain in her right leg and fell on her back by his head. She was panting now the way she did after doing the 200-meter dash twice for physical tests.

She'd won. But she also felt empty. The actual fight might have lasted less than thirty seconds. She wouldn't have survived a longer fight. In any case…she won. That's what mattered.

Takako held her blood-soaked right leg as she looked down at the corpse of Kazushi, who resembled a traveling magician attempting to spit out an ice pick from his throat. Now ladies and gentlemen, I shall spit out what I just swallowed—

"Takako."

The voice came from behind her. Still seated, Takako turned around. She reached out and pulled out the ice pick from Kazushi's mouth (which resulted in Kazushi's head rising a little and then falling to the ground).

Mitsuko Souma (Female Student No. 11) was looking

down at Takako.

Takako quickly looked over at Mitsuko's right hand. Her small hand was holding a large automatic pistol.

She had no idea what her intentions were. But…if like Kazushi Niida she intended to kill her (it was likely, this after all was *Mitsuko Souma*), Takako had no chance of winning. Mitsuko had a gun.

She had to escape. She had to. Takako pulled at her right leg in pain and tried to get up.

"Are you all right?" Mitsuko asked. Her voice sounded terribly kind. She didn't point the gun at her.

But Takako had to be cautious. She moved back and finally managed to get up by holding onto a tree nearby. Her right leg felt incredibly heavy.

She answered, "Well, I suppose."

Mitsuko looked over Kazushi's corpse. Then she looked at the ice pick in Takako's hands.

"You killed him with that? I have to say I'm impressed. Speaking as one girl to another."

She really sounded like she was impressed. It almost sounded cheerful. Her angelic face was beaming.

"I guess," Takako responded. She felt as if her body were off balance. Perhaps it was from the heavy loss of blood from her right leg.

"Say," Mitsuko said. "You never went out of your way to impress me."

Still unable to tell what Mitsuko's intentions were, Takako stared at her. (The two most beautiful girls in Shiroiwa Junior High were staring at each other. Nice jewelry and a boy's corpse. Oh, you're so pretty.)

Mitsuko was absolutely right. Takako couldn't stand sucking up to anyone, so she was never intimidated like the other girls when Mitsuko talked to her. She was too proud and besides, she wasn't scared of Mitsuko.

Then she remembered something an older student she had a crush on a while ago (actually, it ended only a couple months ago) used to say. Whereas her feelings for Hiroki Sugimura were vague, she definitely had a crush on this guy. After getting involved in one of his friend's fights, he showed up all beat up at the team room before one of their meets and said in his unique voice, "There's nothing to be afraid of. Nothing to fear."

Be strong and beautiful....Takako had her eye on this guy ever since she entered junior high and it seemed he'd had a profound effect on her personality. But he also had a girlfriend. Someone very elegant, yes, someone like Sakura Ogawa...someone calm as a serene lake hidden deep inside a forest....Well that was all in the past.

But she thought—the fact that she suddenly recalled his words which hadn't occurred to her even when she was fighting Kazushi Niida just moments ago....Did that mean that...she was...in fact...afraid of Mitsuko?

"I was always a little envious," Mitsuko continued. "You were so pretty, and you were a better girl than me."

Takako listened quietly. She immediately realized there was something wrong. Why was Mitsuko referring to her in the past tense?

"But..." Mitsuko's eyes twinkled playfully. Now she was back to the present tense. "I really like girls like you. Maybe I'm a bit of a dyke. So it's..."

Takako's eyes opened wide. She turned around and began running. Her right leg dragged a little, but it was still a respectable sprint for the track star.

"So it's..."

Mitsuko lifted the .45. She pulled the trigger three times in a row. Takako had managed to run down the hill and through the woods, covering a quick twenty meters when three holes appeared in the back of her uniform. She fell forward as if diving in a head-first slide. Face down, she slid across the ground, and her legs contrasted against each other, the left one white and the right one red as they flew into the air, her skirt fluttering against them. She was lying on the ground.

Mitsuko put down the gun and said, "It's too bad."

24 players remaining

38

Noriko's breathing grew heavier. Shogo's medicine didn't seem to be having much effect. It was close to 2 p.m. All of a sudden Noriko's cheeks appeared sunk in. Shuya used up a water bottle to moisten Noriko's handkerchief, and wiped her sweaty face, and then placed it on her forehead. Noriko kept her eyes closed, but nodded as if to thank him.

Shuya looked back at Shogo. Shogo remained in the same position, leaning against a tree all this time, smoking with his legs crossed. His right hand gently touched the grip of the Remington shotgun resting in his lap.

"Shogo."

"What?"

"Let's go."

Shogo raised his brows. "Where?"

Shuya's lips tightened. "I can't stand it anymore." He pointed to Noriko. "She's getting worse every second."

Shogo glanced at Noriko, who was lying down with her eyes closed. "If it's from septicemia, warming her up and letting her rest won't cure her."

Shuya did his best to restrain his impatience. "According to the map, there's a medical clinic on the island. We might be able to find some better medicine for her there, right? It's way north of the residential area, and it's not in any of the forbidden zones."

"Oh yeah." Shogo exhaled smoke from the corner of his mouth. "That's true."

"Let's go there."

Shogo tilted his head. He took another drag and then rubbed out the cigarette. "That facility is at least one and a half kilometers away. It's too dangerous to go there now. We have to wait until dark."

Shuya clenched his teeth. "We can't wait until dark. What if that area becomes a forbidden zone?"

Shogo didn't reply.

"Hey," Shuya said. He wasn't sure whether it was from impatience or the mere thought of having to risk falling out with Shogo, but he was beginning to stutter a little. He had to say it though. "I-I won't say you're trying to get us killed. But why are you so afraid of taking any risks? Your life that precious?"

Shuya looked him in the eye. Shogo didn't change his calm expression.

"Shuya…"

Shuya heard Noriko's voice behind him and turned around. Noriko had her head turned toward him. The handkerchief on her forehead was lying on the ground.

"Stop it. We won't make it without Shogo," she managed to say in between heavy breaths.

"Noriko." Shuya shook his head. "Don't you see how weak you're getting? You can't die before we can make it out of here." Shuya turned to Shogo again. "If you say you're not coming, I'll take Noriko with me on my own. You can forget about our deal. You're on your own." That was his parting remark as he got ready to get their bags.

"Hold on," Shogo said. He slowly got up,

approached Noriko, and checked the pulse of her right wrist. It was what he did every twenty minutes. He rubbed his increasingly stubbly chin again and looked at them. "You won't know what medicine to use." He tilted his head slightly, looked at Shuya, and said, "All right. I'm coming with you."

24 students remaining

39

Although over half an hour had passed since she'd been shot in the back three times and though she'd lost a large quantity of blood from the arrow wound in her leg, Takako Chigusa was still alive. Mitsuko Souma had disappeared, but Takako couldn't care less about that.

She was half dozing, half dreaming. Her family...her father, mother, and younger sister were all waving at Takako from the front gate of their house.

She could tell her sister Ayako, who was two years younger, was crying. She was saying, "Goodbye, Takako, goodbye." Her handsome father, from whom Takako had inherited most of her features and her mother who shared her looks more with Ayako, were both silent, looking very sad. Their pet dog, Hanako, drooped her head and wagged her tail. Takako had taken care of Hanako, smart female dog, ever since she was a puppy.

Oh shit, Takako thought in her dream, how awful. I've only lived fifteen years. Hey Ayako, look after Mom and Dad, okay? You're so spoiled, so learn from your older sister a little, huh?

Then she saw Kahoru Kitazawa. Her one really close friend, the petite girl she'd been buddies with for seven years now.

Time to say goodbye to you too, Kahoru. That's right. You were the one who said that nothing, not even hell, could scare you as long as you gave it your best shot. That's right, I'm not afraid. But…it's still kinda hard, dying alone like this….

Then Kahoru seemed to be shouting. But she couldn't hear her well. It sounded like, "What about him?"

Him?

Then the scene changed to her track team locker room. She knew it was the summer of her second year because this room had been torn down last fall, replaced by a new clubhouse.

Hey, this is no dream. This actually happened. This…

An older teammate. His buzz-cut hair stood up in front, and he wore a white T-shirt with the words "FUCK OFF!" on it and green track shorts with black lines. Playful but gentle-looking eyes. He was the guy she had a crush on. He was good at running hurdles. Now he was concentrating on taping up his knee which he'd injured a while ago. There was no one else besides them. Takako said, "You have a beautiful girlfriend. You two make a great couple."

Ah well, when it comes to him, I turn into an average girl. How lame.

"Yeah?" he lifted his face and smiled. "You're prettier than her."

Takako smiled, but felt a little odd. She was happy to hear him praise her looks for the first time…but the fact he could tell another girl she was prettier also indicated how strong his relationship with his girlfriend was.

"Don't you have a boyfriend, Takako?" he asked, smiling.

The scene changed again.

She was at the park, but everything appeared very low.

Oh, this must be from my childhood. I must have been in the second or third grade.

Hiroki Sugimura was crying in front of her. He wasn't tall the way he was now. In fact back then Takako was taller. A bully had taken away his brand new comic book.

"Come on, boys don't cry. Don't be such a wuss. Be strong. Come on. Our dog just had puppies. You wanna see them?"

"Okay…" Hiroki wiped his tears and tagged along.

Come to think of it, Hiroki started martial arts school the year after that. He also went through a growth spurt around then and eventually ended up taller than her.

Up until the end of elementary school they often visited each other. Once, when she seemed preoccupied, Hiroki asked her, "What's wrong, Takako? Something wrong?"

Takako thought about it and then said what was on her mind. "Hey, Hiroki, what would you do if someone said they liked you?"

"Hmm. I don't know, since it's never happened to me."

"…don't you have a crush on someone?"

"Hmm. Nope. Not at this moment."

Takako then thought, so I'm not even in the running?

Whatever. She continued, "Oh, really. Well you should find someone you can confess to."

"I'm too chicken. I don't think so."

The scene changed. Junior high school again. They became classmates in their second year. They were talking on the first day of class. At some point, Hiroki asked, "So I heard there's this supposedly hot guy on the track team." Although he didn't directly say it, he was implying she had a crush on him.

"Who told you?"

"Just heard. So how's it going?"

"No hope. He has a girlfriend. What about you? You still don't have a girlfriend?"

"Leave me alone."

…we were always on the verge of being close. We both had a thing for each other but…or am I just imagining things? At least I liked you. I mean, it was different from how I felt about my track teammate. You know what I mean?

Hiroki's face appeared. He was crying.

"Takako. Don't die."

Come on guy, be a man. Boys don't cry. You might be bigger now, but you haven't made much progress.

Was it by the grace of God? Takako came to her senses once more. She opened her eyes.

Hiroki Sugimura was looking down at her in the soft afternoon light. Beyond Hiroki she saw the treetops, and in between them fragments of the blue sky formed complex patterns like those in a Rorschach Test.

The first thing she realized was that Hiroki wasn't crying. Then she started wondering, "How did you..."

As she tried to form words with her mouth, she felt as if she were forcing open a rusty door. She realized she didn't have too long to live.

"...get here?"

All Hiroki said was, "I managed." He knelt down beside her and gently lifted up her head. She'd fallen face forward, but now for some reason she was facing up. The palm of her left hand (her left hand...no, the entire left side of her body was numb now, so she couldn't feel anything...it might have been from Kazushi Niida's blow to the side of her head) felt the sensation of weeds underneath—had he carried her here?

Hiroki then asked quietly, "Who got you?"

That's right. It was important information.

"Mitsuko," Takako answered. She didn't give a damn about Kazushi Niida anymore. "Be careful."

Hiroki nodded. Then he said, "I'm sorry."

Takako didn't understand. She stared at Hiroki.

"I was hiding outside the school...waiting for you." Hiroki said and then tightened his lips as if holding something back.

"But...then Yoshio came back. I...I got distracted for a

split second. Then…you know how you ran at full speed…I lost you. I ran in your direction, calling after you, but…you were too far off by then."

Oh no, Takako thought. So it was true. After she ran away from the school into the woods she thought she'd heard a distant voice. But she was so frantic she thought it was just her imagination—and if it wasn't, then it meant there was someone—so she continued running at full speed.

Oh—

Hiroki had waited for her. Just as she'd suspected, he'd been waiting for her, risking his life. And when he said, "I managed," he probably meant that he'd been looking for her all this time.

The thought made her want to cry.

Instead she did her best to form a smile on her face.

"Really? Thanks."

Takako knew that she couldn't talk much anymore. She tried to come up with the best thing to say, but then an odd question occurred to her and she blurted it out, "Do you have a crush on someone?"

Hiroki's brows moved and then he gently said, "I do."

"Don't say it's me."

Still looking sad, Hiroki faintly smiled.

"No, it's not."

"Well then…"

Takako took a deep breath. She felt as if poison were spreading through her body which strangely felt both chilly and at the same time incredibly hot. "Could you just…hold me tight? It'll be…over soon."

Hiroki tightened his lips and raised her up, hugging her tightly to his body with both his arms. Her head was on the verge of falling back but Hiroki held it up.

She felt like she could say one more thing.

"You have to survive, Hiroki."

Dear God, can I have one more word?

Takako looked into Hiroki's eyes and grinned.

"You've become quite a stud."

Hiroki said, "And...you're the most stylin' girl in the world."

Takako smiled faintly. She wanted to thank him, but she was out of breath. She just stared at Hiroki's eyes. She was grateful. At least she wasn't going to die alone. The last person to stay with her ended up being Hiroki. And she was grateful. She really was.

Kahoru...thanks, I heard you.

Takako Chigusa remained in this position as she died approximately two minutes later. Her eyes remained open. Hiroki Sugimura held her limp, lifeless body and wept.

23 students remaining

40

"Get down," Shogo said. He carefully surveyed the area while holding on to his shotgun.

Carrying Noriko on his back, Shuya obeyed Shogo. The area was shaded by a large elm tree. They must have covered two-thirds the distance to the medical facility by now. They should be in the vicinity of sector F=6 or F=7. If they were headed in the right direction (Shogo was leading them, so they couldn't be far off), the school building should soon appear below them to their right.

Moving along the shore, they first passed through C=4. Then they moved east along the foot of the northern mountain. Moving in broad daylight did turn out to be difficult. They would move a little, quiet down their breathing, and when they had to get through thick vegetation Shogo would throw several pebbles ahead to make sure no one was there. It'd already taken them half an hour just to get this far.

Noriko continued to breathe heavily.

Shuya tilted his head back the way mothers do with their infants and told her, "We're almost there, Noriko."

"Uh huh…," she answered.

"All right, let's go," Shogo said. "We're going for that tree over there."

"Got it."

Shuya got up and proceeded through the soft, grassy soil that must have been a farm field. Shogo was right next to them, holding their belongings with his left hand and his shotgun in his right, indicating directions with the motion of his head. The muzzle of the shotgun would point in the same direction as his head.

They reached a thin tree and stopped. Shuya took a deep breath.

"Are you all right, Shuya?"

Shuya gave him a smile. "Noriko's light."

"We can take a break."

"No," Shuya shook his head. "I want to get there as soon as possible."

"All right," Shogo said, but Shuya felt uncertain. Maybe he was being an idiot. He was always jumping to wrong conclusions, failing to check the important details.

"Shogo."

"What?"

"Does that mark on the map really indicate a clinic?"

Shogo snickered. "I believe you were the one who claimed it was."

"No, that was—"

Shuya was embarrassed, but Shogo immediately said,

"Don't worry, it is. I checked it."

"Really?"

"Yeah, I walked around the island last night until I met you guys. I should have had the foresight to take some more medicine. I didn't think I'd need it."

Shuya let out a sigh of relief. Then he reproached himself. He had to get his act together. Otherwise, he'd end up not only getting himself killed but Noriko as well.

Even as they talked, Shogo was searching for their next spot.

"All right—"

Then they heard the gunfire. Shogo froze. He nervously crouched down and surveyed the area. So...had Shuya been too optimistic, hoping they could reach the medical facility without any obstacles?

But there was no one in sight.

Shuya looked over at Shogo, who stretched out his left arm as if to shield them and looked ahead toward their left, where they were headed. There was a gentle slope leading up to rows of tall pine trees approximately ten meters away, cutting off their view. Did he mean they were going through there?

Shuya finally let out the breath he'd been holding.

"It's all right," Shogo said in a hushed voice. "We're not the targets."

Shuya decided against pulling out his gun and, still carrying Noriko, said, "It's close."

Shogo nodded silently. Then the gunfire continued. Two, then three shots. The third one somehow seemed louder than the first two shots. Then another shot. It was a smaller sound.

"A gun fight," Shogo mumbled. "They're pretty pumped up."

Now that he knew they were safe, Shuya felt relieved, but

he kept on biting his lip.

Whoever they were, his classmates were trying to kill each other again. In fact, it was happening right near them. And he was just trying to stay quiet, waiting for it to end. That was just...

The image of the men in black crossed his mind. Now then, you're next, and you. Fortunately, Mr. Nanahara, your time still hasn't come.

His back facing him, Shogo said, as if he could read Shuya's thoughts (didn't he say something silly about reading his mind on a clear day?), "I hope you're not thinking of stopping them, Shuya."

Shuya held his breath and then mumbled, "No..." That's right. His priority was to take Noriko to the medical facility. If they got mixed up with someone else's fight they'd end up risking their own lives.

Then Noriko suddenly said from behind, "Shuya." Her fever was so high, he could even feel it through his back. She was practically whispering.

Shuya turned his head around. He saw Noriko's eyes squinting right behind his shoulder.

"Let me...stand...," she finally uttered and continued, "We have to see...make sure...whoever it is..."

Her words were cut off by her heavy breathing, but he knew what she was getting at. What if someone who didn't want to participate, in other words, someone innocent, was about to get killed right now? In fact that could be the case with both parties exchanging bullets right now.

The area they were in was a direct southward descent from the northern peak where Yukiko Kitano and Yumiko Kusaka were killed. But they weren't hearing a machine gun now. Therefore, neither of the fighting parties right now had killed Yukiko and Yumiko. But what if...Yukiko and Yumiko's killer heard this gunfire? He could show up at any moment.

More gunfire was exchanged. And then silence again.

Shuya clenched his teeth. He quickly let Noriko down. He had her rest against the tree trunk where they were hiding.

Shogo turned around. "Hey, you're not…"

Shuya ignored him and said to Noriko, "I'll go check it out." He pulled out his Smith & Wesson and said to Shogo, "Look after Noriko."

"H-hey…"

He heard Shogo, but he was already on his way.

He climbed the slope carefully, keeping an eye on all sides, and made his way through the coniferous trees.

There was thick vegetation beyond the trees. Shuya made his way into it. He got down on the ground and proceeded to make his way through the long, sharp needles pricking at him from both sides.

More gunshots. Shuya finally reached the edge of the grove and slowly poked his head out.

There was a house. It was an old wooden, single-story building with a triangular roof. A typical farmhouse. On his left was an unpaved entrance road. The mountain escarpment surrounded the property further down. The area above was covered in deep forest. And even further up, you could see the viewing platform on the northern mountain where Yumiko and Yukiko had been killed.

The farmhouse was on his left side. Hirono Shimizu (Female Student No. 10) was crouched against the wall in front of the building. Hirono was looking beyond the yard at what appeared to be a shack for farm equipment right beside the entrance road. He could make out the figure of a girl beside the entrance. The girl looked up, and that was when he realized it was Kaori Minami (Female Student No. 20). And both of them were holding guns. They were less than fifteen meters apart from each other.

He had no idea how they ended up shooting at each other. It was possible one of them was out to get the other girl, but Shuya could tell this wasn't the case. They probably stumbled into each other, and because neither of them could trust the other, they ended up shooting at each other....

This guess might have just been based on his own favorable opinion of girls, but in any case he couldn't just sit back and let this happen. He had to stop them.

As Shuya tried to grasp the situation, Kaori stuck her head out from the shack's entrance and fired at Hirono. She handled the gun like a kid playing with a water pistol, but unlike a water pistol the gun exploded, and a small brass shell flew into the air. Hirono fired two shots back. She actually handled the gun well, and her shells didn't fly out. One of her bullets hit the post of the shack, which shattered into sawdust. Kaori quickly tucked her head in.

Hirono's body was almost entirely visible from where Shuya was standing, and he saw her open the cylinder of her revolver to extract the shells. Her left hand was soaked crimson. Her arm might have been wounded by Kaori. But she managed to reload her gun quickly with that hand. She aimed her gun at Kaori again.

All of this happened in a matter of seconds, but right before he was about to act Shuya was once again overwhelmed by the sensation of being in a nightmare. Kaori Minami loved pop idols, so she'd often talk about her favorite stars with her friends, or share a photo taken in person that thrilled her to no end. Then there was Hirono Shimizu, who hung out with Mitsuko Souma, so there was something jaded about her. But they were both third-year students in junior high, they both had charming qualities. Now these two...were shooting at each other. Seriously, with real bullets. Obviously.

I have to do something *now*.

Shuya stood up and fired his Smith & Wesson into the air. Oh great, so now I'm playing the sheriff, he thought for a moment. But without hesitating, he shouted, "Stop it!"

Hirono and Kaori froze, and then together looked over at Shuya.

Shuya continued, "Stop it! I'm with Noriko Nakagawa!" He thought it was best not to mention Shogo's name for now. "You can trust me!"

As he said this, he realized how lame his words sounded. But he had no other way to put it.

Hirono was the first to move her eyes away from Shuya to Kaori. And...Kaori was gazing at Shuya.

Shuya realized at that moment how half of Kaori's body was exposed beyond the entrance—she was in the open now.

What happened next reminded him of a traffic accident he once witnessed. It happened on an autumn evening before he turned eleven. Maybe the driver had fallen asleep or something. His truck lost control, rammed through the guardrail, rode up onto the sidewalk, and hit a young girl walking home from school, just like Shuya, who was behind her. It was unbelievable but her backpack came off her shoulders and flew into the air, tracing a different trajectory from the girl's body. The girl landed on the sidewalk before the backpack did, falling on her shoulder. Obstructed by the wayside concrete wall she slid along the edge of the sidewalk and then stopped still. Blood came flowing out, leaving a trail on the bottom edge of the concrete wall over one meter long.

It all looked like—from the time the truck swung off the road and crashed into the girl—as if it was happening in slow motion. Anyone there could tell what was going to happen, but there was nothing anyone could do. That's what it felt like.

Hirono aimed and fired at Kaori, who'd completely let her guard down. Two shots in a row. The first one hit Kaori in the shoulder, making her spin halfway to the right. The second shot hit her in the head. Shuya saw a part of her head—from the top down to her left temple—explode.

Kaori collapsed by the front door of the shack.

Hirono glanced over at Shuya.

Then she turned and ran to his left, westward, where Shuya's group came from. She ran into the bushes and disappeared from sight.

"Damn!"

Shuya moaned. After some hesitation he ran to the shack where Kaori had collapsed.

Kaori was lying down, legs jutting out from inside the shack that only housed a decrepit tractor. Her body remained twisted as blood came flowing out the corner of her mouth, mixed with the blood from her head and shoulder wounds, turning into a puddle on the shack's concrete floor. Tiny dust particles from the floor were floating on the surface of the puddle. Her eyes stared out at the sky. A thin gold chain hung down from her sailor suit onto the floor, and the golden locket attached to it looked like an island in a lake of blood. A famous male idol singer was smiling cheerfully from it.

Shuya was shaking as he knelt down beside her.

Oh, man...what the...so this girl...can't gossip about pop idols anymore, she can't go to their concerts anymore. If he had been more careful...maybe she wouldn't have been killed?

He heard a sound and turned around. It was Shogo, holding Noriko with one of his arms as they looked out from the woods.

Shogo left Noriko there and trotted over to Shuya.

Shogo's expression seemed to be saying, "See, what'd I tell you?" but he didn't say a word. He just calmly picked up Kaori's gun and day pack, and then as if it occurred to him as an afterthought, he crouched down and shut her eyes with his right thumb. Then he told Shuya, "We're going. Hurry up."

He knew it was dangerous. Anyone—especially the killer with the machine gun—could have heard the gunfire and might be showing up now.

Still, Shuya's eyes were glued to Kaori's corpse until Shogo tugged his arm back.

22 students remaining

41

The medical clinic was an old, small, single-story building. The wood walls had turned black, and the black-tiled roof was so worn out with age that the corners had turned white. Like the shack where Kaori Minami had died, it was located in front of the northern mountain at the end of a narrow unpaved road. They'd made their way through the mountain, but they could tell the narrow entrance road led down to the paved road along the island's eastern shore. There was a white minivan parked in front of the facility. Maybe the doctor had used it. Beyond the minivan they could see the ocean.

The afternoon sun was shining on the sea. The color of the ocean was completely different from the murky water that lapped against the concrete sea walls in Shiroiwa harbor. It was a wonderfully brilliant blue tinged with green. There were hardly any waves, and the sparkling dots of light on its surface became increasingly dense in the distance. Other islands floating in the Seto Inland Sea looked remarkably close, but this was probably due, as he was once told, to the optical illusion of reduced distance when objects were absent. So they must have been at least four or five kilometers away.

In any case...they were here. It was a miracle they got here without getting hurt. They'd immediately left the area where Kaori died. No machine gun shots came after them. According to the map they'd traveled a distance of less than two kilometers, but Shuya, who'd been carrying Noriko, accompanied by the pressure of a possible attack, was incredibly tired. He wanted to check to make sure no one was in the area of the clinic as soon as possible, so that not only Noriko but he too could get some rest.

But something caught Shuya's attention.

A ship was floating on the peaceful sea. It was probably the guard ship Sakamochi had mentioned. But...for some reason there were three ships in a row. Sakamochi said there would be one ship on all sides—north, south, east, and west—and on the west side they had only seen one. So what was this?

Still carrying Noriko, Shuya poked his face out from the leaves and asked Shogo, "There're three ships."

"Yeah," Shogo replied. "The small one is a guard ship. The huge one is the ship that will transport the soldiers who were in the school building back to their base. The one in the middle is for the winner of the game. The winner rides that boat. It's the same model as the one from last year."

"So...the Program in Hyogo Prefecture was also held on an island like this one?"

"Yep," Shogo nodded. "Hyogo Prefecture also shares the Seto Inland Sea. It seems like Programs held in prefectures along the Seto Inland Sea coast are always held on islands. I mean, there are at least a thousand islands in this small ocean."

Shogo then told him to wait and descended the slope toward the clinic with his shotgun cocked. He crouched down and first examined the minivan. Then he snuck up to the building and circled it. When he returned he examined the sliding door entrance. It seemed to be locked, so Shogo flipped his shotgun and shattered the frosted glass window with the sawed off gun stock. Then he stuck his hand into the V-shaped opening, unlocked the door, and entered the building.

After watching him do this, Shuya tilted his head back to Noriko, whose head was resting against his back.

"Noriko, we're here." Shuya said, but Noriko could only moan, "Huh..." Her heavy breathing continued.

After five full minutes, Shogo poked his head out of the entrance and signaled Shuya to join him. Shuya cautiously descended the two meter drop so he wouldn't lose his balance and approached the clinic.

A thick, grimy wooden sign with the traces of weather-worn letters that read, "Okishima Island Medical Clinic" hung right beside the entrance. Shuya slipped by Shogo, who kept watch, holding his shotgun. He entered, followed by Shogo, who shut the door tightly.

Right near the entrance, there was a small waiting room. On the left there was a long, green couch with a white cover on the worn out cream-colored carpet. The wall clock made a ticking sound as it approached three o'clock. The right side appeared to be the examination room.

Shogo jammed the door shut with a broom and then signaled Shuya, "Over here."

Although they were supposed to take their shoes off, Shuya stepped up with his sneakers on and entered the room on the right. There was a wooden desk in front of the window, and what appeared to be a doctor's black leather chair. There was a green vinyl stool in front of it. Even though the clinic was small, it still had the sterile odor of disinfectant.

There were two beds beyond a thin green curtain hanging

from metal pipes. Shuya carried Noriko to the bed in front and gently put her down there. He thought of having her take off his school coat, but then decided against it.

After Shogo quickly pulled the curtains shut, he said, "blankets," and gave him two thin brown blankets folded in small squares. Shuya took them and after some thought spread one of them on the other bed. Then he moved Noriko there and spread the other blanket over her. He made sure the blanket went up to her shoulders. Shogo was rummaging through a gray office cabinet that was probably the medicine cabinet.

Shuya crouched down by Noriko's head and combed the sweaty hair against her cheeks back to her ears. She seemed dazed. Her eyes were closed, and she continued to breathe heavily.

"Damn it," Shuya muttered. "Noriko, are you all right?"

Noriko squinted, her eyes glazed at him as she said, "Uh huh…" She might be faint from the high fever, but her mind was clear enough to respond.

"How about some water?"

Noriko barely nodded. Shuya took out a new bottle of water from the day pack Shogo had tossed onto the floor and tore off the seal. He held her up and helped her drink it. Shuya wiped off the water spilling from the side of her mouth with the back of his hand.

"Is that enough?" Shuya asked and Noriko nodded. Then he lay her down and waved to Shogo. "Any medicine?"

"Hold on," Shogo replied. He rummaged through another, lower cabinet and pulled out a cardboard box. He opened it and read the directions. It seemed to be what he was after. He extracted what looked like a small bottle and an ampoule. The bottle was filled with white powder.

"Do you swallow that?" Shuya asked.

Shogo answered, "No, it's for injections."

Shuya was a little shocked. "You know how to use that?"

Shogo turned on the faucet in the back of the room. No water came out, as expected, and Shogo clicked his tongue. He pulled out his water bottle from his day pack and washed his hands. Then he set a needle on a syringe and extracted the contents of the ampoule. "Don't worry, I've done this before."

"…really?" Shuya felt like he was constantly repeating this phrase to Shogo.

Shogo broke the seal of the small bottle and injected it with the syringe, filling it up with the liquid from the ampoule. After removing the syringe, he held the bottle and shook it vigorously. Then he injected the syringe again to extract the liquid mixture.

After preparing another syringe like this, he finally approached them.

"Is she going to be all right?" Shuya asked again. "What about side effects or shock?"

"That's what I'm going to check for now. Just do as I say. Pull out Noriko's arm."

Unsure of the situation, Shuya lifted the side of the blanket and rolled up both the sleeves of his school coat and her sailor suit. Her arm was very thin and her healthy looking dark skin had now become excruciatingly white.

"Noriko," Shogo asked her, "have you ever had any allergic reactions to any medicine?"

Noriko opened her eyes again in a daze.

Shogo repeated, "Are you allergic to any medicine?"

Noriko shook her head slightly.

"Good. I'm going to test you first though."

Shogo held her arm out with her palm up, then took a cotton swab soaked with disinfectant and wiped the area between her wrist and elbow. He slowly inserted the needle, injecting only a small amount of the liquid. A slight bump formed on this area of her skin. Shogo took out another syringe and performed another injection.

"What are you doing?" Shuya asked.

"One of them is real medicine. If she's in the same condition fifteen minutes later, we won't have to worry about side effects. It means we can probably use the medicine. But…"

"But?"

Shogo quickly took out another larger bottle from the cardboard box. He placed it on the small desk nearby, prepared another syringe, and looked over at Shuya. "It's not easy to diagnose septicemia. To be honest I can't tell whether this is from septicemia or just a cold. Antibiotics are pretty potent, and that's why we're testing this on her, but the fact is my experience and knowledge is pretty limited, so injecting her with this syringe could be pretty dicey. On the other hand…"

Holding Noriko's hand, Shuya waited for him to continue.

Shogo took a breath and continued, "If she is suffering from septicemia, then we have to treat her as soon as possible. Otherwise, it'll be too late."

Fifteen minutes passed by quickly. In the meantime, Shogo checked her pulse again and took her temperature. The thermometer read 39 degrees Celsius. No wonder she could barely stand.

Shuya couldn't tell the difference between the two adjacent marks from the syringes. Shogo also appeared to reach the same conclusion and took the larger syringe.

Crouching down slightly, Shogo asked, "Noriko. Are you awake?"

Noriko answered with her eyes shut, "Uh huh…"

"I'll be honest. I don't know if you're suffering from

septicemia or not. I think you probably are."

Noriko nodded slightly. She must have been able to follow Shuya and Shogo's conversation moments ago.

"It's all right…go ahead."

Shogo nodded and inserted the syringe, this time deeply. He injected the liquid and removed the needle. Then he wiped her arm with the cotton and told Shuya, "Hold this."

Shogo took the empty syringe and walked over to the sink to toss it away. Then he came back.

"Now she's got to sleep. You look after her for a while. If she looks thirsty, you can use the whole bottle."

Shuya said, "But that's—"

Shuya shook his head.

"Don't worry. I found a well behind the building. As long as we boil the water we can drink it." Shogo left the room. Shuya turned towards the bed. With his right hand pressing the cotton swab and his left hand gently holding Noriko's hand, he watched over her.

22 students remaining

42

Noriko fell asleep almost immediately. Shuya checked to make sure she wasn't bleeding from the shot, then he tossed the cotton swab, tucked her arm under the blanket, and left the room.

The doctor's living quarters was beyond the waiting room next door. There was a kitchen at the end of the hall on the right. Shogo was in there. The gas stove next to the sink wasn't operating, but on it was a large pot filled with water, and under it a pile of charcoal was glowing red.

Shogo was standing on a table, looking through a built-in

ceiling cabinet across from the sink. That's when Shuya noticed for the first time that Shogo was wearing New Balance sneakers. He'd assumed they were some domestic brand like Mizumo or Kageboshi. New Balance! He'd never seen them before!

Whatever. "What are you doing?" he asked.

"I'm looking for food. I found some rice and miso, but nothing else. The vegetables in the fridge are rotten."

Shuya shook his head. "You're stealing."

"Of course I am," Shogo said dryly and then added while he continued rummaging, "Forget about it. Just be ready. Anyone could show up at any moment. If the machine gun shooter shows up, we'll be dead. So be ready."

Shuya replied, "Yeah, all right."

Shogo jumped off the table. The New Balance shoes squeaked against the floor.

"Is she asleep?" he asked.

Shuya nodded.

Shogo pulled out another pot from under the sink, walked up to the plastic rice container in the corner, and poured rice into the pot.

"So you're boiling rice."

"That's right. Noriko won't recover eating that terrible bread." Shogo scooped up a bowl of water from the bucket on the floor and poured it into the pot. He combed through the rice and only changed the water once. Next to the boiling water, he placed several pieces of charcoal from his day pack onto the other burner, then took out a pack of cigarettes and emptied them into his pocket. Then he crumpled the pack, lit it with his lighter, and stuck it into the charcoal. Once the charcoal was lit, he put the lidded pot of rice on the burner. It was an impressive sight.

"Damn," Shuya said.

Shogo took a break as he lit up a cigarette and

looked at Shuya.

"You're so good at everything."

"Yeah?" Shogo answered lightly. But something else flashed through Shuya's mind. The moment Kaori Minami was murdered...you know what's going to happen but there's nothing you can do to stop it. Slow motion. Kaori spins around and the left side of her head's blown off. It was blown away, did you see that?...If it had been Shogo instead of Shuya, the outcome wouldn't have been so horrible.

"Are you still bummed about Kaori?" Shogo said. Once again, Shogo's psychic powers were on. The sunlight doesn't reach this far inside, but that didn't seem to affect him.

Shogo shook his head. "Don't let it get to you. It was a bad situation. You did your best."

Shogo's voice was kind, but Shuya looked down. The corpse of Kaori Minami, collapsed on her side inside a grimy farm equipment shack. The pool of blood gradually spreading, oozing outward. By now, beginning to congeal. But the body would just stay there, with no ceremony, just left there like a disposed mannequin sprawled inside that shack. Of course in that sense she was no exception to Tatsumichi Oki, Kyoichi Motobuchi, Yukiko Kitano, and Yumiko Kusaka. That's right, everyone else was in the same boat.

He felt like puking. They were all lying there, on the ground. Already close to twenty of them.

"Shogo." The words spilled out.

In response Shogo tilted his head and slightly moved his hand that was holding the cigarette.

"What happens to the dead...their bodies?" Shuya asked. "Are they left there until this stupid game is over? So they just start rotting while the game is going on?"

Shogo answered as if it were an official matter. "That's right. Once it's over, the following day a clean-up crew is hired to take care of them."

"...clean-up crew?" Shuya bared his teeth.

"Yep. I heard about it from someone who works for the subcontractor, so I'm sure it's true. Self Defense Forces soldiers are too proud to perform such menial tasks. Of course, government officials accompany the crew to collect the collars and examine the bodies. You know, so the news media can report the number of deaths by strangulation, all that stuff."

Shuya was pissed. He recalled that final part of the news report. The meaningless causes of deaths and itemization of each student.

But he also realized something and knit his brows.

Shogo saw this and asked, "What's up?"

"Well...that doesn't make sense. I mean these..." Shuya raised his hand up to his neck. His fingers touched the collar's cold surface, its sensation no longer so strange. "I thought these were a secret. Shouldn't they collect them before the hired hands come in?"

Shogo shrugged. "The cleaning crew have no idea what they're for. They probably just assume they're used as markers. The guy I talked to didn't even remember them until I asked him about them. So there's no rush. They can deal with the collars after the clean-up crew's collected the bodies, right?"

It was true. But even so, something else bugged him.

"Hold on. What if one of these is defective? Let's say it breaks down and someone who's alive is assumed to be dead. Couldn't that student escape? Shouldn't they confirm all the dead right after the game?"

Shogo raised his brows. "You talk like you work for the government."

"No...," he stammered. "It's just that—"

"I doubt they could ever be defective. Think about it. If they actually could break down, this game couldn't proceed smoothly. Besides, if a student equipped with weapons turned out to be alive, they couldn't even afford to check the bodies. It'd turn into another battle." Shogo took a drag as he considered it more thoroughly. "This is just my guess, but I think each collar is loaded with multiple systems, so that if one breaks down, another gets switched on. Even if one system became defective—the chances of that being at least less than one in a hundred—if the systems were combined the probability would practically be reduced to zero. In other words," he said, looking at Shuya, "it would be impossible for us to escape that way."

Shuya understood. He saw no reason not to object. (Once again, he couldn't help but be impressed by Shogo's intelligence.)

But then—

The question he promised not to ask crossed his mind. Which was:

How did Shogo plan to beat a perfect, escape-proof system?

Before he could consider it, Shogo said, "Anyway, look, I have to apologize."

"About what?"

"About Noriko. I was wrong. We should have treated her sooner."

"No…" Shuya shook his head. "It's okay. Thanks. I would have been useless on my own."

Shogo exhaled and fixed his gaze on a part of the wall. "We'll just have to wait and see. If it's just a cold, then her fever will go down as soon as she gets some rest. And if it turns out it's from septicemia then the medicine should kick in."

Shuya nodded. He was grateful they had Shogo. Without Shogo, he would have been helpless, doomed to watch Noriko deteriorate. He was also sorry for saying to

Shogo, "You can forget about our deal," and heading off here. It was immature. Shogo must have made his decision after carefully weighing the risk of moving during the day against Noriko's condition.

Shuya decided he should apologize. "Hey, I'm sorry. Saying you were on your own and all. I just got so excited—"

Still looking away from Shuya, Shogo shook his head and smiled. "No. You made the right decision. End of conversation."

Shuya took a breath and decided to let it go. Then he asked, "Is your father still a practicing doctor?"

Shogo shook his head as he took a drag. "No."

"What's he doing? Is he still in Kobe?"

"No. He died." Shogo said it casually.

Shuya's eyes opened wide. "When?"

"Last year, while I was playing this game. By the time I got back he was dead. He probably got in a scuffle with the government."

Shuya's face stiffened. He was beginning to understand the glimmer in Shogo's eyes when he'd said, "I'm going to tear up this fucking country." The moment Shogo ended up in the Program, Shogo's father must have tried some kind of protest. Which must have been met with a shower of bullets.

It occurred to Shuya that the parents of some of his classmates might have ended up the same way.

"I'm sorry. I didn't mean to pry."

"Don't worry about it."

Shuya paused and then asked another question, "Then you moved to Kagawa Prefecture with your mother?"

Shogo shook his head and again replied, "No. My mom died when I was a kid. I was seven. She died from illness. My dad used to cry over the fact that he couldn't even save her. But my dad specialized in surgery, like abortions. Nervous disorders were out of his field."

Shuya apologized again, "I'm sorry."

Shogo chuckled. "Hey, it's all right. We both don't have parents, right? And it's true about getting a lifetime pension. I've got enough to live on. Although they don't give you as much as they say they do."

Bubbles began to form at the bottom of the first large pot. The charcoal under the rice pot was still mostly black, but the charcoal under the large pot was flaming red. The heat reached the table where Shuya and Shogo were standing next to each other. Shuya sat up on the table, which was covered with a flower-pattern vinyl tablecloth.

Without warning, Shogo suddenly said, "You were good friends with Yoshitoki Kuninobu."

Shuya looked over at Shogo and looked at his profile. Then he looked ahead. It felt like a while since he'd last thought of Yoshitoki. He felt a little guilty about it.

"Yeah," he answered. "We've known each other forever." After hesitating a little, Shuya continued, "Yoshitoki had a crush on Noriko."

Shogo continued smoking, listening.

Shuya wondered whether he should continue with what he was about to say. It had nothing to do with Shogo. But he decided to tell him anyway. Shogo was a friend now. It was all right for him to know, and besides, they had time to kill right now.

"Yoshitoki and I were at this orphanage called the Charity House—"

"I know."

Shuya nodded and continued, "There're all kinds of kids there. I ended up there when I was five. My parents were killed in a car accident. But that's unusual. Most of them—"

Shogo understood. "They end up there because of 'domestic' problems. They're illegitimate children."

Shuya nodded. "So you know."

"A little."

He took a deep breath. "Well, Yoshitoki was illegitimate. Of course, no one at the orphanage told him, but there are ways to find out. He was conceived from an 'illicit affair' and both sides refused to take him in. So…"

The water made a gurgling sound.

"I remember something Yoshitoki once said to me. It was a long time ago, probably when we were still in elementary school."

Shuya recalled that moment. They were in the corner of the school playground, rocking back and forth on a big swing made of a wooden log and wire rope.

"Hey, Shuya. I was thinking—"

"What?"

Shuya responded in his usual casual voice, kicking at the ground to rock the log. Yoshitoki didn't put much effort into it, letting his legs dangle from both sides of the log.

"Well…uh…"

"What is it? Spit it out."

"Well…do you have a crush on anyone?"

"Oh, please," Shuya grinned. He knew it was something about girls. "So that's it? What's the matter? You have a crush on someone, huh?"

"Well…" Yoshitoki evaded the question and once again asked, "Well, do you?"

Shuya thought about it and then moaned, "Hmmm."

By then he was "Wild Seven." So he'd gotten several love letters. But at the time he never fell head over heels for anyone in particular. As it turned out, he wouldn't until he met Kazumi Shintani.

He answered, "Well, I think there're some cool girls.…"

Yoshitoki didn't say anything back so he assumed he wanted to hear more. He continued speaking in a light tone, "Komoto's not bad. She actually wrote me a love letter. I haven't, uh, responded though. Then there's Utsumi, who's on the volleyball team. She's pretty cool. That's my type. You know, real outgoing."

Yoshitoki looked pensive.

"What is it? I told you, now you tell me. Who is it?"

But Yoshitoki only said, "No, that's not it."

Shuya knit his brows.

"What is it then?"

Yoshitoki seemed quite hesitant, but then he said, "You see, I never really understood."

"?"

"I mean…" His legs dangled passively as he continued, "I think if you really loved someone you'd marry her, right?"

"Uh, yeah." Shuya replied with an idiotic look on his face. "Yeah. If…if I loved someone, I'd want to marry her…I mean I don't feel that way about anyone."

"Right?" Yoshitoki said, as if it were only natural. Then he asked, "So let's say you just can't get married for some reason. If you ended up having a kid with her, wouldn't you still want to raise the kid?"

Shuya felt a little uncomfortable. He'd just begun to get the idea of how babies were made.

"Having a kid? Hey, you're still a kid. That's dirty stuff. You know I heard that that's—"

That was when Shuya finally remembered Yoshitoki was born as a result of an illicit affair and that neither of his parents wanted him. Startled, he held back what he was about to say.

Yoshitoki was staring at the log between his thighs. Then he mumbled, "My parents weren't like that."

Shuya suddenly felt really bad for him.

"H-hey, Yoshi—" He looked up at Shuya and said somewhat forcefully, "So I-I just don't know. Loving someone. I don't feel like I can trust that sort of thing."

Shuya continued pushing with his legs, but he had no choice but to stare back at Yoshitoki. He felt as if he were being addressed in a language from another planet. At the same time, it sounded like a dreadful prophecy.

"I think—"

His hands by his waist, Shuya gripped the corners of the table covered with the vinyl tablecloth. Shogo continued smoking, squinting his eyes.

"I think Yoshitoki was a lot more mature at that point already. I was just a silly kid. And ever since then, Yoshitoki, even since we entered junior high, and I fell for someone," this was Kazumi Shintani, "he never brought it up. That kind of worried me."

Another gurgling sound.

"But then one day he told me he liked Noriko. I acted like it wasn't a big deal…but I was so happy for him. And that was, that was…"

Shuya looked away from Shogo. He knew he was about to cry.

Once he managed to hold back his tears, he said without looking at Shogo and continued, "That was only two months ago."

Shogo remained silent.

Shuya looked at Shogo again.

"So you see, I have to protect Noriko to the very end."

After staring back at Shuya for a while, Shogo only said, "I see," and rubbed out his cigarette out against the tablecloth.

"Don't tell Noriko. I'll tell her about Yoshitoki once we've gotten out of this game."

Shogo nodded and replied, "All right."

22 students remaining

43

Five hours had passed since the Macintosh PowerBook 150's connection to the internet had been cut off with a warning beep. Shinji Mimura scrolled through a document in one of the windows on the display monitor of the 150 that was now reduced to a word processor.

He'd worked on the phone, checked the connections, and rebooted over and over but the gray monitor responded with the same message. Finally, after disconnecting all the modem and phone cords, he came to the conclusion his cell phone had completely broke down. Without a phone line he couldn't even access his home computer. And of course, calling all the girls he'd ever gone with and sobbing over how he was, "About to die, but I loved you the most," was out of the question. He still believed he could get to the bottom of this and considered taking apart his cell phone—but then stopped.

A chill ran down his spine.

It was obvious now why he wasn't able to dial in anymore. The government had managed to locate the line test number used by the DTT technician, the number used for the special phone with the counterfeit "Second ROM" he'd painstakingly built. They'd cut off all connections including this one. The question was…how had they managed to do this? His hacking had been flawless. He knew that much.

The only way he could imagine the government discovering his hacking was through some method outside their computer's internal security system, their warning system, and other manual monitoring systems. And now that they knew—

The moment Shinji realized what it was, his hand went for the collar around his neck.

Now that the government knew, it wouldn't be all that surprising if the bomb went off, would it? They probably wouldn't spare Yutaka either.

Thanks to this realization, the government-supplied water and bread they had for lunch tasted even worse.

After Yutaka saw Shinji turn off the laptop, he asked for an explanation. Shinji only replied, "It's no good. I don't know why, but it's not working. Maybe the phone's broken."

Ever since then Yutaka's mood became gloomy, and he slouched back to the way he'd been earlier that morning. Other than the occasional gunshots and brief exchanges it remained silent. Shinji's great escape plan that mesmerized Yutaka had completely fallen apart.

But—

I'll still make them regret they didn't kill me right away. No matter what.

He thought a little, then dug into his pants pocket and pulled out an old pocketknife he carried around with him ever since he was a kid. There was a small tube tied to the keyring on the knife. Shinji examined the scratched up tube.

His uncle had given him the knife a long time ago. And the tube was, that's right, like the earring on his left ear, another memento from his uncle. Like Shinji, his uncle had kept it chained to a small knife and always carried it around.

The thumb-sized tube, with its rubber ring under the cap, was a waterproof case used by soldiers. It was normally used to hold a document with name, blood type, and history of illness in case of injury. Others used it as a matchbox. Until his death, Shinji assumed his uncle kept that sort of thing in it too. But after he died, when he opened the tube, Shinji found something completely different inside. In fact the tube's casing itself was carved out of a special alloy and contained two smaller cylinders inside. Shinji took out the two cylinders. He had no idea what they were. The only thing he could tell was that their contents were supposed to be mixed.

The thread of the screw from one of the cylinders fit perfectly into the other one. The reason why they were kept apart was that it was risky to connect them. And once he found out what they were for, after some research (no wonder they were separate—otherwise, you couldn't carry those cases around), he still had no idea why his uncle carried this around wherever he went. It served no particular purpose. Or maybe like the earring Shinji wore, his uncle had merely held onto it to remind himself of someone. Anyway, it was another piece of evidence from his uncle's past for Shinji to ponder over.

Shinji turned the squeaky cap and opened it. He hadn't opened it since his uncle died. He dropped the two cylinders into the palm of his hand. Then he opened the seal of the smaller cylinder.

It had been stuffed with cotton to make it shockproof. There was the dull yellow of brass underneath the cotton.

After examining it, he returned both cylinders back into the larger container and screwed the cap back on. He'd thought that if he ever had to use this, it would be after they escaped the island, or after messing up the school computer. It might have been handy after they equipped themselves and attacked Sakamochi and the others—but now this was all they had.

He flipped out the blade from his pocketknife. The sun had moved west, and the bushes reflecting against the silver steel were dark yellow. Then he pulled out a pencil from his school coat pocket. It was the pencil they all used to write the phrase, "We will kill," before the game began. Because he'd used it to mark the forbidden zones and check off the names of dead classmates, its point was now blunt. Shinji sharpened the pencil with his knife. Then he pulled out his map from another pocket and turned it over. It was blank.

"Yutaka."

Yutaka had been hugging his knees and gazing at the ground. He looked up. His eyes were shining. "Did you come up with something?" he asked.

Shinji wasn't exactly sure why Yutaka's response ticked him off. It might have been the tone of his voice, or maybe the words. Shinji felt like saying, what the hell—here I am banging my head against the wall trying to come up with an escape plan and all you've been doing is sitting on your ass! You swore you were going to get back at them for Izumi Kanai, but you haven't done squat. You think this is a fast food restaurant where I'm working the register? You want some fries with that?

But Shinji restrained himself.

Yutaka's round cheeks were sunken and his cheekbones stuck out. It was only natural. He must have been worn out by the pressure of this game that could end at any moment for them.

Ever since he was a kid Shinji was always the best athlete in the class. (Although this changed in his second year in junior high, when he was joined by Shuya Nanahara and Kazuo Kiriyama. He could beat them in basketball, but he wasn't sure about other sports.) His uncle had taken him mountain climbing ever since he was a kid, and he was confident in any competition that required stamina. But not everyone was built like The Third Man. Yutaka was a poor athlete, and when the cold season came he was often absent. Fatigue must have been overwhelming him, and it might be numbing his thinking too.

That was when Shinji realized something important. Wasn't the fact that he was even a little upset at Yutaka an indication of his own fatigue? Of course, given how their chances of survival were close to nil, it would have been much stranger not to be worn out.

No.

I have to be careful. If this were a basketball game, you'd just feel bad about losing—but in this game you end up dead.

Shinji shook his head.

"What's wrong?" Yutaka asked.

Shinji looked up at him, forcing a smile. "Nothing. Hey, I just want to take a look at the map. Okay?"

Yutaka came over to Shinji.

"Hey," Shinji raised his voice. "There's a bug on your neck!"

Yutaka touched his neck.

"I'll get it," Shinji stopped him and approached Yutaka. He fixed his eyes on the nape of Yutaka's neck—but he was searching for something else.

"Oh, it's moved," he said and got behind him. Shinji examined his neck again.

"Did you get it?"

As he listened to Yutaka's shrill, terrified voice, Shinji took a closer look.

Then he lightly brushed away the nape of Yutaka's neck. He crushed the imaginary bug with the sole of his sneakers and (pretending) he picked it up and (pretending once again) tossed it out.

"I got it," he said. He was now facing Yutaka and added, "Looked like a little centipede."

"Oh man," Yutaka rubbed the nape of his neck and looked over where Shuya had (apparently) tossed it, grimacing.

Shinji broke into a slight grin and said, "Come on, let's look at the map."

Yutaka looked over, then knit his brows when he saw that it was turned over.

Shinji waved his index finger to get his attention and scribbled on the back of the map. His writing wasn't very neat. Several scrawled letters appeared at the edge of the paper.

They can hear us.

Yutaka's face twitched and asked, "Really? How can you tell?" Shinji quickly put his hand over Yutaka's mouth. Yutaka understood and nodded.

Shinji released his hand and said, "I just know. I know a lot about insects. That one wasn't poisonous." Then just to be sure, he scribbled again, *Pretend to check map. Don't say anything to make them suspicious.*

"Well, now that the computer's failed, there's nothing we can do," Shinji said, providing some fake commentary. Then he wrote: *They heard my explanation and cut the Mac connection. I screwed up. They know some of us are going to resist so they're monitoring our conversation. Should have known.*

Yutaka took out his pencil from his pocket and wrote under Shinji's scrawled letters. His writing was much neater than Shinji's.

How can they use a monitoring devise on such a big island? He had copied Shinji's spelling for monitoring, but "device" was spelled incorrectly. Whatever. This wasn't composition class.

"So I think we should look for others. We can't do much on our own. So…" Shinji said as he lightly tapped on his collar with his finger. Yutaka's eyes widened as he nodded.

Shinji then scribbled again: *I checked your collar. It doesn't seem to have a camera. Only listening device. I don't think they're any cameras in the area. Maybe satallites, but the woods are covering us. They can't see what we're doing now.* Spelling wasn't Shinji's strongest suit either.

Yutaka's eyes widened again, and he glanced upward. The branches were swaying, cutting them off completely from the blue sky.

Yutaka's face then stiffened suddenly as if he'd realized something. He gripped his pencil and wrote on the back of the map: *Mac stopped working because you told me about it. If not for me, you would have succeeded!*

Shinji poked Yutaka's shoulder with the index finger of his left hand and smiled at him. Then he scribbled: *Don't sweat it. Should have been more careful. Collars could have gone off the moment they heard, but they're "mercifully" letting us live.*

Yutaka touched the nape of his neck, eyes wide. He stared at Shinji and then tightened his lips and nodded. Shinji nodded back at him.

"I wonder where they're hiding out—"

I'm writing my plan here. Fake our conversation. Just go with the flow.

Yutaka nodded and then quickly responded, "Hmm, but I'm not sure we can trust anyone."

Good going. Shinji grinned. Yutaka grinned back.

"That's true. I think we can trust Shuya. I want to hook up with Shuya."

If comp worked we could have saved others but now we can only worry about saving ourselves. All right with that?

Yutaka considered it and then wrote, *Not looking for Shuya?*

Right. Can't afford to worry about others anymore.

Yutaka bit his lip, but finally nodded.

Shinji nodded back. *If this works out, game will get held up. Might give others chance to escape.*

Yutaka gave two small nods.

"You think everyone's hiding in the mountain like us? Maybe some of them are hiding in houses?"

"Maybe…"

Shinji was deliberating over what to write next when Yutaka wrote, *What's the plan?*

Shinji nodded and gripped his pencil. *I've been waiting for something to happen since morning.* Yutaka tilted his head, his pencil down. *Announcement that game has been canseled. I'm still waiting.*

Yutaka looked surprised and tilted his head in bewilderment. Shinji grinned at him.

When I got access to school comp, I found all backup files. And file search apps. Then before I downloaded, I infected them all with virus.

Yutaka silently formed the word "virus?" with his mouth. Hey, Yutaka, how about writing it out?

Shinji wrote, *Virus would enter school comp system if they search files or backups. Would wreak havoc on the system and freeze game.*

Impressed, Yutaka gave several brief nods. Shinji knew it was a waste of time, but wrote it out anyway, *I designed virus. It's cool. It's like getting athlete's foot, but 100x worse.*

Yutaka held back the urge to laugh, but gave a broad grin.

It'll destroy all data and play "The Star Spangled Banner" on repeat. It'll drive em crazy.

Yutaka held his stomach, doing his best not to laugh, and pressed his hand against his mouth. Shinji also did his best not to burst out laughing.

Now they've discovered me, maybe they won't get those files. Then game will have to stop. But it hasn't. So they've only done routine checks. I didn't go through any main files.

"Why don't we go find them then?"

"Isn't that dangerous?"

"Yeah, but we have a gun."

My plan: make them get files. Will activate virus.

Shinji pulled his laptop over and showed Yutaka the document he'd been looking over. It was a 42-line text file.

The data download had been interrupted, but of all the copied files this was the most important one. The horizontal text. Each row began with a listing on the left, from "M01" to "M21," followed by "F01" to "F21," in succession. Each listing was accompanied by a ten-digit number resembling a phone number, all in succession as well. Finally there were what appeared to be random sixteen-digit numbers. A small comma was inserted between these three listings. The file name at the heading was cryptic.

"guadalcanal-shiroiwa3b"

What's this? Yutaka wrote.

Shinji nodded. *These are the #'s assigned to our collars.*

Yutaka gave a huge nod as if to say, Oh. So "M01" was Male Student No. 1 (Yoshio Akamatsu), and "F01" was Female Student No. 1 (Mizuho Inada, that weird girl).

Collars are like cell phones. Each band has a number and password. Use numbers to set them off. So

Shinji stopped and looked at Yutaka. Then he continued

If data's infected with virus we won't have to worry about collars blowing us up. Virus will keep spreading. If they have backup files they can't stop it. If they reprogram to stop virus we'll be in trouble, but it will still buy us time.

"How about tossing pebbles at certain places to see if someone comes running out?"

"Wait, what if it's a girl? She might scream. That could be dangerous, not just to us, but the girl. I mean, assuming she's not 'bad.' "

"Huh."

How will you make them do it?

Outside school building did you see room for SDF?

Yutaka nodded.

Computers in there, remember?

Yutaka's eyes opened wide again as he shook his head. *I*

couldn't afford to.

Shinji chuckled a little. *I got a good look. They have a row of desktop computers and large server. Someone stuck out though. It was an ensine.* Or was it "ensign"? Forget it. *He had a pin on his uniform. He was the tech. A computer runs this whole game. All we have to do is attack the school so they think we might* ugh, another word I can't spell *aniyulate their data. We need to get materials we can actually blow up the entire computer. So*

Shinji stopped writing. He spread his hands with the exaggerated motion of a magician. Then he wrote on the map

BOMB THE SCHOOL ESCAPE BY SEA

Yutaka's eyes were now bulging. He mouthed the word "Bomb?"

Shinji grinned.

"Maybe we should look for some weapons though. That fork is pretty useless."

"Uh huh. Yeah."

We need gasoline. There's a gas station at the harbor, but we can't get there. There are several cars here though. Maybe have fuel? Worst case use oil. We also need fertilizer.

Yutaka knit his brows, puzzled. Fertilizer?

Shinji nodded and tried to write out the name of the fertilizer compound, but he didn't know how to spell it. He was a casualty of spellcheck. Anyway, what mattered was the molecular formula.

Amoniem nitrate. If we find it, we can make bomb with gasoline.

Shinji pulled out his knife and the tube tied to it. He showed it to Yutaka.

This is a detonater. Too complicated to explain why I have one. I just do.

Yutaka looked thoughtful. Then he wrote *That uncle?*

Shinji grinned and nodded. Yutaka knew because Shinji was always going on and on about his uncle.

Yutaka wrote

How are we going to bomb the school? We can't get near it. Make a giant sling with trees?

Ah ha. Shinji smiled. *No. Not precise enough. Too bad we don't have a bunch of bombs. But we have only one detonater, so we have only 1 chance. Rope and pulley.*

Yutaka opened his mouth as if to say, Oh.

Can't get near school, but can go to mountain area and area on other side of school.

Shinji flipped over the map and indicated the areas to Yutaka. Then he flipped it back over.

Tie rope from flats to mountain. About 300 m. Stretch it tight so we can slide bomb down on pulley. Then cut rope when it's on top of school. My special SLAM DUNK.

Once again impressed, Yutaka nodded enthusiastically.

"It might be best to find weapons during the day."

"Yeah, I think so too. It'll be easier than finding someone."

Let's get to work. There's a pulley by a well I saw. Get gas from cars. Fertilizer and rope? I don't know. Can we find rope that long?

They fell silent, but then Yutaka quickly wrote

Let's go for it.

Shinji nodded and continued

We might kill Sakamochi and soldiers. But all we have to do is make them __think__ *data's damaged. Then* he pointed at his neckband *these can't kill us.*

Then escape by sea?

Shinji nodded.

But I can't swim he looked at Shinji warily.

Shinji interrupted Yutaka's writing and wrote *Full moon tonight. Use tide current. According to my calculations tide will carry us at 6-7 kph. If we swim fast it will take <20 min. to* *reach next island.*

Yutaka's admiration burst beyond the expression in his eyes as he shook his head vigorously.

What about guard ship?

Shinji nodded.

They might find us but because game's run by computers my guess is they will be lax. One ship for each direction is kinda lame. Their weakness. Once computers down they won't know where we are. Guard ship will only be able to chase us on their own. If they have satallites, cameras can't see at night. We don't have to worry about our heads blowing up. We have chance to escape.

It won't be easy.

I have another idea.

Shinji dug into the day pack and pulled out a small transceiver. This was another item he found in someone's house.

I can increase output by customizing. Not hard. At sea I'll send out an SOS.

Yutaka's face beamed. *Some ship will pick us up.*

Shinji shook his head. *No. Government will come at us so we give them false location. We escape in opposite direction.*

Yutaka shook his head. Then he wrote out

SHINJI YOUR AWESOME

Shinji shook his head and smiled.

"All right, then." He looked at his watch. It was already 4 p.m.

"We'll take off in five minutes."

"Uh huh."

Shinji felt worn out from all the handwriting, which he didn't do very often. He tossed his pencil. Like a PC communication log file, the back of the map was filled with letters. (He would have preferred to communicate by laptop, but Yutaka didn't know how to type.)

Then he grabbed the pencil and added

Not a great plan. Our chances are slim. This is all I can think of.
He shrugged and looked at Yutaka.
Yutaka gave him a cheerful smile and wrote
Let's go for it!

22 students remaining

44

On the southern side of the northern mountain, a boy sat on a spot on a slope covered with thick vegetation. He was looking at himself with a mirror he held in his left hand, neatly arranging his pompadour with the comb in his right. Ever since the game began he might have been the only student in class, including the girls, who felt like he could afford to take good care of his hair. But that was only natural. Although he had a thuggish-looking face, he paid an inordinate amount of attention to his personal appearance, and although no one knew exactly why, this boy was known, or no, had been known until now as "Zuki," he was in any case…

Queer.

As for his location, he was at a horizontal distance directly two hundred meters west of where Shinji Mimura and Yutaka Seto were hiding. He was also approximately six hundred meters northwest of the medical facility where Shuya's trio was. In other words, he was right above the farmhouse where Shuya Nanahara had witnessed Kaori Minami get shot by Hirono Shimizu. If he looked up he would have had a clear view of the platform where the bodies of Yumiko Kusaka and Yukiko Kitano were still lying, bathed in the light of the setting sun.

This student arranging his hair had seen the corpses of

Yumiko Kusaka, Yukiko Kitano, as well as that of Kaori Minami. He had actually seen more. Kaori Minami's was the seventh corpse he'd seen.

Ugh, yuck. Leaves stuck in my hair again! Every time I lie down, this happens.

With the pinky of his right hand, the boy brushed the blade of grass from his hair and then looked beyond his own face in the mirror to the woods approximately twenty meters below him.

Ka. Zu. O. Are you asleep?

The boy's thick lips twisted into a smile.

Aren't you being careless? Well, even you could probably never guess that after you'd failed to kill me I'd be following you.

Yes, this queer boy who was holding a mirror and comb was the only member of the "Kiriyama family" who'd escaped Kazuo's massacre by not showing up at the assigned meeting place. And now he, Sho Tsukioka (Male Student No. 14), was the only surviving member of the Kiriyama family. In the shrubbery was Kazuo Kiriyama himself, who'd already finished off six students. For the last two hours Kazuo had remained still, though.

Sho looked back at himself in the mirror, this time checking his complexion as he recalled how Mitsuru would always warn him against referring to Kazuo as "Kazuo-kun." Mitsuru would say something like, "Hey Sho, you have to call the boss, boss." But even bold Mitsuru seemed to have a hard time with a "feminine guy," so as soon as Sho would respond with a casual sidelong glance, saying, "Oh, give me a break. Don't be so picky, it's not very manly," and Mitsuru would just grimace, mumbling and letting it go at that.

Call him boss, huh? Sho thought as he looked over each of his eyes in the mirror. But you ended up getting killed by that so-called boss. You're a fool.

It was true. Sho Tsukioka had been more cautious than Mitsuru. It wasn't as if he had a clear sense of Kazuo the way Mitsuru had imagined right before his death, but Sho had always held the basic belief that betrayals happen all the time. That's how the world is. One could say that, compared to Mitsuru, who was just a good fighter, Sho, who'd seen more of the adult world as a result of going in and out of the gay bar his father ran ever since he was a kid, was more sophisticated.

Instead of heading straight to the southern tip of the island, as Kazuo had requested, Sho moved inward from the coast, weaving his way through the woods. This ended up being a hassle, but it probably only cost him ten more minutes.

He ended up seeing it all from the woods along the beach. Three bodies, two wearing coats and one in her sailor suit, sprawled on the rock stretching out into the ocean across the beach. There was Kazuo Kiriyama, standing quietly in the crevice of the rock, hidden in shadows from the moonlight.

Mitsuru Numai appeared almost immediately. After a brief exchange, he was pummeled by machine gun bullets and left on the rock that was drenched with blood now (its stench even reached Sho)....

Oh my, Sho thought. This is trouble.

By the time he began following Kazuo Kiriyama walking away from the scene, Sho had already decided on his course of action.

To assist him in this course of action, the top candidate was undoubtedly Kazuo Kiriyama. He couldn't hear what Kazuo and Mitsuru were saying to each other, but given how Kazuo had decided to play the game, he was sure Kazuo would be the best. Furthermore, at the very least, Kazuo carried not only a machine gun (was that his supplied weapon or did it belong to one of the three students he had killed?) but also Mitsuru's pistol. No one could win in a direct confrontation with Kazuo now.

Sho had one advantage though, something he knew he was extremely good at. He had a talent for sneaking into places and stealing when no one was looking and was also good at following people. (When he found a boy he liked, he could stalk him endlessly.) A talent to be sneaky—what do you mean sneaky, how dare you?—in all respects. As for the weapon he found in his day pack, it was a Derringer .22 Double High Standard. The cartridge was a magnum, lethal at close range, but not the best gun for a shootout.

So Sho thought, even if Kazuo Kiriyama was going to emerge victorious, he'd have to take on tough guys like Shogo Kawada and Shinji Mimura (definitely my type) who, if they had guns, would probably end up injuring him. And all that fighting should wear him out.

Then...I'll just follow him until the end. At the very end I can just shoot him from behind. The moment he thinks he's finished off the last one, he'll let his guard down and that's when I'll shoot him. Even Kazuo would never suspect someone would be following him, especially me, since I blew him off last night.

That way Sho wouldn't have to sully his hands in this game where you had to kill your classmates off one by one. It wasn't that he felt a strong moral objection to killing them, it was just that, he thought, I don't want to kill innocent kids, it's so vulgar. Kazuo's going to do the killing. I'm just going to stay behind him. He might be killing someone right in front of me, but it's not like I can interfere, that's too dangerous. And so at the very end, I'm going to kill him out of self-defense. I mean, if I don't kill him, he'll kill me. That was his line of thinking.

There was another advantage he had in following Kazuo. If he stayed close to Kazuo, then he wouldn't have to worry much about being attacked. And on the off chance that he was, as long as he dodged the first attack Kazuo would have to respond. All Sho would have to do is flee the scene and Kazuo would take care of the rest. Of course, that would also mean losing track of Kazuo, bringing his plan to an end, so he wanted to avoid this scenario as much as possible.

He decided to maintain a basic distance of twenty meters behind Kazuo. He'd move forward when Kazuo did and stop when Kazuo stopped. There was also the issue of the forbidden zones. Kazuo must have also been considering it, so he'd probably keep a good distance away from the zones. As long as Sho maintained his distance, he should be safe from entering the zones. When Kazuo stopped, he'd check the map to make sure he wasn't in a forbidden zone.

Everything had proceeded according to plan.

Kazuo left the southern tip of the island and after entering several houses in the residential area (probably finding what he was looking for), he decided to head to the northern mountain for some reason and then sat down. In the morning, when he heard the distant gunfire, he looked over there, but decided not to move, perhaps because of the distance. But then a little while later when Yumiko Kusaka and Yukiko Kitano began calling from the peak of the mountain with their megaphone he moved quickly and after making sure no one was responding to their call (now wasn't there another gunshot? Sho believed there was, urging Yumiko and Yukiko to hide. Wow, how wonderful, so there's a real humanitarian out there. He was moved, but not enough to alter his plans) he shot them dead. Then he descended the northern slope. There was another distant gunshot, but he stayed put on this one too. Then, this just happened, just before 3 p.m. he began moving after hearing gunfire on this side of the mountain. But what he (and Sho) found at the source was the dead body of Kaori Minami, lying inside a farm equipment storage shack. Kazuo went down to check the body, probably to go through her belongings, but it looked like someone else had gotten there before them. Then he proceeded to move on—

And now he's in the woods right under me.

Kazuo's plan seemed simple, at least for now. Once he knew where someone was, he'd go there and shoot away. Sho was exasperated by the merciless way he'd killed Yumiko Kusaka and Yukiko Kitano (Kazuo, you have such a plain name but your actions are out of control. And yet my name sounds like a celebrity's, Sho Tsukioka, but I'm just a Plain Jane), but it was pointless to fret over these details. For now he should be happy that Kazuo was completely clueless about his presence.

Kazuo appeared to be resting quietly. He might have been sleeping.

On the other hand Sho couldn't sleep at all, but he felt he was strong in that department as well. Naturally. Girls had more stamina than guys. That's what I read in one of those popular books.

What turned out to be a real drag instead was that he was a heavy smoker. The smell of cigarette smoke, depending on the wind direction, would give him away to Kazuo. No, the sound of his electronic lighter flicking open could be even more fatal.

Sho pulled out his pack of imported Virginia Slims Menthol cigarettes (he liked the name, though of course it was hard to get them in this country, but there were places that carried them, and all he had to do was steal them. He had piles of boxes in his room) and carefully placed the thin cigarette between his lips. He caught a whiff of the faint smell of tobacco leaves and that unique menthol odor and felt mild relief from his withdrawal. He wanted to fill his lungs with smoke—but somehow managed to suppress the urge.

I simply cannot die. There's too much fun waiting for me in my prime.

To distract himself, he lifted the mirror in his left hand and caught a view of his face with the cigarette in his mouth. He tilted his head slightly and examined his sidelong glance.

I am so pretty. On top of that, I'm so smart. It's inevitable I should be the winner of this game. Only the beautiful survive. That's God's—

Out of the corner of his eye, the bushes rustled slightly

Sho quickly removed the cigarette from his mouth and put it into his pocket, along with his mirror. Then he gripped the Derringer and grabbed his day pack with his left hand.

Kazuo Kiriyama's slicked-back head appeared on the edge of the bushes. He looked to his left and right and then northward—directly to the left of Sho—up the slope.

In the shade of the azalea tree covered in pink leaves, Sho raised his brow slightly.

What's he doing?

He heard no gunfire. No strange noise at all. Was there something over there?

Sho looked over there, but saw no movement.

Kazuo emerged from shrubs. He had his day pack on his left shoulder and the machine gun slung over his right shoulder with his hand on its grip. He began climbing the slope, weaving his way in between the trees. He quickly reached Sho's higher position and moved on up. Sho then stood up and began following him.

Not at all in keeping with his large frame, 177 centimeters tall, Sho moved gracefully, like a cat. He carefully maintained the twenty meters behind Kazuo's black school coat that intermittently flashed between the trees. Sho's confidence was justified when it came to this sort of thing.

Kazuo's movement was also very precise and quick. He'd stop in the shade of a tree, check ahead, and where the vegetation got thick, would get on his knees and check underneath before proceeding. The only trouble being that...

...your back's wide open, Kazuo.

They must have covered a hundred meters. The observatory was on the top left. Kazuo stopped there.

The rows of trees in front of him were interrupted by a narrow, unpaved road. It was less than two meters wide, just wide enough for a car.

Oh...this was the path leading up to the peak. We crossed it right before we saw Kaori Minami's body.

On Kazuo's right, where he was looking, there was a space with a bench and a beige prefab toilet. Maybe it was a resting area for climbers on the way to the peak.

Kazuo surveyed the area and then looked behind Sho, but Sho of course had hidden himself away in the shade. Kazuo stepped onto the path and ran up to the toilet. He opened the door and went in. He stuck his head out and looked around again before he closed the door. He left it slightly ajar, maybe just in case he had to escape if something happened.

Oh my. Sho brought his hand to his lips. Oh my. Sho remained crouched, trying hard not to burst into a fit of laughter.

It was true, since Sho had started following him, Kazuo hadn't gone to the bathroom even once. He might have used the toilet in one of the houses he entered before sunrise, but in any case, it'd be impossible to hold it an entire day, so Sho assumed he took care of business hidden in the bushes. (Anyway, that's what Sho did. It was a pain not to make any sound though.) But turned out he was wrong. After all, Kazuo Kiriyama came from a wealthy family. Maybe the thought of going anywhere besides a real toilet was out of the question. He must have remembered seeing this toilet when he passed through here a while ago. That's why he came back here.

That's it, I'm sure. Even Kazuo Kiriyama has to pee. How cute.

He was pissing against the bowl now. Sho could hear it splashing against the bowl. Tee hee. Once again Sho tried hard not to laugh.

Then he remembered something and flipped his wrist over to check his watch. They were near sector D=8, which Sakamochi had announced would turn into a forbidden zone at 5 p.m.

The elegant italic numerals on the women's watch indicated 4:57 p.m. (He'd set his watch to Sakamochi's announcement, so it was accurate.) Sho took out his map and examined the northern mountain area. The mountain road was only marked by a dotted line on the map, and the rest area and public toilet wasn't marked in or outside the lines marking off D=8.

Sho suddenly became tense and unconsciously lifted his hand up to his metallic collar. He suddenly felt the urge to return the way he'd come but—

He looked over at toilet, where the sprinkling sound continued. He shrugged and exhaled lightly.

We're talking about Kazuo Kiriyama here, after all. Even if nature called, he would have checked his position. The reason why he cautiously looked over here before moving out of the bushes where he was hiding was to determine whether the toilet was in D=8 or not. And Sho's position was approximately thirty meters west of the toilet. Kazuo was closer to the zone than he was, so the fact that Kazuo was over there, in other words, meant that he was safe too. That's right. He mustn't lose Kazuo by succumbing to irrational fear. That would ruin his plan.

Sho pulled out the Virginia Slims he'd taken out a moment ago and put it between his lips. Then he looked at the dimming sky. At this time of year, it'd still be another two hours before sundown, but the darkening sky was now tinged with orange from the west, and the tips of several tiny clouds had become bright orange. It was beautiful. Just like me.

The sprinkling continued. Sho grinned again. You must have held it for a long time, Kazuo.

It still continued.

Oh, I really need a smoke. I'd like to take a shower, polish my nails, and mix my favorite screwdriver, and as I sip this drink I'd have a nice relaxing...

It still went on.

Oh geez, I wish he'd stop. Hey, let's wrap it up, come on and let's get to work.

But...it still continued.

That was when Sho finally knit his drooping, thick brows. He took the cigarette out of his mouth and quickly got up. He approached the toilet, moving along the shrubs, and squinted his eyes

The sprinkling sound continued. And the door was left slightly ajar.

Just then a sudden wind blew by, opening the squeaky door. What brilliant timing.

Sho's eyes opened wide.

Inside the toilet a government-supplied water bottle was hanging from the ceiling as it swung in the wind. Kazuo had probably pierced it with a blade because there was a very thin stream of water trickling out, fluttering with the wind.

Sho panicked.

Then he saw the back of a school coat below, weaving

its way through the trees. He saw the unique slicked-back hairstyle which he could recognize even from behind this far away.

Wh-wh-what? Kazuo? But then...hey, but I'm...

As Kazuo disappeared beyond the shrubs, Sho heard a thud. It resembled the sound of a silencer, or a gunshot into a pillow. It was impossible to say whether the sound came from the bomb itself in the government's custom Program collar or from the vibration it made through his body.

Over one hundred meters below, Kazuo Kiriyama didn't even look back as he glanced down at his watch.

Seven seconds past five.

21 students remaining

45

With a brief stir Noriko opened her eyes. It was past 7 p.m. She gazed at the ceiling of the room, now turned dark. Then she looked at Shuya beside her.

Shuya got up a from his seat and removed the damp towel on her forehead. He touched it. Just as it was when he checked last time, her fever was almost gone. Shuya felt a wave of relief. Great. Really.

"Shuya." Noriko's voice was still dazed. "...what time is it?"

"It's past seven. You slept well."

"I..."

Shuya nodded. "Your fever's gone down. Shogo said it probably wasn't from septicemia. It was just a really bad cold. Probably from fatigue."

"I see...." Noriko nodded slowly as if she were also relieved. Then she turned to Shuya. "I'm sorry for all this trouble."

"What are you talking about?" Shuya shook his head. "It's not your fault at all." Then he asked, "Can you eat? We have rice."

Noriko's eyes opened wide. "Rice?"

"Yeah, just hold on. Shogo cooked some." Shuya left the room.

Shogo was sitting on the chair by the window by the kitchen door. The last traces of light, more like particles of blue, closer to indigo, entered the window, but where Shogo was sitting it was almost completely pitch black.

"Noriko's up?"

Shuya nodded.

"How about her fever?"

"She's fine. It seems to be gone."

Shogo gave him a slight nod, then stood up, holding the shotgun as usual. He opened the lid of the pot on the gas stove. Shuya and Shogo had already had their share of cooked rice and miso soup. The miso soup base came from some strange leaves growing in the back of the building.

"Is the food cold?" Shuya asked.

Shogo gave him a brief reply, "Wait five or ten minutes. I'll bring it over."

"Thanks." Shuya returned to the examination room. He sat down by the bed and gave Noriko a small nod. "Wait a little. Shogo's going to bring some real rice."

Noriko nodded. Then she asked, "Is there a bathroom here?"

"Uh…yeah. Over here."

Shuya helped Noriko out of the bed. Supporting her with his arm, he showed her to the bathroom beyond the waiting room. She was still staggering, but she'd definitely recovered from the terrible condition she was in before.

Shuya helped Noriko return to her bed. As Noriko sat

down on the edge of the bed, Shuya wrapped her shoulders with the blanket the way Ms. Anno had done for him at the Charity House when he was a kid.

"Once you've eaten," Shuya said as he pulled at the edges of the blanket, "I think you should get some more sleep. We're going to have to leave this place by 11 p.m."

Noriko stared at Shuya. Her eyes still looked slightly unfocused. "You mean—"

Shuya nodded. "Yeah, this zone's going to be forbidden at eleven."

It was part of the announcement Sakamochi gave at 6 p.m. Other zones included G=1 at 7 p.m. and I=3 at 9 p.m. That meant the southwest border and the southern slope of the southern mountain. Since it was hard to tell exactly where the border of the forbidden zone was, the southwest shore area was all off limits now.

Noriko looked down at her kneecaps and touched her forehead under her bangs. "I was sleeping like an idiot."

Shuya reached out and touched Noriko on the shoulder. "Don't be ridiculous. You were better off sleeping. You need to rest more. Take it easy."

But Noriko glanced up and asked, "Did anyone else— besides Kaori—die?"

Shuya tightened his lips. Then he nodded. "Takako…and Sho and Kazushi."

According to Sakamochi's announcement, these four had died during the six hours after twelve o'clock. Now there were only twenty-one students left. Only eighteen hours had passed since the game began, yet Third Year Class B of Shiroiwa Junior High had been reduced to half its size.

"And one more thing," Sakamochi had said enthusiastically. "Sho Tsukioka was caught in a forbidden zone. So I want you all to be careful."

Sakamochi didn't say where Sho had died, and Shuya

couldn't remember hearing a big explosion in the afternoon. At the same time he couldn't see any reason Sakamochi would lie. That big, boorish-looking guy who oddly enough acted really feminine, "Zuki" of the Kiriyama family, had gotten himself caught in a zone. As a result, his head was blown off. Besides their boss then, the entire Kiriyama family was decimated.

Shuya thought of telling Noriko about this, but after seeing how troubled she looked, he decided not to. He doubted that sharing any news about a guy's head getting blown off would have a good effect on Noriko's recovery.

"I see...." Noriko said quietly and then added, "Thanks for this," and began taking off the coat she'd been wearing.

"Keep it."

"No, I'm all right now."

Shuya took the coat and draped the blanket over her shoulder again.

Shogo came in after a while. Like a waiter, he carried a round tray full of bowls on one hand. Steam rose from the bowls. As he lowered the tray he said, "Here you are, madame."

Shuya chuckled. "So she gets room service?"

"Well, the food isn't exactly first class. I hope it tastes all right though." Shogo put the entire tray on the bed and placed the bowls next to her.

Noriko looked down and asked, "Soup?"

"Yes ma'am," Shogo replied in English, which sounded pretty fluent to Shuya's ears.

"Thanks," Noriko said and took the spoon. She brought the bowl to her lips and swallowed a mouthful. "It's delicious." She raised her voice. "There's egg in it."

Shuya then looked at Shogo.

"It's our special, ma'am."

"Where'd you find that?" Shuya asked. All the fresh food

in the refrigerator was rotten, probably because the government had moved the civilians out a while ago. All the other houses were probably in the same condition.

Shogo looked at Shuya out of the corner of his eye and grinned. "I found a house that kept a hen. It looked like it hadn't been fed in a while and looked pretty weak."

Shuya exaggeratedly shook his head. "When we ate I didn't notice any eggs."

Shogo lifted his brows. "I only found one. Sorry. I'm nicer to girls. That's just how I am."

Shuya laughed, sniggering.

Shogo returned to the kitchen and brought over some tea. Shuya and Shogo drank tea while Noriko ate her meal. The tea had a mild sweetness and a pleasant, nostalgic odor.

"Damn," Shuya groaned. "I feel like everything's fine, the three of us sitting around like this."

Shogo smiled and said, "I'll make some coffee later. Would you prefer tea, Noriko?"

Her spoon still in her mouth, Noriko smiled and nodded.

"Hey, Shogo." Shuya had more to say. Of course the fact was that they were still in this killing game, but now that Noriko seemed to be recovering, he was feeling a little gushy. "Some day the three of us, let's all get together for some tea. We'll sit on the veranda and enjoy the cherry blossoms."

It was highly unlikely. Nonetheless Shogo shrugged his shoulders and said, "I thought you were a rocker. You sound like an old man."

"I know. You're not the first one to tell me that."

Shogo chuckled. Shuya laughed, and so did Noriko.

Noriko finished her meal and said, "Thank you." Shogo gathered her bowls. He signaled with his other hand for Shuya's cup, which Shuya handed over.

"Shogo," Noriko said, "I feel totally fine now. Thank you so much. And I'm so sorry for all the trouble I've caused."

Shogo smiled and replied, "*You're welcome,*" in English. "But it looks like the antibiotic wasn't necessary."

"No. I know this sounds weird, but I think it made me feel secure enough to fall asleep."

Shogo smiled again and added, "Well, you could still be suffering from septicemia. In any case, you should rest a little more. Take it easy." Shogo then said to Shuya, "Do you mind if I catch some sleep?"

Shuya nodded. "You tired?"

"No, not really, but it's best to sleep when you can. Once we leave here, I'll stay up through the night. Is that all right?"

"Yeah sure, that's fine."

Shogo nodded, took the tray, and headed towards the hall.

"Shogo, you should sleep here," Noriko said, signaling towards the bed next to hers.

Shogo glanced back at her from the door and smiled as if saying, no thank you. "I don't want to intrude on you two. I'll sleep on the sofa in this room." He tilted his head in that direction and added, "Please be considerate to your neighbors though if you get intimate."

In the dim room Shuya could see Noriko's face flush.

Shogo then left the room. Beyond the half opened door, Shuya heard him walk out of the kitchen and into the waiting room. It became quiet.

Noriko broke into a smile and said, "Shogo's so funny."

Perhaps it was because of the meal, her face seemed more animated.

"Yeah, he is," Shuya smiled too. "I'd never talked to him until now, but he kind of reminds me of Shinji."

They didn't resemble each other at all physically, but Shogo's crude and blunt speech and his ability to still be humorous through it all resembled The Third Man. Not to mention the way he was the anti-model student and yet managed to be incredibly smart and reliable.

Noriko nodded. "You know you're right. Totally." Then Noriko uttered, "I wonder where Shinji is."

Shuya took a deep breath. He'd been wondering whether there was any way to contact him, but given Noriko's condition he couldn't afford to do anything.

"Yeah, if he were only with us…"

With Shinji along and with Shogo on their side, Shuya thought they couldn't be defeated. And if Hiroki Sugimura were with them they would be fearless and invincible.

"I still remember the class match," Noriko said as she glanced up at the ceiling. "Not this year's, but last year's…the finals. Shinji was on his own against Class D, who had four students on the basketball team. We were thirty points behind, but then you rushed over after your softball game, and together you two guys started an incredible comeback."

"Yeah." Shuya nodded. He noticed how Noriko was becoming talkative. That was a good sign. "I guess that's what happened."

"I was cheering you guys on. When we won Yukie was on her feet shrieking."

"Yeah."

Shuya remembered too. Because Noriko, who was always reserved, was cheering the loudest. And although he wasn't as uncoordinated as Yoshio Akamatsu, the unathletic Yoshitoki Kuninobu was standing apart from Noriko and the others. Shuya saw Yoshitoki, his hands waving and making devil signs. It was a humble gesture, but Yoshitoki's display of support moved Shuya more than Noriko and the other girls' screaming rally.

Yoshitoki…

Shuya gazed back at Noriko, and then realized that Noriko was crying. He reached over to Noriko, touching her shoulder, and asked, "What's wrong?"

"Uh…" Noriko hiccuped slightly. "I was telling myself

not to cry, but…then I was thinking how wonderful our class was.…"

Shuya nodded. It might have been from the still lingering fever, or it might have been from the drugs, but Noriko seemed to be in an emotional state. He kept his hand on her shoulder until she stopped crying.

Eventually Noriko said, "I'm sorry," and wiped her eyes. Then she said, "I didn't tell you because it might end up disturbing you."

"What do you mean?"

Noriko looked into Shuya's eyes. "Did you know a lot of girls have a crush on you?"

The topic of conversation was so unexpected Shuya couldn't help grimacing. "What are you talking about?"

But Noriko continued, her face dead serious. "Megumi…and Yukiko too, I think."

Shuya tilted his head as if puzzled. Megumi Eto and Yukiko Kitano. Two of the players no longer in the running in this game.

"Those…" Was it proper to call them "those"? "What about those two?"

Noriko looked up at Shuya and said quietly, "They both had a crush on you."

Shuya's face stiffened. He hesitated and then mumbled, "…really?"

"Uh huh." Noriko looked away from Shuya and nodded. "It's easy to tell with girls. I just…wanted you to have fond thoughts for them." She added, "I am in no position to be telling you this now, given the situation I'm in."

Shuya had a dim image of the faces of Megumi Eto and Yukiko Kitano. Just a little though. Like, two teaspoons each. "Wow…" He exhaled. Then he said, "I wish you'd told me after we escaped."

"I'm sorry. Did it shock you?

"Yeah, a little."

Noriko tilted her head again, "But...I thought you should know in case I die."

Shuya looked up. His right hand squeezed her left wrist. "Look, please don't assume that. We're in this together till the end. We're going to survive together."

Noriko was taken aback by Shuya's sudden intensity. "I'm sorry."

"Hey."

"Hm?"

"I actually know someone who's got a crush on you."

Now it was Noriko's turn to open her eyes wide. "Really? Why me?" She said this innocently, but the expression on her face vanished quickly. Shuya saw the fading light from the window reflected as an obscure rectangle in her pupils. She asked, "Is he a classmate?"

Shuya slowly shook his head. As he recalled those warm, bulging eyes, he thought, damn, how nice and peaceful it would have been just to be able to get worried over a romantic triangle involving a longtime friend. But that would never happen. No siree. It just won't.

"No."

Noriko looked somewhat relieved as she looked down at the knees of her skirt and only mumbled, "I see." Then she looked up and said, "So who could it be? I wasn't in any clubs or teams. And I don't have friends in any of the other classes."

Shuya shook his head. "I'm not telling. I'll tell you once we're out of here."

Noriko looked slightly skeptical, but didn't pursue the matter.

After they fell silent for a while Shuya looked up at the ceiling. Even though tidiness was mandatory in a clinic, the fluorescent light hanging here had dusty covers. The lights didn't work. They couldn't turn them on anyway even if they did.

"Megumi-san...," he said. He added the polite "san" to her name. Boys can be so fickle. "...and Yukiko-san. If it's true...what could they have possibly liked about me?"

It was becoming pitch black, but Noriko appeared to be smiling a little. "You mind if I share my opinion?"

"Sure."

Noriko tilted her head. "Everything about you."

Shuya chuckled and shook his head, "What do you mean?"

"That's what it means to love someone." Noriko's suddenly sounded serious. "Isn't that how you feel about that girl?"

Shuya thought of Kazumi Shintani's face. He thought about it. He hesitated, but thought he should be honest. "Yeah. Something like that."

"If it's not, then it's not real," Noriko said as if she were amused and then let out a quiet laugh.

"What?"

"I'm jealous. Even in this situation, it's still hard."

Shuya looked at her face that was no longer discernible in the dark and hesitated whether he should tell her, but then decided he should be honest with her.

"I can relate to the guy who had a crush on you though."

Noriko looked up at Shuya. Her well-defined brows seemed to quiver slightly. Her lips seemed to be forming a slightly melancholic smile.

"You're so wonderful," Shuya said.

"That's nice to hear even if it's not true."

"But it is."

"Can I ask you a favor?"

Shuya opened his eyes wide as if asking, "What is it?" but he wasn't sure whether Noriko could see his reaction. Noriko then leaned over slightly and gently put both of her hands on Shuya's upper arms, putting her head against his shoulder. Her shoulder-length short hair brushed up against Shuya's cheeks and ears.

They remained like this for quite some time until the dimness outside the window turned into moonlight.

21 students remaining

46

Before the dusk turned to darkness, Hirono Shimizu (Female Student No. 10) emerged from the thicket she'd been hiding in and proceeded west. It was unbearable. Her body was on fire as if she were walking in a desert under a burning sun.

Water.

She needed water.

Kaori Minami had shot her in the upper left arm. After tearing open the sleeve of her sailor suit drenched in blood, she discovered the bullet had penetrated her arm. The skin on the exit wound was torn up badly. It seemed the bullet had barely missed the major blood vessels. The torn sleeve she wrapped around her arm as a bandage seemed to have stopped the bleeding for a while. But then…the wound started to burn and the sensation spread all over her body. The initial chill was replaced by a numbing heat. By the time Sakamochi made his announcement at 6 p.m. Hirono had finished off her entire supply of water. After she killed Kaori she ran approximately two hundred meters away from Shuya and hid in the thicket, but she ended up using a lot of water in her attempt to clean her wound (which she ended up deeply regretting).

Almost two hours had passed since then. For a while she'd

been sweating profusely underneath her uniform, but now she wasn't sweating at all. Most likely she was approaching dehydration. In other words, unlike Noriko Nakagawa, Hirono was actually suffering from septicemia. And because she hadn't disinfected her wound, it came on quickly. Of course she had no way of knowing any of this.

The only thing she knew was that she needed...water.

As she cautiously moved through the green woods of the mountain, Hirono's head spun with thoughts of hatred towards Kaori Minami. Her burning body and thirst only intensified these thoughts.

Hirono Shimizu had no intention of trusting anyone in this game. Of course she'd been tight with Mitsuko Souma forever, and according to student number she immediately preceded Mitsuko. So if she'd managed to avoid Hiroki Sugimura, who came in between their departures, she could have met up with Mitsuko, but she chose not to. Because she knew how terrifying Mitsuko really was. That's right...like when Mitsuko took on a bad-girl leader from another school (who'd by then become the mistress of a yakuza gangster). That girl ended up getting run over by a car. The injury was nearly fatal. Mitsuko didn't say anything about it, but Hirono knew Mitsuko had some guy do it. There were plenty of guys willing to do anything for Mitsuko....

If Hirono had decided to meet up with Mitsuko, Mitsuko would have probably used her as much as possible only to finally shoot her in the back. Even though she was part of the group too, the somewhat clueless Yoshimi Yahagi might trust Mitsuko (which reminded her of how Yoshimi was dead, and Hirono had a hunch that Mitsuko was the one who killed her), but Hirono was having none of that.

She couldn't imagine trusting anyone else in her class. The ones who acted nice were the ones that wouldn't think twice about killing the others now. She might have only been fifteen years old, but those fifteen years had taught her that much.

At the same time though she wasn't too thrilled about killing off her classmates. She'd done prostitution and drugs, and she constantly fought with her parents who treated her like a lost cause, but murder was taboo. Of course the rules of the game permitted it, so it wasn't a crime here—but while she'd done some bad things, they were never all that harmful towards others. Even though she'd prostituted herself, compared to other girls who pretended to be proper at the same time that they "phone-dated" (she knew Mayumi Tendo was one of those), at least she went the whole nine yards working with professionals through her connection with Mitsuko Souma. As for drugs, what was wrong with asserting her individual freedom to choose? And it wasn't like she was putting the mall's cosmetics department out of business by stealing stuff from there. They have huge capital backing anyway....Yes, she bullied others around, but they deserved it. And as far as her fights with students from other schools, they all knew they were out to hurt each other and what they were in for. I mean, come on, grow up. In any case, she was...

...not the kind of girl who'd go around murdering people. She knew that much.

But, but...

...it was different if she had to defend herself. And if she ended up surviving in this game...then she'd open a bottle of champagne to celebrate. Or if time ran out and she died then...her thoughts weren't very clear on this matter...anyway there was nothing she could do about that.

So she ended up hiding out in that house where she later had that shootout with Kaori Minami.

Once she'd checked it out and saw no one was there, she stayed there. Occasionally she'd look out the window, and once, much to her dismay, she caught a glimpse of someone in the shack across from the building where she was staying.

After several minutes she decided to leave the house (she was good at leaving home). She couldn't stand the thought of someone being near her. There was no back entrance, so she climbed out the window furthest from the shack when...

Kaori was looking out the door of the shack. She suddenly fired at Hirono, who'd done nothing. Kaori's shot hit Hirono's arm, and Hirono nearly rolled outside onto the ground. She somehow managed to get on her feet, and for the first time aimed her pistol and fired back. Then as she remained glued to the wall of the edge of the house...that was when Shuya Nanahara appeared.

That bitch. She was always acting so innocent with her blind devotion to idol groups, and then all of a sudden she has the nerve to pull the trigger on me. Well, I was able to finish her off. (In self defense. The jury's verdict would have been 12-0, no prob.) And if the others are anything like her then I'll have to be merciless, I think.

Then Hirono thought of Shuya Nanahara. At least Shuya didn't point his gun at her (which enabled her to shoot at Kaori). He also claimed he was with Noriko.

Shuya Nanahara and Noriko Nakagawa. Were they going out? Never seemed that way. Are they going to try to escape?

Hirono automatically shook her head.

Ridiculous. Nothing could be more risky than being with someone under these circumstances. If you're in a group, well then, that's just your own fault if you get shot in the back. Besides, it was impossible to escape anyway.

Hirono didn't see Noriko Nakagawa, but if he was telling her the truth, then Shuya Nanahara would soon be killing Noriko Nakagawa. Or perhaps Noriko Nakagawa would be killing Shuya Nanahara. If one of them ended up surviving...then Hirono might end up having to kill one of

them. But right now that didn't matter compared to her…
…thirst.

Before she knew it she had covered a fair distance. The dim sunlight in the western sky was gone. The sky up above was now jet black and the full moon just like last night when the game began shone eerily, casting a pale blue light on this island.

She held onto the revolver that had killed Kaori Minami, a Smith & Wesson Military & Police .38, and ran through the bushes. She held her head low with bated breath. Then she slowly peered out of the bushes. There was a house standing beyond a narrow farm. Hirono was near the northern mountain. There was a foothill on the other side of the house. On the left there were several farms and further beyond two more similar houses. Then the land sloped upward to the southern mountain. According to the map, in front of that mountain there was supposed to be a relatively wide longitudinal road that traversed the island. So given the position of the mountains Hirono was probably near the island's western shore. Just as she had done before moving, she checked her position and was pretty certain she wasn't in a forbidden zone.

Hirono did her best to forget about her thirst and observed the house in front. The area was completely still and silent.

She remained crouched and crossed the farm. The area around the house seemed slightly elevated above the farm. Hirono stopped at the edge of the farm and after looking back she observed the house again. It was your average, old, single-story farmhouse. But unlike the previous house she'd hid inside, the roof was tiled. An unpaved road came in from the left side of the farm. There was a light truck parked in front of the house. She also saw a moped and bicycle.

The water at the first house Hirono hid in wasn't running.

This one was probably no different. Hirono looked to her right and left…

…and found a well at the far end of the area from the entrance road. It even had a beam holding a bucket. There were thin tangerine trees with plenty of leaves surrounding the well. Their branches were high, so she could tell there was no one hiding under the trees.

Since she couldn't use her left hand, she tucked her gun in the front. Then she groped around the farm soil under the moonlight. She found a fist-sized rock.

She tossed it upward. Tracing an arc, the rock crashed against the roof. It rattled down the rows of tiles and fell off the edge onto the ground with a thud.

Hirono gripped the gun and waited. She checked her watch. Then she waited again.

Five minutes passed. No one appeared at the windows or entrance. Hirono quickly stepped up to the property and ran toward the well. Her head was spinning from thirst and fever.

The well was a concrete tube approximately eighty centimeters high. Hirono clutched the brim of the well.

Inside it, the moonlight revealed a small circle six to seven meters down. Her own shadow was also reflected inside the circle.

It was water. Ah, it wasn't dry.

Once again Hirono tucked her revolver into her skirt and removed her day pack from her aching left shoulder with her right hand. It landed on the dirt. Then she held the worn out rope hanging from the bucket beam.

As she pulled the rope, a small bucket appeared on the surface of the water. Hirono frantically tugged at the rope. The bucket beam was equipped with what looked like an ancient pulley which allowed you to retrieve water with two buckets. Her left arm was too numb to move, but with every pull she held the rope against the concrete edge of the well with her elbow and managed to pull the bucket upward.

The bucket finally reached the edge of the well. She held the rope with her elbow once more, grabbed the handle of the bucket, and placed it on the edge of the well. It was water. The bucket was brimming with water. She didn't care if it ended up making her sick. Her body needed water now.

But then she discovered something and let out a small shriek.

There was a tiny fingernail-sized frog swimming in the water. In the moonlight she saw its small, gross eyes and its glistening back. (In broad daylight, their color would have been an disgusting fluorescent green, or a dirty brown.) It was her least favorite animal, and the mere sight of one with its slimy skin was enough to send chills down her spine.

But Hirono did her best to quell her disgust. She didn't have the strength to pull the bucket up again. Her thirst was unbearable now. She would have to get rid of that frog, and then—

The frog climbed onto the edge of the bucket and leapt onto Hirono. Hirono let out a small shriek and twisted her body. So what if this was a matter of life or death. She just couldn't stand frogs. She somehow managed to dodge the frog—but her right hand let go of the bucket, which suddenly fell back into the well with a splash—and that was that.

Hirono groaned and looked over in the direction of the frog. I'll kill it. I'll kill that fucking frog!

But then…something else caught her eye.

She saw a black figure in a student coat stop a mere four or five meters in front of her.

Hirono's back had been facing the house. Now she saw the back door behind the figure was ajar.

With the figure frozen in its footsteps, Hirono suddenly recalled a childhood memory—the game where you have to freeze when the person who was "it" turns around—but that was irrelevant. The issue at stake was that this thin, short, ugly boy—come to think of it, he also resembled a frog—Toshinori Oda (Male Student No. 4) was holding a thin, ribbonlike object with both hands. Hirono realized it was a belt.

Now look at this. Toshinori Oda, the privileged son of a company president whose house was located in the town's wealthy district. He was supposed to be good at violin (apparently he'd won some competition). A pretentious, well bred, quiet boy. And this kid was now...

...trying to kill me!

As if the pause on a frozen video image had been suddenly released, Toshinori moved, swung his belt up, and attacked her. The large buckle sparkled in the moonlight. It could easily gouge out some flesh on impact. The distance between them was only four meters....

Enough.

Hirono's right hand went for her gun. She felt the grip, by now a familiar sensation.

Toshinori was right in front of her. She fired. She fired three times in a row.

All the shots landed in his stomach. She saw his school coat instantaneously rip apart.

Toshinori spun around and fell face forward. Dust flew up into the air and he remained motionless.

Hirono tucked the revolver into her skirt again. The hot barrel burned against her stomach, but she couldn't be concerned about that. Right now the important thing was...water.

She picked up her day pack and entered the house. She'd been foolish exposing her back to the house, but now she no longer had to make sure it was unoccupied. And she could drink Toshinori's water.

She deliberated over whether to use her flashlight, but Toshinori's day pack turned out to be located right behind the back door. Hirono crouched down and opened the zipper with her right hand.

There were water bottles. One of them hadn't been opened and the other was still half full. She felt a wave of relief.

Still on her knees, Hirono opened the lid of the half filled bottle and pressed her lips against it, sucking on it as she tilted the bottle back. Hmm. Was this an indirect kiss with the boy who had tried to kill her—who was, on top of that, dead? Didn't matter. Concerns like that were now as remote as the tropics or the north pole. Or the moon. This is Armstrong. One small step for a man...

She guzzled the water down. It was delicious. No doubt about that. Water never tasted this good. Even though the water was lukewarm, as it gushed down her throat and into her stomach it felt like ice water. It was so good.

She emptied the bottle almost immediately. She took a deep breath.

Something wrapped around her throat. Right above the metal collar. She went into a coughing fit and a mist of water sprayed out between her lips.

As she struggled with her functioning right hand to free herself from the object digging in under her throat, she twisted her head around. Immediately to the right of her face she saw the boy's tense face...which belonged to Toshinori Oda, the boy who just died!

Her throat was getting choked. It took her several seconds to realize what was wrapped around her neck. It was Toshinori's belt.

How how how—how could this guy be alive?

The dark interior of the house was fading into red. She tried to pry the belt loose with her right hand as her fingernails tore off. Blood dripped out of her fingers.

That's right, my gun.

Hirono reached for her gun tucked in the front of her skirt.

But her arm was kicked by the foot of an expensive leather shoe, making a cracking sound. Along with her left arm, her right one went numb too. The belt slackened for a moment—but then it tightened again. She couldn't hold the belt anymore and instead she swung her twisted arm around in a bizarre looking manner.

It was only a matter of seconds. Her arm hung limply. Although she wasn't in the same rank as Takako Chigusa or Mitsuko Souma, she was still quite attractive and she had the appealing, mature look of a high school or college student. But now her face was puffed up from blood congestion, and her tongue was now twice its normal size and hung out from the middle of her mouth.

Nonetheless, Toshinori Oda continued choking Hirono's throat. (Of course he didn't forget to check around occasionally.)

After five minutes or so, Toshinori finally released the belt from Hirono's neck. The breathless Hirono fell forward onto the raised floor. There was a muffled cracking sound. Maybe part of Hirono's face had cracked. Her punkish hair that stood straight up was now going in all directions and fading into the darkness. The nape of her neck above the collar of her sailor suit and her left arm with the torn sleeve were the only parts glimmering white.

Toshinori Oda breathed heavily for a while as he stood still in a daze. His stomach was still in pain, but it wasn't too bad now. When he first opened his day pack he had no idea what this cumbersome strange gray vest was, but it did exactly what the manual said it would. Amazing...

...what a bulletproof vest can do.

20 students remaining

47

The area was pitch black by now, but thanks to the nearly full moon, the cliff extending from the foot of the northern mountain offered a wide open view of the ocean. The Seto Inland Sea Islands floated in the black sea, but there were absolutely no ship lights nearby due to the government's prohibition on traffic in the area. The guard ships were also out of sight, probably because they were moored with their lights off.

He'd seen this view before, but from a lower position. That's right, when he left the school building. Of course, this was neither the time nor place to call it a nice view.

"All right then, over here," Shinji said. He tucked his gun into his belt, and was the first to climb up on the rock. Then he offered his hand to Yutaka. Yutaka was out of breath due to the climb up the mountain as well as from the looming threat of being attacked in the dark, but he managed to grip onto Shinji's hand and struggled up the rock.

They stayed flat on their stomachs and looked down the cliff.

The blackened rows of woods spread out beneath them, and further beyond there was a glimmer of light. It came from the school building where Sakamochi was. It hardly emitted any light because the windows had been sealed off with those steel sheets. It was approximately one hundred meters away. The school's sector, G=7, was already forbidden, so they'd immediately get killed if they entered it, but they were a safe distance away now. By using cross-bearing navigation with his compass and map before the sun went down, Shinji managed to figure out precisely the zone layout. The school, in sector G=7, was nearer the border of F=7, where Shinji and Yutaka were now, and according to the map the shortest distance to the border was approximately eighty meters. Furthermore, with the 6 p.m. announcement of forbidden zones, neither F=7 nor H=7, which surrounded the school, were included.

Which reminded him of Sakamochi's announcement that Sho Tsukioka had gotten caught in a forbidden zone. He was an annoying, queer kid ("Shinji, let's go out on a date"), and right now Shinji really couldn't be bothered by others, but he felt a little sorry for Sho whose head had probably been blown off by a bomb. He wondered where it happened.

He also felt a pang of remorse over the death of Takako Chigusa. She was the prettiest girl in the class (according to Shinji's taste, anyway), and what's more, she was childhood friends with Hiroki Sugimura. Contrary to what most of the class thought—that they were a couple—Hiroki and Takako weren't going out (Hiroki himself told Shinji). Still, it must have come as a shock to Hiroki.

Hiroki—where the hell are you?

Shinji decided to concentrate on the present. He observed the school below and its surrounding geography closely. They would have to stretch a rope from here, over the school, and then over to the other side of the zone. Now that he actually had a view of the area, he realized how much distance they'd have to cover.

Gazing at the gentle light leaking out the steel-plated windows, Shinji thought, damn. That was where Sakamochi and his men were. It was dinner time. For all he knew they could be eating fried udon. (He thought of fried udon because it was his favorite ever since his uncle made it several times for him when he had him over at his small single-bedroom house and that was what Shinji wanted so badly to eat right now.) Bastards.

Shinji and Yutaka already had what they needed.

Although it wasn't indicated on the map (which marked it as just another blue dot), Shinji managed to find a farm coop near the longitudinal road slightly south of the school. The building with slated roof and walls bore a sign that read

"Northern Takamatsu Agricultural Cooperative Association, Okishima Island Branch." (Although Shinji already knew they were on Okishima Island in the Takamatsu-shi Sound, Yutaka was impressed.) It wasn't your typical farm coop. It had no real office, nor were there any ATMs. There was only a tractor, combine harvester, and threshing machine scattered inside the warehouse-like space. The only other equipment they found was an office desk taking up one of the corners. Anyway, that was where they found the ammonium nitrate. Fortunately it was fresh, not at all damp. On top of that, they didn't have to collect gas from cars. They found plenty in the gas containers.

The pulley they took from the well next to the house where Shinji had found the Macintosh PowerBook 150, slightly east of the coop.

The other significant item was rope. If they were going to stretch rope across sector G=7 they would need at least three hundred meters of it. Furthermore, they would have to roll it out with plenty of slack to escape detection by Sakamochi and his men so they needed even more. It wasn't going to be easy finding rope that long. The farm coop had rope but all together it was at most two hundred meters long and— maybe it was used for a greenhouse or something—too thin at a diameter of less than three millimeters to be reliable.

Fortunately though, they managed to find what appeared to be a private fishing-equipment warehouse along the shore south from the harbor, which was now forbidden along with the residential area. In spite of the fishing rope being weathered out from exposure, in spite of its heavy weight and size, given how it was over three hundred meters long, Shinji and Yutaka managed to divide it up, transport it, and hide it in the farm coop.

Leaving these resources behind, they came up here.

Shinji stared into the dark. The foot of the northern

mountain, where they were now, spread out around this side of the school, in other words, the north side, and his right, the west side. To the left of the school, the woods on the east extended up to the northern side of the residential area and the seashore. Beyond the school there were paddy fields. There were clusters of trees here and there, and between them he could see some houses. Beyond the houses, Shinji could barely make out the farm coop warehouse where they had left all their equipment. Immediately to the left the area became gradually crowded with rows of roofs that extended over the border of the forbidden zone into the residential area.

Yutaka tapped him on the shoulder. Shinji looked to Yutaka, who was on his right. Yutaka pulled out his student notepad and began writing something.

That's right, before they started moving, Shinji had warned Yutaka with another message that they mustn't give anything away by talking. After all, if Sakamochi and his men found out they were up to no good again, this time Shinji was sure they wouldn't hesitate to blow their heads off by remote control.

He'd already gone over why Sakamochi chose not to ignite Shinji and Yutaka's collars. It was probably because it was best for the game if *the students fought each other as much as possible*. Shinji had some theories about this. It had to do with a rumor he'd heard that high-ranking government officials placed bets on this game. If that was true, then he was sure the star shooting guard of Shiroiwa Junior High, The Third Man, must have been the top seed. All the more reason why Sakamochi couldn't just finish him off. That was Shinji's hypothesis. Meanwhile Yoshitoki Kuninobu and Fumiyo Fujiyoshi were irrelevant players. Or, to be blunt, no one had placed any bets on them.

Still, even if that were true (what a bastard that "Kinpati

Sakamocho" was), as long as Sakamochi was in charge of this game, he could blow their heads off at any time. Shinji could only pray that wouldn't happen until they managed to bomb the school. Of course Shinji found the idea despicable. The thought of someone else having so much control over him was entirely revolting to Shinji, who learned from his uncle how to be totally self-reliant for everything in his life.

As he looked down at the light from the school though, he shook his head. That was neither here nor there.

He recalled his uncle once telling him, "Don't worry about stuff you can't do anything about. You do what you can even if your chances of success are less than one percent."

Yutaka seemed done writing his message and tapped his shoulder. Shinji turned away from the view and examined the note under the moonlight.

There's no way we can toss that enormous rope over there. Besides we left the rope behind. What are we going to do?

That's right. He hadn't explained that yet. They'd been too frantic in their search for the equipment. Shinji nodded, took out his pencil, and wrote on the student notepad *Wire. I brought some. We'll reel out the wire down to the other side and tie it to the rope. Then we'll draw in the rope by pulling the wire right before we execute our plan.*

He handed the pad over to Yutaka. After reading the note, he looked at Shinji and nodded, as if satisfied. Then he wrote *You're going to tie a rock to the wire and throw it over there?*

Shinji shook his head. Yutaka opened his eyes, surprised. Then after some thought he wrote again *Are you going to make a bow and arrow and shoot the wire across?*

Shinji shook his head again. He took the pad and began scribbling *That might work. But even I can't throw a rock 300m away. And I can't afford to miss. If the rock hits the school we're done. And if the wire gets caught somewhere and we end up breaking it…I have a better plan.*

Yutaka didn't take up his pencil this time and only gazed back at Shinji as if saying, "?" Shinji took the pad and continued *First, tie the wire to a tree here. Then go down the mountain with the other end of wire. Stretch it taut when we're on the other side.*

Yutaka read this but then almost immediately knit his brows skeptically. He wrote quickly, *You can't do that* his note read *It'll get caught in the trees. Somewhere in the middle.*

Shinji grinned.

He couldn't blame Yutaka for doubting him. The path they'd taken here was covered with trees, both large and small. Even if they managed to drag the wire out while avoiding G=7 and tugged on it later, the wire might get caught. It would make for an odd-looking piece of outdoor contemporary art. "This installation piece is gigantic, but five meters away it turns obscure. The piece addresses the delicate balance between nature and humans...." On top of that, sector G=7 was filled with dense forestry bordering up to the school. Unless you were a 100-meter-tall giant (wasn't there a video his uncle had shown him, an old special-effects movie where the superhero saves the world by fighting against monsters as they completely tear up the city? They don't make movies like that anymore) you'd have to cut down all the trees if you wanted to put the wire near the school. It was so obvious. And that was why Yutaka insisted it was impossible.

But Shinji elegantly spread his arms out (given how they were on their stomachs though, the effect wasn't so impressive) and wrote *How about launching an ad balloon, huh, Yutaka?*

Yutaka read the note and knit his brows. Shinji signaled Yutaka to get off the cliff rock and follow him. Once they sat under the rock, he rummaged through his day pack. He pulled out the contents and lined them up on the ground.

A half dozen gas canisters, several hundred-meter reels of thin fishing wire (that was all he found at the farm coop), plastic tape, and a box of black plastic garbage bags.

Shinji took one of the canisters and showed it to Yutaka. It was painted blue with bright red letters which read "VOICE CHANGER" (underneath the ad copy read, "Now you'll be the life of the party!" huh!), and under that there was an illustration of a duck—Shinji recognized where it came from—based on a "Walt Disney" character. A whistlelike object poked out of the canister.

Shinji wrote *I remembered seeing these at the house where I found the PowerBook. You know what this is?*

Before taking the pulley, Shinji had gone into the nearby house to retrieve these canisters. What in the world would the occupant of that house do with all these things, though? The files left on the PowerBook's hard drive offered a clue. Given how they had names like "5th Grade Science" or "Third Term Report Card Drafts," the owner of the machine must have been an elementary school teacher. Yes, he was probably one of the real teachers at that school.

Yutaka touched his throat and opened his mouth. Shinji nodded.

Right. It makes you sound like a duck! It's helium. And this one's a defect. So it's still loaded with gas.

Yutaka still seemed unconvinced. Shinji thought an actual demonstration would get his point across quicker so he tore open the pack of garbage bags and pulled out a bag. He opened it up, inserted the canister valve (which was supposed to be sucked) into it, and taped it to the bag with the plastic tape. He sealed the edge of the bag with more tape. Then he pressed the valve button and the bag began to inflate.

With his finger on the button, Shinji thought, this would be a lot more entertaining with condoms. But even if they had condoms they would have been a little too small. Huh?

Do I have some on me? Well, I mean, come on, this was supposed to be a study trip. Anything can happen, right? You tossed your clothes, but you're still holding onto these? Yeah, I dunno, I do still have them. Well, you never know when they might come in handy. Let's not go into details.

After filling up the bag, Shinji twisted the edge right above the canister and sealed it with tape. He took a reel of fishing wire and tied its end to the end of the bag. Then he removed the tape below to release it from the canister. Just to be sure, he folded the edge over again, sealing it again with more tape.

The garbage bag floated upward. It rose until the wire was taut to the point where it almost seemed to lift the reel—but it stopped right at Shinji and Yutaka's heads.

"See?" Shinji said out loud. Yutaka had probably realized what was going on while Shinji was working on the canister. He'd already nodded several times.

Shinji tied another piece of wire from another reel to the wire stretching under the balloon. Just to be sure, he secured this to the balloon with tape. With the pair of wires in both of his hands, he moved the balloon as if it were walking on a pair of legs. Then he pointed to a nearby tree. He moved the string. Yes, in other words, these were the legs of the giant. They were too frail to crush a city and right now they're shorter than me, but...

Yutaka seemed to understand completely. He gave two huge nods. Then he moved his lips without saying anything. It looked like he was saying, "Awesome, Shinji." Or maybe it was, "Enough already." Whatever, it didn't matter.

Shinji took the memo pad and wrote, *We make one or two more balloons and attach them to each other. But I still don't know how far up the wire can be stretched. There's also the wind. Let's just go for it.*

Yutaka read this and nodded.

Shinji glanced up at the sky. The bags were black, so even

under the moon, Sakamochi and his men wouldn't see them. Right now there wasn't much wind either. But he had no idea what it was like further up there in the sky.

Then he said, "Let's hurry."

Shinji signaled Yutaka to hold onto the first balloon and proceeded to pull out another garbage bag.

20 students remaining

48

Shogo rose a little after 10 p.m.

Shuya had been looking after Noriko, who remained resting in bed. Shuya groped through the nearly pitch black room and entered the waiting room.

"I'll make some coffee," Shogo said as he looked up at Shuya. Then he walked down the hall. He seemed to have good night vision.

Shuya returned to the beds, where he found Noriko up without her blanket.

"You should rest a little more," Shuya said.

Noriko nodded, "Uh huh…" Then she mumbled, "Could you ask Shogo…if he's going to boil some more water if I can get an extra cup?" Noriko was sitting on the edge of the bed with her hands by her thighs. Moonlight spilled in over the curtain from the window. She kept her chin tucked in as she looked over to her side.

"Sure…but what for?"

Noriko hesitated and then answered, "I sweated so much…I just wanted to wipe my body…maybe it's too much to ask for."

"Oh no," Shuya replied and quickly nodded. "No prob. I'll go tell him." He left the room.

Shogo was boiling water in the dark kitchen. The tip of the cigarette between his mouth glowed red, and the charcoal flame under the pot resembled a strange firefly stirring to life.

"Shogo," Shuya said. Shogo turned around. The afterimage of his cigarette traced a thick line before vanishing. "Noriko was wondering if she could have some hot water. She said one cup was enough—"

"Ah." Shogo didn't let him continue. He removed his cigarette from his mouth. Shuya could see Shogo was smiling in the dim moonlight coming through the window. "Sure. A cup or an entire bucket, fine with me."

As he moved he scooped up water with the bowl from the bucket and added it to the pot. He repeated this five times. He kept a low charcoal flame going to keep the water in the pot boiling. Shuya felt some steam drift by.

"She's a girl," Shogo said.

It turned out Shogo wasn't as slow as Shuya was. He knew why Noriko asked for hot water.

Shuya was silent and Shogo unexpectedly continued on his own.

"She wants to stay pretty cause she's with you."

Then he exhaled some smoke.

Shuya remained quiet, but then asked, "Can I help you?"

"No." Shogo seemed to be shaking his head. Squinting his eyes, Shuya could see three cups and a coffee dripper already loaded with a filter on the table. There was also a tea bag for Noriko.

"Hey," Shogo called him.

Shuya lifted his brow, "What is it? All of a sudden you're so chatty."

Shogo chuckled. Then he continued, "I understand how you feel about Yoshitoki, but don't forget about Noriko's feelings."

Shuya fell silent again. The he spoke. For some reason, there was a hint of dissatisfaction in his tone of voice. "I know."

"You have a girlfriend?" Shogo proceeded to ask.

Shuya shrugged. "Nope."

"Then what's the problem?"

Shogo continued to look at the window, smoking his cigarette. "It's not a bad thing to be loved."

Shuya shrugged again. Then he asked, "Don't you have someone?"

His cigarette glowed brightly. He didn't say anything. The smoke drifted slowly through the dark.

"A secret, huh?"

"No…" Shogo began to speak, but then he removed the cigarette from his mouth and tossed it into the bucket of water. "Get down, Shuya," he whispered and crouched down.

Shuya nervously obeyed him. Was someone going to attack? He grew tense.

"Get Noriko. Be quiet though," Shogo whispered again. Shuya was already on his way to the examination room, where Noriko was.

Noriko was still sitting in a daze on the edge of the bed. Shuya signaled her to duck down. She must have immediately understood because she got off the bed, holding her breath. Shuya offered her his hand for support as they moved to the kitchen. He looked over to the entrance on the way there, but there was no one beyond the glass door.

Shogo had already gathered their day packs which he'd packed with refilled water bottles and other items, and now he was on his knees by the back door, holding his shotgun.

"What is it?" Shuya asked in a hushed voice. Shogo lifted his left hand to silence him. Shuya didn't say another word.

"Someone's outside," Shogo whispered. "We'll exit

through whichever door they don't enter."

The only thing visible in the dark was the bright charcoal flame under the pot. Given the location of the sink, it couldn't be seen from outside.

Shuya heard a tapping sound. It came from the entrance. The door wouldn't open because of the stick jamming it. The glass was broken, so the person outside must have realized that someone had entered the building and that it was probably still occupied.

There was a clacking sound, but then it stopped. It sounded like the person had given up.

Shogo groaned. "Damn, we'll be in trouble if this one tries to set this place on fire."

They remained quiet, but there was still no sound. Then Shogo signaled for them to move towards the entrance. He might have heard a slight sound.

They were nearly crawling down the hall.

As they made their way, Shogo, behind the other two, reached out to Shuya who was leading. They stopped. Shuya turned around and looked over his shoulder at Shogo.

"He's circling back to the front." He waved his hand to the back. "Let's go out the back."

So they went towards the kitchen down the hall.

Shogo stopped again before they entered the kitchen.

"Damn, why?" he muttered.

…the person outside was now coming round to the back door again.

The silence continued. Shogo held onto his shotgun. With Noriko between him and Shogo, Shuya also gripped the SIG-Sauer that had once belonged to Kaori Minami. (He'd given the Smith & Wesson to Shogo. Shuya decided to hold onto the gun that had more bullets.)

But the silence was suddenly broken. A voice called from outside the kitchen window. "It's Hiroki," he said. "I'm not fighting. Respond, you three. Who are you?"

It was undoubtedly the voice of Hiroki Sugimura (Male Student No. 11), who along with Shinji Mimura was one of the few classmates Shuya could trust.

"What the?..." Shuya moaned. "That's incredible...."

It was a stroke of luck. He never thought they'd see Hiroki. Shuya and Noriko looked at each other. Noriko looked relieved.

Shogo stopped Shuya as he tried to get up.

"What?"

"Shh. Don't raise your voice."

Shuya stared at Shogo's serious expression and then responded with an exaggerated shrug and smiled. "Don't worry, I'll vouch for him. We can totally trust him."

Shogo shook his head and said, "How did he know there were three of us?"

That thought hadn't occurred to Shuya. He thought it over while looking at Shogo. But he had no idea. That didn't matter though. The important thing was that Hiroki was here. He just wanted to see Hiroki's face now.

"Maybe he saw us go in here, from far away. That's why he didn't know who we were."

"What took him so long to get here then?"

Shuya thought again. "He probably deliberated over whether he should find out who was here or not....In any case, we can trust Hiroki. I'll vouch for him."

Shuya ignored Shogo, who looked like he wasn't satisfied. He raised his voice and directed it beyond the window. "It's Shuya, Hiroki. I'm with Shogo Kawada and Noriko Nakagawa."

"Shuya!...," a relieved voice replied. "Let me in. Where should I come in?"

Before Shuya could answer, Shogo raised his voice, "This is Shogo. Go to the front entrance. Keep your hands behind your head and do not move. Got that?"

"Shogo…" Shuya was about to protest, but Hiroki immediately responded, "Got it." What looked like the upper body of Hiroki crossed the frosted glass window.

Shogo bent down to look out of the cracks in the glass. Holding onto his shotgun, he yanked out the obstructing stick and opened the door.

Hiroki Sugimura was standing with his hands behind his neck. He was slightly taller than Shogo, but more slender. His hair, wavy like Shuya's, went down the middle of his forehead. His day pack was by his feet and for some reason there was a 1.5-meter stick on the ground.

It was true. Shuya shifted his eyes, as if it were a miracle. Shuya's face made Hiroki grin.

"I have to do a body check."

"Shogo, come on.…"

Shogo paid no attention to Shuya's protest and moved forward, holding onto his shotgun. He went behind Hiroki and first checked his hands behind his neck. Then he rubbed his left hand over Hiroki's school coat.

His hand stopped at a pocket.

"What the hell's this?"

"Go ahead and pull it out," Hiroki said with his hands held together. "But give it back to me."

Shogo pulled it out. It was the size and shape of a thick notepad, but it was made of plastic or steel. The cover panel reflected the moonlight. After fiddling around with it, Shogo said, "Ah ha." He moved his body with the object in his hands and then looked down at the cover panel against the moonlight. He nodded and returned it to Hiroki's pocket. Then he thoroughly searched Hiroki down to his pant cuffs. He also checked his day pack and finally announced, "Okay. Sorry about that. You can put your hands down."

Hiroki unlocked his hands and picked up his day pack

and stick. The stick appeared to be his weapon.

"Hiroki." Shuya broke into a smile. "Come on in. We have coffee. You want some?"

Hiroki nodded somewhat hesitantly as he went through the entrance. Shogo looked outside and then shut the door.

Hiroki stood still. With his back to the shoe cabinet that was filled with slippers, Shogo stared at Hiroki. The Remington muzzle was pointed down, but Shuya noticed Shogo's finger still on the trigger and felt slightly annoyed. He did his best not to let it get to him, though.

Hiroki looked at Shuya and Noriko again, and then glanced over at Shogo. That was when Shuya realized that Hiroki was troubled not so much by him and Noriko as he was by them hooking up with Shogo.

Shogo addressed the issue. "Shuya, Hiroki seems to want to ask whether it's all right for you guys to be with me."

Hiroki smiled slightly and looked over at Shogo, and said, "No...I just thought it was an odd combination." Still smiling, he continued, "Shuya would never be with you if you were hostile. Shuya can be pretty stupid when it comes to certain things, but he's not that stupid."

Shogo responded with a grin. He still kept his finger on the trigger though. In any case, for now Hiroki and Shogo were finished introducing themselves.

"Ah, come on, Hiroki," Shuya gave him a smile.

Then Noriko said, "Come on in. It's not our house, so I can't apologize for its messiness."

Then Hiroki smiled, but he stayed at the entrance. Shuya supported Noriko with his left hand and then pointed at the hall.

"Come on in. We'll have to get going soon, but we have a little time. We'll throw you a welcoming party."

But Hiroki stood still there. Shuya realized how he'd forgotten to share an important detail. Hiroki might have been appalled Shuya was using the word "party" in this situation.

"Hiroki, we can get out of here. Shogo is going to help us."

Hiroki's eyes widened a little. "Really?"

Shuya nodded. But then Hiroki looked down. Then he looked up again.

"Thing is...," he said and shook his head, "there's something I have to take care of."

"Something?" Shuya knit his brows. "Why don't you first come on in—"

Instead of taking Shuya up on his invitation, he asked, "Have you three been together all this time?"

Shuya thought it over and then shook his head. "No...me and Noriko were. And then..."

Then he remembered what happened this morning. It'd been a while since the image of Tatsumichi Oki's skull split open assaulted him, and once again he felt a chill run down his spine.

"...yeah. A lot of stuff happened, and we ended up joining Shogo."

"I see." Hiroki nodded and then said. "Hey, have you guys seen Kotohiki?"

"Kotohiki?" Shuya repeated. Kayoko Kotohiki (Female Student No. 8)? The one who, in spite of being into tea ceremony, seemed more playful than elegant?

"No..." Shuya shook his head. "We haven't but..." He thought of Shogo and looked over at him, but he also shook his head, saying, "I haven't seen her either."

Of course Kayoko Kotohiki had to be on this island. As long as her name wasn't announced yet in Sakamochi's announcements, she had to be alive. That's right—unless she was killed after 6 p.m.

Once again he realized how he was letting most of his classmates die and felt awful.

"What about Kotohiki?" Noriko asked.

"Oh…" Hiroki shook his head. "It's no big deal. Thanks. Sorry, but I have to get going." He gave Shuya a parting glance and turned to go.

"Hold on, Hiroki!" Shuya stopped him. "Where are you going? I told you we're safe with us, didn't I?"

Hiroki looked back at Shuya. There was a sad look in his eyes, but they still gave away that humorous trace of irony. It might have been a look all his close friends shared. Yoshitoki Kuninobu (deceased, damn), and of course Shinji Mimura, and—now it seemed—Shogo Kawada.

"I have to see Kayoko Kotohiki about something. So I have to go."

Something. What could that possibly be in this situation where moving around would only increase your chances of dying? Finally Shuya said, "Hold on. You can't go…not with any real weapons. It's too risky. And how are you going to find her?"

Hiroki bit his lower lip. Then he pulled out that object resembling a mobile data terminal from his pocket and showed it to Shuya. "This is the 'weapon' I got in my day pack. Professor Kawada over there could explain." He pointed at his neck while his hand held the device. The silver collars around the necks of Shuya, Noriko, and Shogo were all shining. "Looks like this device detects anyone wearing these collars. Once someone's in the vicinity, they show up on the screen. But you can't tell whose collar it is."

Shuya finally figured out the answer to Shogo's questions. It was thanks to this device Hiroki had been able to announce there were three of them and detect their movements. Like the computer at the school monitoring their positions, it could detect the position of anyone wearing a collar, even if, as Hiroki said, you couldn't tell who it was.

Hiroki put the device back into the pocket. "See you—" He was ready to go when he suddenly stopped, "That's right...beware of Mitsuko Souma," he added. He gave Shuya and then Shogo a stern look. "She's playing the game. I don't know about the others, but I know for sure she is."

"Did you fight her?" Shogo asked.

Hiroki shook his head. "No. I didn't, but Takako...Takako Chigusa said so before she died. Mitsuko killed Takako."

Shuya suddenly recalled how Takako was already dead. After hearing Sakamochi announce her death, he'd been concerned about its effect on Hiroki, but he was so happy to see him he'd forgotten this dreadful fact.

That's right, Hiroki and Takako Chigusa were close. For a while, Shuya actually thought they were going out. But when he'd casually asked him about it, Hiroki chuckled and said, "She's in a different class. We've known each other since we were kids. You know hide-and-seek, that kind of thing. When we used to fight, I'd be the one crying." That sounded (of course Takako Chigusa was an amazing athlete, and pretty aggressive, but her taking on Hiroki, who was now over 180 centimeters tall and ranked in martial arts—a while back, that's right, the only time he visited his house, Hiroki reluctantly showed him how he could split a piece of pine wood with the palm of his hand) preposterously funny.

But now Takako Chigusa was dead. And...given the way Hiroki had just described it, he was there when she died.

"So you were with her?" Noriko asked quietly.

Hiroki shook his head. "Just the very end. I...when we left, I hid in front of the school, waiting for her...but then Yoshio came back, and I got too distracted, so I lost Takako...then...as I looked for Takako I ended up losing my chance to join you, Shuya, and Shinji."

Shuya nodded several times. So Hiroki was in front of the

school until Yoshio Akamatsu returned. He probably hid in the woods. It was dangerous, of course. But that only showed how important Takako was to Hiroki.

"But...," Hiroki continued, "I found Takako...I was...too late though." Saying this much, Hiroki looked down. He shook his head several times. Without being told, Shuya understood that by the time Hiroki had found Takako she was dying from being attacked by Mitsuko.

Shuya thought of telling him how Yoshio Akamatsu had killed Mayumi Tendo, and how he had almost killed Shuya as well, but...it was irrelevant now. Yoshio Akamatsu was dead now too.

"I don't know what to say, but...I'm so sorry," Noriko said.

Hiroki smiled a little and nodded. "Thanks."

"In any case," Shuya said, "Come on in. Let's talk it over, what's the—"

He meant to say, rush, but refrained. If Hiroki wanted to see Kayoko Kotohiki while they were both still alive, what else could he do but rush? While Hiroki's connection to Takako Chigusa was clear, Shuya had no idea why it was so important for him to find Kayoko Kotohiki. But in any case, as they sat here talking, she could be fighting someone, or she might even be dying.

Hiroki grinned. It seemed he knew what Shuya was thinking.

Shuya licked his lips. He glanced over at Shogo and then said, "If you insist..." He looked at Hiroki and continued, "We'll find her with you."

But Hiroki flatly refused. He pointed his chin at Noriko. "Noriko's injured. It's too dangerous. No."

Shuya found the situation unbearable. "But you could be saved with us....How are we going to meet again if you leave?..." That's right. Once they separated it would be nearly impossible for them to meet again.

"Hiroki." It was Shogo. He still held the shotgun, but his finger wasn't on the trigger anymore. Hiroki looked over at him, and Shogo pulled out something small from his pocket with his open hand. He lifted it to his mouth and bit on its metal end, twisting it. It made the chirping sound of a bird. It was a loud, brilliant, and playful sound. Like a robin or chickadee.

Shogo released his hand from his mouth, and Shuya realized that it was Shogo's device—a bird call? Forget why he would have one in the first place…it was one of those things that mimicked the sound of birds chirping.

"Whether you meet Kayoko Kotohiki or not," Shogo said, "if you want to see us, make a fire somewhere and burn raw wood to get some smoke going. Make two fires. Of course, leave as soon as you make them because you'll only attract attention. And make sure you don't cause a fire. Once we see that we'll make this call every fifteen minutes, say, for fifteen seconds. Try to find us by following this sound."

He pointed to the bird call.

"This sound is your ticket out of here. If you're up for it, you can come aboard our train."

Hiroki nodded. "Okay. I will, thanks."

Shogo took out his map. He unfolded it and handed the map and his pencil over to Hiroki. "Also, I'm sorry for keeping you, but I need you to mark where Takako was killed. If you saw anyone else, I need to know those locations too."

Hiroki lifted his brow slightly as he took the map. He spread the map out on the shoe cabinet, under the moonlit window, and held the pencil.

"Give me your map. I'll write in the locations of the bodies we know," Shogo said. Hiroki stopped writing and handed over his map. The two began marking the maps side by side.

"I'll bring some coffee over," Noriko said and left Shuya's arm. She limped down the hall, using the wall as support.

"Did Takako say whether Mitsuko had a machine gun?" Shogo asked as he wrote.

"No," Hiroki answered without lifting his eyes, "She didn't say anything about that. I do know that she was shot several times. It wasn't a single bullet."

"I see."

As the two proceeded, Shuya explained the fates of Yoshio Akamatsu, Tatsumichi Oki, and Kyoichi Motobuchi. Hiroki nodded as he continued to write.

Shogo was done marking Hiroki's map. He pointed at it and explained, "This is where Kaori Minami was killed. Shuya saw Hirono Shimizu escape. She might have done it in self-defense. But either way, you should be careful."

Hiroki nodded. Then unexpectedly he said, "I saw Kaori too," and pointed at the map. "Before noon. She fired at me, but I think she was in a panic."

Shogo nodded and exchanged Hiroki's map with his.

Noriko came out into the hall, holding a cup. Shuya went down the hall and took it from Noriko, who walked unsteadily. He offered it to Hiroki, who took a sniff, whistled lightly, and then held it. "Thanks," he said and took a sip. Then he put the cup on the raised entrance floor. It was nearly full.

"I'll see ya."

"Hold on." Shuya pulled out his SIG-Sauer from under his belt. With its grip pointed at Hiroki, he offered it to him. He also pulled out an extra cartridge from his pocket. "If you still insist on going take these, okay? We have a shotgun and one more gun."

The first gun was Kyoichi Motobuchi's, and the Smith & Wesson was now with Shogo. Shuya's handing over the SIG-

Sauer gun would decrease their fighting capacity, but Shogo didn't intervene.

But Hiroki shook his head. "You need that, Shuya. You better protect Noriko all right. I can't take that. Even if someone attacks me, I just can't do it." He tilted his head and then examined both Shuya and Noriko. He broke into a slight grin and then added, "I always wondered why you two weren't going out." Then he nodded at each of them and quietly opened the entrance door.

"Hiroki," Noriko called. Her voice was quiet. "Be careful."

"I will. Hey, thanks. And best of luck to you guys."

"Hiroki…" Shuya was getting choked up, but managed to say, "We'll meet again. That's a promise."

Hiroki nodded and left. Shuya held Noriko and stepped through the front entrance, watching Hiroki as he quickly ascended the mountain.

Without a word, Shogo gestured to Shuya and Noriko to move back and close the door.

Shuya took a deep breath and turned around. He could barely see the steam still rising from the cup Hiroki had left on the floor.

20 students remaining

49

The moon was high in the center of the sky. There wasn't a single cloud. The white light from the nearly full moon cast a thin film over the rest of the sky, obscuring the stars.

Shogo, who was leading, stopped. Shuya, who was supporting Noriko with his shoulder, stopped too.

"Are you all right?" Shuya asked Noriko.

She nodded. "I'm fine." But Shuya could tell she

was still unsteady.

Shuya looked at his watch. It was past 11 p.m. now, but they'd already left G=9, which was now a forbidden zone. They had to find another place to settle down.

They were tracing their way back along the foot of the northern mountain. The area was scattered with trees. A little further down and they'd be near where Kaori Minami was killed. Immediately to their left, Shuya saw a flat, narrow area that extended from the island's residential area on the eastern shore. The flat land spotted with houses then became increasingly narrow, like a triangle. The road traversing the island supposedly passed through this pivot and headed to the western shore.

Shogo turned around. "Now what do we do?" Noriko's blanket was tied to the top of the day pack on his shoulder.

"Can we stop at a house, like we did just now?"

"A house, huh." Shogo looked away from Shuya and squinted. "It's really not a good idea. As the number of zones decrease so do the number of houses. The moment someone needs something, they'll want to enter a house. Whether it's to eat or whatever."

"Hey, if you're worried about me, I'm fine now. Even outside," Noriko said.

Shogo flashed a smile and then silently looked over the flat land. He looked as if he was taking Hiroki's marks on his map into consideration as he took in the view.

Along with the bodies he'd seen, Hiroki had given detailed explanations of how they had died. The body of Kazushi Niida was right near where Takako Chigusa had died. Along with his eyes being gouged out (!), his throat had been stabbed. In the residential area that was now forbidden was Megumi Eto. Her throat had been slashed by a blade. (Shuya felt a pang in his chest over this one, since Noriko had told him how

Megumi had a crush on him.) To the east, Yoji Kuramoto and Yoshimi Yahagi were killed where the eastern shore's residential area met the southern mountain. Yoji was stabbed in the head, and Yoshimi had been shot. At the southern tip, Izumi Kanai, Hiroshi Kuronaga, Ryuhei Sasagawa, and Mitsuru Numai were all found dead together. Mitsuru Numai was shot several times, while the others' throats were slashed. Three of Kiriyama's group had died together, the only exception being Sho Tsukioka, who got caught in a forbidden zone.

"Shogo," Shuya said. Shogo looked back. "Do you think Mitsuko Souma killed Yukiko and Yumiko?"

Even now, as he asked this, it all felt so unreal. He didn't believe a girl could do such horrible things. Of course he had no doubt, since it was Hiroki who'd informed them, but he still couldn't restrain the urge to dismiss it all as a delusion.

"No," Shogo shook his head. "I don't think so. After Yukiko and Yumiko got killed by that machine gun, you know how we heard pistols going off? That was to finish them off. But Hiroki said Takako was alive after being shot when he found her. Which means her killer wasn't as thorough. Of course she might have let Takako go, knowing she was going to die anyway. But given the times and locations, I just don't think Mitsuko Souma's the one with the machine gun."

Shuya recalled the machine gun fire he heard before 9 a.m. The killer was still roaming around the island. And the distant gunfire they heard a little afterwards...was that Mitsuko Souma?

"Eventually we'll...," Shogo forced a grin and shook his head, "...meet him or her. Then we'll know for sure."

Shuya recalled something else that had been bugging

him. "When Hiroki showed us his radar, I was thinking how Sakamochi must know we're together and our positions as well."

Shogo answered as he surveyed the flat land, "That's right."

Shuya moved his shoulder to give Noriko better support. "Won't that hinder our escape?"

Shogo chuckled with his back to Shuya. "Nope. Not at all. Don't worry." Shogo looked over the flat land again and said, "Let's go back to where we were."

He continued, "A common strategy players in this game take is to show up anywhere they hear some action. That's because of the 24-hour deadline. Because of that limitation, they kill when they can. And the fact that they're on a killing spree means they're on their own, so they can't afford to sleep much. So the match has to be kept short. If something happens near them, they go there, and if there's a fight already going on, they sit back and then they finish off any survivors. That's why we should stay somewhere we can avoid confrontations. If we get mixed up with someone who's panicking then one of the top players is bound to show up. If we go back where we were it's unlikely we'll meet anyone. Since Tatsumichi Oki and Kyoichi Motobuchi, who'd been hiding there, are no longer around, that area is pretty much uninhabited."

"But Hirono ran in that direction."

"No, I doubt she's gone that far. It wouldn't be necessary." Shogo pointed to the flat land with his thumb. "But we'll avoid this mountain where she might be hiding. We'll take a different route."

Shuya lifted his brow. "Is it safe for us to move through the flat land?"

Shogo smiled and shook his head. "The moon may be shining, but this isn't daylight. I think we're safer there than in the mountain, where there's too much cover."

Shuya nodded. Shogo took the lead and began descending the slope. Shuya held the SIG-Sauer tightly in his right hand and followed Shogo as he supported Noriko.

The trees turned into a field of short grass. The first farm they came across had a field full of squashes. Beyond this field there was a wheat field. This island was so small these probably weren't for domestic consumption. Of course the Republic of Greater East Asia was incessantly issuing orders to promote national self-reliance, so even a small farm like this might contribute a little to the effort. As they moved along the edge of the farm, the soil under their sneakers felt dry. Maybe it was because several days had passed since the area had been evacuated. Still, Shuya was struck by the pleasant, rich odor of wheat drifting through the evening air, anticipating the summer.

It was a nice smell. Especially after having smelled so much blood.

There was a tractor to their left. Beyond the vehicle there was a house.

It was an ordinary, two-story house and appeared relatively new. It was probably one of those cheap, mass produced buildings resembling Banana Homes or Vertebrae Houses. Even though it was in the middle of the farm, it was enclosed by a concrete wall.

Shuya looked at Shogo's back as he moved forward.

Something irked him.

He looked back. Noriko was leaning on his left shoulder as she walked, but he noticed something high above her head in the middle of the sky. Something flashing in the moonlight, tracing an arc. This object came flying at them.

20 students remaining

50

What made Shuya such a star athlete in his Little League days was his incredible ability to perceive objects in motion. Even in this dim light Shuya could tell that the object flying towards them right now resembled a can. Of course, they were in the serene Seto Inland Sea region, so it couldn't possibly be an empty can falling from the sky from a hurricane. There was no way it was an empty can.

No.

Shuya suddenly released his shoulder, which was tucked under Noriko's right armpit. He couldn't even afford to call on Shogo, who must have realized something odd though, because he also suddenly turned around, while Noriko tottered without Shuya's support.

Shuya dashed out. His jumping ability was quite extraordinary. Just as in the past, during the Little League prefectural semifinals, he could make the ultimate play from any given position, stealing the opponents' winning home run in the bottom of the eleventh inning.

Shuya caught the ball—no, the can—in mid-air with his left hand. He put it in his right hand, and as he came down he twisted his body and threw it as far as he could.

Before Shuya landed a bright light shined through the night.

He felt the air burst as a sonic boom tore through his eardrums. The bomb blast blew him away before he could land, and he fell sprawling onto the ground. If he'd waited for the hand grenade to fall, he, Noriko, and Shogo would have all been mincemeat now. Although Sakamochi's crew might have reduced the grenade's explosive power so that it couldn't be used against the school, it was more than capable of killing human beings.

He raised his head. He realized, he heard nothing. His

ears were screwed up. In this state of silence, Shuya saw Noriko collapsed on his left. Then he lifted his face to look back at Shogo and saw...another can flying at them.

Another one! I have to...but it was too late now.

His disabled ears all of a sudden heard a definite but muffled bang, almost simultaneously followed by another explosion in the air. This sound was also muffled, but this time it felt a little further off and Shuya wasn't blown away. Right beside him Shogo was on one knee, holding his shotgun. He had shot the hand grenade, as if he were skeet shooting, blowing it to bits before it managed to explode.

Shuya ran over to Noriko and held her up. She was grimacing. She seemed to be moaning, but he couldn't hear her.

"Shuya, get back!"

Shogo waved his hand and fired his shotgun with his right hand. Shuya then heard a different sound, rattling gunfire, and the wheat heads right in front of him scattered into the air. Shogo fired another two shots. In a state of confusion, Shuya pulled Noriko into the shade of the ridge marking off the farm. He got down. Shogo slid to his side, firing several shots as he went. The rattling continued, and the ridge soil blew up, grains flying into his eyes.

Shuya pulled out his SIG-Sauer and looked out from the shade of the ridge. He fired blindly in the direction Shogo was firing.

Then he saw him. Less than thirty meters away, the unique slicked-back hair behind the break in the house's concrete wall.

It was Kazuo Kiriyama (Male Student No. 6). And although Shuya's hearing was impaired, he could recall the sound of the rattling gunfire. It was the same sound he heard from far away when Yumiko and Yukiko fell at the northern mountain peak. Of course he might not have been the only one with a machine gun, but even so, Kazuo, who was right in front of their very own eyes, had just tried to kill them without warning, with of all things a hand grenade!

Shuya was certain Kazuo was the one who'd murdered Yumiko and Yukiko. He thought of how they were killed and felt a flash of rage.

"What the…what's the hell's he doing!?"

"Stop shouting, just shoot!" Shogo handed the Smith & Wesson to Shuya and reloaded his shotgun.

Shuya held a gun in each hand and began shooting at the concrete wall. (Two-hand shooter! This is crazy!) First the Smith & Wesson, then the SIG-Sauer ran out of bullets. He had to reload!

Having waited for this moment, Kazuo got up. *BRRRRATTA.* Sparks flew out from him. Shuya ducked, and Kazuo revealed part of his body that was behind the wall.

Shogo blasted his shotgun away. Kazuo's body once again vanished. The swarm of shotgun pellets blew off part of the wall.

Shuya ejected the empty magazine from his SIG-Sauer and pulled out a loaded magazine from his pocket. He opened the Smith & Wesson cylinder and pushed the rod in the center of the cylinder to release its spent shells, puffed up from the explosions. One of the shells nearly singed part of his right thumb. It didn't matter. He quickly loaded the .38 caliber bullets Shogo had rolled over his way. Then he aimed at Kazuo's house.

Shogo shot again, blowing off another part of the wall. Shuya also fired several shots into it with his SIG-Sauer.

"Noriko! Are you all right!?" Shuya yelled. Right next to him, Noriko answered, "I'm okay." He could make out her response, which made Shuya realize his hearing was back. He saw her in the corner of his eye reloading 9mm Short bullets into the SIG-Sauer's empty magazine. Of all the things he'd seen since the game began this one really sent his head reeling. How could a girl like Noriko be participating in a battle like this....

A hand appeared from the other side of the wall. The hand was holding a machine gun. It rattled again. Shuya and Shogo ducked.

Kazuo got up. As he continued shooting, he came forward. Then he ran behind the tractor. The distance between them was shrinking.

Shogo fired a shot, blowing off the tractor's driving panel.

"Shogo," Shuya called, after shooting twice.

"What?" Shogo answered as he reloaded his shotgun.

"How fast can you run the hundred-meter dash?"

Shogo took another shot (annihilating the tractor's rear light) and answered, "I'm pretty slow. Maybe thirteen seconds. My back's strong though. What?"

Suddenly Kazuo's arm stuck out from behind the tractor. Sparks flew as Kazuo revealed his head, but as Shuya and Shogo fired back, he ducked again.

"We can only retreat into the mountain, right?" Shuya spoke quickly. "I can run a hundred meters in almost less than eleven seconds. You and Noriko go ahead. I'll keep Kazuo there."

Shogo glanced at Shuya. That was all. He understood.

"At the place we were, Shuya. The place where we talked about rock," Shogo said quickly. He gave Shuya his shotgun and retreated into a ducking position. He moved around over to Noriko.

Shuya took a deep breath and shot three times into the tractor with the shotgun, prompting Shogo to lift Noriko and run in the direction they'd come from. Noriko's eyes flashed by Shuya's for a moment.

Kazuo's upper body appeared from behind the tractor. Shuya fired his shotgun several times. Kazuo, who had his gun pointed at Shogo and Noriko, ducked. Shuya realized he was out of shotgun shells so he picked up the Smith & Wesson instead and began shooting again. He immediately used up five bullets. He opened the SIG-Sauer and loaded the extra magazine Noriko had loaded with bullets and began shooting again. It was crucial he keep on shooting.

He saw Shogo and Noriko disappear into the mountain.

The SIG-Sauer was empty, and there were no more extra magazines. He could only reload bullets....

But then this time Kazuo's arm appeared from behind the tractor's blade. The Ingram machine gun rattled away. Just like before. Kazuo was running towards him!

Shuya had to get out of this gunfight. He held onto only the empty SIG-Sauer (he still had seven more individual 9mm Short bullets), turned around, and ran. If he could reach the mountain where there was plenty of cover, Kazuo wouldn't be able to get too close to him. Shuya decided to head east. Noriko and Shogo would be headed west to get where they were yesterday. He wanted to lead Kazuo as far away from them as he could.

It all came down to his sprinting speed. He had to get as far away from Kazuo as possible in a short span of time. A machine gun basically offered a shower of bullets so it was impossible to dodge at a close distance. What mattered was how far he could get.

Shuya ran. As the fastest runner in the class (at least he thought so. He was even a fraction of a second faster than Shinji Mimura, unless, that is, if Kazuo wasn't really trying during his test), he could only rely on his speed.

Right when he thought he was five meters away from a tree he heard a rattling sound. He felt a severe blow against the left side of his stomach.

Shuya groaned as he began losing his balance, but he kept on running. He ran into a row of tall trees and made his way up the slope. The rattling resumed and this time his left arm reflexively flinched up. He realized he'd been shot right above his elbow.

But he still ran. He continued east—hey, yo, that's a forbidden zone—and moved north. More rattling. A thin tree to his right crackled and burst into matchstick-sized splinters.

More rattling. This time he wasn't hit. Or maybe he was. He couldn't tell anymore. He only knew he was being chased. At least he was buying time for Noriko and Shogo.

He made his way through the trees and vegetation, climbed a hill, and then descended it. He couldn't even afford to worry that there might be someone else hiding in the dark, waiting to attack him. He had no idea how far he'd gotten. He wasn't even sure which direction he was running. Sometimes it seemed like he could hear—sometimes it seemed like he couldn't—the rattling sound. He couldn't tell maybe because his hearing had been impaired by that explosion. In any case now was not the time to be relieved. Farther. He had to get farther.

Suddenly Shuya slipped. He'd somehow reached a cliff, and all of a sudden realized that the slope just dropped off. Just as he'd done when fighting Tatsumichi Oki, he tumbled down the steep slope.

He landed with a thud. He was no longer holding the SIG-Sauer. And as he tried to stand up...

He realized he couldn't. He wondered, in a daze, am I delirious from blood loss? Or...did I hit my head?

Impossible. I'm not injured so badly I can't stand up....I have to get back to Noriko and Shogo....I have to protect Noriko, I promised Noriko...

As he tried to get up though, he fell forward...

...and lost consciousness.

20 students remaining

51

It was almost pitch dark, but beside the dimly moonlit window Shinji tossed the item in his hand once again onto the floor. The sound of it hitting the floor was muffled by the thick folded blanket, but there was a popping sound along with a ring.

Shinji immediately picked it up off the floor and then tucked the small plastic item inside the blanket. The sound stopped.

"Come on, let's go," Yutaka said. He'd been watching over Shinji, but Shinji signaled him to calm down. He repeated the test again.

Pop, zing. It made the same sounds. Shinji picked it up, and it stopped.

Was it all right? But if this malfunctioned, then all the careful preparations they'd made would come to nothing. One more try—

"We have to hurry…," Yutaka said again, and Shinji's face was about to flush with anger—but he managed to suppress it. Although he wasn't entirely satisfied he said, "All right," and concluded his test. He unhooked the lead wire connecting the battery and mini-motor which was used for the test and began peeling off the plastic tape attaching the motor unit to the battery.

Shuya and Yutaka were back at the "Northern Takamatsu Agricultural Cooperative Association, Okishima Island Branch."

Along with the school and harbor fishery coop, it might have been one of the largest buildings on the island. The space, unlit of course and enveloped in darkness, was the size of a basketball court, and there was farming equipment strewn all over the area, including a tractor and combine harvester. There was also a light truck with a missing wheel lifted on a jack, probably to be repaired. Then in the corner were piles of sacks of various kinds of fertilizer. (And hazardous ammonium nitrate was further beyond them, stored in a large cabinet with a provisional lock that Shinji had busted open.) The slate walls were at least five meters high, and there was an upper floor attached along the north wall where more fertilizer, insecticide, and other supplies had been stored. On the opposite, or east, wall was a steel staircase diagonally descending from the second floor, and underneath the stairs was a large sliding warehouse door. Next to this sliding door, in front of the stairs in the southeast corner, was an officelike space made up of partition walls. Beyond its open door he could make out office equipment, including the outlines of a desk and fax machine.

Setting the wire across sector G=7 where the school was turned out to be a hassle. First, Shinji tied the end of the wire to the tip of a tall tree behind the rock they'd climbed on. Then he took the other end and began walking between the trees, but then a gust in the upper region of the sky acted up, so guiding the garbage-bag balloons proved to be difficult. There were at least ten occasions where he had to climb up a tree to loosen the wire. On top of that, given how the enemy could be anywhere in the dark, he had to worry about Yutaka, so the endeavor ended up exhausting him.

But he'd managed to set the wire after a full three hours, when he heard the gunfight. It was past 11 p.m. He heard an explosion as well, but he couldn't afford to get involved, so he hurried back to the farm coop with Yutaka. By then the gunfire had ceased.

Finally Shinji began building the electric detonator, but this also turned out to be difficult. He didn't have the proper tools, and furthermore the device required a delicate balance. Electric current had to run through the device at the moment of impact against the school, but at the same time he had to make sure it wasn't so sensitive it'd be ignited in the middle of the rope cable by, say, a bump or knot in the rope.

But somehow he managed to build it, using a motor (which he removed from an electric razor) instead of the detonator for the test. It was right when he began testing, in other words, only moments ago, that the midnight announcement was made. The only one who died was Hirono Shimizu (Female Student No. 10), whom Shinji saw immediately after the game began. He thought it might have been a result of that intense gun battle, but in any case Sakamochi had announced something far more urgent, at least to him and Yutaka. Sector F=7, which included the cliff rock they'd climbed up on to survey the school, was designated to be a forbidden zone as of 1 a.m.

No wonder Yutaka was so impatient. If they couldn't enter that area then all their preparations would amount to nothing. It would be the end for them. He didn't want to be in the situation of, after a clever play, being just one move away from checkmate only to fall into a fatal trap.

Shinji quickly pulled out the electric detonator from the tube chained to his knife. He connected the two cylinders—their dull metallic exterior shone in the dark—and peeled off the insulation from the lead wire. Then using tape, he first secured the small plastic spring serving as the electrical switch, then took the end of the lead wire extending from the detonator and tied it to the wire from the charge device. He taped the connection over and over so it would be completely secure. Then next to the battery he installed a condenser circuit board taken from the flash component of a camera. In order for the detonator to be absolutely reliable, he needed a high voltage output. He connected the wires to this device as well. To prevent any accidental detonation, he decided he would work on the remaining wire from the electric detonator at the top of the mountain, taping the exposed end of the wire to the side of the battery.

"All right."

Shinji stood up, and then put the completed detonation device in his pocket.

"Let's hurry. It's time."

Yutaka nodded. Just in case, Shinji tossed his equipment, including the electrical pliers and extra lead wire into his day pack, and then lifted several piles of rope they had divided up onto his shoulder. He looked down. There was a gas can filled up with a mixture of gasoline and ammonium nitrate. To add oxygen, he stuffed in insulation material filled with air and folded in pleats. The opening was shut with the lid, but next to it another rubber lid functioning as the detonator holder was tied to it with a plastic cord dangling from the handle.

Then he looked at his watch. It was 12:09. They had plenty of time.

Okay then. He was trembling from excitement. It took a lot of effort, but now they had everything they needed. They would connect all the ropes they had, tying one end to a tree in H=7. Then they would tie the other end of the rope to the end of the fishing wire secured by the weight of a rock. They would unravel the rope and leave it there and then go around the school, going up the mountain into F=7. He would take the wire tied to the top of the tree and reel it in immediately. The rope stuck to the wire would then come to them. He would proceed to attach the pulley to the gas-can gondola with the detonation device and thread the rope through it. Then he would stretch the rope taut with one swift motion and secure it to a tree. Then the rest is...party time, dude. Have fun! Here we go! Make it happen!

Once they had done some damage to the school's computer, or its electrical current or wiring, Sakamochi's staff would suspect a system failure, no, given the power of explosives here once the entire computer, no, in fact half the school was blown up, then they would take the tire tubes they'd already hidden behind the rock in F=7 and run towards the western shore, escaping by sea as planned. If they could mislead the government by sending a false SOS signal using their transistor radio and get to the next island, Toyoshima, in less than a half an hour as calculated, then they would take a boat. (He had experience with a motor boat. He was really appreciating all the wisdom his late uncle had imparted.) Then they would probably escape into Okayama, hopefully landing on an obscure shore, and then they'd be fine. They could take a freight train heading to the countryside. Or they would furnish themselves with a car passing by. After all, he had a gun. Carjack. Nice.

Shinji looked down at the Beretta M92F tucked into his belt. He was planning on slipping through by misleading the government, but just in case they were found at sea, he'd filled several Coke bottles with his special ammonium nitrate-gasoline mixture and stuffed them into his day pack. But without a detonator they were basically just Molotov cocktails. If they were detected, it would be best to swim toward the guard ship and get on board to fight. If all went well they could get their hands on the enemy's weapons, and if they could operate the ship, it could provide their means of escape. But he would have to be a good shot to accomplish this.

He was a little…concerned. He'd been running all over the island with his Beretta, but come to think of it, he hadn't fired it once. And even his uncle didn't have a gun, so he'd never learned how to use one.

But Shinji shook his head. The Third Man, Shinji Mimura. No prob. The first time he held a heavy basketball and tossed a free throw, the ball swooped right through the basket.

"Shinji." Yutaka called him.

Shinji looked up. "Are you ready?"

"No...," Yutaka said pitifully. And then he nervously wrote something on the memo pad.

Shinji read it under the moonlight by the window. It read, *I can't find the pulley.*

He glanced at Yutaka. For all he knew he might look really mad. Yutaka suddenly drew back.

Yutaka was in charge of half of the rope supply and the pulley. Ever since Shinji took the pulley from the well, Yutaka had been in charge of it, bringing it over here and putting it somewhere.

Shinji put his bundles of rope and day pack down again. He began searching the area on his knees. Yutaka did the same.

They groped in the dark, looking beyond the tractor and below the work desk, but they couldn't find it. Shinji stood up and checked his watch again. Instead of 12:10, it was approaching 12:15.

Finally, he decided to take out the flashlight from his day pack. He cupped the bulb area with his hands and turned it on.

He did his best not to let any light leak out, but the interior of the warehouselike pseudo farm coop glowed a faint yellow. Shinji saw Yutaka's worried face and then beyond his shoulder, he easily located the pulley, lying beyond the moonlight from the window on the floor by the plain wall behind the desk. It was less than a meter away from Yutaka's day pack on the floor.

Shinji signaled Yutaka and quickly turned off the flashlight. Yutaka snatched up the pulley.

"I'm sorry, Shinji," Yutaka said apologetically.

Shinji forced a grin, "Get it together, Yutaka."

Then he shouldered the day pack and rope once again. He lifted the gas can. He was confident about his strength, but two of these items were pretty heavy. Carrying the rope would only be partway, but he would have to carry the twenty-kilogram gas can to the top of the mountain. And they had to hurry too.

Yutaka carried his bundle of rope (the heavy load made him look like a tortoise weighed down by its shell. Well, Shinji looked no different), and they walked to the sliding door on the east side of the building. The door had been opened approximately ten centimeters, letting in a thin ray of pale blue moonlight.

"I'm so sorry, Shinji," Yutaka said again.

"It's all right. Don't worry. Let's just make sure we get it right from here on."

Shinji shifted the gas can to his left hand, put his right hand on the heavy steel door, and slid it open. The pale light spread out.

Outside there was an unpaved parking lot. Its entrance was on the right. The farm coop faced a narrow road. Near its entrance was a station wagon. The wide longitudinal road traversing the island was slightly south of this road.

In front of the door, east of the parking lot, was a farm made up of several houses. Beyond that area was another cluster of houses, and even in the dark you could see them.

To his left Shinji saw a small storage shack at the end of the property, and further on up was the school, and above it, as if it were embracing it, the cliff. There were some trees right by a two-story house in front of the school. They were planning on tying the rope to the tallest tree there. They had secured the wire near the farm's waterway immediately left of the tree. So the wire went by the school and directly up into the center of the mountain, where the overlooking rock was, covering an amazing distance of three hundred meters.

I can't believe I came up with this plan. I wonder though, whether that wire will really lift the rope up to the mountain without getting cut?

Shinji took a breath and then after considering it, he decided to say something. It wouldn't matter whether they heard him say this.

"Yutaka."

Yutaka looked up at Shinji. "What?"

"We might die. Are you prepared for that?"

For a moment Yutaka fell silent. But then he answered immediately, "Yeah, I'm ready."

"Okay."

Shinji gripped the handle of the gas can again and was about to form a smile…

…that froze when he saw something in the corner of his eye.

Someone's head emerged from the farm east of the parking lot.

"Yutaka!"

Shinji grabbed Yutaka's arm and ran back behind the sliding door into the slate-walled farm coop building. Yutaka teetered for a moment, partially due to the heavy rope, but managed to follow him. By the time they were crouched over behind the sliding door, Shinji already had his gun aimed at the figure.

The figure shrieked, "D-don't shoot! Shinji! Please don't shoot! It's me! Keita!"

Shinji realized it was Keita Iijima (Male Student No. 2). Keita, relatively speaking, was friendly and got along with Shinji and Yutaka (after all they'd been classmates since their first year), but Shinji wasn't relieved someone was joining them. No, he felt like this meant trouble. That's when he realized he hadn't given much thought to the possibility of others joining them until now. Damn, why now!

"It's Keita, Shinji. Come on, it's Keita."

Shinji thought Yutaka's excited voice sounded a

little inappropriate.

Keita slowly stood up and proceeded toward the farm coop premises. He held his day pack in his left hand and what looked like a kitchen knife in his right. He spoke cautiously.

"I saw the light."

Shinji clenched his teeth. It must have come from the flashlight he'd used just that one time to find the pulley. Shinji chided himself, how could he have screwed up like that, rushing to use that flashlight?

Keita continued, "So I came here and saw that it was you guys…what are you doing? What were you carrying? Rope? Let me…let me join you guys."

Knowing how their conversations were monitored, Yutaka knit his brow and looked over at Shinji, his eyes opened wide, realizing how Shinji hadn't lowered his gun.

"Sh-Shinji, what's going on?"

Shinji moved his open right hand and signaled Yutaka not to move forward. "Yutaka. Don't move."

"Hey," Keita said. His voice was shaking. "Why are you pointing that at me?"

Shinji took a deep breath and said to Keita, "Don't move." He could tell Yutaka was getting tense.

Keita Iijima's pitiful face was visible in the moonlight as he took a step forward.

"Why? Why won't you let me? Have you forgotten who I am, Shinji? Let me join you guys."

Shinji cocked his gun with a click. Keita Iijima stopped. They still had plenty of distance, seven or eight meters.

"Don't come near us," Shinji slowly repeated. "I can't let you join."

Yutaka whined right beside him, "Why, Shinji? We can trust Keita."

Shinji shook his head. Then he thought, that's right,

there's something you don't know about us, Yutaka.

It wasn't a big deal. In fact it was a trivial incident.

It happened during their second year near the end of the term in March. Shinji went to Takamatsu to see a movie (there was no movie theater in Shiroiwa) with Keita Iijima. Yutaka was supposed to go too, but he had a cold that day.

That was how Shinji encountered three tough-looking high school students in a back alley off the main street near the shopping arcade. Shinji and Keita had already seen the movie, and once they were done checking out the book and record stores (Shinji bought imported computer books. They were lucky finds. Even though they were technical books, the government strictly prohibited books from the West so they were difficult to come by), they were heading over to the train station when Keita realized he'd forgot to buy a comic book and went back to the bookstore alone.

"Hey, you got any dough?" one of the high school students asked. This guy was at least ten centimeters taller than Shinji, who at 172 meters was short for a basketball player.

Shinji shrugged. "I think I have 2,571 yen."

The interrogator looked at the other two as if saying, how lame. Then he leaned over by Shinji's ear. Shinji was annoyed. Maybe it was from getting wasted on paint thinner or some wacky drug that was hip these days, in any case the guy's gums were receding, and the smell of his breath coming between his teeth reeked. Brush your teeth, man.

The guy said, "Give it up. Come on, now."

Shinji gave an exaggerated look of surprise and said, "Oh, so you guys are homeless! You know you should be content with twenty yen then. I actually might give you something if you get on your knees and beg for forgiveness."

The guy with a gap in his teeth looked surprised while the other two grinned.

"You still in junior high, right? You should learn to respect your elders," the guy said and grabbed Shinji by the shoulder. He kneed Shinji in the stomach. Shinji tightened his stomach muscles to take the blow. It didn't hurt that much. It was just a threatening knee kick. These guys could never take on someone their own age.

Shinji calmly pushed the high school student away. Then he said, "What was that? A Russian hug?"

The guys probably didn't even know where Russia was. But the guy with the gap in his teeth seemed irked by Shinji's tone of voice, and his thin, ugly face contorted.

"That's it." He punched Shinji in the face. This also didn't hurt much, though the inside of Shinji's mouth got cut.

Shinji stuck his fingers in his mouth to check the wound. It stung a little. He pulled out his fingers and found blood on them. It was nothing.

"Come on, give us your wallet."

Still looking down, Shinji broke into a grin. He looked up. When their eyes met the guy with the gap in his teeth looked intimidated.

Shinji said playfully, "You made the first move," and then with the motion of a short hook punch he swung the hardcover imported book in his hand into the guy's filthy mouth. He felt the guy's teeth break, his head fly back.

It took ten seconds for the fight to end. Of course his uncle's teachings had included fighting lessons too. It was trivial.

What wasn't trivial was something else.

As he glared at the passers by who were staring at the high school students on the ground, Shinji headed back to the book store and found Keita in the comics section. The book he went back for was already in a shopping bag. He seemed to be browsing aimlessly, and when Shinji called on him, he said, "I'm sorry. I remembered there was another book I wanted…." Then his eyes opened wide and he asked him, "What happened to your mouth?"

Shinji shrugged and said, "Let's go home." He knew though that Keita had actually turned the street corner for a split second and ducked back when he saw Shinji surrounded by three high school students. Shinji had thought Keita might have gone to call the police. (Well, given how they were so occupied with the suppression of civilians instead of criminals they weren't all that dependable anyway.) Oh, so there was another book you wanted. I see.

Thanks to this incident, the train ride back to Shiroiwa-cho wasn't much fun.

Keita probably thought Shinji could take on three high school students without any problem. And he was right. Keita probably didn't want to get hurt by getting involved in the fight. And okay, Shinji could understand how the high school students might take note of Keita's face if he'd called the cops. Uh huh. And Keita had no intention of apologizing to Shinji. Sometimes you need to lie to make the world go around.

These things happen. As his uncle often used to say, cowards can't be faulted for being sly. They can't be held responsible for everything.

But the cover was torn on the technical book Shinji bought. On top of that, the edge was stained with the guy's saliva and dented by his teeth. That really got Shinji. Every time he'd open that book he'd have to recall that annoying face. On top of that, and he might be called anal retentive for this, but he hated it when his books were torn or dirty. He always put covers on them when he read them.

His uncle also said this. When you can't accept the results, then you have to punish whoever was responsible for them. Even the score.

So from then on as a form of punishment Shinji decided

to keep his distance from Keita. It wasn't such a severe punishment. After all, it wasn't like he decided they were enemies. They were both better off this way.

So it was a trivial story. And he'd never shared the incident with Yutaka.

But maybe trivializing a story like that one could get you killed in this game. This isn't revenge, Uncle. This is what you'd call the real world. I simply can't be friends with him.

"That's right." In response to Yutaka's statement, Keita Iijima spread his arms. The kitchen knife in his right hand reflected the moonlight. "I thought we were friends."

Shinji still refused to lower the muzzle of his gun.

Seeing how adamant Shinji was, Keita looked like he was about to burst into tears. He threw the kitchen knife onto the ground. "See! I don't want to fight. Do you see now?"

Shinji shook his head. "No. Scram."

Keita's face flushed with anger. "Why? Why won't you trust me?"

"Shinji——"

"Shut up, Yutaka."

Keita's face froze. He turned quiet…and then said, his voice trembling, "Is it because of what I did that time, Shinji? When I ran off? Is that why you don't trust me, Shinji?"

Shinji aimed the gun at him without a word.

"Shinji…" Keita's voice once again turned pathetic. He was practically sobbing, "I'm sorry about that Shinji. I'm so sorry, Shinji—"

Shinji's lips tightened. He wondered whether Keita was being sincere or whether he putting on an act. But then he dismissed the thought. I'm not alone. I can't risk Yutaka's life too. There was an aphorism he'd heard claimed by a Defense Minister of some nation, "We must defend ourselves according to our opponents' ability, not their intentions." They were approaching 1 a.m.

"Shinji, what is going on—"

Shinji held Yutaka back with his right hand.

Keita proceeded forward. "Please. I'm so scared. Please let me join."

"Don't come any closer!" Shinji shouted.

Keita Iijima shook his sad face left and right and stepped out. He was approaching Shinji and Yutaka.

Shinji pointed the gun downward and pulled the trigger for the first time. The shell popping out of the Beretta traced a pale white arc in the moonlight and a cloud of dust rose in front Keita's feet. Keita stared at it as if it were some rare chemistry experiment.

But then he started walking again.

"Stop! Just stop!"

"Please let me join. Please."

Like a wind-up doll Keita stepped forward. Right, left, right.

Shinji clenched his teeth. If Keita was going to pull out something besides his knife, it would have to come from his right arm.

Can you aim well? This time it won't be a threat. Accurately?

Of course.

There was no time left. Shinji pulled the trigger again.

He felt his finger slip.

A split second before the popping sound, Shinji suddenly realized that he was sweating. He was sweating from the tension.

It happened so suddenly. Keita Iijima bent over as if his upper body had been punched in. He spread out his arms like a shotputter does right before throwing a shot, then bent his knees and fell on his back. Even in the dark Shinji could clearly see the blood spurting out of the hole in the right side of his chest like a small fountain. This was also instantaneous.

"Shinji! What'd you do!" Yutaka screamed and ran to Keita. He knelt beside him and put his hands on Keita's body, his mouth agape. Then after hesitating for a moment he touched his neck. His face went pale. "He's dead...."

Shinji remained frozen, still holding onto his gun. He felt like he wasn't thinking, but he was. How lame, the voice echoed in his head. Although it was irrelevant, the voice echoed the way it does when you talk to yourself in the shower.

How lame. I thought you were supposed to be The Third Man, Shinji Mimura, who never missed a shot. The star shooting guard of Shiroiwa Junior High, Shinji Mimura, right?

Shinji stood up and began to walk forward. As if he'd suddenly turned into a cyborg, his body felt heavy. One day Shinji Mimura woke up to find out that he had become the Terminator. Great.

He slowly walked over to Keita Iijima's body.

Yutaka glared back at Shinji.

"Why, Shinji! Why'd you kill him!?

Standing motionless, Shinji answered, "I thought we'd be in trouble if Keita had another weapon besides the knife. I aimed for his arm. I didn't mean to kill him."

Hearing this, Yutaka checked Keita Iijima's body. As if to make a point, he looked through Keita's day pack too. Then he said, "He had nothing! How could you, Shinji!? Why didn't you trust him!?"

Shinji suddenly felt hollow. But...it was necessary. Hey, Uncle, I didn't do anything wrong, did I? Right?

Shinji looked down at Yutaka without saying a word. But—that's right—they had to hurry. They couldn't let their mistakes drag them down.

Right before he was about to say this, something

changed in Yutaka's face.

His lips trembled. He said, "Oh no, Shinji, don't tell me you—"

Shinji had no idea what he was referring to. He asked, "What?"

Yutaka quickly stepped back. He distanced himself from Shinji.

Yutaka spoke through his trembling lips, "Shinji, you didn't do that on purpose—"

Shinji's lips tightened. He gripped the Beretta in his left hand.

"You're saying I shot Keita to buy us time? That's…"

Yutaka frantically shook his head. Then he slowly retreated. "No…no…this whole plan—"

Shinji knit his brows and stared at Yutaka. Yutaka, what is it you're getting at?

"This whole thing about our escape, that was just, that was—"

Yutaka still didn't make any sense, but Shinji whose brain's CPU was amazingly fast finally had understood what Yutaka was thinking.

No, it can't be—

But what else could it be?

Yutaka was accusing Shinji of having no intention whatsoever to escape, that he had been planning all along to "play" this game. That's why he shot Keita.

Shinji's face gave a look of absolute dismay. His mouth might have been hanging open for all he knew.

Then he shouted, "Don't be stupid! Why the hell would I be with you then!?"

Yutaka was trembling, shaking his head. "That's…that's…"

Yutaka didn't say anymore, but Shinji understood that too. He probably wanted to say that Shinji was using him to survive, for instance by having him keep watch so Shinji could sleep. But waitasec here, I used the laptop to take on Sakamochi, and even after that failed, I came up with this other plan. So you're saying since I'm smart I was playing around with the cell phone and laptop to gain your trust and that my hidden intention was to use the gasoline and fertilizer to protect myself and win the game. That since I only had one gun, a special explosive would come in handy to survive in this game? That right before executing the plan to bomb the school I was going to say, "Nah, let's not"? Just like how I'd said, "It's not working" when I was computer hacking? Look, waitasec though, what about that wire we installed by the school? Are you saying I wanted to start a wire-can phone business on this island where all the phone circuits have been shut off? Or you're just saying that was another act? Or that I had some plan you couldn't even conceive of?

When I said I'd help out after you told me you were going to avenge Izumi Kanai's death, you cried. So my response was another deception?

That's too much, Yutaka. I mean there's no end to suspicion once you get going. But you're going too far. This is absurd. Really, it's hilarious. Funnier than your jokes. Maybe you're losing it from fatigue.

That's what Shinji thought on a rational level. And if he could have gone through each explanation step by step then Yutaka would have realized how foolish every one of his suspicions were. In fact, everything Shinji could come up with might not have corresponded to Yutaka's suspicions. It might have been a simple case of fatigue combined with the shock of witnessing his close friend die suddenly giving way to a suspicion lurking somewhere in the back of Yutaka's mind. But...it came to surface because it had been there in the first place, his suspicion towards Shinji. And the thought of suspecting Yutaka had never even occurred to Shinji.

All of a sudden, the exhaustion he felt was overpowering. A horizontal twelve-cylinder turbo engine. This level of exhaustion is top-class, yessir, it really is a steal, sir.

Shinji uncocked the Beretta and tossed it over to Yutaka. Yutaka hesitated but received it.

Emptied out, Shinji threw his hands onto his knees.

"If you don't trust me then shoot me, Yutaka. I don't care, just shoot me." Crouching, Shinji continued, "I shot Keita to protect you, Yutaka. Damn."

Yutaka suddenly looked at him blankly. Then ready to burst into tears, he uttered, "Oh...oh..." He ran to Shinji.

Yutaka put his hand on Shinji's shoulder and began sobbing out loud. Shinji stared down at the ground with his hands on his knees. He realized his eyes too were filled with tears.

Somewhere in the back of his mind, he was telling himself, hey hey, don't you have more urgent matters to attend to? Look how vulnerable you guys are bickering like this. Have you forgotten, you're surrounded by enemies? Look at your watch for crying out loud, you're out of time...the voice resembled his uncle's.

But Shinji's nerves were too worn out, his body too tired, and emotions too rattled from Yutaka's suspicion against him to take heed of this warning.

He merely cried. Yutaka. I was trying to protect you. How could you suspect me? I trusted you...but then again, maybe Keita Iijima felt the same way. How horrible to be suspected by someone you trust. I did an awful thing.

Amidst these worn out emotions of sadness, exhaustion, and regret, Shinji heard a rattling that sounded like the tapping of an old typewriter.

A split second later, he felt as if burnt tongs were poking through his body.

The wounds were fatal by then, but the pain made Shinji come to his senses. Yutaka, who had his hand on Shinji's shoulder, fell to the ground. Over at the far end of the farm coop parking lot was a figure in a school coat. He held a gun—something bigger than a pistol. It looked more like a tin box. Shinji realized he'd been shot—of course with bullets, damn—with bullets that had exited through Yutaka's body.

His body felt hot and stiff (the guy just lanced me with lead bullets, duh), but Shinji reflexively fell to his left and picked up the Beretta Yutaka had taken and dropped. He aimed it at the figure, Kazuo Kiriyama (Male Student No. 6) and fired several times at his stomach.

Kazuo Kiriyama shifted to the right before the shots got to him, though. Then along with the rattling sound, the tips of his hands flashed like out-of-season fireworks.

The blows he felt in the right side of his stomach, his left shoulder, and chest were much worse than the one he'd just felt a moment ago. The Beretta fell from his hand.

But by then Shinji had already begun running toward the farm coop. He staggered for a moment, but then crouched down and dashed off, leaping through the sliding door head first. A stream of bullets chased after him and right when Shinji thought he'd escaped them, it managed to blow off the tip of his right foot's basketball sneaker. This time Shinji grimaced in agony from the pain shooting through his body.

But he had no time to rest. He grabbed the gas can in the shadow of the sliding door and retreated through the dark where the tractor and combine harvester were, practically crawling on his left arm and left leg. He dragged the gas can with his right hand.

Blood was pouring out of his mouth. There were at least ten bullets in his body. And despite the sharp pain that shot up from his right foot he managed to glance at the vanished tip of his basketball shoes and thought, I guess I can't play ball anymore. Impossible now. Even if I could I'll never be in the starting lineup. So much for my basketball career.

But Shinji was more concerned about Yutaka. Could he still be alive?

Kazuo—Shinji coughed up blood as he clenched his teeth—so you've decided to play the game, you bastard. Then come after me. Yutaka can't move, but I can. You can take care of Yutaka later. First come after me. Come on, come after me.

As if responding to his wish, Shinji could see from underneath the tractor a figure in the blue pale belt of light coming in through the sliding door.

Then along with the rattling sound, lights flashed like camera flashes, and bullets scattered across the building. A part of some farm equipment was blown to bits, and the window across from him was smashed into fragments.

It stopped. He was out of bullets. But Kazuo would reload another magazine.

Shinji grabbed a screwdriver near him and tossed it to his left. It made a clanging sound and tapped onto the floor.

He thought Kazuo would shoot over there, but instead he scattered bullets across in an arc around the screwdriver. Shinji ducked, praying he wouldn't be hit. The shooting stopped again. Shinji looked up.

Now...he could tell Kazuo was inside the building.

That's right, Shinji's blood-drenched lips formed a smile. I'm over here. Come over here—

Shinji lifted the gas can with his right hand and placed it on his stomach. He moved back again with his left arm and left leg, trying his best not to make any sound. His back hit a hard, boxlike object, and he slid around it as he continued to retreat. His movements weren't completely silent. Kazuo already knew he was hiding somewhere in the dark here. The blood dripping out of him was a dead giveaway.

Kazuo crouched down and checked under various farm tools and the pickup truck as he approached Shinji.

Shinji surveyed the area. He could barely make out the outline of the upper floor on the opposite side of the building as well as the steel stairs that led up there from the door. If his body was in adequate condition he could have jumped on him from up there. But that wasn't possible anymore.

There was a cart on the east wall. It was a pushcart with four small wheels used to carry equipment. The office in the corner with partitions was beyond the pushcart and next to it was an exit. The sliding door, if fully opened, was large enough for a car, but this one was only for people. The door was shut.

That door...I locked it along with the other windows and every other door. How long would it take me to unlock it?

He had no time to think it over. Shinji dragged his body over to the pushcart. Once he was there he placed the gas can on it. He opened its lid. He pushed in the rubber object dangling from a plastic cord.

He took out the detonation device in his pocket. His fingers were clumsy—probably due to his wounds—but they finally managed to peel off the tape on the side of the battery, revealing an exposed wire dangling from the detonator tube. Shinji connected it to the wire tip of the condenser circuit. He pulled off the insulation of the battery case. As he heard a faint, high hum from the rapid charge of the condenser, he quickly peeled off the tape on the charge device switch and shoved the detonator tube deep inside the gas can's rubber cap. He left the rest of the unit, including the charge device, the battery case, and circuit, on top of the gas can. He had no time to secure it. He could see Kazuo's feet to the right of the threshing machine.

His chances were slim. But now that Yutaka and me are injured there's no way we'll ever make it up the mountain. So...

...here's a special something for you, Kazuo.

Shinji kicked the pushcart with his left leg as hard as he could. As the cart skimmed by the other equipment, Shinji leaped for the exit door without even checking to see if the cart was heading towards Kazuo.

He unlocked it in 0.2 seconds. He even utilized his right leg with its missing foot tip to crash through the door and leap out of the building.

The slate walls of the farm coop behind him suddenly burst with an explosion that shook the entire dark island. The sound of Kazuo's hand grenade that had temporarily disabled Shuya's hearing was nothing compared to this explosion. Shinji realized, whoa, there go my eardrums.

His body slid on the ground from the blast of the explosion, scraping off the skin on his forehead. Fragments and scraps blew by. Still, Shinji managed to look back quickly and see, right where the building's wall should be, the light truck floating in the air upside down. Probably due to its raised position from the jack, the blast had slammed it with incredible pressure, blowing it upwards. It spun around slowly in air filled with fragments of glass, slate, and concrete (he felt as if they were also stuck into his body too, but the ones he saw now didn't come flying out directly, but were blown up into the sky), traced an exaggerated arc, and crashed on its side in the middle of the parking lot. It rolled over another ninety degrees and stopped, completely upside down. The back carriage was nearly torn off, twisted up like a wrung out rag, and the wheel with a missing tire somehow managed to still spin around and around.

Fragments continued showering down. Immersed in clouds of smoke the farm coop was now reduced to only its frame. The only wall remaining was part of the one on the north side, along with the upper floor. But the upper floor was completely exposed behind the smoke. The south side of the roof was completely blown away, and the machines, including the farm equipment, were scattered around on their sides. Even in the dark Shinji could tell they were burnt black. He saw several bright flames. Maybe something was on fire. The side exit Shinji used to escape through was barely connected to the remains of the wall by the bottom hinges, bent over his way, as if bowing. The office with partitions had completely vanished without a trace. Well, actually there was the office desk still hanging on, glued to the part of the wall that escaped destruction, pushed from behind by the combine harvester that was also probably blown away by the explosion.

Something must have been blown up high in the sky because, completely out of sync with the other debris, it was finally landing somewhere in the smoke with a high metallic ring. Although Shinji could hardly hear it.

Next thing he knew, Shinji was struggling to get up from the debris of wall and other materials, staring at the ruins of the building. He gasped.

Yes, the handmade gasoline can bomb was well made. With that kind of destructive force it would have certainly annihilated the school.

But that was all over now. The important thing now was that he'd defeated the enemy coming after him. And even more urgent was—

"Yutaka…"

He mumbled as he finally got up, kneeling on his right knee on the debris. The moment he opened his mouth, blood came gushing out between his teeth, and he felt an incredible surge of pain running from his chest down to his stomach. It was a miracle he was still alive. But he stretched out his arms and put his right leg down on its heel and then stretched out his left leg and somehow managed to stand up. Shinji looked over to the edge of the parking lot where Yutaka was lying...

...when he saw the overturned light truck's door—it must have been busted—open with a dull creaking sound. (He could hear it faintly. Some of his hearing seemed to be coming back.)

Kazuo Kiriyama stepped down onto the ground. He held the tin-box-like machine gun in his right hand as if nothing had happened.

Hey—

Shinji felt like he should burst out laughing. For all he knew his blood-soaked lips might have even formed a smile.

You gotta be kidding.

By then Kazuo fired. Shinji this time met a full frontal parabolic shower of 9mm bullets and staggered back into the ground covered with debris. Something was pressing into his back. As of now there really was no need to check it, but he thought it was the front of the parked station wagon. The station wagon had also been blown up by the blast, its back stuck into a wooden telephone pole now lopsided from the impact. Another object seemed to have smashed into its windshield, which resembled a spider's web.

Surrounded by the bright flames burning in the building, Kazuo calmly stood still. Then beyond him Shinji saw Yutaka lying on his face, half buried in the debris. Right near him was Keita Iijima lying on his back, his face staring at Shinji.

He thought, Kazuo, damn, so I ended up losing to you.

He thought, I'm sorry Yutaka, I let my guard down for a moment.

He thought, Uncle, how lame, huh?

He thought, Ikumi, fall in love and be happy. Looks like

I won't be able to...looks like...

Kazuo Kiriyama's Ingram burst out once again and Shinji's thoughts came to an end. The bullets had torn apart his cerebral cortex. Near his head, the cracked front windshield was now shattered, most of its fragments sliding into the car, but some of the finer mistlike particles fell on Shinji's body already covered with dust and debris.

Shinji slowly fell forward on his face. Debris bounced up on impact. It took less than thirty seconds for the rest of his body besides his brain to die. The memento of his beloved uncle—the earring worn by the woman he loved—was now stained in blood running down Shinji's left ear, reflecting the glow from the building now consumed in red flames.

And so the boy known as The Third Man, Shinji Mimura, was now dead.

17 students remaining

PART 3

FINAL STAGE

17 students remaining

52

In the bushes with her blanket over her shoulders, Noriko hugged her knees and stared at the ground. It was still very dark and insects were humming the way a fluorescent light sputters out before it dies.

Sakamochi's midnight announcement came on right after they reached this area. He announced the death of Hirono Shimizu (Female Student No. 10), who had—although Noriko herself didn't see it—killed Kaori Minami and fled from Shuya, followed by the addition of three forbidden zones. At 1 a.m. F=7, at 3 a.m. G=3, and at 5 a.m. E=4. Noriko and Shogo's sector, C=3, was still safe. Shuya's name wasn't mentioned, but...

Ten to twenty minutes later, there was distant gunfire again and then the sound of that machine gun. Noriko's heart froze. The sound continued.

She couldn't forget it. It was unmistakable—the sound of Kazuo Kiriyama's machine gun. Unless someone else had the same gun. Regardless, the sound was enough to make her wonder whether Kazuo had finally caught up to Shuya.

Before Noriko could mention this to Shogo though, there was an incredible explosion. The hand grenade they encountered when they were fighting Kiriyama was nothing compared to this. And then there was the faint sound of the machine gun, once or twice. After that the island returned to silence.

Even Shogo seemed surprised by the sound. He was carving an arrow-like object with his knife when he suddenly stopped and said, "I'm going to go have a look. Don't move," and walked out of the bushes. He came back immediately and told her, "A building's on fire on the east side."

Noriko started to ask, "Could it be?...," but Shogo shook his head and said, "It's quite a ways south from where Kiriyama was. Shuya escaped into the mountainside, so it can't be him. Let's wait for him here."

Noriko felt relieved for the time being. But nearly an entire hour had passed since then. Shuya still hadn't returned.

Noriko held her wrist under the coin-sized moonlight coming through the branches and checked her watch. It was 1:12 a.m. She'd been repeating this gesture as if it were a magical ritual.

Then she buried her head between her knees.

A horrible image flashed by in her thoughts. Shuya's face. His mouth half-open and eyes looking off into the distance, the way he looked singing a song called "Imagine" (Shuya said it was a rock standard) during one of their breaks in the music room, out of the teacher's sight. But this face had a large, black dot similar to one worn by a Hindu worshipper. Without warning, red liquid came oozing out of the dot. The large dot was in fact a very dark and deep hole. The blood poured out from his brain, covering his face…like cracks running through a piece of glass.…

Noriko shivered and shook her head, dismissing the thought. She looked up at Shogo, who was leaning against a tree trunk, smoking a cigarette. There was a handmade bow next to him and several arrows stuck in the ground.

"Shogo."

He looked like a silhouette in the dark. He removed the cigarette from his mouth and rested his right wrist on his upright knee.

"What is it?"

"Shuya should be here by now."

He put his cigarette in his mouth again. Its tip reddened, faintly lighting up his calm face. Noriko felt impatient. His face darkened again and smoke drifted out of his mouth.

"Yeah."

His calm tone also irritated her. But then she reminded herself how he'd saved her and Shuya several times over, so she restrained herself.

"Something must have...happened."

"Probably."

"What do you mean, 'probably'?"

His silhouette raised its arms. The lit cigarette moved. "Calm down. That was definitely Kazuo's machine gun. Unless they supplied an identical machine gun to someone else. And given how the explosion occurred over there, it means that Kazuo was fighting someone besides Shuya. Shuya escaped from Kazuo. I know that much."

"But then why isn't he—"

He interrupted, "He's probably hiding somewhere. Or he might have gotten lost."

She shook her head. "He might be hurt. Or even worse..."

She felt a chill run down her spine. She couldn't continue. The image of Shuya with the red spider-web face and half-open mouth flashed by again. Shuya might have escaped from Kazuo, but he might have been severely wounded, he might be dying right now. Even if that wasn't the case, what if he was attacked by someone while he was running through the mountains...or what if he fell unconscious somewhere, and what if that was in a forbidden zone, then Shuya would end up dead. That's right...Shuya might have run into the base of the northern mountain which was in sector F=7, directly north of the school, sector F=7 which was a forbidden zone as of 1 a.m. And now it was past 1 a.m. Which meant...

She shook her head again. That couldn't be. Shuya couldn't die. Because...Shuya was like a holy man with a guitar. He was always kind to everyone, he was always so sympathetic to the sorrows of others, but he would never lose that powerful smile, he was so upright and transparent and innocent but also tough. He's like my guardian angel. How could someone like that die? There's no way he could...but still...

Shogo quietly said, "He might be, he might not be."

She turned her wrist and nervously checked her watch again. She moved her leg painfully and sidled up to Shogo. She squeezed Shogo's left hand, which was on his knees, with both hands.

"Please. Can't we go...can't we go look for him? Will you come with me? I can't do this on my own. Please."

Shogo said nothing. He only lifted his left hand slowly, returning Noriko's hands to her thighs, and tapped them lightly. "We can't. Even if you insist on going alone, I won't let you. Shuya wanted me to look after you. He took a big risk making us leave before him. I don't want to jeopardize all he did for us."

She bit her lower lip and stared at him.

"Don't give me that look. You're making this hard on me." Shogo scratched his head with his hand holding his cigarette and said, "You care about Shuya, right?"

She nodded. She didn't hesitate.

He nodded back and said, "Then let's respect his wishes."

She bit her lip again, but then looked down and nodded. "All right. We can only wait, right?"

"That's right." He nodded.

They were silent for a while but then he asked, "Do you believe in sixth sense?"

The topic was so unexpected Noriko widened her eyes. Was he trying to distract her?

"Well...a little. I don't really know though," she responded. "Do you?"

He crushed his cigarette into the ground. Then he said, "Absolutely not...well, I don't think it matters either way. All that stuff about ghosts, the afterlife, cosmic power, sixth sense, fortune telling, psychic powers, that's just the talk of fools who can only deal with reality by avoiding it. I'm sorry. You said you believed a little. That's just my opinion. But…"

She looked at his eyes. "But?"

"But sometimes without any apparent reason I'm certain about things I can't know for sure. And for some reason I've never been wrong when this happens."

She remained silent and stared at him.

He said, "Shuya's still alive. He'll be back. I know it."

Her face suddenly relaxed. He might have been making this up on the spot, but even so she was touched he made the effort.

"Thanks," she said, "You're kind, Shogo."

He shrugged. "I'm just telling you how I feel." Then he said, "Shuya's a lucky guy."

She looked over at him. "Hm?"

"Lucky that someone loves him this much."

She smiled just a little. "You got it wrong."

"What?"

"It's unrequited. Shuya likes someone else. I'm nothing compared to her."

"…really?"

She looked down and nodded. "She's really awesome. I don't know how to describe her. She's so strong and beautiful. I'm jealous, but I can understand why he's attracted to her."

He tilted his head and said, "I don't know." He flicked his lighter several times and lit another cigarette and added, "I think Shuya cares about you now."

She shook her head. "Oh no."

"When he comes back," he smiled, "you should let him have it, call him a jerk for making you worry like this."

She smiled a little again.

He blew out smoke. "Now lie down. You haven't fully recovered yet. Once you're drowsy, get some sleep. I'll stay up all night. If Shuya shows up, I'll tell him to wake the princess with a kiss."

"Uh huh." She smiled and nodded. "Thanks."

She still sat up another ten minutes. Then she wrapped herself in the blanket and lay down.

She still couldn't sleep though.

17 students remaining

53

Hiroki Sugimura was getting exhausted. He'd been walking without stopping ever since the game began, so it was only natural. But every time he heard Sakamochi's announcement, his level of exhaustion rose as if he were climbing a staircase. Now only twenty were left...no, as far as Hiroki knew, the number was down to seventeen. It was hard to believe, but Shinji Mimura was dead, along with Yutaka Seto and Keita Iijima.

After he left Shuya's group at the clinic, Hiroki headed towards the island's northwest shore, which he'd never checked out. Then a little past 11 p.m. he heard heavy gunfire and moved back east of the island's central area in pursuit of the sound. But the noise stopped before he got there, so he couldn't find anything. Then the midnight announcement came, and the additional forbidden zones were announced. Hiroki decided to comb through each of those zones. As he was entering the north side of the school, sector F=7, which would be forbidden at 1 a.m., he heard a gunshot and then...that machine gun sound.

Because he was in the mountain, looking over the flat

area, Hiroki saw a repeating flash, what seemed like a muzzle flashing in the farm immediately west of the housing area. As he descended the slope he heard an ear-shattering explosion. The night sky above the trees lit up. Then he heard the rattling sound again.

As he left the foot of the mountain, he saw a building on fire where the light had been flashing. Hiroki thought the assailant with the machine gun might still be there, but as he'd done with Megumi Eto, he had to find out what happened. He cautiously wove his way through the farm, approaching the area where...

...he found the body of Shinji Mimura. The area was flickering with flames. The warehouse building—that must have been what exploded—was blown apart. Large and small debris were scattered all over what appeared to be a parking lot. Shinji was lying face down in front of a station wagon in the lot. His body was riddled with bullets. Later Hiroki found the bodies of Yutaka Seto and Keita Iijima in the debris.

There was no trace of the assailant with the machine gun, but Hiroki thought it was likely someone who was "playing the game" would show up soon, so he quickly left the area.

It was only after he'd crossed the island's latitudinal road and entered the base of the southern mountain that he thought about Shinji, the death of *the* Shinji Mimura. There was something unbelievable about it, since Hiroki knew him pretty well. It sounded offensive now, but he'd always thought Shinji was immortal. Hiroki went to the town martial arts school and learned martial arts, but that in the end was just a matter of technique. It was nothing against Shinji's inborn athletic prowess. Even if they'd fought according to martial arts rules, and even though Hiroki was ten centimeters taller, Shinji would have easily defeated him in a match. Besides, Shinji was much smarter than him. Even if Shinji couldn't escape the game (although it was likely he'd considered it), Hiroki firmly believed no one else would be able to kill Shinji. And yet the machine gun shooter somehow managed to do just that.

He couldn't afford to mourn over Shinji, though. What mattered now was finding Kayoko Kotohiki. He had to find her soon—if the machine gun shooter found her, someone like Kotohiki would get instantly killed.

Since sector G=3, forbidden at 3 a.m., was on the northern side of the southern mountain peak, Hiroki decided to head over there.

He'd already entered this mountain several times now. Takako Chigusa's body was still lying in sector H-4 in the region right before sector G=3. He couldn't even bury her body. He'd only managed to close her eyes and cross her arms over her chest. Her body was still outside the forbidden zone.

As he cautiously moved forward through the darkness, Hiroki thought, I'm so awful. He wasn't even able to stay by his closest childhood friend. He'd probably be walking by her as he headed towards sector G=3.

I'm so sorry, Takako. I still need to take care of something. Right now I just have to see Kayoko Kotohiki. Please forgive me....

Then something else occurred to him. It concerned Yutaka Seto.

Yutaka's seating number immediately followed his, so Yutaka had exited right after Hiroki. But Hiroki was still in the middle of checking out the premises, frantically searching for a hiding place that gave him a clear look at the school exit, so Yutaka was gone by the time he could afford to look back. Hiroki decided Takako would be his priority, and so he let Haruka Tanizawa (Female Student No. 12) and Yuichiro Takiguchi (Male Student No. 13) pass by. (But in spite of his extreme caution, Yoshio Akamatsu's surprise appearance had made him panic enough to lose Takako.) Yutaka had managed to join up with his friends Shinji Mimura and Keita Iijima. But Yutaka was now dead along with Shinji.

I have to hurry, he thought. I can't let Kotohiki die.

He stopped by a bare tree and checked the radar in his left hand again. With the moon providing the only source of light, the unlit liquid crystal display was difficult to read, but by squinting his eyes he found he could make out faint traces of the crystal particles.

Nothing changed on the screen, though. There was only the star mark indicating his position. Hiroki sighed.

Maybe he should just shout for Kotohiki. Hiroki had considered doing this several times, but then decided against it. When he found Takako, it had been too late. He didn't want that to happen again.

No. It wouldn't work. He couldn't. First of all, Kotohiki wouldn't necessarily respond to his call. In fact, she might run away. Furthermore, although he didn't care about someone coming after him once he called for her, if Kotohiki were to come at the same time she might end up getting attacked.

In the end, he could only rely on the government-supplied radar. And without this equipment, he would have been even worse off. He absolutely despised the government for throwing them into this stupid game, but he had to admit he benefited from his equipment. What's this called? A stroke of luck in hard times? Or more like, a light in a tunnel of fury?

He went up and down a low cliff covered in bushes and came out onto a gentle slope scattered with trees. He knew he was entering sector H=4, where Takako was resting in peace. Hiroki raised the radar, moving it slightly to catch the moonlight on the crystal display.

He saw a blurred double image of the star mark indicating his position at the center of the display. Oh no, I'm getting tired. Even my vision's going now.

...

Hiroki was still looking down when he realized he was wrong. At the same time, he turned around and swung his stick in his right hand. Following the martial arts technique he had learned so thoroughly, his elegant swing traced a graceful arc.

The stick impressively landed on the arm of the figure standing behind him. The person groaned and dropped the object, a gun, in their hand. Someone had snuck up behind him when his guard was down for that brief moment.

The figure made a dash for the gun on the ground. Hiroki thrust the stick out in front of him. The figure froze and then staggered back—

Hiroki saw it. First, it was only the sailor suit. Then the beautiful face, brightly lit by the moon—angelic—it was unmistakably hers. It was right after he left the school, when he still hadn't managed to find a hiding place....Hiroki had been lurking in the corner of the athletic field when he saw the face of Mitsuko Souma (Female Student No. 11) as she emerged from the school building after him.

Mitsuko lifted both of her hands and stepped back. "Please don't kill me! Please don't kill me!" she shouted. She staggered and fell on her behind, revealing her white legs up beyond her thighs under her pleated skirt. She continued coquettishly to move back in the pale blue moonlight.

"Please! I was just trying to talk to you! I wouldn't think of killing anyone! Please help me! Help me!"

Hiroki looked down at her without saying a word.

Maybe she'd taken his silence to be a sign he meant no

harm. Mitsuko slowly lowered her hands. Her eyes had the intimidated look of a terrified mouse, and tears were gleaming in them.

"You believe me, don't you?" she said. A ray of moonlight fell on her tearstained face. Her eyes were faintly smiling. Of course, it wasn't the proud victorious smile of deception, but a smile brimming with relief that she felt deep in her heart.

"I...I...," she said but then pulled on her skirt with her left hand as if she'd finally realized her thighs were exposed. "I thought I could trust you...so...I've been so scared...all alone...this is so awful...I'm just so terrified...."

Without saying a word, Hiroki picked up the gun Mitsuko had dropped. He saw it was cocked, so he uncocked the hammer with one hand and walked over to Mitsuko. He offered her the handle of the gun.

"Th-thank you...." Mitsuko reached out.

But the gun froze.

Hiroki flipped it around with his hand. Now the muzzle was pointed right between her brows.

"Wh-what are you doing, Hiroki?"

Mitsuko's face was twisted with dismay and horror—at the very least it looked contorted. She was priceless. It wouldn't matter how many sordid rumors you heard about Mitsuko Souma, most people (particularly guys) would have to believe her once this angelic face of hers pleaded for mercy. No, even if you didn't believe her, you'd still end up doing anything you could for her. By no means was Hiroki an exception. Still, he had special circumstances.

"Forget it, Mitsuko," Hiroki said. He held the gun and stood upright. "I saw Takako right before she died."

"Oh..."

She looked up at him, her perfectly shaped eyes trembling. Even if inside she was regretting not having finished Takako off, she gave no indication whatsoever of any regret. She just maintained that terrified look...a look seeking understanding and protection.

"N-no! That was an accident. Sure, I saw some of the others. But...when I encountered Takako...it was her...she...she tried to kill me...that gun's really Takako's...so...so I..."

Hiroki recocked the Colt .45 with a click. Mitsuko's eyes squinted.

"I know Takako. Takako would never try to kill someone, nor would she ever panic and go on a shooting spree. Even in this stupid game," Hiroki said.

Mitsuko tucked in her chin. She looked up at Hiroki and formed a smile. While it sent chills down his spine, it was precisely then that Mitsuko looked even more beautiful.

Ha, she faintly laughed. "I thought she died instantly," she said.

Hiroki didn't respond and kept pointing the gun at her.

Still sitting, Mitsuko pinched the edge of her skirt with her left thumb and index finger, pulling it back slowly, once again revealing those enticing legs.

Hiroki looked up.

"How about it? If you help me, you can do what you like with me. I'm not bad, you know."

Hiroki remained frozen, holding the gun. He examined her face.

"I guess not," Mitsuko said. She said lightly, "Of course not. I mean I'd kill you the moment you let down your guard. Besides, how could you sleep with the girl who killed your girlfriend—"

"She's not my girlfriend."

Mitsuko looked at Hiroki.

Hiroki continued, "But she was my best friend."

"Oh really?" Mitsuko raised her brow. Then she asked, "Why won't you shoot me then? Is it because you're some kind of feminist? Can't shoot women?"

Her supremely confident face was still beautiful. It was totally different from Takako's, who, that's right, had the graceful beauty of a war goddess in Greek or Roman myth. Here we had a teenage sorceress. She's charming, innocent, angelic, yet completely frigid. Under the moonlight, her eyes were like gleaming ice. Hiroki felt dizzy.

"How..." He could tell his voice was hoarse. "How could you kill someone so easily?"

"You fool," Mitsuko said. She sounded as if she could care less about the gun pointed at her forehead. "Those are the rules."

Hiroki squinted and shook his head. "Not everyone's playing by them."

Mitsuko tilted her head again. Then she said, still smiling warmly, "Hiroki." It sounded so plain and friendly, the way a girl who ended up sitting next to her crush would call him, looking for some topic to bring up before homeroom began.

"You're probably a good person, Hiroki," she said.

Hiroki didn't understand and knit his brows. His mouth might have been open.

Mitsuko continued, lightly, as she were singing, "Good people are good. In some respects. But even those good people can turn bad. Or maybe they end up being good their entire lives. Maybe you're one of those people."

Mitsuko looked away from Hiroki and then shook her head.

"No, that's beside the point. I just decided to take instead of being taken. It's not a question of good or bad, wrong or right. It's just what I want to do."

Hiroki's lips trembled. They were twitching uncontrollably.

"…why though?"

Mitsuko smiled again. "I don't know. But if I have to come up with some explanation. Well, for starters…" She looked into Hiroki's eyes and then said, "I was raped when I was nine years old. Three guys taking turns, three times each, oh, wait, one of them might have done it four times. One of you did it. Although they were middle-aged men. I was just a skinny kid back then, my chest was flat, and my legs were like sticks, but that's what they wanted. And when I started screaming that only excited them more. So even now when I'm with perverted men like that I still pretend to cry."

Hiroki stood frozen as he stared at Mitsuko who'd just revealed so much but continued wearing her pleasant smile. He was shocked by this devastating story.

It was—

Hiroki might have been on the verge of saying something. But before he could, a silver light flashed out of Mitsuko's hands. Hiroki realized Mitsuko had managed to reach behind her back with her right hand, but by then the double-bladed diver's knife (this used to be Megumi Eto's weapon) was already planted in his right shoulder. Hiroki let out a groan, and although he still held the gun, he staggered back in pain.

Mitsuko instantly got up, ran past Hiroki, and into the woods behind him.

Hiroki quickly looked back and caught a glimpse of her…as she vanished into the dark.

He knew if he didn't kill Mitsuko Souma now then Kayoko Kotohiki might be the next one to fall into her trap. But Hiroki couldn't bring himself to do it. Instead, he pressed his left hand against his right shoulder where the blood from the knife wound began to soak through his school coat. He stared into the dark where Mitsuko had disappeared.

Of course…Mitsuko might have made up that story to stall him. But Hiroki couldn't buy that. Mitsuko told him the truth. And he'd only heard…part of it. Hiroki had been puzzled over how a third-year junior high school girl his age could be so merciless. It turned out she had acquired the psyche of a grown adult a long time ago. A twisted adult's, no, maybe it was more accurate to say a twisted child's psyche?

The blood oozed down his sleeve then down the Colt .45 and began dripping from the tip in a thin line, landing onto a pile of moldy leaves by his feet without a sound.

17 students remaining

54

Slightly past 3:30 a.m., Toshinori Oda (Male Student No. 4) left the house he was hiding in. Immediately after he hid there, he surmised it was inside sector E=4. Sakamochi had announced the sector would be forbidden at 5 a.m.

Before he opened the back door to leave, he glanced over at Hirono Shimizu's body, which he'd dragged into the corner. All he did was glance at the body lying face down. He didn't feel particularly sorry for her. After all this was a serious competition. You get what you deserve. Hirono Shimizu didn't even think twice about shooting him the moment she saw him. Of course, he'd been the one who snuck up behind Hirono to choke her.

Although he wasn't sure where his next resting spot should be, Toshinori finally decided to move east towards the residential area. The area on the map was approximately two hundred square meters. According to the map, the narrow flat land extending outward from the residential area turned into farm fields spotted with houses. Once he was well beyond this zone then all he had to do was hide in one of these houses. After all, he came from a privileged family and lived in what was probably the nicest house in the prefecture (Kazuo Kiriyama's house was probably the nicest, but Toshinori would never admit this). Hiding in bushes was beneath him. Entering a house was dangerous, given how someone might already be hiding there, but he wasn't worried. Now he not only had a bulletproof vest (with a certificate of high quality) but the revolver he'd taken from Hirono. Furthermore...

...he was now wearing a full-face motorcycle helmet he'd found inside the house.

A thin cloud appeared in the sky. Its tip was already slowly beginning to cross the low full moon. After checking the chin guard of his superdeluxe helmet, he crossed the yard and made his way down the edge of the narrow field next to it.

He could see the flat land continuing down to the eastern shore. It wasn't completely flat, though. It went up and down. Most of the area was covered with farms visible by their various moonlit shades. On the left, a hundred meters away, was a house by the base of the northern mountain. There was another house another hundred meters to its right. Further left were two more houses. There were no other houses in the vicinity. Three to four hundred meters away were farms spotted with houses. He couldn't see very well because his view was blocked by a hill and the woods, but this geography seemed to continue out to the residential area on the island's east side. The flames from the intense explosion that came immediately after Sakamochi's midnight announcement were located immediately to the right of the hill. But the flames must have gone out, because now the area sank back into darkness.

On the south side, to his right, were two adjacent houses.

But this was—if you assumed the blue dots indicated residential houses—on the borderline between sectors E=4 and F=4. Behind him the northern and southern mountains were connected—or to be more accurate, the base of the northern mountain stretched out like a cliff along the western shore without any houses in sight. According to the map though, there were supposed to be a couple houses up in the mountain.

Unless he'd misread the map, he'd be outside the forbidden zone if he got to the third or fourth house to the east. But if he found out they were dumps, then he might have to consider moving further on. First of all, he couldn't stand dirty houses, and second of all, he was certain a vulgar place would only attract vulgar people.

Toshinori decided to move over there.

He crouched down and walked cautiously along the field ridge of the farm. But he was appalled at the sensation of dirty soil. The dull pain he felt from Hirono Shimizu's shot in the stomach area of his bulletproof vest only infuriated him more. Why did he have to be thrown into this coarse game and writhe around on the ground with the "vulgar masses"? (This was an expression his father, who ran the largest food company in the eastern part of the prefecture, often used at home, but it was a favorite phrase Toshinori himself used to express his scorn for the "vulgar masses." Of course, he *was* well bred, so he could never say it out loud.)

Whether he had a right to claim it or not, it was true he possessed a unique gift, unique even among his talented classmates who ranged from being star players of their teams and clubs to being leading delinquents, or even being queer (this one was dead now, he was a very vulgar queer too). In fact, it was unique to the entire school.

He'd started private violin lessons when he was four years old, and now he was one of the leading junior high school players in the entire prefecture. He wasn't a genius, but he wasn't mediocre either. Arrangements were made for him to enter a highly distinguished high school in Tokyo that had its own music department. As for his future career, he thought he'd at the very least become the prefectural government symphony conductor.

This gave him—so he believed—all the more reason not to die. He would attain the status of conductor, marry a beautiful, refined woman, and mingle with rich, elegant people. (His older brother Tadanori was going to inherit the company. Of course, the thought of making a lot of money as president was attractive, but I don't need to deal with food products, yuck. I'll let my vulgar brother deal with that.) He was different from his loser classmates. Their deaths wouldn't mean a thing, but he was *gifted*. He was *precious*. And even in biological terms, the superior species was destined to survive, right?

At first he only had this bulletproof vest, oddly supplied as a weapon, so all he could do was sneak away and hide, but now he had a gun. He was going to be merciless. What's this about the noble soul of a music lover? That's totally naïve! It was true he was only fifteen, and he hadn't seen much of the world, but he knew what the music world was like. For those who weren't geniuses it was all about money and connections. It was all about crushing other competitors to survive.

Whether this was objectively true or not, this was what Toshinori Oda believed.

Of course, he had no close friends in Third Year Class B that was filled with the vulgar masses. In fact, he despised his vulgar classmates. Especially Shuya Nanahara.

Toshinori did not take part in the Shiroiwa Junior High Music Club, which was filled with vulgar masses who were especially vulgar. All those losers played was popular music (apparently the club office was cluttered with music sheets of illegal foreign music). That's right. Especially Shuya Nanahara.

Toshinori was vastly superior to him in term of music ability, given his ear training and understanding of music theory. And yet, in spite of that, the vulgar bitches in his class would scream out indecently at the sound of Shuya Nanahara plucking out kindergarten-level chords on his guitar (I mean come on those bitches who listen to Shuya Nanahara playing during the short break before music class, they might as well have printed on their foreheads in thick Gothic font: "Oh, Shuya, do me now, right here"). In contrast, they'd only politely applaud when Toshinori finished playing an elegant passage from an opera at the music teacher's request.

For one thing, those loser bitches could never appreciate classical music, and for another, it was only because Shuya Nanahara was good-looking (although Toshinori would never admit it, deep down inside he couldn't stand his own ugly face).

Fine. That's what women are like anyway. They're just a different species. Just a tool to produce children (and of course to provide pleasure for men when they need it), and if they were good-looking then they were just ornaments to place beside successful men. Yes, it all came down to...money and connections. And my talent is worth the investment of money and connections. Therefore...

...I deserve to be the survivor.

He heard gunfire at times throughout the night, and there was that amazing explosion to top it all off, but now the island was immersed in darkness and silence. Toshinori quickly circled the first house, passed it, and approached the second one. He could tell it was pretty old even though he could only make out its silhouette. The house was surrounded by a circle of trees, and on the west side in front was an extremely large broadleaf tree, its branches spread out. Its circumference was four to five meters, and it was seven to eight meters tall.

There shouldn't be anyone…here.

Toshinori gripped his gun and slowly moved forward, cautiously checking the house as well as the tree. Of course he didn't forget to stop and look in all directions. You never knew where the vulgar masses might show up. Just like cockroaches.

After spending a full five minutes passing by the side of the house, he looked over his shoulder and checked the house, which was surrounded by trees of various sizes. There were no suspicious movements that he could see through his open helmet's square window.

All right.

He could see the third house, the one he wanted, nearby.

…

Toshinori turned around one more time.

He thought something round and black stirred near the ground between the trees surrounding the house. It was

…someone's head, he realized, but by then he was aiming his gun over there. But this one was wandering in an area that would become a forbidden zone soon. Who could it possibly be?…

It didn't matter.

He pulled the trigger. Holding the Smith & Wesson Military & Police's wooden grip, he felt a sudden jerk in the palm of his hand. The gun popped with an orange flash, sending a sting down Toshinori's spine. Although he despised the ignorant, vulgar masses, he had a hobby that wasn't so refined, much less refined than playing the violin. He still had his model gun collection. His father owned several hunting rifles, but he was never allowed to handle them, so this was the first time he'd ever pulled the trigger of a real gun. It was real. Damn, I'm shooting a real gun!

Toshinori shot twice and his opponent crouched down, unable to move, it seemed. The person didn't shoot back either. Of course not, if he had a gun he would have shot me from behind. That's what let me pull the trigger in the first place.

Toshinori slowly approached the figure. It shouted, "Stop!"

He could tell from his voice it was Hiroki Sugimura (Male Student No. 11). That tall guy (Toshinori by the way hated tall guys too. His height was only 162 centimeters and next to Yutaka Seto he was the shortest guy in their class. He couldn't stand: [a] good looking guys, [b] tall guys, and [c] all-around vulgar guys) who practiced that vulgar karate-like sport. He was supposedly going out with Takako Chigusa who tastelessly dyed her hair and wore all that gaudy jewelry—oh, that's right, she was also dead now. She wasn't bad looking though.

Hiroki continued, "I'm not fighting this game! Who are you? Yuichiro?"

Hiroki had guessed it was Yuichiro Takiguchi (Male Student No. 13), who was the next shortest guy to Toshinori. Yes, since Hiroshi Kuronaga had died a while ago, the only ones left alive who were his height were Yuichiro and Yutaka. In any case, Toshinori wondered for a moment, what's this about not fighting? Impossible. Not playing this game would be tantamount to committing suicide. Is he trying to fool me? Even if he was, as long as he doesn't have a gun...

Toshinori changed his course of action. He lowered his gun.

With his left hand he pulled down on the chin guard of the helmet and said, "It's Toshinori." Then he thought, oh, I should probably stutter a little. "S-sorry I did that. A-are you hurt?"

Hiroki Sugimura slowly got up, revealing his large frame.

Like Toshinori he had his day pack on his right shoulder. His right hand held a stick. His right sleeve was missing, maybe it was torn or maybe he'd torn it off. His shirt was missing underneath and his right arm was bare. A white cloth was wrapped around the shoulder. With his bare right arm holding the stick he resembled a naked primitive tribesman. A vulgar naked tribe.

"I'm all right." Then he asked, looking at Toshinori's head, "Is that a helmet?"

"U-uh yes." As he answered, Toshinori came forward, stepping onto the farm soil. All right, three more steps.

"I-I've been so scaaaared." Before he finished saying "scared" Toshinori raised his right hand. Five meters away, he couldn't miss.

Hiroki's eyes opened wide. Too late, too late, you vulgar karate bastard. You're going to die a vulgar death, end up in a vulgar grave, and I'll offer you the most vulgar flowers I can find.

But Hiroki wasn't there at the end of the muzzle of the exploding Smith & Wesson. A split second before the shot, Hiroki had unexpectedly ducked to his left—Toshinori's right. Toshinori of course had no idea Hiroki had used a martial arts move, but in any case...he was incredibly fast.

From this crouched position, Hiroki held up, instead of the stick in his left hand, a gun in his left hand (Toshinori also had no way of knowing that—although, in contrast to Shinji Mimura, he had "fixed" it—Hiroki was originally in fact left-handed). So he already had a gun...then why didn't the fool use it in the first place? Before this thought barely crossed his mind a small flame exploded.

The gun was suddenly gone from his right hand. The next moment he felt a searing pain and his right ring finger exploded. Toshinori shrieked. He fell on both his knees and held the painful stump with his left hand...and realized his ring finger was gone. Blood spurted out. He might have been wearing a bulletproof vest and a helmet, but his fingers were unprotected.

Argh...that bastard...my finger...my right finger that elegantly guides the violin bow is!...that can't be...in the movies fingers never get blown away in gun fights!

Hiroki approached him, gun in hand. Toshinori held his right hand and gazed at it, his eyes inside his helmet terrified and delirious. His face was getting clammy from the sweat breaking out under his helmet.

Hiroki said, "So you're totally up for this. I don't want to shoot...but I have no choice. I have to."

Toshinori had no idea what Hiroki meant at all, and although he was in terrible pain, he still felt confident. Because...the gun was pointed at his chest. Of course, it would be. He wore the helmet not so much because it was bulletproof but because it would force his enemy to aim at his body instead. And under his school coat he was wearing the bulletproof vest. As long as his vest stopped the bullet, then all he would have to do is wait for a chance to retrieve his gun and then—since his index finger was still working—he could pull the trigger and win.

His gun was by his feet.

With Toshinori glaring at him, Hiroki Sugimura still paused a few moments...but Hiroki pursed his lips tightly and calmly squeezed the trigger. Toshinori recalled his fight against Hirono Shimizu and considered how he should play "dead."

But it ended much more than abruptly than he'd expected. Hiroki's gun only made a small metallic click.

Hiroki looked confused. He nervously cocked the gun and pulled the trigger. Again, click.

Toshinori's lips twisted into a smile hidden under the helmet. Karate bastard. That was a dud. With that automatic you'll have to pull the breechblock and reload the chamber.

Toshinori went for his gun by his feet. Hiroki immediately responded with the stick in his right hand but instead—maybe he thought it was too far—he turned around and ran toward the mountain beyond the house.

Toshinori picked up the gun. His crippled hand ached, but he still managed to hold it. He fired. Because his hold on the grip wasn't tight he couldn't fix his aim on Hiroki, but he could tell he hit him in the thigh, right near his butt. Did it only scrape him? In any case, Hiroki suddenly tottered, but he didn't fall. He continued running. Toshinori also started running and fired another shot. This time he missed. The recoil of the gun so pleasurable only moments ago now sent a sharp pain through his injured hand which infuriated Toshinori. He shot again. He missed again. In spite of being shot in the leg, Hiroki was faster than him.

Hiroki disappeared into the woods at the foot of the mountain.

Damn it!

Toshinori deliberated whether he should chase him—and decided not to. His opponent was injured but so was he. The gun grip was slippery from the blood pouring from the stump of his former ring finger. Besides, if he entered the mountains now, Hiroki would reload his gun and shoot back. In that situation, it'd be too dangerous to expose himself like that with nothing to hide behind. He nervously crouched down.

He had to get to the first house—the house he'd decided to enter. And he had to make sure Hiroki wouldn't see him enter it.

Toshinori clutched his right hand, which was still holding the gun, and staggered over there, enduring the pain. As he traveled down the footpath the pain became more and more excruciating. He felt dizzy. First thing was his hand. He had to treat it. He had to come up with a different strategy. Oh, but, damn, even if he were able to play the violin after rehabilitation this crippled hand would stick out during a performance, especially if they televise it and zoom in. So now I'm going to be joining that lame group—the disabled. What a nice melody, how he's overcome his disability. How lame!

He was approaching the house. Toshinori looked over his shoulder again. He looked closely, but didn't see any sign of Hiroki. He was safe now. Hiroki wasn't coming after him.

Toshinori looked back at the house.

He saw a guy standing on the farm field six to seven meters away, right in front of the house he wanted. The guy had appeared suddenly out of nowhere. He had slicked-back hair that reached a little too far behind his neck and cold, gleaming eyes.

By the time he realized it was Kazuo Kiriyama (Male Student No. 6) (another guy he couldn't stand, category [a] good looking), a heavy burst of fire came out of his hands along with a rattling sound, slamming against Toshinori's torso. Toshinori was blown back and fell backward. Because his grip on the gun had loosened from the pain he'd been feeling in his right hand, he dropped it and heard it knock against something. His back scraped against the dirt. His head wearing the helmet hit the ground.

The echoing gunfire faded into the night air. All was quiet once again.

But of course Toshinori Oda wasn't dead. He held his breath and lay down, frozen, trying his best to restrain his urge to snicker. Now that he was overwhelmed by this wicked pleasure, the agonizing pain from his right hand, not to mention his anger at letting Hiroki Sugimura escape, or his anger at being suddenly attacked by a guy in category (a), his emotional faculties were a complete mess, but his body (with the exception of his right ring finger), just as it had been with Hirono Shimizu, was completely intact. So he was right to wear the helmet. Kazuo had aimed at Toshinori's torso, which was protected by the bulletproof vest. Just as Hiroki had done, Kazuo probably assumed Toshinori was dead.

His eyelids nearly shut, his field of vision resembled a widescreen movie. He could see at the far end of his field of vision the S&W flash faintly against the moonlight. And now he could feel the stiff shape of the kitchen knife (which he found in the house where he'd killed Hirono Shimizu) he had tucked in back. It would take less than a second to unwrap the cloth around it.

As he continued to sweat, which was the one thing he couldn't hold back, Toshinori thought, all right, now pick up that gun lying over there. Then I'll slash that vulgar windpipe of yours. Or will you turn around and leave? Then I'll pick up the gun and dig a nice tunnel through that vulgar skull of yours. Come on. Make your choice. Just hurry up and choose.

But for some reason, instead of approaching the gun, Kazuo came straight at Toshinori.

...

He was coming straight at him. Staring at him with those cold eyes.

Why? Toshinori wondered. I'm supposed to be dead. Look how good I am at playing dead.

Kazuo didn't stop. He kept on approaching. One step, two...

But I'm supposed to be dead! Why!?

The faint sound of his steps on the soil became louder and his field of vision was now filled with the figure of Kazuo.

!...

Suddenly overcome with panic and fear, Toshinori frantically opened his eyes.

Kazuo's Ingram once again let out a burst of fire into Toshinori's shielded head. Some of the point-blank shots turned into colorful sparks from scraping against the reinforced plastic shell of the helmet while others, after exiting Toshinori's skull, ricocheted inside his helmet, rattling Toshinori's head along with the helmet (his body was dancing a strange boogie. Toshinori himself would have been irritated by this kind of vulgar dancing). And of course by the time it was all over...Toshinori's head was crushed inside his helmet.

Toshinori no longer played dead. He remained frozen. Blood dripped out from under the helmet, which resembled a bowl of sauce.

And so this boy who despised the ignorant, vulgar masses, foolish Toshinori Oda, had overestimated the value of his bulletproof vest and underestimated Kazuo Kiriyama's calm actions. As a result he died easily. If he'd thought about how Yumiko Kusaka and Yukiko Kitano had died yesterday morning, he would have realized that his assailant would have followed up on his enemy to deliver a coup de grâce, but he wasn't so perceptive. Furthermore—it was quite irrelevant now—he had no idea his killer, Kazuo Kiriyama, had, in his mansion that was much larger than Toshinori's home in Shiroiwa-cho, mastered the violin at a level far superior to Toshinori's a long time ago (and then tossed his violin into the trash).

16 students remaining

55

Some chatting. The sound of someone moving. She'd even settle for the faint sound of someone desperately trying to hold his or her breath. Instead, Mitsuko Souma (Female Student No. 11) ended up hearing the sound of liquid running through grass. She could tell it was someone pissing in the grove nearby (unless there was a dog on the island). Dawn was approaching. She glanced up and saw a faint blue beginning emerge in the dark sky.

After encountering Hiroki and somehow managing to escape him, Mitsuko first decided she needed a gun. She'd accidentally come across Megumi Eto and, upon hearing Yoshimi Yahagi and Yoji Kuramoto in the middle of their fight, she'd killed them and managed to get her hands on a gun (if she'd had a gun in the first place she would have gone back to the school and killed off everyone that came out one by one). Once she had a gun she could confidently move around the island, so it was easy to kill Takako Chigusa, who'd just finished fighting Kazushi Niida. (She should have finished her off though. She'd have to be more careful next time.)

But now she was unarmed. She had used Megumi Eto's knife, and the only thing in her hand now was her original sickle from the beginning of the game. She had to get a gun because she wasn't the only one who chose to play this game. There was the machine gun shooter who killed Yumiko Kusaka and Yukiko Kitano. She had just heard it go off again only thirty minutes ago.

Of course, thanks to the shooter, she didn't have to kill off as many of her classmates. She could just let the assailant take care of that. She'd only kill when it came easy. In fact, after midnight, when she heard the machine gun's rapid gunfire along with the explosion afterwards, she decided it was best to avoid that area. A handgun against a machine gun, she'd be outmatched. So she decided to move somewhere she could view the area from a distance, and that was how she ended up finding and following Hiroki

Sugimura. And that was supposed to be an easy kill but...

It was highly likely she'd end up having to take on this machine gun shooter. Not having a gun would be a major disadvantage. Forget about gun against machine gun, it'd be hopeless with a sickle against a machine gun.

Of course, she could have pursued Hiroki, but she thought it'd be too much trouble to get the gun back from him. His background in martial arts or whatever it was was no joke. Her right hand still stung from his blow. And this time, if he saw her, he'd be merciless and shoot her.

So Mitsuko moved west along the longitudinal road and then entered the northern mountain, trying to find someone else. Approximately three hours had passed.

And now she finally heard someone making noise.

Mitsuko made her way through the thicket and moved forward, cautiously though. She mustn't be heard.

The thicket ended. There was a small, open, mat-sized space in the middle of the bushes. The grove continued on and beyond her right. And to the left as well—in the corner of the space, a boy in his school coat had his back toward her. He nervously looked to his right and left as the dripping sound against the leaves continued.

He was probably scared he might be attacked by someone. She could tell it was Tadakatsu Hatagami (Male Student No. 18). He was on the baseball team. Nothing exceptional, just an average guy. He was tall and well-built, and his face was average. His hobbies were...actually she had no idea, and besides there was no point asking now.

The crucial thing was that, as Tadakatsu was attending to his business, Mitsuko realized he held something tightly in his right hand.

It was a gun. It was a fairly large model, a revolver. She once again broke into that fallen angel's grin.

Tadakatsu still wasn't done. He might have been holding

it in for quite a while. He continued to look left and right while he emptied his bladder.

Mitsuko quietly but quickly took out her sickle with her right hand. Tadakatsu would have to use both of his hands to zip up his pants. Even if he tried using one hand, he'd be vulnerable.

It looks like this'll be the end of you. Didn't someone in a detective show get killed this way?

The drips became sporadic. It stopped…and then another drip, and then it stopped completely. Tadakatsu once again looked around and then quickly moved his hands to the front.

By then Mitsuko had already snuck up behind him. The back of his head, with short spiked hair, was right in front of her. She raised the sickle.

She heard someone from behind say, "Whoa," and Tadakatsu suddenly turned around, along with Mitsuko. She (of course) put the sickle down and looked back at the speaker behind her.

It was Yuichiro Takiguchi (Male Student No. 13). He was shorter than Tadakatsu and had a cute, boyish face. He held what appeared to be his weapon, an aluminum bat, in his right hand and stared at Mitsuko, his mouth agape.

Tadakatsu saw Mitsuko and also said, "Whoa," and then muttered, "Damn," and pointed the gun at her. Seeing how Yuichiro's appearance didn't surprise him, Mitsuko realized they were together. Mitsuko cursed herself. Tadakatsu had left Yuichiro just to take a piss. How stupid could I have been not to check! Come on, you're both boys, can't you just pee next to each other!?

This wasn't the time or place to lecture them. Tadakatsu's revolver (which, although it hardly mattered, was a Smith & Wesson M19 .357 Magnum) was pointed directly at Mitsuko's chest.

"Tadakatsu! Stop it!" Yuichiro said, his voice trembling, probably from her sudden appearance and his fear of seeing someone get killed in front of his very own eyes. Tadakatsu looked like he was ready to pull the trigger at any moment, but his finger on the trigger stopped a fraction of a millimeter before the hammer fell.

His gun still pointed at Mitsuko, Tadakatsu looked over at Yuichiro.

"Why!? She just tried to kill me! Look! A sickle! She's holding a sickle!"

"N-no." Mitsuko croaked as if her words were stuck in her throat. She made sure her voice was high-pitched and trembling, and of course, she didn't forget to flinch her body back. Once again, the star actress had a chance to show off her talents. Watch me now.

"I-I..."

She thought of dropping the sickle, but decided not to, since it would look more natural holding it.

"I was just trying to call you. Then I-I realized you were peeing, so I..." Mitsuko looked down and made her face blush. "So..."

Tadakatsu didn't lower the gun. "You're lying! You were trying to kill me!" His hand holding the gun was trembling. He'd restrained himself from shooting her because he'd never shot someone. The moment he saw her he probably would have fired reflexively, but now that Yuichiro had intervened he had time to think and hesitate. And that meant...

...he would lose.

"Stop it, Tadakatsu," Yuichiro pleaded with him, "Didn't I already say how we have to join up with others—"

"You got to be kidding." Tadakatsu shook his head. "There's no way I can be with this bitch. Don't you know who we're dealing with? She might have been the one...who killed Yumiko and Yukiko."

"N-no...I would never..." Mitsuko made her eyes brim with tears.

Yuichiro said frantically, "Mitsuko isn't carrying a machine gun. She doesn't even have a gun."

"We can't know for sure! She might have tossed them once she ran out of bullets!!"

Yuichiro fell silent for a while, but then said, "Tadakatsu, you shouldn't raise your voice." His voice sounded different from before. It was calm and kind. Tadakatsu opened his mouth slightly as if he'd been caught off guard.

Mitsuko was also a bit surprised. Yuichiro Takiguchi was into anime. He was the otaku of their class, but now he sounded quite dignified.

Yuichiro shook his head. "You shouldn't be so indiscriminately suspicious," he continued as if admonishing Tadakatsu. "Think about it. Mitsuko might have sought you out because she really trusted you."

"But then..." Tadakatsu knit his brows. His gun was still pointed at Mitsuko, but the tension of his fingers on the trigger seemed to wane. "Then what do you suggest we do?"

"If you insist she can't be trusted, then we can take turns keeping an eye on her. I mean, even if we were to tell her to leave, you'd still be worried she might attack you later when she has the chance."

Well, I'll say, I'm impressed. He's sharp and articulate. I mean, putting aside whether he's making a good call (which in fact would be to shoot me now).

Tadakatsu then licked his lips a little.

"Come on. We need more people on our side. And then we have to figure out a way to get out of here. Once we spend some time with her we'll see whether we can trust her, right?" Yuichiro insisted and finally

Tadakatsu nodded, still eyeing her suspiciously. He said in a tired voice, "Well, all right."

Making herself look relieved, she let her body unwind. She rubbed her left hand against her eyes deliberately filled with tears. Yuichiro let out a sigh of relief too.

"Get rid of that sickle," Tadakatsu said, and Mitsuko immediately tossed it to the ground. Then she nervously alternated glances at Tadakatsu and Yuichiro.

Tadakatsu said, "Search her, Yuichiro." Mitsuko looked back at Tadakatsu, her eyes opened wide as if she didn't understand. Then she looked at Yuichiro who stood still in astonishment. Tadakatsu repeated himself. He aimed the gun at her. "Hurry up. Don't be so bashful. This is a matter of life and death. You know that."

"Okay…all right." Yuichiro put his bat down and reluctantly came forward. He stood right beside Mitsuko.

"Hurry," Tadakatsu insisted.

"Uh huh."

His dignified manner was gone now. He'd gone back to being his usual weak otaku self.

"But—"

"Hurry!"

Yuichiro said, "U-uh, Mitsuko, I'm really sorry. I really don't want to do this, but I have to," and he ran his hands lightly over her body. Even in the dim light at dawn, she could tell his face had turned bright red. How cute. Of course, she didn't forget to act all embarrassed too.

After he was done searching, he lifted his hands. Tadakatsu said, "Look under her skirt too."

"Tadakatsu—" Yuichiro protested, but Tadakatsu shook his head.

"I'm not trying to get my rocks off. I just don't want to die."

So Yuichiro blushed even more and said, "U-uh, I was

wondering, could you lift your skirt up a little?"

Oh my, let's not have a heart attack here, little boy.

But Mitsuko only answered in a meek voice, "O-okay," and lifted her skirt bashfully again up to where her underwear was nearly visible. Geez, this was turning into one of those adult videos titled *Fetish Special! Starring Real Junior High School Girls!*

I've actually been in them.

After making sure Mitsuko had nothing to hide, Yuichiro said, "I-I'm done."

Tadakatsu nodded and said, "All right. Yuichiro, I want you to tie up her hands with your belt."

Yuichiro gave Tadakatsu another reluctant look, but Tadakatsu refused to give in, aiming his gun at her.

"Those are my conditions. If you can't accept them, then I'll shoot her now."

Yuichiro looked at Mitsuko, then at Tadakatsu, and licked his lips. Then Mitsuko said to Yuichiro, "Yuichiro, go ahead. It's all right."

Yuichiro looked at Mitsuko, but then nodded, pulled out his belt, and held Mitsuko's hands. "I'm sorry, Mitsuko," he said.

Tadakatsu still pointed his gun at her, and said, "You don't have to be so polite with her," but Yuichiro seemed to ignore his warning as he gently wrapped the belt around her wrists without saying another word.

As she innocently offered her hands, Mitsuko was thinking how lucky, in spite of the situation, she was to have been discovered right before lifting her sickle. (She had also wiped the blood off the sickle earlier. Now that's luck.)

Now then, what's my next move?

16 students remaining

56

"So that's how I thought we had to seek other classmates," Yuichiro said and stopped, glancing at Mitsuko. Dawn had already broken, and she could see how his face was grimy with dirt.

They were sitting next to each other in the shrubs. Of course, Mitsuko's hands were tied up with the belt, and her sickle was tucked in the back of Yuichiro's pants. Tadakatsu Hatagami was in a deep sleep. He still held onto his gun which he had in fact tied to his hand with a handkerchief.

After she ended up with this duo, Tadakatsu was the one who insisted on taking turns sleeping.

"I agree we have to find others, but let's get some sleep. We've been up all this time. We'll lose our ability to make sound judgments." Once Yuichiro agreed Tadakatsu said, "First, it's going to be Yuichiro or me. Then Mitsuko can sleep after us," and Yuichiro responded, "I can sleep later," so the order was decided. Holding his gun (which should have been handed over to Yuichiro who was keeping watch, but Tadakatsu didn't even mention it, nor did Yuichiro protest), Tadakatsu lay down and fell asleep within a matter of seconds.

Mitsuko had an idea how they hooked up. Tadakatsu hadn't slept at all until he met Yuichiro, and he probably couldn't sleep after joining him. Why? Because he was probably afraid Yuichiro might attack him by surprise. And even though Mitsuko might be much more threatening than Yuichiro, now that she was with them, even if Tadakatsu slept, Mitsuko and Yuichiro would have to keep an eye on each other so long as he held onto his gun and remained cautious. He could still get some sleep. (Of course, Mitsuko hadn't slept at all either, but it was nothing to her. She was much tougher than your average wimpy junior high school kid.)

Yuichiro and Mitsuko remained silent for a while, but then Yuichiro told her how he'd ended up joining Tadakatsu.

It turned out that Yuichiro also didn't move at all during the day, but then assuming he was safer at night (of course, Mitsuko thought, it could go either way. You could escape detection at night, but that also meant it was hard to detect your opponent too. But of course, if you were in a tight spot and had to run away, night was better), he cautiously began to move and encountered Tadakatsu only two hours before Mitsuko encountered them. The two tried to concoct an escape plan but came up with nothing...and so Tadakatsu stepped out to pee, but because he was taking so long Yuichiro got worried and checked on him. And that was how he found Mitsuko.

"I was so scared at first, I thought I couldn't trust anybody. But then I realized most of us probably just want to escape."

Yuichiro stopped and glanced at Mitsuko. The otaku of Class B, Yuichiro Takiguchi avoided direct eye contact in his conversations. He always looked down. Still, from the way he talked to her, Yuichiro didn't seem to be all that cautious towards her. For some reason.

And so Mitsuko pretended to look somewhat relieved and asked him, "So Tadakatsu had that gun."

Yuichiro nodded. "That's right."

"Weren't you scared of Tadakatsu?" Okay, now act even more relaxed and a little more intimate. "No, I mean even now. He won't let go of it."

Tadakatsu grinned. "Well, first of all, Tadakatsu didn't shoot at me or anything. He did point his gun at me. I was classmates with him in elementary school. So I know him pretty well."

"But..." Mitsuko made her face look slightly pale. "You saw how Yumiko...Yumiko Kusaka and Yukiko Kitano died.

Some of us are playing this game. How can you be sure Tadakatsu isn't one of them?" She nodded and then said, "…he even suspects me."

Yuichiro tightened his lips and nodded several times. "That's true. But if we just sit still we'll end up dying. It's best to try. I can't be like Yumiko and Yukiko, but I was thinking how we could get others to join us gradually."

He glanced into Mitsuko's eyes for a moment and then looked down. He seemed even more withdrawn than usual, maybe because he wasn't used to looking at a girl's face so close up. (She was probably right on the mark, and on top of that, he was dealing with the most beautiful girl in the class.)

"You can't blame Tadakatsu for holding onto that gun. He's scared out of his wits."

Mitsuko tilted her head and forced a smile. "You're so good."

Yuichiro glanced at her out of the corner of his eye.

Still wearing her smile, Mitsuko continued, "You have to be brave to be like that, to be able to empathize with others like that."

Yuichiro looked down bashfully again and nervously ran his right hand through his messy hair and said, "I don't think so." Then without looking at her, he said, "So…could you cut him some slack for suspecting you? I think he's really scared. He trusts no one."

Trust no one. The phrase really tickled her and she grinned.

Then she said as if sighing, "I guess he can't help it. I have a reputation. You probably don't trust me either."

Yuichiro paused and then turned to Mitsuko. This time he looked at her a little longer. Then he said, "No." He looked down at the ground after saying this, and continued, "Well, I mean, I'm even suspicious of Tadakatsu when it comes down to it. I mean…" He pulled out some grass by his feet. Then he tore the grass that was moist with morning dew into small strands. "I mean, yeah, I haven't heard great things about you. But that's so irrelevant in this situation. I mean, sometimes it's the respectable ones who end up breaking up under stress." He tossed the torn grass by his feet. Then he looked up at Mitsuko. "I don't think you're such a bad person."

Mitsuko tilted her head. "Why?"

Maybe it was because she was staring at her, Yuichiro nervously looked away again. Then he said, "Well…it's your eyes."

"Eyes?"

Still looking down, Yuichiro began tearing out more grass. "You always had a scary look in your eyes."

Mitsuko forced a smile. She tried to shrug her shoulders, but it didn't work because of the belt around her wrists. "I guess."

"But…" The grass was torn into quarters, then eighths. "But sometimes your eyes look really sad and kind."

Mitsuko stared at the side of his face and listened without responding.

"So," he tossed the grass again and continued, "I've always thought you weren't as bad as everyone said you were. Even if you'd done bad things, I was pretty sure you did them because you couldn't help it, because there was some reason behind it that wasn't your fault."

He was stuttering, his voice incredibly shy and tense as if he were confessing his love to a girl. Then he added, "I just don't want to be so foolish I couldn't understand that reason."

Mitsuko sighed inside. Of course, she was thinking, boy, you are naïve, Yuichiro. But then…

…she smiled and said warmly, "Thank you." Even she was surprised by the kindness in her voice. Of course, it was deliberate, but maybe the reason it sounded too real to be an act was that there was a little bit of true feeling in her words.

But...that's all it was.

Yuichiro then asked, "What about you, Mitsuko? What were you doing till now?"

Mitsuko replied, "Well..." She moved a little and felt the morning dew on the grass soaking through her skirt. "I've been running away. You know, away from the gunfire. That's why...that's why when I saw Tadakatsu I was so scared...but I was also so tired and scared of being alone and I thought of calling out to him...I thought maybe he'd understand...but I just couldn't tell whether it was the right thing to do or not...I just didn't know...."

Yuichiro nodded again. He glanced at her again and looked down. "I think you did the right thing."

Mitsuko smiled and said, "I think so too." Their eyes met and they smiled at each other.

"That's right," Yuichiro said, "I'm sorry. I forgot. You must be thirsty. You lost your bag, right? You probably haven't had any water in a while."

She had left her day pack behind when she fought Hiroki Sugimura. She was actually pretty thirsty. She nodded. "Could I...could I have some water?"

Looking away from her, Yuichiro nodded back, reached out for the day pack and picked it up. He pulled out two water bottles and after comparing them he chose the sealed bottle and tucked away the other one. He broke the seal off the new bottle.

Mitsuko put up her belt-bound hands. Yuichiro was about to hand over the bottle to her...but then stopped. He glanced over at Tadakatsu who still seemed sound sleep, then looked down at the plastic bottle in his hand.

Then he put the bottle down by his leg.

Hey there, aren't you going to let me have a drink? You decided not to spoil the prisoner because that might upset tough Sergeant Hatagami?

Yuichiro took her hands without a word instead, had her raise them, and fingered the belt around her wrists. He began to unfasten it.

"Yuichiro…," Mitsuko said as if surprised (which in fact she was), "…are you sure this is okay? Tadakatsu will be really mad."

Concentrating on her wrists, Yuichiro answered, "It's all right. I have your weapon. Besides, how can you drink with your hands bound like that?" Yuichiro glanced up at Mitsuko again.

She smiled warmly and said, "Thank you," making her cheeks blush as she looked down.

The belt came loose. Mitsuko rubbed each of her wrists. Because the belt wasn't tight they were fine.

Yuichiro offered his bottle to Mitsuko. Mitsuko grabbed it and took two brief, delicate sips. She returned the bottle.

"That's all?" he asked and stopped wrapping his belt around his waist. "You can drink more. If we run out, we can always get more from some house with a well."

Mitsuko shook her head. "Oh no, I'm fine."

"Okay."

Yuichiro took the bottle. After he stuffed it into his day pack, he buckled his belt around his waist.

Mitsuko said to Yuichiro, "Yuichiro." He looked up.

Mitsuko quickly reached out her free hands and gently held his right hand. Yuichiro appeared to tense up, not because he suspected her of some ulterior motive, but more simply because a girl was holding his hand.

"Wh-what?"

Mitsuko smiled warmly. She opened her nicely shaped lips and gently spoke, "I'm so glad I'm with someone like you. I was so scared I've been shaking all this time…but now I'm safe."

Yuichiro seemed to break into a grin. His tense mouth quivered and he finally managed to blurt out, "You're safe." It seemed like he wanted to take his right hand back, but Mitsuko refused to let go, clutching onto it. Yuichiro had a hard time speaking and his voice sounded nervous, but then he managed to utter, "I'll protect you, Mitsuko."

He added, "We have Tadakatsu too. He's pretty worked up right now, but once he calms down, he'll see you couldn't possibly be our enemy. Then the three of us can work on finding the rest of the class. Then we'll come up with some way of escaping."

Mitsuko gave a warm smile. "Thank you. I'm so relieved."

She squeezed her grip on Yuichiro's hand. Yuichiro blushed even more and glanced away again. He said, "U-uh, Mitsuko. Y-you know, you're really p-pretty."

Mitsuko raised her brow. "No…really?"

Yuichiro nodded repeatedly. Rather than nodding, he seemed to be trembling from the unbearable tension. This made Mitsuko smile and she realized this smile had no ulterior motive.

Well, almost none.

16 students remaining

57

Sakamochi's 6 a.m. announcement woke up Tadakatsu. He hadn't even slept two hours, but insisted it was enough and untied the handkerchief from his wrist to get a good grip on the gun. Then he sat by Mitsuko and Yuichiro. Yuichiro insisted on her sleeping before him, but Mitsuko abstained, so Yuichiro ended up lying down. (By this time, they had learned that four students—Keita Iijima, Toshinori Oda,

Yutaka Seto, and Shinji Mimura—had recently died. The new forbidden zones were not in their vicinity.)

Tadakatsu was dismayed to find out the belt on Mitsuko's wrists had been unfastened, but Yuichiro managed to convince him it would be okay. Of course, even if Yuichiro hadn't unfastened the belt, Mitsuko had plans to have it unfastened anyway...using Tadakatsu.

Now then.

She couldn't really afford to take her time. If Hiroki Sugimura showed up he'd completely blow her cover. (She wondered, what is he doing wandering around like that anyway? Is he, like Yuichiro and Tadakatsu, trying to find others to hook up with?) And there was...that machine gun shooter.

Although Yuichiro had said to Mitsuko with a smile, "I might not be able to sleep," he went out like a light in five minutes. Given how he was an otaku boy, he couldn't have much stamina. He must be tired. Unlike Tadakatsu who snored, Yuichiro fell into the hushed deep sleep of a little baby.

Tadakatsu kept a good distance of three meters on her left, sitting against a tree. He had short, cropped hair and light acne above his cheekbones. And the eyes above them...were cautiously watching Mitsuko. The revolver in his right hand was no longer pointed at her, but his finger was definitely on the trigger, as if to indicate he could shoot her at any moment.

Mitsuko waited another half hour...and then after making sure Yuichiro, whose back faced them, was still asleep, she turned to Tadakatsu and quietly said, "You don't have to look at me like that. I'm harmless."

Tadakatsu grimaced. "You never know."

As if responding to Tadakatsu's retort, Yuichiro's body stirred a little. For a while Mitsuko and Tadakatsu looked at Yuichiro's back. His deep breathing resumed, though.

Without looking over at Tadakatsu, Mitsuko took a deep breath to indicate her fatigue. Then she moved her legs, putting her right knee down on the ground and bringing her left knee up.

Her pleated skirt smoothly slid down, revealing most of her white thighs, but Mitsuko just looked around, pretending not to notice.

She could tell Tadakatsu had tensed up. Ha. Maybe you can see my panties? They're hot pink silk.

Mitsuko stayed in this position. Then she slowly looked over at Tadakatsu.

Tadakatsu nervously looked up. Of course…until then his eyes had been glued to her thighs.

But Mitsuko still acted as if she were clueless and said, "Hey, Tadakatsu."

"What?"

Tadakatsu seemed to be doing his best to maintain his intimidating stance, but now there was a slight tremble in his voice.

"I am so scared."

She thought Tadakatsu would say something nasty again, but he didn't respond and only stared at her.

"Aren't you scared?"

Tadakatsu's brow moved a little, but then he said, "Of course, I am. That's why I'm being so careful with you."

Mitsuko looked sadly away from Tadakatsu. "So you still won't trust me."

"Don't hold it against me," Tadakatsu said, but his tone of voice wasn't even half as hostile as it had been. "I know I'm repeating myself, but I just don't want to die."

Mitsuko quickly looked back at Tadakatsu. She said a little emphatically, "I'm in the same boat too. I don't want to die. But if you don't trust me, then we'll never be able to cooperate and find a way to save ourselves."

"Uh, well…" Tadakatsu nodded as if relenting. "Well…I know that but…"

Mitsuko smiled warmly. She looked into her opponent's eyes and her well-formed, red lips smiled.…It was different from the one she wore during her somewhat idyllic conversation with Yuichiro. This one was Mitsuko Souma's special fallen angel's smile. Tadakatsu's eyes were glazed, seduced.

"Hey, Tadakatsu," she continued as she returned to her terrified-girl face. This constant switch between expressions, the virgin and the whore, day and night. Wow. Sounds like a movie title.

"Wh-what?"

"I know I keep on saying this, but I'm just so scared."

"U-uh huh."

"So…" She looked at him directly again.

"So?"

Any trace of antagonism and suspicion was now gone from Tadakatsu's voice and face.

Mitsuko tilted her head slightly and asked, "Can we talk a little?"

"…talk?" He knit his brows. "Aren't we doing that right now?…"

Mitsuko hissed, "Don't be stupid. Do I have to spell it out?" Her eyes glued on Tadakatsu, she pointed her chin at Yuichiro. "Not here, okay? I want to talk to you, but not with Yuichiro here."

His mouth slightly open, Tadakatsu gazed over at Yuichiro…and then looked back at Mitsuko.

"Okay?" Mitsuko said. She got up, looked around, and decided the thicket behind Tadakatsu would be best. She walked over to Tadakatsu, tilted her head slightly, and then proceeded forward. She wasn't sure whether he would take the bait…but then after a while she could tell he was nibbling.

Mitsuko stopped approximately twenty meters away from where Yuichiro slept. Just like the previous area, it was a small opening surrounded by bushes.

When she turned around, Tadakatsu appeared, wading through the thicket. His eyes were glazed. But maybe it was subconscious....He still kept a tight grip on his gun.

Mitsuko immediately pulled down the side zipper of her skirt. Her pleated skirt fell to the ground, exposing her thighs in the dull morning light. She could tell he was holding his breath.

Then she removed her scarf and undressed. Unlike the other girls she'd never be so square as to wear an undershirt, so she only had her underwear on now. Oh right, she had to take off her shoes. After she took them off, she stared at Tadakatsu with her fallen angel's smile.

"M-Mitsuko..." Tadakatsu barely managed to utter.

Mitsuko decided to make sure. "I'm so scared, Tadakatsu. So..."

Tadakatsu awkwardly approached Mitsuko.

Mitsuko looked down at his right hand, pretending to suddenly notice the gun, and said, "Put that thing somewhere else."

Tadakatsu lifted his hand, as if he suddenly became aware of its existence, and gazed at it. Then he put it down, away from them.

He approached her again.

Mitsuko gave a nice smile, spread out her arms, and wrapped her hands around his neck. His body trembled but the moment Mitsuko offered her lips, he immediately began sucking on them. Mitsuko received him by breathing heavily.

After a while their lips separated.

Mitsuko looked up at Tadakatsu's eyes and said, "This is your first time, huh?"

"So what?" Tadakatsu said, his voice trembling.

They fell down on the grass, Mitsuko underneath.

Tadakatsu immediately went for her breasts.

You idiot, you're supposed to make out for a while before you do that, Mitsuko thought. Instead she moaned, "Ahh…" Tadakatsu's rough hands slipped off her bra and clutched at her well-endowed breasts, now exposed. Then his face went down there.

"Ahh…ahh…"

She continued pretending to be turned on (in exaggerated porn-video style), but meanwhile her right hand was reaching down to her panties….

Her fingertips touched a hard, thin object.

Gang girls probably didn't use such cheap, clunky weapons anymore. But it'd been Mitsuko's weapon of choice for a long time now. The most useful weapon right now for her was in fact something she could hide in her panties.

Tadakatsu was preoccupied with kissing Mitsuko's breasts. His left hand reached between her legs. Mitsuko then let out a moan…but Tadakatsu's eyes were concentrating on her breasts. His scalp was exposed.

Mitsuko slowly moved her right hand near his neck.

Sorry, Tadakatsu. But at least you get to go out with a nice memory, so you can forgive me, right? Too bad we won't go all the way, though.

Mitsuko's right ring finger gently touched Tadakatsu's neck. The object was between her index and middle finger.

Kaw kaw, a bird cried, unfortunately, to her right.

Tadakatsu raised his head reflexively and glanced over in that direction.

It was only the sound of a bird crying. What really made Tadakatsu's eyes open wide was of course…

…the razor blade in Mitsuko's hand right in front of his face.

Damn it!

How bad can my timing be, the thought sort of crossed her mind, but Mitsuko didn't care as she automatically swung the blade.

He groaned and pulled away from Mitsuko. The blade skimmed his neck, but the cut was way too shallow to be fatal. My oh my, good reflexes. That's right, you're a baseball jock.

Tadakatsu stood up, his eyes open wide, staring down at Mitsuko, her body half raised. He appeared to be on the verge of saying something but seemed at a loss for words.

She could care less about Tadakatsu's state. She leaped up and made a dash for the revolver immediately to her right.

But Tadakatsu's body flew in front of her in a head-first slide. He scooped the gun from the ground, rolled over, and got up on his knees. Ever since elementary school Tadakatsu played the shortstop position formerly occupied by Shuya Nanahara (even though she and Shuya went to different schools Shuya's reputation as a star player in Little League was so widespread even Mitsuko had heard of him), so the Shiroiwa Junior High School baseball team is in good hands, huh? Well, at least you didn't take off your pants. You would have looked pretty pathetic naked.

That was besides the point, though. Once Mitsuko realized Tadakatsu would get the gun before she did, she changed course. She heard gunshots behind her, but they missed as she ran into the thicket.

She could hear Tadakatsu chasing her. He would catch up. That was for sure.

She got out of the thicket. There was Yuichiro Takiguchi. He looked like he'd heard the gunfire, got up, and then realizing Mitsuko and Tadakatsu were gone, was looking around, but the moment his eyes found her, they opened wide. (Of course. She was half naked. What a bonus! Mitsuko Souma's One Night Show. Oh wait, but it's morning.)

"Yuichiro!" Mitsuko raised her voice and ran towards Yuichiro. She didn't forget to crumple up her face.

"Wh-what happened, Mitsuko?"

By the time Tadakatsu Hatagami made his way through the bushes, Mitsuko was behind Yuichiro's back. Because Yuichiro was only four or five centimeters taller than her, she couldn't really hide behind him, but oh well.

"Yuichiro!" Tadakatsu stopped and held his gun, groaning. "Get out of my way!"

"H-hold on." His face still drowsy, Yuichiro spoke quickly perhaps because he didn't fully grasp the situation. Mitsuko grabbed his shoulders from behind and pressed her half naked body against his back.

Yuichiro said, "What is wrong with you?"

"Mitsuko tried to kill me! I told you, man!"

Still hiding behind Yuichiro, Mitsuko said in a feeble voice, "Th-that's not true. Tadakatsu tried to force me to…he threatened me with that gun. Please, help me, Yuichiro!"

Tadakatsu's face contorted in dismay. "I-it's not true, Yuichiro! Th-that's right. Look!" Tadakatsu pointed at his neck with the fingers of his empty left hand. The narrow cut had a slight blood stain. "She went at me with a razor blade!"

Yuichiro turned around and looked at Mitsuko out of the corner of his eye. Mitsuko shook her head (as cutely as possible, as if terrified, now she was playing the virgin).

"I was so desperate…I had to use my nails on him. Then…Tadakatsu got mad…and tried to shoot me…."

She had already gotten rid of the razor blade in the shrubs. Even if she were forced to take off all her clothes (she was nearly naked anyway now) for a body search, they'd find no evidence.

Now Tadakatsu's face flushed red with anger.

"Move, Yuichiro!" he shouted. "I'm shooting her!"

"Hold on," Yuichiro said, trying his best to sound calm, "I...that's right...I can't tell who's telling the truth."

"What!?" Tadakatsu raised his voice, but Yuichiro wasn't intimidated. He reached out his right hand to Tadakatsu.

"Give me your gun. Then we'll see who's telling the truth."

Tadakatsu's face contorted as if he were on the verge of crying out of misery. And wearing this face he screamed at Yuichiro, "We can't afford to take our time here! You're going to get killed too if we don't get rid of her now!"

Mitsuko cried out, "That's awful. I would never do that. Help me, Yuichiro." She squeezed his shoulders tightly.

Yuichiro patiently extended his hand. "Give it to me, Tadakatsu if you're telling the truth."

Tadakatsu grimaced again.

But eventually, after taking a long, deep breath, letting his shoulders down, he exhaled and lowered his gun. He put his finger on the trigger guard, flipped the gun grip forward, and offered it to Yuichiro as if he had no choice.

Of course she still wore her weepy face...but there was a faint glimmer in her eyes. The key moment would be when the gun was in Yuichiro's hands. It should be easy to take away from him. The question was how.

Yuichiro nodded and came forward.

But then...

It was a move that was almost identical to the one Hiroki Sugimura had made with the Colt Government against her. Like a magic trick, the gun flipped over in his hand. Simultaneously, Tadakatsu got down on his right knee and leaned sideways. The gun was pointed directly at Mitsuko, its line of fire passing right by Yuichiro's left shoulder. Now that she wasn't clinging to Yuichiro's back Mitsuko was completely exposed.

Yuichiro followed the gun's target and quickly looked back at Mitsuko.

Mitsuko's eyes opened wide.

I'm dead now—

Without hesitating, Tadakatsu pulled the trigger.

Gunfire. Two shots.

Yuichiro's body fell down slowly as if in slow motion right in front of her.

Beyond it was the frightened face of Tadakatsu.

By then Mitsuko had picked up the sickle Yuichiro had beside him when he went to sleep.

She threw it. It spun through the air. Its banana-shaped blade lodged into Tadakatsu's right shoulder. He groaned and dropped his gun.

Mitsuko didn't waste a single moment. She picked up the bat and dashed forward. She leapt over Yuichiro, who was lying face down, ran towards Tadakatsu, and with this forward momentum took a full swing at his head as he staggered, clutching his right shoulder.

Hey there. Here's something familiar, a bat. Hope you like it.

Thud. The end of the bat landed in the center of his face. She'd crushed in his nose cartilage and cheekbones, tearing out several of his teeth.

Tadakatsu fainted. Mitsuko swung at his forehead. KRAK! His forehead caved in. His eyes bulged out and his hands balled up into fists. One more swing, this time she aimed at the bridge of his nose. Mitsuko Souma's Special Training for One Thousand Catches. Come on, come on, this next one's going into center field.

Blood burst out of Tadakatsu's nostrils with this blow.

Mitsuko put the bat down. Tadakatsu's entire face was immersed in blood. He was dead by now. Thick streams of blood came dripping out of his ears and his deformed nose.

Mitsuko tossed the bat and picked up the pistol lying to her left.

Then she walked over to Yuichiro who was lying down on his face.

The blood stain spread all over the grass underneath.

He had shielded Mitsuko. That one instant.

Mitsuko slowly knelt down by Yuichiro. She could tell he was still breathing as she bent over.

After some consideration, Mitsuko moved over to block Yuichiro's view of Tadakatsu's corpse. Then she grabbed his shoulder to turn him over.

Yuichiro moaned, "Urgh," and opened his eyes in a daze. His school coat had two holes, one in the left chest and the other in his side. Blood came pouring out, absorbed by the black fabric. Mitsuko held Yuichiro up.

His eyes wandered around for a while. Then he looked at Mitsuko. His short breaths came intermittently, matching his heartbeat. "M-Mitsuko...," he said, "wh-what about Tadakatsu?"

Mitsuko shook her head. "He panicked after he shot you and just ran away."

Tadakatsu had tried to kill Mitsuko so this explanation didn't make much sense. But...maybe he couldn't think much anymore. Yuichiro seemed to nod slightly.

"R-really..." His eyes seemed out of focus. He might only have a partial image of Mitsuko now. "Y-you didn't get hurt, I hope?"

"I'm fine." She nodded. And then said, "You saved me."

Yuichiro seemed to form a slight grin. "I-I'm so sorry. I-I don't think I can protect you anymore. I-I can't m-m-move...."

Foams of blood came bursting out the sides of his mouth. His lungs must have been punctured.

"I know." She leaned over and gently hugged his body.

Mitsuko's long black hair fell onto his chest, its ends stained by the blood pouring out of his wounds. Before she pressed her lips against his, Yuichiro's eyes moved slightly but then they shut.

This kiss was different from the whore's kiss she gave to Tadakatsu moments ago. It was soft, warm, and kind even though it might have been mixed with the taste of blood.

Their lips parted. Yuichiro opened his eyes again in a semi-daze.

"I-I'm sorry...," he said, "it looks like..."

Mitsuko smiled. "I know."

BLAM! BLAM! BLAM! With these dull gunshots Yuichiro's eyes opened wide.

Staring up at Mitsuko's face, and probably having no idea what had just happened, Yuichiro Takiguchi was now dead.

Mitsuko slowly removed the smoking revolver from Yuichiro's stomach and held Yuichiro's body again. She looked into his now vacant eyes.

"You were pretty cool. You even made me a little happy. I won't forget you."

She closed her eyes. Almost remorsefully, she once again gently pressed her lips against Yuichiro's. His lips were still warm.

The sunlight was finally shining on the western slope of the northern mountain. Under Mitsuko's head, blocking this light, Yuichiro's pupils dilated rapidly.

14 students remaining

58

Shuya Nanahara (Male Student No. 15) suddenly woke up.

He saw the blue sky framed by brilliant green grass.

He got up. Beyond the grass surrounding him, there was the familiar sight of Shiroiwa Junior High School in the pleasant sunlight.

Several students were on the school field in their gym gear. Maybe they were playing softball for gym class. He could hear their cheering.

He was in the garden at the edge of the courtyard. He saw the large leaves of the phoenix tree looming above him. This was where he took a nap sometimes, either during lunch or when he cut class.

He stood up and checked his body.

He had no wounds at all. Flakes of grass were stuck to his coat. He brushed them off.

A dream…

Shuya shook his head, still in a daze. Then he knew for certain.

It was all a dream. All of it.

He wiped his neck with his hand. It was moist with sweat. He was drenched in sweat as if he'd had a nightmare.

What…what a horrible dream! Killing game? We were selected for that "Program"!

Then he realized. The ones in the field…gym class?

He checked his watch. Afternoon classes had started. He'd overslept!

He quickly left the garden and trotted over to the school building. Today…today was…he checked his watch while running and saw it was Thursday.

The first Thursday afternoon period was literature. He felt relieved. He liked literature, and he did pretty well in that class. Plus his teacher, Kazuko Okazaki, liked him. So all he'd have to do is bow apologetically.

Literature. Favorite subject. Grades. Ms. Okazaki.

These words passing through his mind triggered a nostalgic feeling.

Shuya really did like literature. Even if the stories and essays in the textbooks were inundated with slogans in praise of the Republic or some silly "ideology," Shuya managed to discover words he liked. Words were just as important to him as music. Because rock couldn't do without lyrics.

Speaking of words...the top student in literature, Noriko Nakagawa, wrote beautiful poetry. Compared to the song lyrics he struggled to come up with, her words were so much more concise and brilliant...they could be open and gentle on the one hand and harsh and strong on the other...he thought they represented the nature of girls in general. Sure, Yoshitoki Kuninobu had a crush on Noriko, but what really struck Shuya was this part of her.

Which made Shuya realize, oh, that means Yoshitoki is alive. Realizing how silly the whole ordeal was, he was about to cry from relief as he trotted over. How silly. I can't believe I could dream of Yoshitoki dying.

And how did I end up with Noriko?...Hey wait, since when did I stop calling her "Noriko-san"? How presumptuous...in that stupid dream, he thought. They were linked together in the dream...so does that mean I have some feelings for her beyond admiring her poetry? Uh oh, that means I'll end up fighting with Yoshitoki. That's trouble.

Still, this idle thought made him grin.

Shuya entered the school building, now hushed because classes were in session. He ran up the stairs. Third Year Class B was on the third floor. He skipped every other step.

He reached the third floor and turned right into the hall. The second classroom was Class B.

Shuya stopped by the door for a moment, trying to come up with an excuse for Ms. Okazaki. He was feeling sick...no, he had a dizzy spell. So he had to lie down and rest. Would she believe him, given how he was always in perfect health? Yoshitoki would give an exaggerated shrug, and someone like Yutaka Seto would say something like, "I bet you were sleeping," Shinji Mimura would snicker, and Hiroki Sugimura, his arms folded, would look mildly amused. Noriko would smile at Shuya as he scratched his head. All right, that's what I'll go with. So what if it's embarrassing.

Shuya put his hand on the door, made himself look as apologetic as possible, and gently slid it open.

Right before he looked up from the formal posture he assumed, a stench assaulted him.

He looked up. He slid the door open with all his might.

The first thing he saw was someone lying by the lectern. Ms. Okazaki...

It wasn't Ms. Okazaki. It was their head instructor, Masao Hayashida. And...

His head was missing. There was a puddle where it was supposed to be. Only half of his eyeglass frames were lying beside him.

Shuya tore his eyes off of Mr. Hayashida's corpse and examined the rest of the class.

There were desks and chairs lined up as usual.

The strange thing was that his familiar classmates were all sprawled over their desks. And...

The floor was covered with blood. An intense stench wafted up.

After standing still for a moment, he quickly reached out for Mayumi Tendo—and realized that an antenna-like silver arrow was planted in her back. Its tip was poking out of her stomach while blood dripped down and off her skirt onto the floor.

Shuya moved forward. He shook Kazushi Niida's body. Kazushi's body tilted with a jerk, revealing its face.

Shuya felt a chill run up his spine. Kazushi's eyes were

now two dark-red holes. Blood and a slimy egg-white-like substance oozed out of them. Then...there was a gimlet-like object with a thick handle stabbed into his mouth.

Shuya screamed and ran to Yoshitoki Kuninobu's seat. There were three holes in his back, each one blooming with flowers of blood. As he held him up, Yoshitoki's head slumped over onto his shoulder. His bulging eyes gazed up at the ceiling.

Yoshitoki!...

Shuya raised his voice. Then he looked around frantically.

Everyone was either slouched back in their chairs or lying on the floor.

Megumi Eto's throat was slashed like sliced watermelon. A sickle was planted in Yoji Kuramoto's head. Sakura Ogawa's head was split open like an overripe fruit. Only half of Yoshimi Yahagi's head existed. An axe was planted in Tatsumichi Oki's head, his face cracked down the middle, left and right out of alignment like a split peanut. Kyoichi Motobuchi's stomach looked like a sausage-factory trash bin. Tadakatsu Hatagami's face was completely crushed and covered in blood. Hirono Shimizu's face was swollen black, and her sea-slug-sized tongue dangled out from the side of her wide open mouth. The body of The Third Man, Shinji Mimura, was covered with bullets.

Basically, everyone...was dead.

Something caught Shuya's eye. Shogo Kawada—that standoffish transfer student with the bad reputation—had deep stab wounds all over his chest. His eyes were half-open and looking down at the floor...they were out of focus.

Shuya took a deep breath and looked over at Noriko Nakagawa's seat. It was right behind Yoshitoki's, so he could have noticed earlier. For some reason though, it felt as if his classmates' seats were swirling around with the corpses. He finally managed to locate Noriko.

She was still sprawled on top of her desk.

Shuya ran to her and held her up.

THUD. Her head fell off. Leaving behind her body, it landed with a thud on the floor and rolled around in a pool of blood...and then looked up at Shuya. With eyes full of resentment. I thought you said you would save me, Shuya. But I ended up dying. I really loved you, too. I really did.

His eyes glued to Noriko's face, Shuya held his head and opened his mouth. He felt he was going crazy.

He could tell a scream was welling up inside.

Suddenly, he saw something white.

As he became physically aware that his body was in fact horizontal, his vision came into focus, and Shuya finally realized it was the ceiling. On the left side he saw a fluorescent light.

Someone gently touched his chest.

He realized how heavy he was breathing. His eyes followed the hand up to the arm, the arm up to the shoulder, and finally discerned a sailor-suit figure with braided hair— female class representative Yukie Utsumi (Female Student No. 2), smiling warmly.

"Looks like you're up. What a relief," she said.

14 students remaining

59

Shuya tried getting up, but the pain all over his body immediately assaulted him, and he fell back. He realized then he was lying on a soft bed with fresh sheets.

Yukie gently touched Shuya's chest again, then lifted the puffy blanket up to his neck. "Don't exert yourself. You're injured pretty badly....You seemed to be having a bad nightmare. Do you feel okay?"

Shuya wasn't able to respond coherently. Instead he surveyed the room. It was small. There was cheap fabric wallpaper on the left wall, and on the right behind Yukie was another bed, but besides that there wasn't much else. There was a door near the foot of the bed, but it was closed. The wooden frame gave it an old look. There seemed to be a window above his head letting in a dull light which illuminated the room. Given how dull the light was it seemed cloudy outside. But…where was he?

"I don't get it," Shuya said. He realized he could speak now. "I don't remember checking into a hotel with the student representative."

He was still in a half daze, but Yukie gave a sigh of relief. Then her full lips erupted into a soft chuckle. "You would say that, wouldn't you? I'm so relieved you're all right though." Looking at Shuya, she added, "You were out for quite some time. Let see…it's been," she looked down at her watch on her left wrist, "about thirteen hours."

Thirteen hours? Thirteen hours. Thirteen hours ago I was—

Shuya's eyes opened wide. His memory and the present locked in. He was fully awake now.

There was something he needed to find out. Right away.

"What about Noriko, Noriko Nakagawa? And Shogo Kawada?"

Shuya said this and took a deep breath. Were they still alive?

Yukie gave him a funny look and then said, "I think Noriko…and Shogo are still alive. We just heard the afternoon announcement but their names weren't announced."

Shuya let out a deep breath. Noriko and Shogo had managed to escape. Kazuo had chased after him and ended up losing Noriko and Shogo. Kazuo was—

Shuya then looked up at Yukie.

"Kazuo. It's Kazuo!" His voice was half panicking. "Where are we? Are you alone here? We have to be careful!"

Yukie gently touched Shuya's right hand, which was sticking out from under his blanket. "Calm down." Then she asked, "Did Kazuo do this to you?"

Shuya nodded. "He's the one who's been attacking us. He's totally up for this."

"Really…" Yukie nodded and continued, "We're safe here. They're six of us here, not including you. Everyone else is keeping watch, so don't worry. They're all close friends of mine."

Shuya raised his brow. Six?

"Who?"

"Yuka Nakagawa," Yukie mentioned the cheery girl who had the same last name as Noriko. Then she continued, "Satomi Noda and Chisato Matsui. Haruka Tanizawa. And Yuko Sakaki."

Shuya licked his lips. Yukie saw the expression on his face and asked, "What? You can't trust them? Which one? Everyone?"

"No…" Shuya shook his head. "If they're your friends I trust them."

But how did six girls, all good friends with each other, manage to get together?

Yukie smiled and squeezed his hand. "Good. I'm glad to hear that from you, Shuya."

Shuya smiled too. But his smile receded almost instantly. There were other things he had to know. He'd already missed three—the midnight, 6 a.m., and noon announcements.

"Who…died?" he asked. "I-I mean, at midnight, 6 a.m., and noon, there were three announcements, right? Did anyone else…die?"

Yukie's mouth stiffened. She took some paper from the

small side table right beside them. It was a map and student list. The folds and mud stains looked familiar. He realized it was the one he'd kept in his school coat pocket.

Yukie looked over the list and said, "Hirono Shimizu. And then Keita Iijima, Toshinori Oda, Yutaka Seto, Yuichiro Takiguchi, Tadakatsu Hatagami, and Shinji Mimura."

Shuya's mouth hung open. Of course the game had proceeded, but he was shocked it now left only little more than a dozen students. Plus he'd been teammates with Tadakatsu Hatagami in Little League, but what really took him by surprise was...

"Shinji's..."

The Third Man, Shinji Mimura, had died. It was hard to believe. He thought if anyone could survive it would have been Shinji.

Yukie nodded silently.

At the same time Shuya was struck by how he wasn't all that shaken up. He'd gotten used to it. That must have been it. Still, he remembered Shinji's special grin. Then he recalled that serious expression Shinji wore as he sent him a signal, warning him to calm down when they were back in the school building.

So we're never going to see the awesome play of The Third Man, Shiroiwa Junior High's star shooting guard, again, he thought, and felt a pang of sorrow.

"When was Shinji's name announced?"

"In the morning," Yukie answered. "Keita Iijima and Yutaka Seto were also in the morning. They might have been together. They were such good friends."

"I see..."

Shinji had still been alive at midnight. And as Yukie said, he might have been with Yutaka Seto and Keita Iijima.

Yukie added, "There was an incredible explosion last night. And a lot of gunfire. That's where it might have come from."

"Explosion?"

Shuya recalled the hand grenade Kazuo threw at them. "That was...Kazuo actually used a hand grenade. Maybe that's what you heard."

Yukie raised her brow. "So...that's what that was. That was a little past eleven, right? No, the one I'm talking about actually happened after we brought you here. It was past midnight. It was much worse than the one we heard around eleven. The one who kept watch said the entire center of the island just lit up."

Shuya pursed his lips, but then he realized he still hadn't managed to find out exactly where they were.

Before he could ask though, Yukie handed him the map and student list. "This is yours. I marked off the map too."

As he took it, Shuya realized, yes, there were more forbidden zones. He spread the map out.

"The place where we talked about rock."

That place, sector C=3, near the western shore, was crossed out with a pencil along with several other sectors. The small writing, "23rd, 11 a.m." meant that it was forbidden as of this morning at eleven, while Shuya had been asleep.

Shuya pursed his lips. Noriko and Shogo weren't there anymore—his thoughts were finally getting clearer—if they haven't died between noon and now. Of course they were alive...but then he recalled how he'd seen Shogo and Noriko dead along with Yoshitoki and Shinji in his dream. He felt a chill run down his spine.

But in any case they should be alive. All he could do was believe they were all right. But how in the world would he find them?

Shuya put the map down on his chest. He couldn't afford to waste any time deliberating, under these circumstances. The first thing was information.

And since he wasn't alone there might be a way.

He looked up at Yukie. "Where are we anyway? How did I end up in this bed?"

Yukie looked up at the window and said, "This is a lighthouse."

"Lighthouse?"

"That's right. On the northeast end of the island. It's marked on the map. We've been staying here ever since the game started."

Shuya looked at his map again. Just as Yukie said, the lighthouse was located in sector C=10, jutting out from the northeast side of the island. The area was practically devoid of forbidden zones.

"So Shuya, about last night. The front of this lighthouse is a cliff, and that's where you fell. The person keeping watch found you…and took you in. You were injured pretty badly. Covered with blood. I thought you were going to die."

Shuya finally realized his torso was naked and that his throbbing left shoulder was bandaged. (Given how it felt, he deduced the bullet shattered his shoulder blade and was now lodged in there.) The right side of his neck—he felt a burning sensation right below his collar where there was another bandage (but this bullet wound must have been a minor scrape). And then on top of his left elbow. (It felt heavy. The bullet had most likely exited, but perhaps because the bone or tendon was torn off, it felt paralyzed.) Also his left side. (The bullet had pierced it, but it seemed to have missed his vital organs.) Shuya awkwardly moved his unscathed right arm and lifted his blanket, confirming he was indeed covered with bandages.

He returned the blanket and asked, "So you treated me."

"Yes," Yukie nodded. "We found an emergency first-aid kit in the lighthouse. We stitched your wounds a little. Not a great job, since we didn't know what we were doing and we could only use the string and needle from a sewing set. It looks like the bullet in your shoulder…is lodged in there. We couldn't do much. I thought what you really needed was a blood transfusion. You were bleeding so badly."

"Thanks a lot."

"Oh no," Yukie smiled kindly. "I can't believe I got to touch a guy's body! I even got to take off your clothes."

Shuya chuckled. While she was both very smart and considerate, she could also say bold stuff like that. That's right, she'd been like that ever since he got to know her on a rainy day in the elementary school gym, negotiating the space allocated for Little League practice and girls' volleyball. And that's right, at the time he'd said to Yoshitoki, "Then there's Utsumi, who's on the volleyball team. She's pretty cool. That's my type. You know, real outgoing."

Of course right now he wasn't supposed to be indulging in idle emotions. But when Yukie said, "Oh, yeah, here," and offered him a cup of water, Shuya couldn't resist whistling. He was in fact really thirsty. The cup was already there, on the side table beyond his field of vision.

He thought, how impressive, Representative. You'll be a wonderful wife some day, no, a wonderful woman. No, you might in fact be a wonderful woman now. I've actually thought that for a while.

He took the cup, raised his head, and drank. His neck wound hurt as he swallowed and grimaced. But he drank it all.

"I might be asking for too much," he said, returning the cup, "but I think I should drink a lot more. And also…do you have any kind of painkiller? Anything. It'll help me."

Yukie nodded. "Sure. I'll go get some."

Shuya wiped his lips and then said, "It's amazing your friends accepted me. I mean, I could be an enemy."

Yukie shook her head. "We couldn't just let someone die.

Besides…" She stared into Shuya's eyes and smiled playfully. "It was you, Shuya. I'm leading this group, so I forced everyone to agree."

Did that mean that…she also thought there was something special about them ever since that time at the elementary school gym?

Shuya probed further. "Which means…that some of them were reluctant. I knew it."

"Well, come on. Given the circumstances." Yukie looked down. "Don't take it the wrong way. Everyone's very agitated."

"Yeah." Shuya nodded. "I know."

"But I convinced them." She looked up and smiled again. "So you should be thankful."

Shuya was nodding when he noticed Yukie, who'd just been smiling, was now for some reason suddenly on the verge of tears.

She stared at him and said, "I was worried sick. I thought you might die, Shuya."

Shuya was taken by surprise and looked at her.

Yukie continued, "I just wouldn't know what to do if you died."

Her voice was now sobbing.

"…do you understand what I'm saying? Do you see why I had to save you, no matter what?"

Shuya stared at Yukie's tearful eyes and slowly nodded. Then he thought, geez, I can't believe how popular I am.

Of course…this might have been a psychological result of their confinement. Under these circumstances, they were probably going to die soon (no, according to the rules, they were definitely going to die. He'd never heard of someone else besides the winner surviving the hellish Program), and now that the survivors were becoming fewer and fewer, maybe a boy that you liked "a little" ever since having an exchange in the corner of an elementary school gym might turn into somebody you'd "die for."

No, that probably wasn't the case. She couldn't have opposed her friends unless she really cared for him. Besides, how else could she have trusted him?

"I understand. Thanks," he said.

Yukie wiped her tears with the lower palm of her right hand. Then she said, "Tell me. You asked about Noriko and Shogo. You said, 'we.' Does that mean you were with them?"

Shuya nodded.

Yukie knit her brows. "I get Noriko…but don't tell me you were really with Shogo."

Shuya knew what she was getting at. "Shogo's not a bad guy," he said. "He saved me. Noriko and me survived thanks to him. I'm sure Shogo's protecting Noriko right now….That's right. There's something more urgent," he continued enthusiastically. "I forgot. We can be saved, Yukie."

"Saved?"

Shuya nodded emphatically. "Shogo's going to save us. He knows a way out of here."

Yukie opened her eyes wide. "Really? Really? What is it?"

Shuya stopped suddenly. Shogo had told him, I can't tell you till the end.

Come to think of it…Shuya had nothing to support it. He trusted Shogo, but he wasn't so sure his explanation would persuade Yukie, who hadn't been with Shogo. As Shogo himself constantly reminded him, she might suspect Shogo was using Shuya and the others.

Shuya decided though to explain everything from the beginning.

He told her how he'd been attacked by Yoshio Akamatsu from the very beginning, how he'd been with Noriko ever since then, how he'd fought Tatsumichi Oki, and how, while Kyoichi Motobuchi was shooting at him, Shogo had saved him and how the three were together ever since. He told her about the escape plan, how Shogo was a survivor of the Program last year, how Noriko had a fever, and how they went over to the clinic. That's right, and then about Hiroki Sugimura. How Hiroki told them that Mitsuko Souma was dangerous. And then how they were attacked by Kazuo Kiriyama while they were on the move.

"So Tatsumichi..." After he was done she brought up Tatsumichi Oki first for some reason. "...that was an accident?"

"That's right. Just as I described it," he replied and knit his brows, looking at her. "What about it?"

Yukie shook her head. She said, "It's nothing," and changed the subject, "I'm sorry for being so blunt, but I can't just all of a sudden trust Shogo. I mean, that there's a way out of here."

Shuya still didn't understand why Yukie had asked him about Tatsumichi, but he figured it couldn't be all that important so he let it pass and accepted Yukie's skepticism.

"I don't blame you. But I think we can trust Shogo. It's hard to explain, but he's good," he impatiently waved his uninjured right hand by his face. "You'd understand if you were with him."

Yukie pressed her right fingers against her lips and said, "All right. It sounds like we should at least hear him out. I mean it's not like we have any other option."

Shuya looked at her. "What were you planning on doing?"

Yukie shrugged. "I thought it was hopeless. We were just discussing whether we were better off trying to escape or staying here a little longer. But we haven't made any decisions."

Shuya then realized he'd forgotten to ask something else he'd forgotten. "How did you guys get together? All six of you?"

"Oh," Yukie nodded. "I went back to the school, and I called on everyone."

Shuya was surprised. "When?"

"That would have to be right after you and Noriko ran away. Actually, I saw Kazushi Niida run...I really wanted to get back in time to contact you, but anyway, that's how I saw...those two dead right in front of the school entrance."

Shuya raised his brow. "Yoshio was only unconscious, right?"

Yukie shook her head. "I wasn't able to get a close look...but he looked dead at that point. There was an arrow...stuck in his neck."

...

"Then Kazushi—"

Yukie nodded. "I think so."

Shuya then asked, "Weren't you scared there'd be others like Yoshio?"

"Of course the thought occurred to me...but I just couldn't come up with any other option other than forming a group. So I went to the woods in front. I figured if I hid there I wouldn't be seen. And if I was, then that was just too bad."

Shuya was deeply moved. He had to look after Noriko, who was injured, but still, he'd passed on the others and ran away. Hiroki Sugimura said he'd waited for Takako Chigusa, but he was a guy, and he also practiced martial arts.

"Wow. I'm amazed, Representative."

Yukie smiled.

"You call Noriko by her name, but with me it's 'Representative,' huh?"

Shuya didn't know what to say. "Oh well—"

"Don't worry, it's all right."

A smile flashed across her face. Then she continued a little sadly, "Then Yuka Nakagawa came out...and I called her."

"Were you able to convince her right away? Don't get me wrong—I think you have a good reputation."

"Oh, well." Yukie nodded. "I didn't come back alone. I

was really shaken up at first, but I just had to come back, and on the way back, I totally lucked out, I found Haruka. You know how Haruka and I are best friends."

Shuya nodded. Haruka Tanizawa and Yukie were both on the volleyball team.

"I talked to Haruka. When I told her we should go back she resisted at first, but we had weapons. I had a pistol in my pack. When Yuka heard the two of us call she managed to trust us."

After some consideration, Shuya mentioned that "rule": "But…you can't necessarily trust someone who's paired up in this game."

Yukie nodded. "Yes, that turned out to be true."

"What do you mean?"

"Well, we decided not to have boys…sorry…we discussed it and decided boys could mean trouble. So we let them go, and then there was Fumiyo—" Yukie stopped. Fumiyo Fujiyoshi (Female Student No. 18) had died before their departure. "After her came Chisato. So there were five of us. We also called on Kaori Minami but…"

Shuya filled in the rest, "She ran away."

"Yes, she did."

Shuya realized he hadn't told her that he'd seen her die. He thought of telling her—but decided not to. Now that Kaori's killer Hirono Shimizu was also dead, it didn't seem relevant and besides, it wasn't a pleasant memory. Also, as awful as it sounded, he couldn't afford to waste any more time talking about the dead.

"So Yoshimi reacted the same way as Kaori?" Shuya uttered the name of the last female student seat number, Yoshimi Yahagi, along with Kaori's and suddenly felt a chill run down his spine. Names of the dead. Both of them. Both…of…them. Jesus. The smiling face of the man in the black suit made a sudden appearance in Shuya's mind. It'd been a while. Hey there, Shuya. So you're still alive? You're a tough one.

"Well…" Yukie looked away from Shuya and pursed her lips. She squinted. "That was different."

"How so?"

Yukie took a deep breath. "I said we should call on her. But some of the girls protested. You know Yoshimi was friends with Mitsuko. They couldn't trust her."

Shuya fell silent.

Yukie said looking away. "So she's dead. We let her die."

Shuya said, "No, you're wrong."

Yukie looked back at Shuya.

"It was beyond your control. It's no one's fault."

He knew it didn't sound very convincing, but that's all he could say .

Yukie grinned wryly and sighed. "You're kind. You've always been so nice."

They nearly fell silent, but then Shuya had to say something, "You should have called on Shinji." Yukie's group could have at least called on Shinji Mimura, who was at the tail end of the student list. "He could have been trusted."

Yukie sighed again. "I thought so too…but Shinji didn't have a very good reputation…among the girls. You know, he was kind of a playboy. And his intelligence was kind of intimidating. You know how he intervened when Noriko was injured? One of the girls said that might have been calculated."

It was the same explanation Shogo gave when he mentioned he'd seen Shinji.

"Before we could decide, Shinji was gone." Yukie shrugged. "In any case, we'd decided against boys. So we didn't call on Kazuhiko either."

That's right. Kazuhiko Yamamoto, who went out with Sakura Ogawa, who despite his good looks was kind and unpretentious, and therefore must have been popular with the girls. Yukie's group decided against contacting him too, though. And given this policy, it was only to be expected there'd be some friction over taking in Shuya here.

Shuya realized Yukie only accounted for five of them. She hadn't mentioned Yuko Sakaki (Female Student No. 9).

"What about Yuko? You haven't mentioned her."

Yukie nodded and looked back at Shuya. "That was luck too. We came here yesterday morning....Nice fortress huh? Last night, I think it was around 8 p.m., Yuko just stumbled by here. She was totally terrified."

Yukie stopped as if she had something else to say. Shuya was about to ask her what was wrong, but Yukie continued, "...in any case, everyone knows Yuko. So it wasn't a problem."

That summed up her account. Shuya thought of asking more about Yuko Sakaki but decided not to. If she'd been alone until last night then she might have encountered something horrible. Did she survive someone's attack, or did she see students killings each other, or did she come across a corpse torn up from fighting?...

Shuya nodded slightly several times. "I get it now."

"There's one thing I don't get," Yukie said. "It's not a big deal but...Hiroki was saying he needed to see Kayoko Kotohiki, right? And that was why he didn't join your group."

Shuya was worried about him ever since he summarized his situation to Yukie. Hiroki was still alive and so was Kayoko Kotohiki. Did he manage to find her?

"He had to see her. I wonder why."

Shuya shook his head. "We didn't ask. He was in a hurry. We were wondering too—"

As he spoke Shuya couldn't help but wonder, did Hiroki manage to find Kayoko Kotohiki? If he did then—

Shogo's voice suddenly returned: "This sound is your ticket out of here. If you're up for it, you can come aboard our train."

Shuya opened his eyes wide and exclaimed, "The bird call."

"What?"

Shuya looked over at Yukie. "I know a way we can join Noriko and Shogo."

"Really?"

Shuya nodded. Then he struggled to move his body. He could explain later. "I have to contact him now. I have to get going."

"Hold on," Yukie stopped him. "You need to rest."

"I can't. The more I lie around—"

"I said hold on. You might want to listen to the girl who's in love with you." She managed to say this as she blushed a little with a playful smile. "We took you in here because even if you woke up you wouldn't be able to move. Your sudden burst of energy might terrify some of the girls."

Shuya's eyes opened wide. But then again it made sense. That was probably why the other girls let Yukie stay with him alone here.

Yukie continued, "In any case, just stay put for a while. I'll tell them everything you told me. I'll insist you and Shogo can be trusted and convince them. As for contacting him and Noriko, I can't let you do that alone. That's just too dangerous. I'll discuss that with them too. So you just stay here." Then she asked him, "Can you eat?"

"Yeah."

In fact he was famished. He was worried about Noriko and Shogo, but he thought he should eat first. It would help his immune system fight against his gunshot wounds.

"If you have any food to spare I'd really appreciate it. I do feel pretty weak."

Yukie smiled. "We're preparing lunch right now. I'll bring you some. I think it's something like stew. Is that all right?"

"Stew?"

"Yeah, this place is loaded with food even though it's all just preserved canned food and retort food. But we found water and solid fuel, so we were able to cook it."

"Awesome. That's great."

Yukie's hand left the edge of the bed. She walked over to the door and said, "I'm really sorry but I'm going to have to lock the door."

"Huh?"

"I'm sorry. There's someone who's terrified. So please, just wait," Yukie said. She smiled kindly as she opened the door and went out. Her two braids of hair swung like some mysterious animal's tail, and he caught a glimpse of a gun stuck in the back of her skirt.

There was a clacking sound from beyond the door. It might have been bolted shut. Was that how they locked him up?

Shuya managed to raise his upper body with his right elbow and looked up at the window above his head. The window was sealed with wooden planks and light leaked in through the gaps. This was done to keep intruders out—but right now it also served as an ideal place to lock him up.

The fingers of his near paralyzed left arm reflexively formed guitar chords under the blanket. The chords from that hit tune sung by the rock star the middle-aged man, the one who gave him his guitar, worshipped, "Jailhouse Rock."

Shuya took a deep breath and lay down on his bed. The slight movement was enough to send sharp pain through the wound in his side.

14 students remaining

60

The Okishima Island lighthouse was old but durable. It faced north with a tower seventeen meters high, and the living quarters, a single-story brick building, had been built as an annex to the tower on its south side. The dining-kitchen-living room was immediately south of the tower, and further south was the storage room and bathroom. Further down were two bedrooms, one large, the other small, along with another storage room right near the front entrance. The hall running on the west side of the building connected these rooms. (Shuya was resting in the small bedroom by the entrance.)

In the corner of the kitchen-living room, which was at least as large as a classroom, was a small table that looked out of place. Yuko Sakaki (Female Student No. 9) was sitting on one of the stools around the table, slumped over the white tabletop as if she were dozing off. Unlike the other five girls, she had wandered around the island for hours on end, so a single night here had hardly alleviated her fatigue. No wonder. She had a reason for not sleeping at all last night.

Yukie Utsumi's team used this room as their living quarters and slept here too. Someone had to keep watch at the top of the tower, but otherwise Yukie decided that everyone should stick together.

Right behind Yuko, Haruka Tanizawa (Female Student No. 12) and Chisato Matsui (Female Student No. 19) were busily preparing the preserved food in front of the stove, where solid fuel was lit up in place of the shut-off gas. At 172 centimeters tall, Haruka was an attacker on the volleyball team. She and Yukie, who was a setter, formed a great duo. She had short hair, so next to the long-haired, petit Chisato they almost looked like a couple. The meal was a retort stew mixed with canned vegetables. Above them were planks of wood they found in the storage room and hastily hammered into the frosted glass window, which let in the dull light of the cloudy sky. The planks were there to keep intruders out. As soon as they had arrived Yukie and the girls immediately sealed off every entrance and exit from the inside of the building. (The front entrance was designated as their primary entrance-exit, which was where they took Yuko in, but now it was barricaded with desks and lockers.)

Yuko had a clear view of the other side of the room where there was a writing desk with a fax machine and computer. To the left of it, Satomi Noda (Female Student No. 17) was sitting on a sofa placed against the wall, while the table that had been in front of it was now used to barricade the front entrance. Along with Yukie, Satomi was a model student, and although she always seemed a little frigid, now she looked pretty exhausted as she raised her wire-rimmed glasses and drowsily rubbed her eyes.

To the left of the sofa, the kitchen's side door connected to the hall that led to the front entrance. On Yuko's right, the far door on the other side led to the bottom of the tower, and the first several steel stairs leading up to the lantern room were visible. Yuka Nakagawa (Female Student No. 16) was up there, supposedly keeping watch. Yuko hadn't kept watch yet, but Yukie had told her that since the lighthouse faced the ocean, and since there was only one narrow path from the harbor behind the building, the rest of the area surrounded by mountains, it wasn't very difficult to keep watch. Yukie was now in the room right by the entrance where they'd kept Shuya Nanahara.

Shuya Nanahara.

Yuko felt the tremor of fear returning. Along with it the image that was burnt into her memory. The cracked head. The bloody axe removed from it. And the boy who held this axe.

It was a chilling memory. And this boy—Shuya Nanahara—was now in the lighthouse, the same building she was in. That was—

No, it's all right. It's all right.

Trying to keep herself from trembling, she stared at the white tabletop and reminded herself, that's right, he's dying, he can't possibly wake up after so many injuries and so much bleeding.

Someone tapped her on the shoulder and she looked up.

As Haruka Tanizawa sat down next to her, she stared at Yuko and asked, "Did you get any sleep?" She was taking a break from cooking. Chisato Matsui seemed to be checking the cooking instructions, examining the package of preserved food. (Chisato had in fact been quietly weeping this morning. Haruka Tanizawa had whispered to her it was because of the 6 a.m. announcement of Shinji Mimura's death. Until then Yuko hardly knew Chisato had a crush on Shinji Mimura. Her eyes were still red.)

Yuko forced a smile and answered, "Yeah, a little." It was all right. As long as she was with these other five friends she was all right. She was safe here. Even if that safety would expire when their time ran out. Still—

Haruka brought up the matter. "What you said about yesterday."

"Oh…" Yuko smiled. "It's all right now."

That's right. It was fine now. She didn't even want to think about it. Just the memory sent chills down her spine. But…in any case…

Shuya Nanahara wasn't going to wake up again. Then it was all right. Just fine.

Haruka smiled ambivalently. "Well then, okay."

That's right…When Shuya Nanahara was discovered unconscious in front of the lighthouse yesterday, Yuko had vehemently opposed taking him in. She had explained (she was shouting rather than explaining) what she'd seen, Tatsumichi Oki's split-open skull, how Shuya Nanahara had removed the axe, how dangerous he was, and how he would try to kill them if they let him live.

Yuko and Yukie were on the verge of fighting, but then Haruka and the others insisted they couldn't just let someone die, so they brought Shuya in. Yuko looked on, face ashen, keeping her distance, while the others carried the blood-drenched Shuya. It was as if they were welcoming a strange, scary monster that haunted you in your childhood dreams into your house. No, that's exactly what it was like.

But…as time passed Yuko convinced herself Shuya was dying. After all, he couldn't possibly survive those wounds. Knowing he would die of course was unappealing, but in any case she managed to hold herself back. The one condition she insisted on, though, was that his room be locked.

Haruka continued. It was the same question they had asked several times yesterday. "You say you saw Shuya kill Tatsumichi, but it might have been in self-defense, right?"

That was true. She'd been hiding in the bushes when she heard the thudding sound. By the time she looked, the only part she really witnessed was Shuya removing the axe from Tatsumichi Oki's head. Then she immediately ran away.

In other words, as Haruka said (which was based on Yuko's own description), Yuko had only seen the aftermath. It was possible he had done it in self-defense. However…

…no matter how many times Haruka and Yukie said this to her, Yuko just couldn't see it that way. No, she simply rejected the idea.

What do you mean, "possible"? I saw that cracked skull. I saw Shuya Nanahara holding that axe. The bloody axe. The dripping blood.

Her thoughts revolved around this scene now. Yuko couldn't be rational about Shuya Nanahara anymore. It was like a natural disaster, like a flood or tornado. The moment Yuko began thinking about Shuya, that scene and her fear would just wash it all away. The only thing left was an axiom that was nearly visceral— that Shuya Nanahara was dangerous.

Yuko had her reasons. She abhorred violence. She couldn't stand it. Hearing a friend talk about a splatter film in Class B (was it Yuka Nakagawa? "Of course, it was funny, but, it wasn't a big deal, it should have more gory, ha ha ha") she felt sick enough to be taken to the school nurse.

It was probably related to her memory of her father. Even though he wasn't a stepfather—he was her real father—he drank heavily and abused her mother, her older brother, and Yuko herself. She was too young back then...so Yuko didn't understand why. She was never able to ask her mother why he was like that. She didn't even want to remember it. Well, maybe there were no reasons at all. She didn't know. In any case, when her father was stabbed to death by a yakuza over some gambling dispute—Yuko was still in first grade—she felt more relieved than bereaved. Ever since then she, her mother, and brother led a peaceful life. They could invite friends over. They finally felt safe with the disappearance of their father.

But she still sometimes had dreams about him. Her bleeding mother being beaten with a golf club (even though they were poor, this was the one expensive item in their home). Her brother being beaten with an ashtray, nearly losing his sight. And...herself, suffering cigarette burns, paralyzed with fear (her mother who tried to intervene would then be beaten again).

Maybe all of that was related, maybe not. In any case, Yuko was absolutely convinced Shuya Nanahara was dangerous.

"Right?" She heard Haruka say that emphatically, but her

words didn't register. A chill ran through her body, accompanied by a vision. Everyone including herself, the six of them lying on the floor, their skulls cracked open, and Shuya Nanahara grinning with an axe in his hand…

No, no. It's going to be over. Shuya Nanahara won't be around for long.

"Yes." She looked up and nodded. In fact, she had no idea what Haruka was talking about. But in any case as long as Shuya couldn't recover there was no reason to throw the team off balance. Haruka seemed to be seeking some indication she was convinced.

"Y-yes. It was just me. I was so tired too."

This seemed to put Haruka at ease. She said, "Shuya's a good guy. They're aren't too many around like him."

Yuko looked at Haruka as if she were a mummy exhibited in a museum. She had thought so too, until recently. Shuya seemed strange, but all in all there was something very likable about him. In fact, she'd even thought he was kind of cool.

But any memory of this feeling had completely fallen by the wayside now. Maybe it was more accurate to say the cracked-skull scene had smothered out all her other memories.

What? What are you saying, Haruka? That he's good? What are you talking about?

Haruka looked into Yuko's eyes dubiously, but added, "So even if he gets up, don't provoke him, okay?"

Yuko was horrified. There was no way he was going to wake up. If…if that ever happened…

But a portion of her rational faculties were still intact enough for her to nod and say, "I'm fine. No problem."

"Good. I feel much better."

Haruka nodded back, turned towards Chisato without getting up, and said, "Smells good."

Along with the steam, the smell of the stew came

drifting from the stove pot.

Chisato turned her head around and said in her quiet, thin voice, "Yes, it looks pretty good. It might be better than yesterday's soup."

She had been crying over Shinji Mimura for a long time, but she seemed all right for the time being. Even Yuko could see that.

Right then, the door to the hall opened up. It was Yukie Utsumi. As usual she maintained her perfect posture and walked forward confidently. After Yuko's arrival, Yukie still did a good job leading the group, but she seemed a little tired. Ever since they took in Shuya she looked even more distressed. (It was in fact because she was on the one hand happy to see Shuya, but on the other worried his wounds might prove to be fatal, but this was beyond the scope of Yuko's perception.) Yuko felt like it'd been a while since she last saw Yukie so energetic, but now her face was beaming.

Yuko felt as if a caterpillar was crawling up her spine. She had a bad feeling about this.

Yukie stopped, put her hands on her waists, and looked around at everyone. Then she comically cupped her hands against her mouth in the shape of a megaphone.

Then she said, "Shuya Nanahara has arisen."

Haruka and Chisato cried out with joy while Satomi got up from her sofa, but next to her...

...Yuko turned pale.

14 students remaining

61

"Really? Can he speak?" Haruka asked.

"Uh huh. He says he's hungry too." Yukie nodded and

then looked over at Yuko and said, "It's all right. I locked the door to his room so you wouldn't have to worry."

She wasn't being sarcastic. It sounded more like she was doing what she should do as the leader.

But that wasn't the point, Yuko thought. No, actually she had considered it over and over last night. While she was certain he would never recover, what if he did? Then how would she deal with it? And…then the odor drifted by.

What timing. They were about to eat. Besides…it wouldn't be that odd for a guy in critical condition to die suddenly, would it?

Yuko forced a smile (indeed, it was impeccable) and shook her head. "I'm not worried," she continued, "I'm sorry. I was all screwed up yesterday. I won't hold anything against Shuya anymore."

This seemed to relieve Yukie. She took a deep breath.

"Well then, I guess I didn't need to lock the door." She smiled at Yuko and added, "What happened with Tatsumichi Oki was an accident. That's what Shuya said."

Hearing Tatsumichi's name, Yuko had a flashback of that scene which sent another chill down her spine, but she managed to keep her smile and nodded. An accident. Well, I suppose it was quite an accident for Tatsumichi Oki.

Yukie then said to Haruka, "Hey, Haruka, can you go get Yuka? There's something I need to discuss."

Haruka asked back, "Shouldn't she be keeping watch?"

"It's all right," Yukie nodded. "The building is sealed, so we're fine. It'll be brief."

Haruka nodded and entered the room leading up to the lantern room. You could hear footsteps clang up the steel stairs.

While Satomi and Chisato asked in succession, "How is he?" and "Can he eat the same stuff we're eating?" Yuko quietly stood up from her chair and walked over to the sink.

There was a stack of several deep dishes right beside the steaming stew pot. Chisato and Haruka had taken them out of the dish cabinet.

Yuko dug her hand into her skirt pocket and touched the object inside. The weapon she found in her day pack was a telescoping spring baton, but what she now held was this item labeled "special bonus," the item she had thought was useless. Even after she was welcomed here she didn't think there was much point in mentioning it. But when Shuya Nanahara showed up she came up with this idea, so she kept it a secret.

In the past…her father's violence, his terrorization of the rest of her family, ended unexpectedly. That was how her family finally attained peace.

Now there was another threat. She had to put a stop to it. Once she did…she would be safe again. She wouldn't have to be terrified anymore.

She felt no hesitation. Oddly enough, she was calm.

She removed the cork lid of the tiny bottle inside her pocket with one hand.

14 students remaining

62

"Hey," Yuko called over to Yukie. Yukie, who was speaking to Satomi and Chisato, looked over at her.

Yuko continued, "Maybe we should bring Shuya his meal first?"

Yukie beamed a smile at her. "That's a good idea. Let's do that."

Yuko then added very casually, "The stew looks ready, so how about I start serving it up?"

She held the dish. The dish.

"Sure—oh that's right," Yukie said as if she suddenly remembered. "You know, there's a medicine kit in the desk drawer over there. I think it has some painkillers. I should bring Shuya some painkillers with his meal."

"...sure." Yuko then let go of the dish. It clicked against the sink. "Okay. Hold on."

The writing desk, equipped with a computer and phone, was across from the sink, in the corner of the room. Yuko made her way around the table to get there.

Clanging footsteps descended the steel stairs. Haruka and Yuka Nakagawa entered the room. Yuka Nakagawa had a short-barreled gun resembling an expanded automatic gun with an extended stock slung over her shoulder. (It was an Uzi 9mm submachine gun. It was Satomi Noda's supplied weapon, but because it seemed like the most powerful weapon they had, whoever keeping watch held onto it.)

"I heard Shuya's up!" Yuka said in her usual cheerful voice, placing the Uzi on the table. A little chubby and, thanks to her tennis team practice in the outdoor courts, tan, Yuka somehow managed to stay cheerful even in these dire circumstances.

"Yes." Yukie nodded happily.

"Well, you must be relieved, Representative," Yuka teased her.

Yukie blushed a little. "What are you saying?"

"Oh, come on. You're beaming."

Yukie frowned and then shook her head. Suddenly realizing something, Yuka looked over at Chisato and fell silent. Chisato had lost Shinji Mimura, the boy she loved, and now she stared down at the floor.

Yuko hardly paid attention to this exchange as she took the wooden medical kit she found in the desk drawer. She placed it on the desk and opened it up. It was stuffed with various kinds of medical supplies, gauze, poultices. The only things missing were the bandages, since they were almost entirely used up to treat Shuya Nanahara.

Painkillers…which one were the painkillers? Of course, it didn't matter. It didn't matter because…

"Wow, it smells great," she heard Yuka say, trying to change the mood. But she hardly paid noticed to that either.

Painkillers…ah, here we go. Right here. For headaches, menstrual cramps, toothaches…oh…come to think of it, my stomach's been aching. I'll take some later. After things settle down a little. That's right, once things calm down.

"So what is it?" Satomi asked Yukie in her slightly husky voice.

"That's right. What is it?" Haruka asked.

"Oh, right. Let's see, where do I begin?" Yukie said.

It was only when Yuka said, "Let's have a taste then," that Yuko suddenly looked up.

She turned around…and saw Yuka lift the dish and put it against her mouth. She should have used the ladle if she wanted a taste. Instead she had to put her mouth against *that dish*, the one she'd sprinkled with the half-transparent powder.

Yuko turned pale. She was about to raise her voice…but it happened too fast.

Yuka dropped the dish and the stew splashed against the floor with a crashing sound. Everyone looked over at her.

Yuka held onto her throat and coughed out the stew she had just swallowed. Then she coughed more violently onto the white table. Now the substance was bright red. The red splattered out in a circle against the white table and resembled the national flag of the Republic of Greater East Asia. And then she crashed onto the floor covered with stew.

"Yuka!"

Everyone — besides Yuko, who was speechless —

cried out and ran to Yuka.

Yuka balled up on her side and coughed up blood again. Her tan face became more and more pale. Red foam spilled out the side of her mouth.

"Yuka! Yuka! What happened!?"

Yukie shook her body, but the dark-red foam only continued to spill out the side of her mouth. Her eyes were open as wide as possible, as if on the verge of popping out, but now even the whites of her eyes were turning red. For some reason—inflammation or broken capillaries—dark-red and black spots began appearing all over her blue face, transforming it into the mask of some grotesque monster.

But besides this, there was something else that was indisputable. It was obvious.

Yuka had stopped breathing.

Everyone fell silent. Yukie's trembling hand touched Yuka's throat. She said, "She's dead...."

Behind Yukie, who crouched down beside Yuka and Haruka, Yuko stood still, her face completely pale. She was shaking. (Of course it was very possible the other four were also in the same state.)

Oh, how could...how could this...this is all a mistake...mistake...how could...you only had a mouthful...how could it be this strong...I didn't...this is a mistake...I killed her...by mistake...it was a mistake...I didn't mean to...I wanted to get rid of—

"It couldn't have been from food poisoning...could it?" Yukie continued, her voice trembling.

Chisato responded, "I...just tasted it. Nothing happened...this...this...could this be..."

Haruka followed up, "...poison?"

That sparked it off. Everyone (to be more accurate, it was everyone besides Yuko, but the other four didn't realize this) looked at each other.

There was a thump. Satomi Noda had grabbed the Uzi and was now aiming it at the others. The other four, including Yuko, reflexively moved to the side or backed away from Yuka's corpse.

Satomi screamed. Her eyes behind her glasses were wide open with fear. "Who!? Who did it!? Who poisoned this stew! Who's the one trying to kill us!?"

"Stop it!" Yukie yelled.

Yuko saw her hand reach for the gun (Browning High Power 9mm. This was Yukie's supplied weapon and because she was the team leader she held onto it) tucked in the back of her skirt. Yukie was about to move forward but stopped and stepped back. "Put your gun down. That can't be."

"Oh yes it can," Satomi shook her head. Satomi who always seemed so calm had completely lost control. "The last announcement said there were only fourteen of us left. It's getting down to the wire. So our enemy's finally rearing its ugly head." Then she looked over at Haruka and said, "You were the one cooking."

Haruka shook her head violently. "I wasn't the only one. Chisato also…"

"That's horrible," Chisato said. "I would never do such a horrible thing! Besides…" She seemed to hesitate, but then she said, "Satomi and Yuko also had plenty of chances to poison the food."

"…that's right," Haruka turned back to Satomi, then hissed at her, "Aren't you getting a little too upset?"

"Haruka!" Yukie stopped her, but it was too late. Satomi was now completely upset.

"What was that?"

"That's right," Haruka continued, "First of all, you've hardly slept. I know. When I got up in the middle of the night, you were up. Doesn't that mean you don't trust us? That's proof, right there!"

"Please, stop it, Haruka!" Yukie pleaded. She was nearly shrieking now. "Satomi! Put down the gun!"

"Oh, please." Satomi pointed the Uzi at Yukie now. "Stop pretending you're the leader. So this is the act you put on after your plan to poison everyone goes awry? Is that it?"

"Satomi…" Yukie said desperately.

Yuko raised her hand up to her mouth and stepped back in a daze. Her body was numb from the sudden turn of events. But…she had to say it, she had to explain the truth…or else this…something terrible was going to happen.

Suddenly, Chisato moved…to the side table against the wall on the right side of the sink. There was the remaining gun—a Czechoslovakian CZ75. (It was in fact Yuka's weapon.)

The rattling sound echoed through the room. Chisato was shot in the back three times as she crashed against the side table, slid down, clutched onto its edge, and fell face forward onto the floor. There was no need to check.…She was dead.

"Satomi! What are you doing!?" Yukie's eyes opened wide as she screamed. Her voice was breaking.

"Oh, please." Satomi held her smoking Uzi and glared at Yukie. "She went for the gun. Because she was guilty."

"So did you though!" Haruka screamed. "Yukie! Shoot Satomi!"

With a clicking sound, Satomi pointed the Uzi at Haruka. Her face darkened. She seemed ready to shoot Haruka at any moment.

Yukie looked anguished. At that moment she had her hand on the Browning in the back of her skirt. After hesitating, she must have…intended to shoot Satomi's arm or some other part of her body.

Satomi then quickly shifted the Uzi and fired…at Yukie.

Yukie was blown back with the rattling sound. Blood

burst out of the holes in her chest and she fell backwards.

Haruka stood still for only a moment and then made a dash for the Browning Yukie had dropped. Satomi's Uzi followed her body and burst out, blowing off Haruka's side along with the fabric of her uniform. Her body slid against the floor.

The table was in between them now. Satomi pointed the Uzi at Yuko. She said, "What about you?...You're different, right?"

Yuko could only tremble. As she trembled, her eyes were fixed on Satomi's face.

There was a pop. There was a hole on the left side of Satomi's forehead. She opened her mouth...and looked down at her left hand. Blood burst out of the hole in her forehead, splashing against the inside of her glasses. Then it continued to drip downward.

Yuko's neck moved stiffly like some gadget as she followed Satomi's eyes and found Haruka, her torso raised in pain from her fallen position, somehow still holding the Browning.

Satomi's Uzi burst out. It wasn't clear whether she pulled the trigger intentionally or whether it was from her nerves twitching. Rows of bullets tore along the floor and pierced Haruka's body which got tossed over and back. A bloody mist burst upward, nearly tearing off Haruka's neck above her metal collar.

Satomi's body fell forward slowly and landed with a thud over Yuka Nakagawa's corpse. She remained absolutely still.

Completely alone in the room, Yuko just kept on trembling. Her body was stiff as a rock. With the look of a child wandering into a freakish museum exhibition, she gazed at the floor covered with the corpses of five of her classmates.

9 students remaining

63

When he heard the shattering sound, Shuya just thought, oh, one of those clumsy girls must have dropped a dish, but when the sound was followed by an argument, he got up from his bed.

He felt a sharp pain run through the left side of his stomach and his shoulder blade. Shuya groaned, but using his right arm he managed to get out of the bed and stepped onto the floor with his bare feet. He was only wearing his school uniform pants. The heated argument continued. He thought he heard Yukie shouting.

Shuya walked over to the door and put his hand on the doorknob. The knob turned and as he pushed...the door seemed blocked. Through the one-centimeter gap he could see a wooden plank diagonally set against the door. As Yukie had warned him, they had constructed a makeshift bolt lock.

Shuya grabbed the doorknob and shook it vigorously several times, but the door wouldn't budge. He poked his fingers through the gap, but the plank, set against the door, refused to move.

On the verge of giving up, he took a deep breath when he heard the all-too-familiar rattling sound through the gap. There were several screams.

Shuya turned pale. Were they being attacked...but if that was...in any case, something was wrong!

Shuya managed to keep his injured body from tottering over. He raised his right foot and kicked the door with the heel of his bare foot, using the front kick technique he'd learned from Hiroki. But the door easily spurned his kick, throwing him off balance. He fell back onto the floor and felt a searing pain go up his side. He also realized he needed to pee, but that would have to wait.

BRRATTA. More rattling. And then more BRRATTA.

Shuya turned back to the bed, stood up, and lifted the edge of the bed that was made of steel pipes with his right hand. The bed landed on its side with a thud and the blanket and sheets slid off.

Shuya dragged the bed, pressed one end against the door, and went around to the other end. He then shoved it against the door with all his might. The door made a cracking sound. One more shove.

Bang. Gunfire. This time, one shot.

The bed pummeled into the wooden door. The door bent in half with a crack and opened into the hall. Shuya yanked the bed from the front of the door with his right hand and let it fall against the floor.

The typewriter-like rattling gunfire was now clearly audible through the open door.

Shuya came out into the hall. The shades were drawn on the windows that had been nailed shut with wooden planks so the unlit hall was dim. The entrance was on his left. There were three doors down the hall on his right. The far door was slightly ajar, and light leaked into the hall, forming what looked like a cold puddle of light.

Shuya picked up one of the longer pieces of broken planks in front of the door, approximately one meter long. He dragged his aching body down the hall. It was completely quiet now. What the hell happened? Did someone attack, or...

Shuya cautiously approached the door. He peeked through the gap and saw the room with kitchen equipment where Yukie Utsumi and Haruka Tanizawa were sprawled out by the center table. Beyond them was Yuka Nakagawa (what's up with that face!). Chisato Matsui was against the wall on the right. Someone was lying face down in the shadow of the table. That someone had to be Satomi Noda, because the relatively thin body standing still with her back towards him and silky, straight, shoulder-length hair belonged to—unless Shuya was mistaken— Yuko Sakaki.

There were several guns scattered around the collapsed bodies of Yukie's group. He was assaulted by the stench of blood splattered across the floor.

Shuya froze in shock. That overwhelming numbness was identical to the way he felt when he saw Mayumi Tendo's body right in front of the school.

What happened? How could this have happened? Yukie who had just said to him, "You might want to listen to the girl who's in love with you," was lying over there. Four others had fallen too. Were they dead? Did they die?

Yuko, her back facing Shuya, didn't have a gun. She was just standing still like a Venusian suddenly dropped onto Pluto.

Shuya was in a daze as he slowly clutched the doorknob, opened the door, and stepped into the room.

Yuko turn around. She gazed at Shuya with bloodshot eyes, but then went for the gun lying on the floor between Yukie and Haruka.

Shuya also came out of his daze. He tossed the plank he'd been holding with his uninjured arm the way he'd pitch a perfect fastball in Little League. (He wasn't sure anymore whether such a game existed on earth. It seemed to take place on a distant planet in the remote Andromeda Galaxy where the inhabitants played this game using three arms out of five, although the use of one's tail was permitted in the final inning.)

His body suddenly ached all over, and he grimaced. The plank hit the floor right in front of Yuko and bounced up. Yuko stopped as she shielded her face with her hand and fell back onto the bloody floor.

Shuya dashed for the gun. He knew that in this chaos Yuko holding a gun would only make matters worse.

Yuko shrieked and retreated. She got up, turned around, and ran to the other side of the room. She passed by the table and disappeared through an open door further down. There was a metallic clang. Were they...stairs?

Shuya gazed over there for a moment after she disappeared. But then he dashed over to Yukie and knelt down beside her.

He could tell her chest was ridden with holes. The blood was oozing out under her body already, and her eyes were shut peacefully as if she were sleeping. Her mouth was barely open—

She wasn't breathing anymore.

"Ahh," Shuya cried. He reached out his uninjured right hand to her peaceful face. He felt tears welling up for the first time ever since the game began. Was it because they'd just talked minutes ago? Or was it because of what she'd said:

"I just wouldn't know what to do if you died....Do you understand what I'm saying? Do you?"

Her tearful but relieved face. Her melancholic face. And now her oddly peaceful face right beside him.

He looked around. There was no need to check. Yuka Nakagawa's face had changed color. A bloody foam dripped from her mouth. Satomi Noda lay face down, a puddle of blood under her head. Chisato Matsui's back was covered with bullet holes, and Haruka Tanizawa...her neck was nearly torn off.

How could...how could this be...

Shuya looked back at Yukie. His nearly paralyzed left arm supported his right arm so he could hold her up. It might have been a meaningless gesture. But Shuya had to do it.

As he held her body, he heard the blood dripping onto the floor from the holes in her chest. Her head hung back and her braided hair touched his arm.

"Do you understand what I'm saying?"

Shuya burst into tears as they fell onto her uniform.

"Ungh," Shuya bit his lip and gently let her down onto the floor. He picked up the Browning Yuko had attempted to grab. He walked to the door at the far end of the room where Yuko had gone. His body felt incredibly heavy. It wasn't just because he was injured. He wiped his eyes with his bare right arm, which was also holding the Browning.

He entered. It was a cylindrical space made of bare concrete. The tower. This was the lighthouse. There was a thick steel column in the center and a spiral steel staircase winding around it. There were no windows, only a sliver of light from above.

"Yuko!" Shuya yelled. He began climbing the stairs as he yelled, "What happened, Yuko!?"

Yuko wasn't there at the top of the stairs. But...he heard the sound of her scream "AIEEE" echo through the cylindrical space of the tower. Shuya knit his brows...and began quickly climbing the stairs. The wound in his side began to ache. He thought he might be bleeding because his bandages now felt damp.

9 students remaining

64

Yuko Sakaki ran out of breath as she climbed up the stairs to the top of the lighthouse. The Cyclops-like Fresnel lens was at the center of the landing, and there was enough space to move around it. She saw the cloudy sky beyond the windproof windows of the lantern room. On her left was a low door that led to a narrow balcony, and frantically she opened it. She was outside now.

Maybe it was the height, but the wind was stronger than

she'd expected. She caught a strong whiff of the sea breeze.

The ocean was right there in front of her. Reflecting the cloudy sky, the sea was dull indigo, and the white waves were woven into it like some fabric. Yuko edged over to the right. The northern mountain was right in front of her. There was a small, open lot in front of the lighthouse building. On her left an unpaved road stretched out around the foot of the mountain, and there was a white light truck right by a barely functional gate in front of the road.

Yuko held onto the steel handrailing around the balcony. The room she was inside only moments ago was down below. She saw the roof of the single-story building annex. Following the railing, she continued circling the lantern room, but didn't find what she thought she would—a steel ladder. Yuko never had the chance to keep watch so she didn't know the exterior of the lighthouse. There was no way out. She was standing, facing the sky. She was trapped now. Realizing this, she was about to panic, but she clenched her teeth and held herself together. If there was no ladder…then she'd have to jump.

She was panting. She ended up returning to her previous position. She looked down again.

It was high. It wasn't as bad as leaping to the ground, but it was still high. In fact, it might have been impossible to jump at this height, but before she could make a rational choice the image flashed across her mind again. This time it was *her* head, alone, split open. Blood spraying up. Shuya's face covered with its blood. She had to escape. No matter what. She just had to escape. She had no time to lose.

Yuko crouched down and slid between the haphazardly installed steel fence. Its bars were widely spaced. She got through. Holding onto the railing from outside, she cautiously stood on the edge of the balcony barely ten centimeters wide, but…

...the view below her feet made her dizzy. It was way too high...jumping down was out of the question...it was just way too high...

Her view suddenly shook. Her feet slipped. The side of her shin hit the concrete edge of the balcony (she felt her skin scraping off), and Yuko's body flew out into the sky. "AIEEE," Yuko shrieked. Simultaneously, her hands groped around and managed to grab a thin steel bar from the steel fence. Yuko's body hung from the edge of the balcony.

Holding onto the railing, Yuko was panting. She nearly...nearly died.

However, she took a deep breath and put all her might into her hands. First, that's right, first she had to lift her body up and get back to the other side of the railing. Then she would have to figure out some way to fight Shuya Nanahara. That was the only—

The strong wind whistled by and shook her body. She shrieked, "AIEEE," but it didn't do much. Her hands clutching onto the steel bar slipped, and now the palms of her hands barely managed to hold onto the edge of the balcony. Now she couldn't even reach for the steel bars.

She was appalled to find her palms were oozing sweat. She was overcome with fear and panic. How, how, how, how could she be sweating now? Her hands...her hands were slipping....

Her right pinky slipped off the edge of the balcony.

"No!" Yuko screamed. Then her ring finger. Then her entire right hand fell off the railing (she felt the nail of her index finger catch, but it peeled off and that was that). Her body swung, her left hand now the fulcrum. And now her left hand too...

"Ahhhhhh—" As she screamed, Yuko was overwhelmed with a dreamlike sensation that she was falling.

But then she felt an impact run down her arm to her

shoulder. Her fall came to a halt less than half a meter below.

Swinging like a pendulum on her left arm, Yuko gazed up…and then saw Shuya Nanahara beyond the railing extending his body, stretching his right arm out, holding her wrist.

For an instant Yuko gazed at Shuya's face, but then the next moment she screamed, "No—!"

Of course if she let go she would die, but it was Shuya Nanahara holding her hand!

"No! No!"

Her eyes wide open, her hair tossed around, Yuko continued screaming as she wondered, why? Why are you trying to save me? Is it because you want to use me to survive? Or, oh, I get it. You want to kill me with your very own hands!

"No! Let me go!" Yuko screamed. Any trace of rational thought had all but disappeared. "No! I'd rather die here than let you kill me! Let me go! Let me go!"

Whatever he thought in reaction, or maybe he wasn't thinking at all, in any case, his expression stayed the same, and he yelled, "Don't move!"

Yuko gazed up at Shuya again…and realized the bandage under the silver collar covering his neck wound oozed with blood now dripping down his bare shoulder.

The blood dripped down his arm and reached her left hand.

"Ugh," Shuya moaned. He gripped Yuko's hand tighter. His face was breaking into a sweat. That's right, it wasn't just his neck, his entire body was covered with severe wounds. Given how he was not only holding her entire weight with his right arm but attempting to pull her up, he had to be in incredible pain.

Yuko's jaw dropped. Why? Why would you try to save me when you're in so much pain? That's—

Strangely enough, it suddenly all came to her. The black mist clouding her thoughts suddenly cleared as if blown away by the sea breeze blowing against her body. The image of Shuya holding the blood-soaked axe, looking down at Tatsumichi Oki's corpse, suddenly vanished as if shredded by the wind, and all her previous (although it was only two days ago) memories of the Third Year Class B classroom along with the cheerful expressions of Shuya Nanahara came back to her. How he joked around with his friends Yoshitoki Kuninobu and Shinji Mimura, how he looked so serious repeating a difficult guitar line while practicing in the music room, how he posed triumphantly at second base after making a perfect hit down the third base line during gym class, which she managed to see from the gym where she was playing volleyball. And then when she was pale from menstrual cramps, how he'd gently said to her, "What's wrong, Yuko? You look pale," interrupted their English teacher Mr. Yamamoto, and called on the nurse's assistant, Fumiyo Fujiyoshi. How he looked so concerned then.

Oh no. Yuko finally understood the situation. This is Shuya. Shuya is trying to save me. I...why? Why did I have to think I had to kill Shuya? Why did I believe that? It's Shuya. And I always thought he was kind of cool...that he was really nice but no—

Then a different thought occurred to her. The action she took and its results. Yuko once again turned pale.

I...my mind was all screwed up...and...and that's how I ended up -

Yuko burst into tears. Shuya saw this and looked puzzled.

"Shuya!" she screamed. "I-it was me! I tried to kill you!"

Shuya looked surprised as Yuko looked up with despondent tears in her eyes.

Yuko continued. "I-I-I thought you'd killed Tatsumichi...I saw you two...and I was scared. I was so scared. So I tried poisoning your food…but Yuka ended up eating it…and then everyone…everyone…"

Shuya then understood everything. Hiding in a nearby bush, Yuko had seen him extract the axe from Tatsumichi Oki's head after fighting him. She didn't see how Kyoichi Motobuchi and Shogo appeared afterwards. She'd only witnessed that one moment. She could have interpreted it as an act of self defense on Shuya's part or as an accident, but Yuko was too frightened to trust Shuya. And so she poisoned the food to kill him, but Yuka ate this by mistake…and everyone panicked with suspicion. The culprit, Yuko, ended up being the only survivor….

"It's all right!" Shuya shouted. "It's all right, just don't move! I'll pull you up!"

Shuya was nearly lying flat on the balcony, his body jutting out between the bars, but because his left arm was useless, he couldn't grab onto the railing. Still, he twisted his body, and finally managed to tuck his right knee up to his body so he could rely on his back. He did his best to hold onto Yuko's wrist. The pain from the wounds all over his body, his side, his left shoulder, and the right side of his neck was mounting. But…

Her face soaked with tears, Yuko shook her head. "No. No. It was my fault everyone…everyone…," she said, and suddenly her hand began to pry his fingers loose. The tight grip he'd finally managed to get on her came loose. Shuya gripped tighter in response, but…the blood dripping down from his neck suddenly made his hand slip.

Yuko's hand left Shuya's. The weight on Shuya's arm suddenly vanished.

Yuko's face looking up at Shuya receded—

With a thud, Yuko fell on her back onto the roof of the single-story building below. Instead of slipping from his hand, she seemed to have appeared there suddenly via time-lapse photography.

Her body wrapped in her sailor shirt and pleated skirt was sprawled out…and her neck was crooked, which made her head look oddly disjoined from the rest of her body. The top-right side of her head spurted out a red substance in the shape of a shriveled up maple leaf.

"Ah…"

Shuya stared down at her, his right arm still hanging over the balcony.

8 students remaining

65

Hiroki Sugimura (Male Student No. 11) took a deep breath.

He'd heard the rapid gunfire approximately ten minutes ago. He'd been wandering around the northern mountain, but he quickly headed east toward the shots. Then…by the time he arrived it was already quiet at the lighthouse. He knew it was there from the map, but he assumed Kayoko Kotohiki would never hide there alone in such a conspicuous location, so he'd ignored it until now. He wasn't sure whether this was where the gunfire occurred. He looked down from the cliff over the lighthouse and saw a girl lying on the roof of the brick annex by the lighthouse. Even from a distance he could make out the red color…and see that she was dead. The short hair and petite body resembled Kotohiki, as Megumi Eto's corpse did when he discovered it.

He slid down the edge of the cliff. As he descended, the corpse on the roof disappeared from view. He reached the front entrance of the lighthouse. There was a pile of chairs and desks beyond the open door. Someone had formed a barricade, but for some reason this barricade was also torn down. He looked at the window that was sealed shut with planks and cautiously walked down the hall. (There was a room with a bed right by the entrance, and for some reason its door had been knocked down.) His detector responded. Six. Hiroki proceeded cautiously—

And stood frozen in the room splattered with blood.

The bodies of five girls were scattered all over what appeared to be a kitchen. There was the female student representative Yukie Utsumi on her back by the center table. To her right was Haruka Tanizawa, her head nearly torn off (!). And further down Yuka Nakagawa, whose face had turned nearly black. Chisato Matsui was lying face down in front of the side table to his right, her pale blue face turned his way. And then one more girl was lying face down behind the table, covered in blood.

The four girls, including Yukie, were clearly dead. But this one whose face he couldn't see was...

Hiroki cautiously checked the room once again. He listened for any sounds beyond the opened door on the other side of the room. There didn't seem to be anyone else hiding.

He tucked the gun in his left hand in back, walked between the bodies of Yukie Utsumi and Haruka Tanizawa, passed by Yuka Nakagawa's body, and walked around the table. The soles of his shoes splashed against the blood all over the floor. He crouched down beside the girl lying face down, put aside the stick in his right hand, and lifted her body. He felt a sharp pain from the wound in his right shoulder where Mitsuko Souma had struck him. The gunshot wound Toshinori Oda had inflicted on his thigh though was only a scrape, so there wasn't much bleeding or pain there. Hiroki tried to ignore the pain, in any case. He turned over the body.

It was Satomi Noda. There was a red hole in the left side of her forehead, and her glasses, though crooked, managed to stay on her face. The left lens probably shattered when she fell. Of course she was dead.

Hiroki put her down and looked over at the opened door on the far side of the room. That was where the tower was. That led up to the lantern room.

The other person on the detector was that girl on the roof. She was no doubt dead as well, but he had to check and make sure...as long as she resembled Kayoko Kotohiki.

Hiroki took his gun and entered through the door. There was a steel staircase. He quickly climbed them with hushed footsteps. Someone might still be up there. He held the stick and radar in his right hand, checking it as he went up.

There were no new responses as he came out into the lantern room. Hiroki put the radar in his pocket, tucked his gun also in back, and came out onto the balcony around the lantern room.

He put his hand on the steel railing. He took a deep breath, leaned over the railing, and looked down.

There was the corpse in the sailor suit. Her neck was twisted in an odd way and blood spread out from under her head but the corpse...wasn't Kayoko Kotohiki's. It was Yuko Sakaki.

Still...

He gazed at the sea. There was a strong breeze. Six girls had all died here at once. There were no guns in the room, but given how they were wounded and how the walls and floors were ridden with bullet holes, he was certain the gunshots he'd heard had occurred here. The most logical scenario was that...the girls somehow got together and cooped themselves up here, but then someone attacked them. The five girls were shot down there first, and then Yuko Sakaki managed to get this far and fell to her death without being attacked by the assailant. Then the assailant left before Hiroki got here....

But given how they'd formed a barricade at the entrance—the planks nailed over the windows, every entry point probably sealed—why would they tear the barricade down? Did the assailant shove it away as he left? But then how could he or she have entered in the first place? Could it be...there were seven of them? And one of them had suddenly betrayed the rest—no, revealed his or her true intentions? No, that can't be....The other thing was that Yuka Nakagawa didn't look like she died from gunshots. She looked like...she'd been choked. The blood splattered all over the table also didn't make any sense. How could that large amount of blood end up there? There was more. The door to that room right next to the entrance. Why was it torn down?

There was no use trying to figure it out. Hiroki shook his head, checked the roof of the building, and returned to the lantern room.

As he descended the steel spiral staircase in the dim tower and gazed at the inner walls of the lighthouse, Hiroki felt a light sensation of vertigo as if the spiral movement of the stairs were internalized. It might have been from fatigue, but still...

So now there were six students less. Sakamochi said there were fourteen students left, as of the noon announcement. Then there were at most eight students left now.

Was Kayoko Kotohiki still alive? Wasn't it possible she might have died between noon and now in some area he didn't know about?

No, Hiroki thought, she has to be alive.

Even though he could hardly justify it, for some reason he was nearly certain. Eight students remaining, possibly even less. But I'm alive, and so must be Kotohiki. This is taking too much time. It's been a day and a half since the game began, and I still haven't managed to find Kotohiki. But...I will eventually. Once again he was nearly certain.

Then he thought of Shuya's trio. None of their three names had been announced. Shogo Kawada had said, "If you're up for it, you can come aboard our train."

...was there really a way out? And would he really be able to reach that station with Kotohiki? He wasn't sure. But at the very least he wanted Kotohiki to board that train.

Shall I offer you a hand then, mademoiselle?

It sounded like something Shinji Mimura would have said. Now he saw how Shinji could be good friends with Yutaka Seto. Shinji liked to kid around. The jokes were different from Yutaka's, of course. They were more sarcastic and at times biting. Shinji seemed to value "the importance of laughing it off." At the closing ceremony before New Year's, when they were in their second year, during the regional education representative's dull speech, Shinji said, "My uncle once said laughter is essential to maintain harmony, and that that might be our only release. Do you understand that, Hiroki? I still can't quite get it."

Although he could relate to it a little, he also felt he didn't fully get it. It might have been because he was young. But in any case Shinji Mimura and Yutaka Seto were both dead now. He could no longer give Shinji a reply.

As he pondered these thoughts, soon enough he was back in the kitchen filled with five bodies. Once again Hiroki looked over the room covered in blood.

He hadn't noticed because of the stench, but now he saw the gas stove pot and caught a whiff of the appetizing odor. There was no gas of course, so they were probably in the middle of cooking using solid fuel. He went to take a look. The flame under the pot was out, but there was still steam rising from what looked like stew.

Ever since the game began he'd only had the bread the government had supplied (when he ran out of water he retrieved some from a house well), so he was famished, but he shook his head and peeled his eyes off the pot. He just couldn't bring himself to eat it. Not in this terrible room. Besides, he had to hurry...and find Kotohiki. Hurry up...and leave.

He staggered out into the hall. Not having slept at all, he was feeling dizzy.

Someone was standing at the entrance at the far end of the long corridor. Because the hall was dim, this person looked like a silhouette outlined from behind by the light.

Hiroki leaped to his side before his eyes could even open wide and crashed his way into the kitchen. All at the same time, flames came bursting from the silhouette's hands. A row of bullets raced past the tips of Hiroki's feet flying out of the hall.

Hiroki grimaced from the sudden surprise. He got up, crouched, and then closed the door and locked it.

The gunfire sounded familiar. It was the sound he'd heard before and after that incredible explosion. After he escaped Toshinori Oda, he heard the sound of gunfire behind him...in other words it was whatever killed Toshinori Oda. It was also the gunfire he'd heard when Yumiko Kusaka and Yukiko Kitano were killed. He'd heard the gunfire several other times. It all came from "that classmate." Like Hiroki, the assailant had probably come here after hearing gunfire. Or maybe the student was here to kill the assailant who'd killed Yukie Utsumi's group. Or maybe—the assailant himself was returning.

Kneeling down on the floor, Hiroki reached around his back and gripped his gun with his left hand. He'd found the bullets in the day pack Mitsuko left behind, so it was now fully loaded, but he couldn't find an extra magazine. Maybe Mitsuko had put it in her pocket. Colt Government .45 Single-Action Automatic. Seven rounds in the magazine, plus one in the chamber. He couldn't afford to reload the bullets individually. The moment he did he'd be wasted by the assailant's machine gun or any other gun on him or her.

His back against the wall, Hiroki looked at the kitchen where the girls' corpses were. Unfortunately, the windows were sealed with planks from the inside. It would take too much time to tear them off and escape. He looked over at the door leading to the tower. No, that was impossible. It was too high for him to jump off the top of the lighthouse. It would be insane. He'd end up sun bathing right next to Yuko Sakaki. No, wait…what was this "someone" trying to do? Was he tiptoeing behind the door, approaching, or was he taking his time waiting for Hiroki to come out? No, he had to be in a rush too. He had to get rid of Hiroki before he might be shot from behind by someone else arriving as a result of the gunfire—

Hiroki was right. The wood around the doorknob was blown to bits. (In fact, several of the bullets exiting the door tore off the shoulder and side of Chisato Matsui, who was lying directly in front of the door.)

The door crashed open.

The dark figure leaped into the room.

As it tumbled over once and got up, Hiroki realized it was Kazuo Kiriyama (Male Student No. 6). Ignoring the corpses in the room, he pointed his machine gun to the side of the door which was his blind spot, and immediately began firing away.

After five or six bullets tore through the wall…the gunfire stopped…because he saw no one there.

Now was his chance. Hiroki swung his stick up and leaped onto Kazuo Kiriyama from above. At the last instant he'd decided to climb to the top of the high shelf installed beside the door. He'd decided against using the gun since he wasn't used to it and had tucked it away again. The important thing was to stop the assailant—who turned out to be Kazuo Kiriyama—from shooting anymore.

Kazuo responded by looking up. He lifted the muzzle of his machine gun, but the handle of the broom Hiroki held struck Kazuo's wrist. The Ingram M10 9mm crashed onto the floor, slid, and stopped beyond the table where Satomi Noda was.

Kazuo tried to pull out another gun (it was a large automatic pistol, different from the revolver Toshinori Oda had), but Hiroki, who'd landed and balanced himself, quickly swung the tip of his stick and struck this gun down too.

A rapid assault! I'll strike him down!

The stick came swinging down, but Kazuo quickly bent back and somersaulted backwards. He leaped over Yukie Utsumi's body with the grace of a kung fu master, and after tumbling once he was standing in front of the center table. By the time he was standing he had a revolver in his right hand, the one that belonged to Toshinori Oda.

But even Kazuo couldn't have foreseen Hiroki's agility. He'd immediately moved within eighty centimeters of Kazuo.

"Yahh!" Hiroki swung his stick, striking the gun in Kazuo's hand three times. It flew into the air. Before it landed on the floor, the other end of Hiroki's stick swung at Kazuo's face. There was a table behind Kazuo. He couldn't retreat anymore.

But—the stick stopped several centimeters before hitting Kazuo's face. A third of the stick flew by Kazuo's face. Strangely enough, he only heard it crack later. Kazuo had chopped off the stick with his left hand.

The next moment, Kazuo formed a spear fist with his right hand to strike Hiroki in the face. He was aiming for Hiroki's eyes.

It was a miracle he managed to duck and dodge it. That was how fast Kazuo's fist was.

But Hiroki had managed to dodge it. When he dodged it, he grabbed Kazuo's wrist with his hand that had dropped the stick. The next moment, he twisted his wrist back. Simultaneously, he kneed Kazuo in the stomach with all his might. The absolutely calm Kazuo gasped slightly.

With his left hand restraining Kazuo's arm, Hiroki pulled out his gun and cocked the hammer back. He pressed the gun against Kazuo's stomach and pulled the trigger.

He kept on pulling the trigger until he used up all his bullets. With every shot Kazuo's body flinched.

When the gun's breechblock held up, the eighth shell fell onto the floor with a clink, rolled, and then clicked against another shell.

He could feel Kazuo's right arm and the rest of his body slowly going limp. His slicked-back hair and the rest of his head fell forward. Once Hiroki let go, Kazuo's body would slide against corner of the table and fall onto the floor.

But right now Hiroki stood still facing Kazuo as if dancing a strange dance, panting, his chest heaving.

I won.

He won against *the* Kazuo Kiriyama. The Kazuo Kiriyama whose athletic prowess was probably superior to Shinji Mimura or Shuya Nanahara's, who'd never lost a fight as far as he knew. He'd defeated him.

I defeated—

Suddenly a sharp pain pierced the right side of Hiroki's stomach. He groaned, gasped...then opened his eyes wide.

Kazuo was looking up at Hiroki. And in his left hand...was a knife digging into Hiroki's stomach.

Hiroki slowly shifted his eyes from this hand over to Kazuo's face. Kazuo stared back with eyes that were as always beautiful and cold.

How…could he still be alive?

Of course it was because Kazuo Kiriyama was wearing Toshinori Oda's bulletproof vest, but Hiroki couldn't have known, and right now there wasn't much point trying to figure this out.

Kazuo twisted the knife and Hiroki moaned. His left hand's grip on Kazuo's right wrist was loosening.

Oh no, this is not good…at all.

But Hiroki managed to squeeze some strength out into his arm. He swung down his right hand that was still holding the emptied gun.

His bent right elbow struck Kazuo's lower chin.

Kazuo flew back and slid across the white table covered with blood. The blood stain that resembled the Republic of Greater East Asia's national flag now looked more like the stripes of the American flag. Simultaneously, the knife in Hiroki's stomach, after tearing off approximately thirty grams of Hiroki's flesh, was torn out. Blood came bursting out. Hiroki gasped, but immediately turned on his heel and ran to the door leading out to the hall.

Right as he was entering it he heard gunfire, and the door frame cracked open. Kazuo didn't have any time to pick up the guns scattered on the floor. So he must have had a fourth gun (probably attached under his pants, tied to his ankle or something).

Hiroki ran, ignoring the gunfire.

He leaped over the scattered pile of chairs and desks. Right before he emerged outside he heard that all-too-familiar machine gun fire, but the shots missed him because he was crouched over.

The sky was cloudy enough to expect rain, but for some reason it looked bright to him.

Hiroki ran as fast as he could into the grove beyond the gate where the light truck was parked. He left behind a trail of red spots on the white sand.

He heard the machine gun rattle again, but by then he'd leaped into the grove.

Of course he couldn't afford to rest now.

8 students remaining

66

It began to drizzle. Rain washed over the bushes covering the island, and in the dim light a dark sheen fell through the drops of water and thick clouds.

Shuya slowly wove his way through the bushes. The area to his right was open and offered him a view of the sea, which was dull gray behind the white curtain of rain.

He now wore his shirt, school coat, and sneakers, which he found in the room where Yukie's group was. Raindrops falling off tree branches dripped onto his coat. He had the Uzi slung over his shoulder, his right hand on the grip, and kept the CZ75 tucked in front. The Browning and the bullets he'd collected were inside the day pack on his shoulder.

Shuya left the lighthouse immediately, and as he'd expected fifteen minutes later, right when he began collecting wood to build a fire on a cliff near the northern tip of the island, he heard gunfire coming from the lighthouse. Despite the fact that the massacre of Yukie's group had occurred inside the lighthouse, he surmised at least two students had arrived upon hearing the shots and ended up fighting.

After some hesitation, Shuya started heading back to the lighthouse. It sounded like the all-too-familiar gunfire of Kazuo Kiriyama's machine gun. He doubted

Noriko and Shogo would go out of their way to follow the gunfire, but there weren't too many students left. Supposing one was Kazuo, there was a good chance the other was Hiroki Sugimura. Of course, it also could have been Mitsuko Souma.

But the gunfire ceased immediately. Shuya stopped. He decided not to return to the lighthouse after all. Even if he went back, there wouldn't be anyone there. Or at best there might be another corpse in addition to the bodies of Yukie's group.

It began raining when Shuya had finished preparing two fires on the cliff rock. He found a lighter in the lighthouse, but it was difficult to get the fire going because of the rain.

The rain grew heavy, so Shuya gave up and left the area. Noriko and Shogo probably hadn't moved much. C=3 was forbidden, but the adjacent D=3 and C=4 were still safe. They were probably in that area, so he could make another fire once he was in the vicinity.

With this thought in mind he began walking. That was when we heard the distant chirping sound of a bird as he turned westward on the north shore of the island around 2:30 p.m. Shuya listened closely…and quickly glanced down at his watch. The seconds hand moved seven degrees, and the faint chirping stopped. Shogo had said fifteen seconds. Given the time it took for him to look at his watch, its duration corresponded to that length of time. Besides, he doubted there were many birds chirping in the rain. And he heard none of those little birds that he'd heard during the day ever since the game began.

Shuya continued along the northwest shore of the island—and once again heard the same chirping. This time it was clear. Exactly fifteen minutes had elapsed since the last one—and it stopped exactly fifteen seconds later. It was Shogo. There was no need for the smoke signal. Shogo was using the bird call.

The third fake chirping occurred only three minutes ago. It sounded close. According to the map, Shuya was moving from B=6 to B=5.

Shuya rested a little, tucked the Uzi's barrel under his left wrist, and lifted his left arm. It was easier that way because he didn't have to exert his muscles. The watch hands, out of focus from the raindrops against the glass, indicated it was 3:05 p.m.

The chirping sounded closer to the mountain than it was to the sea. Shuya glanced at the sea, then moved towards and then up the gentle slope. As he looked up, he noticed that the northern mountain in front of him looked different, which made him realize he'd been moving along the foot of the mountain and was now approaching the western shore.

Just a little more. He'd barely covered 1.5 kilometers, but he still felt woozy from all the blood he'd lost. The pain in his body was so severe he felt like throwing up (he really had to stop and rest). But he was almost there. Almost.

He made his way through the grove and his fatigue became overwhelming. Of course…he could be attacked at any point from the bushes. But he couldn't afford to worry about that. If that happened…he would just have to pull the trigger of the Uzi.

The low bushes became sparse and then were cut off. Shuya stood still. It wasn't as if there was someone holding a gun…but there was something strange in this narrow opening.

At first it looked like two stiff gray clumps to Shuya. On top of that, they seemed to be moving. He stared at them. There were black pants and sneakers poking out of these two clumps.

He realized they were corpses. Two boys had died here.

A flash of red color flew up from the stiff gray clump and

cried, "KAW!" It was a large heron-sized bird, its head drenched in red. The birds were feeding on the corpses!

Shuya reflexively raised his Uzi at them. He put his finger against the trigger—but decided against it. He walked over.

The birds flapped their wings and flew away from the two corpses.

Shuya stood still in the rain by them…and lifted his right hand up to his mouth. He felt a sudden urge to vomit.

It was a chilling sight. The birds had picked away at their exposed faces. Their red flesh broke out of their skin. They were covered in blood.

Shuya held back his nausea and somehow managed to look at them. He saw they were probably Tadakatsu Hatagami and Yuichiro Takiguchi. Then he noticed something about Tadakatsu's face, which was in worse condition than Yuichiro's. The birds weren't responsible for his deformed skull. His nose, unharmed by the birds, was also crushed.

He looked around and found a bat lying on the grass. Even though it was washed by the rain, the tip of the bat was still tinged with red. Given the state of Tadakatsu's face, he was most likely beaten to death. With the gear of his sport— a baseball bat.

Compared to him, Yuichiro's face was in relatively good shape. Of course…Shuya had a feeling his lips and eyeballs were gone by now.

One of the birds landed on top of Tadakatsu's face. Then several more birds came by. Given how Shuya remained frozen, they probably assumed they were safe.

Safe? You got to be kidding!

Shuya once again put his finger on the trigger of the Uzi…but restrained himself. The important thing was for him to get back to Shogo and Noriko.

More birds reappeared.

Were they feeding on the other bodies sprawled all over the island? Or was it just because they were near the sea?

Peeling his eyes off the two corpses, Shuya staggered around them and entered the bushes ahead. He heard the birds cry, "KAW!"

As he moved, he felt the urge to vomit once again. By now he was getting used to people dying, but the thought of these birds, these sky rats, feeding on them…I'll never sit on the beach and gaze peacefully at seagulls again. Even if I write my own songs, I'll never ever sing about birds. I might not even be able to eat chicken for a while. Man, birds…suck.

But then he heard that chirping sound again. He looked up. Large raindrops hit his face.

Ah—birds suck but…I guess a little bird's all right, huh?

Another full fifteen seconds passed and the chirping ceased. This time it sounded really close.

Shuya looked around. The bushes continued along the gentle slope. It must be…around here. They had to be somewhere near here. But…where?

Before he could think, the nausea he'd held back surged up. The two corpses, their faces messed up. And their soft flesh would be the birds' afternoon snack. Yummy.

I can't puke. I'm weak enough as it is…but…

Shuya knelt down on the ground and vomited. Because he hadn't had anything to eat, it was all gastric juices. There was a sharp, acidic stench.

Shuya threw up more. A pinkish substance was mixed into the yellow liquid like a drop of paint. For all he knew, his stomach might be screwed up by now.

"Shuya."

He looked up. Reflexively, he pointed the Uzi over there. But the muzzle fell again.

Between the shrubs he saw that thuggish face. It was

Shogo. In his left hand, Shogo held a bow which seemed to be carved out of wood, and in his right hand he was about to put down the arrow fixed to the bow. That was when Shuya realized, oh, I get it, I must have gotten caught on Shogo's tripwire.

"Hangover, huh?" Shogo said. His humorous remark was tinged with kindness.

There was a rustling sound. Noriko appeared behind Shogo. She gazed at Shuya through her rain-drenched hair, her eyes and mouth trembling.

Pushing Shogo aside, Noriko dragged her leg as she ran to him.

Shuya wiped his mouth and staggered up. He released the Uzi and extended only his right hand, hugging Noriko. On impact Noriko's body sent a jolt of pain through his side, but he didn't care. They were having their reunion right above some fresh puke, but that didn't matter either. Her body against him felt warm in the cold rain.

Noriko looked up. "Shuya…Shuya…I'm so glad…I'm so glad…" She was crying. Tears came streaming out of the corners of her eyes along with the raindrops falling against her face.

Shuya gently smiled. Then he realized he was on the verge of crying too. Too many people have died…too many people have died in this game, but how wonderful, how incredibly wonderful these two were still alive.

Shogo came up to him and offered his right hand. For a moment Shuya was puzzled by the gesture…but then he understood. He reached out his hand over Noriko's shoulder and held it. It was, as always, a large, solid hand.

"Welcome back," Shogo said warmly.

8 students remaining

67

Exposed rocks appeared where the woods headed toward the sea. Now a low wall formation of those rocks faced the sea. Shogo seemed to have worked on it with his knife. Two large branches had been stuck into the rock wall, and on top of them were leafy branches serving as a roof to block the rain. Raindrops came flowing off the branch tips.

After he was given strong painkillers that Shogo had brought from the medical clinic, Shuya told him about the lighthouse. Shogo boiled water in a can with charcoal, and its gurgling sound overlapped with the sound of pouring rain.

When Shuya was done, Shogo said, "I see." He took a deep breath, and put another Wild Seven into his mouth. He held the Uzi in his lap. They decided it was best Shogo hold onto it. Shuya held the CZ75, and Noriko had the Browning.

Shuya shook his head feebly. "It was awful."

Shogo blew out some smoke and removed the cigarette from his mouth. "Yukie forming such a large group ended up backfiring."

Shuya nodded bitterly. "It's so hard to…trust someone."

"Yes, it is." Shogo looked down. "It's very hard." He continued smoking and appeared pensive. Then he said, "In any case, I'm glad you made it."

Shuya recalled Yukie's face. He was alive. He was alive thanks to Yukie's group, but they were gone now.

Shuya looked at Noriko, on his left. Hearing about the deaths of her friends Yukie Utsumi and Haruka Tanizawa must have been hard on her. Once she saw the water was boiling, she took out some dried bouillon Shogo must have found and tossed two cubes into the can. The smell of broth came drifting up.

"Can you eat, Shuya?" Noriko asked.

Shuya looked at Noriko and raised his brow. He knew he had to eat, but he had just thrown up—and besides the images of the stiff gray lumps around Tadakatsu Hatagami and Yuichiro Takiguchi still flashed through his mind. (He hadn't told them about that. The "lumps" were at work only a hundred meters or so away from them....He only said that he threw up from the pain of his wounds.) He couldn't work up an appetite.

"Eat, Shuya. Noriko and I already had lunch," Shogo said, cigarette in mouth. His stubble had thickened. He grabbed the edge of the can with a handkerchief, poured the soup into a plastic cup, and offered it to Shuya.

Shuya took it and slowly put it against his mouth. The taste of broth spread through his mouth. Then the warm liquid slid down his throat and into his stomach. It wasn't as bad as he'd expected.

Noriko offered him bread. Shuya took a bite. Once he started chewing, he was surprised to find he could eat. He ended up eating it all instantly. Regardless of the mental state he was in...his body had been starving.

"Would you like more?" Noriko asked and Shuya nodded. "A little more soup." He raised the empty cup. Noriko refilled it this time.

Taking the cup, Shuya said, "Noriko."

She looked up at him. "What is it?"

"Are you feeling all right now?"

"Uh huh." She smiled. "I've been taking cold medicine. I'm fine."

Shuya looked at the side of Shogo's face. Shogo nodded, cigarette dangling between lips. He'd taken another antibiotic syringe kit from the medical clinic, but it turned out that was unnecessary.

Shuya turned around to Noriko again and smiled back at her. "That's great."

Then she asked the same question she'd been repeating over and over. "Shuya, are you really all right?"

Shuya nodded. "I'm fine."

In fact, he wasn't, but what else could he say? He could see over his cuffs how his left hand had grown pale compared to his right hand. He wasn't sure whether it was due to his shoulder wound or elbow wound. Or it might simply be because the bandage was too tight around his elbow. He felt his left arm get stiffer and stiffer.

He had another sip of the soup and put the cup down by his feet. Then he called Shogo.

Shogo, who was checking the Uzi, raised his brow and looked at Shuya. "What is it?

"It's about Kazuo."

That's right. As he contemplated the events that had occurred since yesterday, the question that had been occupying him right before he split up with Shogo and Noriko suddenly came back to him. The gunfire he'd heard right after he left the lighthouse also reminded him. In other words—as he'd yelled out before, "What the hell's he doing!?"—meaning, what kind of person was Kazuo Kiriyama?

As far as he could tell, Kazuo wasn't the only one willing to participate. Tatsumichi Oki, whom Shuya had fought, possibly Yoshio Akamatsu, and if Hiroki was right, Mitsuko Souma might also be in the same category. But...Kazuo was absolutely merciless. His coldness and calmness. The strange vibe he always got from Kazuo suddenly exploded in this game and assaulted them. Shuya once again recalled the flames erupting from the machine gun, and the cold eyes behind them. He felt a chill run down his spine.

Shogo remained silent, so Shuya continued, "What...what's up with him? I just don't get it."

Shogo looked down and tinkered around with the Uzi's

safety device, equipped with a full-auto/semi-auto switch.

Didn't Shogo say there was no need to understand? Shuya wondered whether Shogo would give him the same reply.

But Shogo had a different response this time.

He looked up. "I've seen people like him before."

"In the previous game?"

"No." Shogo shook his head. "Not there. Totally outside of this game. You see a lot of things when you're the son of a doctor working in the slums." Shogo took out another cigarette and lit it. He exhaled and said, "A hollow man."

"Hollow?" Noriko asked.

"That's right," Shogo nodded. "There's no place in his heart for logic or love, no. For any kind of values. That kind of person. On top of that...there's no reason for the way he is."

No reason, Shuya thought, or did he mean he was just born that way? That's—

Shogo took a puff and exhaled. "Hiroki warned us about Mitsuko Souma, right?"

Shuya and Noriko nodded.

"We still haven't seen for ourselves whether Mitsuko's really up for this game. But from what little I've seen at school, I think Mitsuko and Kazuo are similar. The only difference is that Mitsuko's abandoned all reason and love. There was probably something behind that. I have no idea what it was. But Kazuo doesn't have any cause. The difference is crucial. There's no explanation behind Kazuo."

Shuya stared at Shogo and mumbled, "That's scary."

"Yeah, it's scary," Shogo agreed. "Just think about it. It's probably not even his fault. Of course you can say that about anyone. But in his case he probably could never grasp 'an unknown future.' Nothing could be more terrifying than to be born that way."

Shogo then continued, "What I mean is that, even a dumb ass like me can think everything's pointless. Why do I get up and eat? It all ends up shit anyway. Why am I going to school and studying? Even if I happen to succeed I'm going to die anyway. You wear nice clothes, you seek respect, you make a lot of money, but what's the point? It's all pointless. Of course, this kind of meaninglessness might suit this crappy nation. But...but, you see, we still have emotions like joy and happiness, right? They may not amount to much. But they fill up our emptiness. That's the only explanation I have. So...these emotions are probably missing from Kazuo. He's got no foundation for values. So he merely chooses. He doesn't have a solid foundation. He just chooses as he goes....Like for this game he might just as well have chosen not to participate. But he decided to. That's my little theory."

He said all of this at once and then concluded, "Yeah, it is scary that someone could live a life like that...and that we have to take on someone like that right now."

They fell silent. Shogo took one more drag from his shortened cigarette and then rubbed it out against the ground. Shuya took another sip from his cup of soup. Then he looked up at the cloudy sky over the edge of Shogo's thatched roof.

"I wonder if Hiroki is all right."

He'd mentioned the gunfire he heard after he left the lighthouse. He was still worried about it.

"I'm sure he's all right," Noriko said.

Shuya looked at Shogo. "I wonder if we'll be able to see any smoke."

Shogo nodded. "Don't worry. We can see smoke coming from anywhere on this island. I'll check periodically."

Shuya then remembered the bird call. It led him to them. But why did Shogo have such an odd thing to begin with? He was about to ask him when Noriko said, "I wonder if Hiroki met up with Kayoko Kotohiki."

"If he did, we'd be seeing smoke," Shogo answered.

Noriko nodded and then mumbled, "I wonder why he had to see Kotohiki."

This came up when they were in the medical clinic. Shuya's response was the same. "Beats me."

"They didn't seem all that close."

But then Noriko said, "Oh...," as if she'd realized something.

Shuya looked up. "What?"

"I don't know for sure." Noriko shook her head. "But maybe..." She emphasized her last vowel. Shuya knit his brows.

"Maybe what?"

"That would be..."

Shogo interrupted them. Shuya looked over at him. Shogo was tearing the seal off a new pack of cigarettes and continued, his eyes glued to the pack, "...too corny...in this fucking game."

"But...," Noriko continued, "...it's Hiroki, so..."

Shuya looked back and forth at them, utterly perplexed.

8 students remaining

68

Kayoko Kotohiki (Female Student No. 8) was hugging her knees in the bushes. She was on the southern slope of the northern mountain, in sector E=7.

Evening was approaching, but the light coming through the bushes didn't change much. It just stayed dark. In the afternoon, the area was covered with thick clouds, and just two hours ago it finally began raining.

Kayoko wrapped a handkerchief around her head to shield herself from the rain. Thanks to the branches over her, the rain didn't hit her directly, but her shoulders were drenched. She was cold. And of course more importantly...she was terrified.

Kayoko had first hidden on the eastern side of the northern mountain peak, in sector C=8. So of course she witnessed Yumiko Kusaka and Yukiko Kitano getting killed in front of her very own eyes. She held her breath. She knew that their killer was near, but she instinctively thought she would be risking more by moving. She stayed absolutely quiet. As noon and then night passed, she managed to avoid any attacks.

She moved twice in accordance to the forbidden zone announcements. The second time she moved was immediately after noon today, because the southern side of the peak, sector D=7, was going to become forbidden at 1 p.m. So the northern mountain peak was now surrounded by three forbidden zones. Her allocated area was definitely shrinking.

She hadn't met anyone yet. She heard a lot of gunfire, sometimes in the distance, sometimes near. She even heard an explosion, but she just remained still and absolutely quiet. The announcement every six hours made it clear though, the number of her classmates was steadily diminishing.

At noon there were supposedly fourteen remaining. And then there was more gunfire. Was it now just twelve? Or ten?

Kayoko put the heavy gun (Smith & Wesson M59 Automatic, manual included, but Kayoko of course could care less about the gun's name) down by her feet and massaged her right-hand fingers with her left hand. She'd been holding the gun all this time, and now the muscles in her fingers had gone numb. The palm of her hand was flushed red and imprinted with the gun-grip pattern.

She was completely exhausted, both from sleep deprivation and the threat of attack. Because she was too scared to enter a house that might be occupied, the only food she ate was the bread and water that came supplied with her day pack. She was hungry and thirsty. Her water intake was grossly inadequate. She did her best to save the supplied water and only drank over a liter since the game began. If there was one good thing about the rain, it was that she could collect water by putting the recently emptied water bottle under a dripping branch, but it wasn't even a third full. She would intermittently remove the handkerchief from her head and wet her dry lips with it, but of course this did nothing to relieve her dehydration.

Kayoko let out a long, weary breath, combed back her short, shoulder-length hair, and took up the M59 again. She was in a daze.

As she sat, dazed, she thought of that face again. She kept on thinking of that face ever since the game began. He wasn't as familiar as her parents and older sister, whom she thought of as well, but he was very important to her.

She just began learning tea ceremony when she first saw "him" at an event conducted by the school where she attended tea ceremony class. It was the fall of her first year in junior high.

Sponsored by a government park for an autumn holiday, the tea ceremony was held outdoors for tourists. The actual practitioners performing that day were all adults, so Kayoko and other students her age took care of menial tasks, like arranging outdoor seating and preparing biscuits. "He" was one of the masters of the tea ceremony.

He arrived around noon, much later that day. He was good looking, but he still looked boyish, as if he were still a college student. Kayoko thought, oh, this guy must be helping out too. But he addressed Kayoko's teacher (a 42-year-old woman) at her seat, "I'm sorry I'm late," took her place, and prepared the tea.

His preparation was very impressive. He handled the tea whisk and bowl incredibly gracefully, and his posture was impeccable. Despite his age, he didn't look odd in traditional clothes.

Kayoko put her tasks on hold and was gazing at him when someone tapped her on the shoulder. She turned around and saw her senior in the Tea Ceremony Club at Shiroiwa Junior High, the one who'd invited her to attend the tea ceremony school.

"He's pretty hot, huh? He's the grandson of the headmaster. Well, to be more accurate, he's the master's mistress' grandson. I'm a fan too. I mean, basically I've been going to tea ceremony class just to meet him."

The senior informed her how he was nineteen years old, and how after graduating from high school he was already ranked as an "instructor" with many disciples. Kayoko's only reaction at the time was, *Oh, he's from another world, so there're people like him*. That was all but then...

She began spending more hours in front of the mirror whenever there was a tea ceremony school event, or whenever she knew he would be appearing as a guest in her class. Given her age she didn't use makeup, but she did wear her traditional kimono immaculately, kept a comb in her hair, and carefully inserted her favorite dark-blue hair clip. Her flowing brows, and although not very large, curved eyes, and although short, well-shaped nose, wide lips, nicely shaped at the center, she thought, sure, I might not be stunning, but I do look pretty mature....

The reason she fell head over heels for this man adored by adolescent girls to middle-aged women alike may have been pretty simple. After all, he was handsome and intelligent, cheerful and considerate, basically the kind of ideal man you hardly believed existed. On top of that, he apparently didn't even have a girlfriend.

Kayoko had two important encounters with this man (although from someone else's perspective they might not have seemed all that special).

The first one occurred at the tea school's demonstration ceremony the spring she became a second-year junior high school student. The ceremony was held at the headmaster's home in Shido-cho near Shiroiwa-cho. Almost immediately after the event began, there was a problem. A special guest, the central government's regional cultural representative, suddenly began complaining about the tea ceremony. It wasn't the first time. They were government officials who announced their "absolute loyalty to preserve the nation's absolute sanctity," but many of them in fact abused their power. Some would even request kickbacks in return for arranging increased national traditional arts funding which the headmaster would politely refuse, so this could have been a way to get back at them by stirring up trouble.

The problem was that the headmaster was absent because he was hospitalized. The heir who substituted for the headmaster and his heir were both so completely intimidated their incompetence could have led to the school being shut down. But the nineteen-year-old master saved the day. He took the belligerent official to another room, then returned alone and said, "The official has left. He seems satisfied now, so there's no need to worry, everyone."

He said no more, and the attending established members of the school also refrained from inquiring any further. As a result the rest of the ceremony proceeded smoothly. But Kayoko was concerned. Knowing him, he could very well have assumed full responsibility, saying something like, "I am in charge of today's ceremony," and if that were true then the official could get back at him by concocting a report and arranging his arrest for being a malign influence against the government (and as a result sending him to one of those "reeducation camps").

After the ceremony came to an end with no further

interruptions, they began to clean up the area, and she waited for him to be alone. When he went to move the seat cushions, she decided to call on him.

"Sir..."

He stopped, still holding the cushions, and elegantly turned around towards Kayoko. His sad eyes made Kayoko's heart race, but she managed to continue, "Is everything all right, sir?"

He seemed to understand what she was getting at and broke into a smile. Then he said, "I appreciate your concern. It's all right though." Her concern was suddenly eclipsed by the thrill she felt in having her first real conversation with him.

Then she asked, "But...but that government official looked so mean, what if?..."

But he stopped Kayoko and said something sophisticated, as if admonishing her. "That official doesn't necessarily get a kick out of doing what he does. I'm sure this kind of thing happens all over the world...but the way this country is...it twists people....We're supposed to strive for harmony and that's what the art of tea is supposed to accomplish...but it is very, very difficult to achieve in this country." Near the end, he almost seemed to be addressing himself. Then he looked back at Kayoko and continued, "Tea ceremony is powerless. But it's also not such a bad thing either. You should enjoy it while you can." He smiled kindly, turned, and proceeded to walk away.

Kayoko was in a daze and stood still for a while. The unpretentious way he talked made her feel at ease...and even though she didn't completely understand what he was saying, it impressed her, and she thought, wow, he's so mature.

In any case, she might have made an impression on him because ever since that encounter he would always give her a warm smile whenever they met.

The crucial encounter occurred during the winter of her second year. Kayoko came out into the old temple garden of another tea ceremony and gazed at the camellia flowers there. (In fact, she was thinking about him again.) Suddenly she heard suddenly someone from behind say, "They're beautiful," in a transparent voice now familiar to her. At first she thought she'd imagined it, but when she turned around she couldn't believe he was there...smiling at her. It was the first time he addressed her without any reference to teaching tea ceremony or official duties.

And so they had a conversation.

"So you find tea ceremony interesting?"

"Yes, I love it. But I'm not very good."

"Really? I've been impressed with your excellent posture during your preparation. It's not just that your back is upright. There's a kind of intensity."

"Oh, no, I'm really no good at all...."

With his hands tucked inside his sleeves, he still wore his kind smile and glanced up at the camellia. "No, I really do mean it. Yes...just like those flowers. There's something strained...but there's beauty in that. Something like that."

Of course, she was still just a child, and he might have only been complimenting a hobbyist dabbling in the school's tea ceremony. But that didn't stop her from getting excited. Right on! (She snapped her fingers only later in the bathroom.)

From that point on Kayoko began to practice tea ceremony more seriously. She thought, I can do it. Of course, I'm still just a kid, but once I'm eighteen he'll be twenty-four. That would totally work....

And so that was her memory of him.

Kayoko buried her face into her skirt. A warm liquid which wasn't rain oozed into the area covering her kneecaps. Kayoko realized she was crying. Her hand holding the gun trembled. How could all this be happening?

She wanted so badly to see him now. Sure, she was still a kid. But in her own adolescent way, she really did love him. This was the first time she ever had serious feelings for someone. She wanted a single moment with him so she could tell him this much. She wanted to tell this person—kind enough to describe her as "beautiful" even if it was only referring to her tea ceremony skills—"I'm still a kid, so I may not understand what it really means to be in love. But I think I am in love with you. I really love you." Something like that.

Something rustled in the bushes. Kayoko looked up. She wiped her eyes with her left hand and got up. Her feet moved automatically and took a step back from the source of the sound.

A boy in a school coat—Hiroki Sugimura (Male Student No. 11). His face and torso emerged from the bushes. The sleeves of his coat and shirt were torn off, revealing his right arm. The white cloth wrapped around his shoulder was stained with blood and—perhaps it was because of the rain—it oozed pink. And his hand was holding...a gun.

Hiroki's jaw dropped, but what really caught her attention when she saw his grimy face were his eyes. They were gleaming.

Kayoko felt a sudden surge of fear. How could she have not noticed sooner before he got this close, how—

"Kotohiki—"

Kayoko let out a shriek and turned on her heels. She entered the bushes. She didn't care about the branches scraping against her face and hair, or getting drenched in the rain. She just wanted to escape. If I don't...I'll get killed!

She made her way through the bushes. There was a twisting path approximately two meters wide. Kayoko instinctively decided to run down there. If she ran uphill, he would catch up, but if she ran down then maybe...

She heard a rustling sound behind her. "Kotohiki!" It was

Hiroki's voice. He's coming after me!

Kayoko summoned all her strength from her tired body and ran as fast as she could. I can't believe this, I should have been jogging instead of learning tea ceremony if I'd known this was going to happen.

"Kotohiki! Stop! Kotohiki!"

If she had been calmer—that is, if this were a scene in a movie and she were in the theater watching the actor performing as she munched on some popcorn—then it would have been obvious he was pleading with her. But right now it sounded like he was saying: "Kotohiki! You better stop! I'm gonna kill you!"

She wasn't going to stop. The path forked. She took the left one.

The area opened up on her left. Rows of tangerine trees spread out in the dull light coming through the silky rain. Beyond them was a thicket of short trees. If she could enter that area—

It's impossible, she thought. She had at least fifty more meters to get there. It was hopeless. While she struggled through the uneven rows of tangerine trees, Hiroki Sugimura would catch up to her and shoot her from behind with his gun.

Kayoko clenched her teeth. She didn't want to, but she had to. After all, he was trying to kill her.

She stopped on her right foot and spun around to her left.

By the time she had turned around the gun was in her hands. That thing called the safety had been released ever since she'd read the manual. The manual said you didn't have to raise the hammer, all you had to do was pull the trigger. The rest was...up to her.

Less than ten meters away, Hiroki Sugimura stood still on the slope, his eyes wide open.

It's too late. You think I won't shoot?

Kayoko extended her arms and squeezed the trigger. With a pop, a small flame exploded from the muzzle, and her arms jerked back from the recoil.

Hiroki's large frame spun around as if he were hit. He fell back.

Kayoko ran over to him. She had to finish him off, finish him off! So he wouldn't get back up again!

Kayoko stopped approximately two meters away from him. There was a small hole in the left side of his chest (she'd actually aimed at his stomach), and the fabric around it had turned dark black. But his sprawled right hand still held his gun. He still might raise it. The head. I have to aim for his head.

Hiroki turned his head around and looked at Kayoko. Kayoko pointed the gun and pulled the trig—

She stopped...because Hiroki had tossed his gun aside. If he'd had that kind of strength he could have pulled the trigger. What was going on?

The gun spun around once and landed on its side.

Huh?

Kayoko stood still, holding the gun, her short hair drenched in the rain.

"Now listen." He lay on the messy path ridden now with puddles as he said painfully, somehow fixing his eyes on Kayoko, "You have to burn some fresh wood. Build...two fires. I have a lighter in my pocket. Use that...then you'll hear a bird call."

Kayoko heard him, but she had no idea what he was talking about. She had no idea what was going on.

Hiroki continued. "Follow that bird call. Then you'll find Shuya Nanahara...Noriko Nakagawa, and Shogo Kawada. They'll help you. You got that?"

"Wh-what?"

Hiroki seemed to be smiling. He repeated patiently,

"Build two fires. Then find the bird call."

He awkwardly moved his right arm, pulled out a small lighter from his school coat pocket, and tossed it over to Kayoko. Then he painfully closed his eyes.

"Okay, now go."

"Whaaaat?"

Hiroki suddenly opened his eyes wide and yelled, "Go now! Someone might have heard the shot. Go!"

Then as if fitting the pieces of a complex jigsaw puzzle into place, Kayoko finally managed to get it. This time she got it right.

"Oh…oh…"

She dropped the gun and fell on her knees beside him. She scraped her knees but she didn't care.

"Hiroki! Hiroki! I…I can't believe…I can't believe I did this to you!…"

She burst into tears. Sure, there was something intimidating about Hiroki Sugimura. He seemed tough since he studied martial arts, plus he didn't talk much, and when he did he was always gruff. When he spoke to other boys, like Shinji Mimura and Shuya Nanahara, he would smile but otherwise he looked grumpy. She also heard he was going out with Takako Chigusa, and they looked so close. Kayoko only thought, I don't get Takako's taste, I wonder maybe if you're that pretty, you're attracted to someone intimidating. In any case…that was her impression of him. So in this situation where her classmates were being killed off one by one she was absolutely terrified of Hiroki Sugimura. But then…it turned out…

He closed his eyes again and said, "It's all right." He was smiling. He looked content. "I was going to die soon anyway."

Kayoko then finally noticed he had another wound on his side, soaked in liquid that wasn't rain.

"So…go now. Please."

Kayoko sobbed convulsively and touched his neck gently. "Let's go together. Okay? Stand."

Hiroki opened his eyes and looked at her. He seemed to be smiling. "Forget about me," he said. "I'm just glad I got to see you."

"What?" Kayoko opened her tear-stained eyes wide. What? What did you just say? "What...what do you mean..." Her voice was trembling.

Hiroki exhaled deeply, as if to bear the pain, or maybe it was a long sigh. "If I tell you, will you go?"

"What? I don't get it. What do you mean?"

Hiroki said without hesitating, "I love you, Kotohiki. I've loved you for a real long time."

Kayoko once again didn't understand Hiroki. What's he talking about?

Hiroki continued. He was looking up at the sky raining down on them. "That's all I wanted to tell you. Now...go."

Kayoko then uttered, "But I thought...you and Takako..."

Hiroki looked into her eyes again. He said, "You're the one."

She finally got it. She was blown away as if struck by a huge wrecking ball swinging from a demolition crane.

Love, me? You wanted to tell me...don't tell me you were trying to find me? Is that true? If so...then what did I just do?

Her breath was raspy. She kept on getting choked up, but finally she managed to cry out, "Hiroki...Hiroki!"

"Hurry," Hiroki said and coughed out a mist of blood, spraying Kayoko's face. Hiroki opened his eyes again.

"Hiroki...I...I...I..."

Her body was supposedly dehydrated from lack of water, but the tears kept on gushing out.

"It's all right," Hiroki said kindly. He closed his eyes

slowly. "Kayoko…," he called her by her first name as if it were a precious treasure. It was probably the first time he had ever called her by her first name. "I don't mind at all…dying because of you. So please, please go. Or else…"

Kayoko kept on crying, waiting for Hiroki to continue. "Or else"?

Hiroki didn't say anything. Kayoko slowly reached out for him. She held his shoulders and shook them. "Hiroki! Hiroki!"

In a TV drama when someone died their words would be cut off, like, "Or el—" but Hiroki managed to say in a painful but clear voice, "Or else." So there had to be more. Or else?…

"Hiroki! Hey, Hiroki!"

Kayoko shook his body one more time. Then she finally realized he was dead.

Once she realized this, the dam restraining her torrent of emotions suddenly collapsed. A shriek was welling up inside.

"AHHH!" On her knees, Kayoko fell over Hiroki's body and cried.

He loved me…he loved me so much he sought me out at the risk of being attacked. Any encounter could have led to an attack on him. In fact, the wound in his side…the wound on his shoulder…came as a result of him trying to find me.

No…there's more. Kayoko stopped sobbing for a moment.

I was the one who attacked Hiroki. At the very end, when Hiroki managed to achieve his goal.

Kayoko shut her eyes and cried again.

He loved me…just like I wanted to tell "that guy" how I felt about him, Hiroki was thinking the same thing about me, looking for me. Someone in my class cared for me that much. And yet…and yet….

Suddenly, Kayoko recalled a scene. It was when they were doing their cleaning tasks. Kayoko was wiping the blackboard with a wet rag and when she couldn't reach the top, Hiroki, who had been slacking off, rested his chin against his hands that were holding the upright broom as if it were a cane, and said, "You're too short, Kotohiki." He took the rag from her and wiped the area she couldn't reach.

The scene came back to her.

Why...why didn't I see how kind he was? How could I not notice how someone loved me so much? If I'd thought about it, I would have realized if Hiroki wanted to kill me he could have immediately shot me with his gun. But I couldn't tell. I wasn't able to understand. I am so stupid. I—

Another memory came flashing by.

When she was telling some of her classmate friends about "that guy," Hiroki, who was nearby looking out the window, muttered, "You're being foolish, getting so worked up like that." It made her mad at the time, but in fact he was right, she was being foolish. And yet...and yet Hiroki told her he'd cherished this fool.

She simply couldn't stop crying. She pressed her cheek against his warm cheek and continued to sob. Hiroki told her to go, but she couldn't bring herself to do that. I'm going to keep on crying, I'm going to cry over the dedication (it was irreplaceable) of this boy who loved me and my foolishness (I was such a kid thinking I was actually in the running for "that guy"), I'm going to keep on crying. Even if it was suicidal in this game.

You plan on dying with him? A voice whispered to her in her thoughts.

That's right, yes, I'm going to die with him. I'm going to die for the sake of Hiroki's love for me and my foolishness.

"Then why...don't you go ahead?" the voice said.

Kayoko suddenly trembled and turned around. She saw the long, beautiful, rain-drenched hair of Mitsuko Souma (Female Student No. 11), gazing down at her, gun in hand.

BAM BAM, two dry pops formed two holes in Kayoko's right temple. Kayoko's body then landed on Hiroki Sugimura's body.

Blood slowly began flowing out of the holes in her head. The blood continued flowing down her face against the rain washing it away.

Mitsuko lowered the Smith & Wesson M19 .357 Magnum and said, "You really were a fool. You should have understood him."

Then she looked over at Hiroki's face.

"Long time no see, Hiroki. Are you glad you got to die with your beloved?"

She shook her head, disgusted, and proceeded to walk forward to pick up the Smith & Wesson M59 Kayoko dropped and the Colt Government .45 (which had been Mitsuko's) Hiroki had tossed aside.

She looked down at the intertwined bodies and put her finger against her lips.

"Now what was that about…building a fire?"

Then she shook her head. With her foot she brushed away Kayoko's skirt covering part of the M59 and reached for the blue gun, when she suddenly heard the rattling sound of an old typewriter.

6 students remaining

69

Her back was pummeled, repeatedly. Her chest burst open with blood. She staggered…and she felt something hot expand inside her, like burning embers.

She didn't feel so much the painful shock as she felt dismayed. How could she not have heard someone sneaking up behind her in this mud?

The bullets had done enough damage, but Mitsuko managed to turn around.

There was a boy in a school coat. The unique slicked-back hair, the well-defined face, the gleaming, frigid eyes. It was Kazuo Kiriyama (Male Student No. 6).

Mitsuko squeezed her right hand holding the M19. Her muscles were nearly disabled, but she summoned all her remaining strength and attempted to raise the gun.

Suddenly Mitsuko's thoughts—despite the fact that she was in a life-or-death confrontation—slipped into another dimension. It only lasted for a split second.

When I spoke to Hiroki Sugimura I said:

"I just decided to take instead of being taken."

That's what I said.

When did I...become like that? Was it after the time I told Hiroki about, when I was raped by three men? That day I was raped by those men with the video camera in a rundown apartment room in the shabby outskirts of town? Or maybe the moment my drunken mother (I never had a father) left the room when she received the thick envelope (it couldn't have been that thick) after taking me to that room before "it" happened? From then on? Or...was it after my elementary school teacher, the one person I thought I could trust, kindly addressed me, nearly numb from trauma, and I finally told him exactly what happened, when the look on his face changed, and it happened again? From that point on? In that small, dark reading room after school? Or after my best friend saw it (at least part of it) and instead of offering consolation, spread a rumor (which led to the teacher leaving the school)? Or was it three months later when I resisted my mother, who was trying to take me to do "it" again and accidentally ended up killing her? After getting rid of all the evidence and doing everything to make it look like a break-in, I sat on a swing in the park. From that point on? Or after being taken in by distant relatives, I was repeatedly harassed by their kid, and when the kid accidentally fell from the roof, the mother accused me of killing her since I was with her? From that point on? The father intervened and defended me, but then after a while, this father started fooling around with me. From that point on? Or...

Little by little, no, more like in big chunks, everyone took from Mitsuko. No one gave Mitsuko anything. And so Mitsuko ended up an empty shell. But...

...that didn't matter.

I am right. I will not lose.

Her arms were suddenly strengthened, and she lifted the gun. The tendons in her wrist rose up, resembling violin strings. Then she pulled the—

The rattling Ingram M10 in Kazuo Kiriyama's hands fired away a row of four holes that ran from her chest up to the middle of her head. Blood sprayed out of Mitsuko's mouth. Her upper lip tore. She bent backwards.

Still Mitsuko managed to smile. She regained her footing and pulled the trigger. Over and over.

The four bullets from the chamber struck Kazuo Kiriyama's chest.

But...Kazuo remained calm as he staggered only slightly. Mitsuko didn't understand why. Kazuo's Ingram then fired away again.

Mitsuko's face, once so beautiful, was torn up as if a strawberry pie had been flung into her face. This time her body was blown back—and the next moment she fell back onto the wet ground. By then she was dead. In fact, she may have been dead a while ago. Physically, several seconds ago, mentally, ages ago.

Kazuo Kiriyama walked up to her slowly, and then calmly removed the gun from her hand. He also picked up the Colt

Government .45 lying by Hiroki Sugimura's hand and the M59 Kayoko Kotohiki had tossed aside. He didn't even bother glancing at the three rain-drenched bodies.

5 students remaining

70

Mizuho Inada (Female Student No. 1) cautiously looked out from the shade of the bushes. Due to the relentless rain her neatly cropped hair stuck to her forehead.

Beyond the bushes there was a narrow farm field, and through the light sheet of rain she saw the back side of a school coat in the middle of the field. His slicked-back hair was also wet from the rain. It was Kazuo Kiriyama (Male Student No. 6).

Kazuo Kiriyama had formed what appeared to be two piles of branches. Now he sat arranging one of the piles.

Mizuho calmed her breathing. It was cold, and she was tired, but she didn't really mind. After all, she was about to execute her most important mission...

...as a space warrior.

Are you ready, warrior Prexia Dikianne Mizuho?

In her mind, the God of Light Ahura Mazda asked her this. Apparently, this voice came from the spindle-shaped magic crystal (in fact the mail order item was made of glass but Mizuho believed it was crystal) she wore.

Of course. Mizuho responded. I saw that demon walk away after killing Yumiko Kusaka and Yukiko Kitano. I lost track of him, but just found him. And I saw him kill that other demon who killed Kayoko Kotohiki. I must defeat this enemy. And I have followed him this far.

Very well then. So you understand your mission?

Of course, sir. I received your message from the local fortune teller, that I would become a warrior destined to fight evil. I didn't understand what it meant at the time. But now, now I understand completely.

Very well then. Are you not scared?

No, sir. With your guidance I have nothing to fear.

Very well then. You are a surviving member of the Holy Dikianne Tribe. You are a chosen warrior. The light of victory will shine upon you soon. Hm? What is it?

No, no. It's just that, great Ahura Mazda, my fellow warrior, Lorela Lausasse Kaori was killed (in their former Class B classroom, Kaori Minami, who spent some time hanging out with Mizuho Inada, would restrain herself from yawning every time Mizuho told her, "You're the warrior Lorela," but whatever). She...

She fought to the very end, Mizuho.

Ah. Oh, I thought so. But, but, she was defeated by the evil forces.

Uh, well, yes. Well, that was because she was a mere commoner in origins. You are different. In any case, let's not fuss over the details. The important thing is that you must fight for her sake. And you must win. All right?

Yes, sir.

Okay then. The light. You must have faith in the cosmic light. The light that engulfs you.

The light grew inside her. The great warm cosmic power that encompassed everything.

Mizuho nodded again in her brief repose. Yes. Yes. Yes.

Then she pulled the double-bladed knife (when she found the weapon in her day pack she thought it most becoming for a warrior) out of its sheath. She held it up in front of her face. A white light covered the blue blade, and Mizuho looked at Kazuo beyond the light.

She saw Kazuo's back. It was wide open.

Now then. You must cut down the enemy!

Yes!

In order to keep quiet, Mizuho dodged the bushes and dashed towards Kazuo. A light burst out from the short blade that had been barely fifteen centimeters in length, and it suddenly transformed into a legendary sword at least one meter long. This sword of light would pierce the evil monster with a single thrust.

As Kazuo Kiriyama adjusted the branches with his left hand, his right hand calmly pulled out the Beretta M92F. Without even turning around, he reached around and pulled the trigger twice.

The first shot hit Mizuho in the chest, stopping her, and the second shot went right through her head.

Mizuho fell back as her wounds burst into gently curved red lines drawn through the air. The rain immediately began washing away the blood. Then the warrior Prexia Dikianne Mizuho's soul transmigrated to the Land of Light.

His back still facing her, Kazuo Kiriyama put away his gun and continued arranging the branches.

4 students remaining

71

It continued to rain. Shuya was slouched against the wet rock wall as he watched the rain dripping off the edge of the thatched roof. He heard rapid gunfire. Then about five minutes ago he heard gunfire again, this time two single shots. Both times it didn't sound too close, but it didn't seem too far away either. It was probably somewhere in the northern mountain, where they were camping.

A large raindrop slid along one of the "roof" leaves and

fell by Shuya's stretched out foot wearing Keds sneakers, splashing against the muddy water.

"Maybe Hiroki likes Kotohiki."

That's what Noriko had said. "If I were him…I would have done the same thing." She glanced at Shuya. "I would find the person I cared about."

Was it true? Did Hiroki like Kayoko Kotohiki? Why, when he was so close to the prettiest girl in their class, would he be into a Plain Jane like Kayoko?

Well, maybe that's how it was. After all, Billy Joel sang, "Don't imagine you're too familiar…I'll take you just the way you are."

Then…who was involved (the second series of shots sounded like it was just one assailant shooting away) in those rounds of gunshots he just heard? If he were to include the gunfire he heard immediately after leaving the lighthouse, it meant he'd heard guns go off three times since noon. (This wasn't including what happened to Yukie Utsumi's group.) It would be reasonable to assume at least three people had died. Then there were only five left? Which three got killed? Or maybe no one died at all, maybe there were just confrontations, and everyone managed to escape each other. Then eight students, including Shuya's group, were left.

"Are you tired, Shuya?"

They were sitting next to each other in a row, but Shogo, who was on the other side of Noriko, asked, "Maybe you should sleep a little."

Shuya looked back at them. "No." He gave a smile. "I slept a lot until noon. I bet you haven't had much sleep."

Shogo shrugged. "I'm fine. But Noriko. She didn't sleep at all waiting for you."

Shuya looked over at Noriko, but she waved her palms at Shuya and smiled. "That's not entirely true. I dozed off a little here and there. Shogo's the one who hasn't slept for my sake."

Shogo chuckled and shrugged. Then he held his right hand up to his chest in a salute and said, "I shall always guard you, Your Highness."

Noriko grinned, touched his hand, and said, "The honor is mine, Shogo."

Shuya raised his brow and observed their interaction. It was odd how close Noriko and Shogo seemed now. Ever since the game began, Noriko seemed to speak to Shogo mostly through Shuya, but now things seemed different. They seemed like a good pair on their own. It was only natural though, given how they'd spent over half a day without Shuya.

Shogo suddenly pointed at Shuya and said, "Uh oh. Shuya's getting jealous."

Noriko opened her eyes wide and looked at Shuya. She smiled and said, "No..."

Shuya blushed a little. "I am not. What are you talking about?"

Shogo shrugged. He raised his brow and said to Noriko in mock exasperation, "He says he trusts you, out of love."

"..."

Shuya wanted to say something, but he was speechless. Shogo began laughing. Cracking up, really. Despite the urge to protest, Shuya ended up going along with it and chuckled too. Noriko was smiling too.

It was a brief but wonderful moment. It was the kind of conversation and laughter you'd share with your longtime friends, hanging out with them after school at your favorite café. Of course, looming over them was the feeling that they were all here only after attending a friend's funeral....

Still smiling, Shogo looked down at his watch and went outside to check again for a signal from Hiroki.

Noriko grinned and looked at Shuya. "Shogo likes to kid around."

Shuya smiled. "Yeah. but…" He squinted at the open space.

I might have been jealous.

Shuya looked back at Noriko again. He was about to tell her in a joking way, "I may have been jealous." Then Noriko would probably laugh and say, "Yeah right."

Shogo returned to the front of the roof. His stubbly face was moist with raindrops. "I see smoke," he said and immediately turned around.

Shuya quickly got up. He helped Noriko up with his uninjured right arm. They walked to where Shogo was standing.

The rain was light now, so he could make out the smoke drifting in the sky. As he followed Shogo's eyes…he saw a white column of smoke on the opposite side of the northern mountain. Two columns, in fact.

"Right on!"

Without thinking, Shuya gave a little holler out as if singing a rock and roll song. His eyes met Noriko's. Noriko, no less enthusiastic, broke into a grin and said, "So Hiroki's safe."

Shogo took out the bird call from his pocket and teaked it as he observed the smoke. The cheerful chirping of a little bird rose and spread out into the rain covering the island. As he continued, Shogo checked his watch. Fifteen seconds later he stopped.

Shogo then looked over at them.

"Let's wait a little more here. My guess is he won't hear this sound unless he's close. It'll take time."

They returned underneath the roof.

"Hiroki probably found Kayoko," Noriko said. Shuya was about to nod but stopped when he saw Shogo's mouth stiffen. Noriko also stopped smiling.

"Shogo…," Shuya said.

Shogo looked up. Then he shook his head. "It's nothing. I just think things might not be what they seem."

"Huh? But..." Shuya raised his opened right palm. "Hiroki would never give up though."

Shogo nodded. "That might be true." He stopped and then looked away from them. "But he might have only found Kayoko Kotohiki dead."

Shuya's face became tense. He was right. Kotohiki seemed to be alive up until noon...but there was all that gunfire. They'd just heard those single shots. After searching around for two weeks, Hiroki might have ended up discovering Kayoko Kotohiki had died.

Shogo continued, "Or there might have been a totally different outcome."

Noriko asked, "What do you mean?"

Shogo took out a pack of cigarettes and answered curtly, "It's very possible Kayoko didn't trust Hiroki."

Shuya and Noriko both fell silent.

Shogo lit his cigarette and continued, "Well, in any case, let's just hope Hiroki can make it back here. We'll see then whether he's with Kayoko or not."

Shuya was hoping Hiroki would return with Kayoko Kotohiki. Then...there would be five of them. Five of them could escape.

Only five.

Shuya then recalled that Mizuho Inada was still alive, at least she had been at noon.

"Shogo."

Shogo glanced at Shuya.

"Inada is still alive. I wonder if we can't contact her."

Shogo shrugged. "I keep on saying this, but it's best not to trust the others too much in this game. To be honest, nothing against Hiroki, but I don't necessarily trust Kotohiki either."

Shuya bit his lip. "I know but—"

"Well, if we can afford to, then I'll come up with some way to contact Mizuho, but," he blew out smoke, "don't forget, we may not be around to do that."

That's right, Shogo had said, "At the very end. Once everyone else is dead, there's a way out." That meant no matter what, they would have to confront Kazuo again and also take on Mitsuko Souma. He wasn't sure about Mitsuko, but there would be no way around fighting Kazuo. There was no way Kazuo could die easily. Which mean that...everyone in Shuya's trio might not survive fighting him.

Shogo puffed on his shortened cigarette and said, "I'm going to ask you again, Shuya." He exhaled a puff of smoke and continued to stare at Shuya, "Even if we manage to hook up with Hiroki, we're probably going to have to fight Kazuo again and Mitsuko....Are you prepared to be merciless?"

So that's what it came down to. They could afford to contact Mizuho Inada only after they'd defeated Kazuo and Mitsuko. Although he wasn't comfortable with how he'd gotten used to the idea of killing his classmates no matter how extreme the circumstances were...

...Shuya nodded and responded, "I am."

4 students remaining

72

Shogo tweaked the bird call. It was the third time. The rain was now lightening up, and the drops falling off the edge of the roof became less frequent. The time was already past 5 p.m.

After he heard the same bird sound four times Shuya managed to join up with Noriko and Shogo.

But that was because he had some idea of their location. It could take Hiroki longer to find them since he didn't have that information.

Shogo returned under the roof and lit a Wild Seven.

He blew out smoke and asked out of the blue, "Where do you want to go?"

Shuya looked at Shogo, who was sitting on the other side of Noriko. Shogo turned towards him.

"I forgot to mention it, but I have a connection. Once we get out of here we can stay there for the time being."

"Who's that?" Shuya asked and Shogo nodded.

"A friend of my dad's," he continued. "He'll see to it that you get out of this country....I'm assuming you'll want to do that. You'll get killed if you stay in this country. You'll be hunted down like rats."

"Escape the country...," Noriko said, surprised. "We can really do that?"

Shuya also asked, "Who's this friend of your father's?"

Shogo looked at them, as if considering something as he held the cigarette to his mouth with his left hand. He removed the cigarette from his mouth and said, "Right now isn't a good time to tell you." Then he continued, "In case we end up splitting up during our escape it'd be bad if either of you get caught and share our plans with the government. It's not that I don't trust you. But once they torture you, you'll eventually end up confessing. So I'll be in charge of getting us there."

Shuya thought about it and then nodded. It seemed like he was making the right call.

"But...let's see," Shogo said. He bit his cigarette and pulled out a piece of paper from his pocket.

It looked like the sheet on which they'd all written that statement, "We shall kill each other." Shogo tore it in two and then scribbled onto both pieces. He folded them up neatly and offered one to Shuya and the other to Noriko.

"What's this?" Shuya asked and began opening it up.

Shogo stopped him, saying, "Hold on. Don't look at it now. It's our contact method, just in any case. The time and locations are written on it. Go to that place and time every day. I'll do my best to get there too."

"We can't look at it now?" Noriko asked.

"Nope," Shogo said. "Look at it only in case we end up splitting up. In other words…your note and Shuya's have different information. It's best you two don't know what's on each other's note. Just in case one of you gets caught."

Shuya and Noriko looked at each other. Then Shuya turned to Shogo. "I'm going to be with Noriko no matter what."

"I know I know," Shogo grinned wryly, "but we can't rule out the possibility you might get separated again, like you were when Kazuo attacked us."

Shuya pursed his lips and looked over at Shogo…but ended up nodding. He exchanged glances with Noriko and put away the memo. So did Noriko.

It was true. Anything could happen. Escaping this island in the first place was going to be incredibly difficult. But if that were the case then shouldn't he and Noriko also come up with their own place and time to meet? Without telling Shogo? Then again, if Shogo ended up getting caught by the government then their situation would be hopeless anyway.

Shogo asked, "So…where do you want to go?"

Shuya recalled how Shogo wanted to know their ideal destinations once they fled the country. He folded his arms and thought about it. Then he said, "It'd have to be America. It's where rock came from. I always wanted to go there, at least once." He thought, I didn't think I'd be escaping there, though.

"I see." Shogo nodded. "What about you, Noriko?"

"I don't really have anywhere in mind but...," Noriko said and glanced over at Shuya.

Shuya nodded back. "Let's go together. All right?"

"Oh..." Noriko's eyes opened wide. Then she formed a smile and nodded. "Sure, if you're all right with that."

Shogo smiled. He took another drag from his cigarette and asked, "What will you do once you get there?"

Shuya thought about it. Then he answered with a grin, "I'll be busking with my guitar. At least I'll make some change."

Shogo chuckled, "Huh." Then he said, "You best be a rocker. You're talented. From what I hear, in that country the odds aren't stacked so high against you even if you're an immigrant or exile."

Shuya took a deep breath and gave him a skeptical grin. "I'm not that talented. I don't have what it takes to be a pro."

"I don't know about that."

Shogo smiled and shook his head. Then he looked over at Noriko. "What about you, Noriko? Anything you want to do?"

Noriko pursed her lips. Then she said, "I've always wanted to be a teacher."

Her reply caught Shuya by surprise since he'd never heard about it. He exclaimed, "Really?"

Noriko turned to look at Shuya and nodded.

Shuya continued, "You wanted to be a teacher in this lousy country?"

Noriko grimaced, "There are good teachers too. I...that's right," she looked down and continued, "I thought Mr. Hayashida was a good teacher."

It had been a while since Shuya recalled the corpse of Mr. Hayashida, whose head was half crushed. "Dragonfly" died for their sake.

"...you're right," Shuya agreed.

Shogo said, "It might be difficult to become a teacher as an exile. But you might be able do research at some university. Ironically enough, the rest of the world seems very interested in this country. Then you might be able to teach." He continued staring ahead, then tossed his cigarette butt into the puddle by his feet. He put another cigarette in his mouth and lit it. He continued, "So you should go for it, both of you. Be what you want to be. Follow your heart and give it your best shot."

Shuya thought what he said was kind of cool. Follow your heart. Do your best. The way the late Shinji Mimura would also say something sometimes that hit the mark.

Then he realized something.

"What about you?" He asked anxiously, "What are you going to do?"

Shogo shrugged his shoulders. "I told you. It's payback time against this country. No, that's not it. They owe me, and they're going to pay me back. No matter what. I can't join you guys."

"No...," Noriko said with anguish.

Shuya responded differently, though. He clenched his teeth and said, "Let me join you."

Shogo looked at Shuya for a moment...then he looked down and dismissively shook his head. "Don't be stupid."

"Why not?"

Shuya said insistently. "You're not the only one with a grudge against this fucking country."

"That's right," Noriko insisted. Her response surprised Shuya. Noriko looked at Shogo and continued, "We'll do it together."

Shogo looked at them. He heaved a deep sigh. He looked up and said, "Look. I think I told you before that this country might be fucked up, but it's well run.

It's almost impossible to take it down. No, I'd say it's absolutely impossible right now, but I…" He turned around and then looked beyond the roof at the sky turning white from the receding rain. Then he looked back at them. "To use a cliché, I just want to take a stab at it. I'm getting back at them. I'm only doing it for my own sake, which isn't such a bad thing." He stopped and then said, "No, it's not bad at all."

"So then—" Shuya said but Shogo interrupted him, raising his hand.

"I'm not done."

Shuya shut up and let him speak.

"I'm saying you'll die if you join me. You just said you're going to be with Noriko. Which means…" He looked at Noriko. Then he looked back at Shuya. "You still have Noriko. You protect her, Shuya. If she's in danger then fight for her. Whether your assailant's a burglar, the fucking Republic of Greater East Asia, or an extraterrestrial alien." Then he turned to Noriko and said kindly, "You too. You still have Shuya, right? Protect him, Noriko. It's foolish to die pointlessly." Then he looked at Shuya again. "You understand? There's nothing left for me. So I'm just doing it for my sake. It's different for you guys." The last statement sounded adamant. He checked his watch, tossed another cigarette into the puddle, got up and went out from under the roof. The chirping bird call rang out.

As he listened Shuya recalled a song by a mainland Chinese rocker that went: "Perhaps you are saying/You love me even though I have nothing at all."

But what did Shogo mean when he said he had nothing?—

After tweaking the bird call for exactly fifteen seconds, Shogo went back underneath the roof and sat down.

Noriko asked Shogo, gently, "Don't you have someone you care about?"

That's right. That's what he wanted to ask too.

Shogo opened his eyes and then forced a grin. "I wasn't planning on telling you, but...," he said and then took a deep breath. He continued, "No, maybe I did want to tell you." He reached behind for his back pocket and pulled out his wallet. He removed a photo with frayed edges.

Noriko took it. She and Shuya looked at it.

The photo included Shogo. He was wearing a school coat, and his hair was as long as Shuya's. He was smiling, wearing a bashful smile that was hard to imagine on him now. And on his left was a girl in a sailor suit uniform. Her black hair was bundled over her right shoulder. She looked assertive, but her smile was incredibly charming too. In the background were a road, gingko-like trees, a whiskey billboard ad, and a yellow car.

"She's beautiful...," Noriko exclaimed.

Shogo rubbed the tip of his nose. "Really? She's not what you'd call typically beautiful, but I always thought she was pretty."

Noriko shook her head. "Well, I think she's very pretty and very...mature looking. Is she the same age as you?"

Shogo broke into a bashful grin that was reminiscent of the one he wore in the photo. "Yeah. Thanks."

Shuya gazed at the two smiling faces next to each other in the photo and thought, hey, what do you mean you have nothing? But Shuya had overlooked something crucial.

"So is she in Kobe?" Shuya asked and then Shogo grimaced. He shook his head and said, "Remember, Shuya? I played this fucking game once before. And I was the 'winner.' "

That was when Shuya realized. And Noriko probably did too. Her face stiffened.

Shogo continued, "She was in my class. I wasn't able to save Keiko."

They fell silent. Shuya finally felt he could truly understand Shogo's anger, the sheer depth of it.

"So you see now," Shogo said, "I really have nothing. And it's payback time against this country for killing Keiko." Shogo put another cigarette in his mouth and lit it. Smoke drifted by.

"So her name was Keiko," Shuya finally asked.

"Yeah," Shogo gave several small nods. " 'Kei' means 'joy.' "

Shuya realized it was same kanji character as the first character to Yoshitoki's name.

"Were you...," Noriko gently asked, "...with her until the very end?"

Shogo smoked silently. After a while he replied, "That's a hard one to answer." He continued, "Her last name was Onuki. The roll call started with No. 17 in that game. Whatever. Anyway, Keiko's number came before mine, so she left three numbers before me."

Shuya and Noriko listened quietly.

"I thought...she might be waiting for me somewhere near the departure point. She just might be. But she wasn't there. I mean it couldn't be helped. Just like with this current game. It was dangerous to hang around the departure point." He took a drag from his cigarette and exhaled. "But I finally found her. The game took place on an island like this one, but I found her." He took another drag and exhaled. Then he continued, "But she ran away."

Shuya was shocked. He looked at Shogo. His stubbly face remained calm. It seemed like he was doing his best to restrain his emotions.

"I tried chasing her...but I was attacked by someone else. I managed to kill that person...but I ended up losing sight of her."

He took another drag and then exhaled.

"Keiko couldn't trust me."

He still wore his poker face, but there was a tense look in his eyes.

He continued, "But I still looked for her. The next time I found her...she was dead."

Shuya understood. Once he was back here Shuya had told them about Yukie Utsumi's group and observed, "It's so hard to...trust someone," to which Shogo responded by saying, "Yes, it is....It's very...hard." Shuya now saw why Shogo looked so uneasy then. He also understood why Shogo said Hiroki might have found Kotohiki dead, or that she might not necessarily trust him.

"You asked me, Shuya," Shogo said. Shuya looked up. "Why I trusted you guys, when we first met, right?"

"Yeah." Shuya nodded. "I did."

"And I believe I said you two made a nice couple," Shogo said and glanced up at the roof. By the time he lowered his eyes, the tension in his cheeks was gone. "It's true. That's how you two looked. So I decided I wanted to help you guys out, unconditionally."

"Uh huh." Shuya nodded.

After a while Noriko said, "I bet..." Shuya looked over at Noriko, who continued, "...she was just terrified...and confused."

"No." Shogo shook his head. "I...I really loved Keiko. But there must have something about the way I treated her when we were going out. That's what I think it came down to."

"That's so wrong," Shuya adamantly insisted.

Shogo looked over at him, his arms folded over his pulled-up knees. The smoke from the cigarette in his hands drifted up gently like silk.

"There was a misunderstanding. A small misunderstanding, I'm sure. Given how fucked up this game is. The odds were against you. That's what it really came down to, right?"

Shogo grimaced wryly again and only replied, "I don't know. I'll never know." Then he tossed his cigarette into the puddle and took out the bird call from his pocket. "This...," he said, "...unlike most city kids, Keiko loved to go on mountain walks. The Sunday after the week that fucking game happened she was supposed to take me bird watching." He raised the bird call between his right thumb and index finger up to his eyes and examined it as if it were a jewel. "She gave this to me." He smiled and looked at Shuya and Noriko. "This is the only thing I have left of hers. It's my lucky charm....Didn't bring much luck, I guess."

As he put it away, Noriko returned the photo. Shogo put it back in his wallet, which he tucked into his back pocket.

Noriko said, "Hey, Shogo." Shogo looked up at her. "I don't know how Keiko felt at the time. But..." She flicked her tongue against her lips to moisten them. "But I think Keiko loved you in her own way. She had to...I mean, she looks so happy in that photo. Don't you think?"

"Yeah?"

"Of course, she did." Noriko nodded. "And if I were Keiko...I would want you to live. I wouldn't want you to die for me."

Shogo grinned and shook his head. "Well, that's just a difference in opinion."

"But," Noriko insisted, "please take it into consideration. Okay, please?"

Shogo's lips moved as if he were on the verge of saying something...but then he shrugged and smiled. Sadly.

He checked his watch and went out from under the roof to tweak the bird call.

4 students remaining

73

It had stopped raining completely by the sixth time Shogo tweaked the bird call. It was now 5:55 p.m., but the light which now seemed brilliant, compared to the preceding hours, enveloped the island. They removed the thatched roof from the rock wall.

After sitting against the rock wall, the open sky up above, Noriko said, "The sky's clear." Shuya and Shogo both nodded.

A soft breeze rustled by.

Shogo put another cigarette in his mouth and lit it.

Staring at Shogo's profile, Shuya hesitated over whether he should bring it up or not. He decided to speak out. "Shogo."

The cigarette dangling from one end of his mouth, Shogo looked up.

"What about you? What did you want to be?"

Shogo snickered as he exhaled. "I wanted to be a doctor. Like my old man. That's right, I thought at least a doctor could help people, even in this fucked up country."

Shuya felt relieved. "Then why don't you become one? You're certainly talented enough."

Tapping the ashes off his cigarette, Shogo shook his head, as if to say this discussion was over.

Noriko said, "Shogo." He looked at Noriko. "I know I'm repeating myself, but I have to say it. If I were Keiko, this is what I'd say." She looked up at the sky, now tinged with orange, and continued, "Please live. Talk, think, act. And sometimes listen to music...." She stopped, then she continued, "Look at paintings at times to be moved. Laugh a lot, and at times, cry. And if you find a wonderful girl, then you go for her and love her."

It was poetic. Pure poetry.

And then Shuya thought, oh. These are Noriko's words.

And words along with music had an incredible, holy power.

Shogo listened without saying a word.

Noriko continued. "Because that's the Shogo that I really loved." Then she looked over at Shogo. She seemed slightly embarrassed, but added, "That's what I would have said."

The ash on Shogo's cigarette grew longer.

Shuya said, "Come on, Shogo. Aren't there ways to tear up this country without dying? It might be a roundabout way but still…" He continued, "I mean we got to be such good friends. We'd really miss you. Let's go to America, the three of us."

Shogo fell silent. Then realizing his cigarette was burnt down to the filter, he tossed it away. He looked up at them. He was on the verge of saying something.

Shuya thought, that's right, come with us, Shogo. We'll be together. We're a team.

"Hey—"

It was the all-too-familiar voice of Sakamochi.

Shuya quickly lifted his left arm with his right hand and checked his watch. The muddy display read 6 p.m., exactly, five seconds past the hour.

"Can you hear me? Well, I guess there aren't too many of you left who can hear. Now then, I will announce the dead. Now in the boy's group…"

Shuya was already thinking. There were only four boys left, Shuya, Shogo, Hiroki, and Kazuo Kiriyama. (Of course the same was true with the girls, Noriko, Kayoko Kotohiki, Mitsuko Souma, and Mizuho Inada.) Kazuo couldn't die so easily. And Hiroki had sent the signal. So none of the boys were dead. But…

"…we have only one. No. 11, Hiroki Sugimura."

Shuya's eyes opened wide.

4 students remaining

PART 4

FINISH
4 students remaining

74

"Now then, with the girls, the body count was pretty high. No. 1, Mizuho Inada, No. 2 Yukie Utsumi, No. 8 Kayoko Kotohiki, No. 9 Yuko Sakaki, No. 11 Mitsuko Souma, No. 12 Haruka Tanizawa, No. 16 Yuka Nakagawa, No. 17 Satomi Noda, and No. 19 Chisato Matsui."

Shuya's eyes met Noriko's. Her eyes were trembling. They had already been prepared to hear about Yukie's group, but Hiroki and Kayoko too? And Mitsuko Souma…and Mizuho Inada. Basically…did it mean the only ones left were them and Kazuo?

"That can't be—" Shuya uttered. Ever since the smoke signal went up, there hadn't been any gunfire. Or was Hiroki stabbed? Or…did he not hear Sakamochi's announcement correctly? Were his ears playing tricks on him?

No. Sakamochi continued, "All right then. Now there are four students remaining. Can you hear me, Kiriyama, Kawada, Nanahara, and Nakagawa? Wonderful work. I'm really proud of you all. Now then, I'll announce the new forbidden zones."

Before Shuya could mark his map, Shogo said, "Gather your stuff."

"Huh?" Shuya asked, but Shogo only signaled for him to hurry up. Sakamochi continued, "From 7 p.m…"

"Get up. It's Kazuo. It's likely he somehow found out about Hiroki's method to contact us. We might have been sending our signal to Kazuo all this time."

Shuya immediately got up. Noriko was carrying her day pack on her shoulders. Then right before or after Sakamochi finished his announcement saying, "All right then, do your best. Just a little more to go—" Shuya saw Shogo's eyes glance at that alarm system consisting of notches cut into thin trees wrapped with thin wire.

And then he saw this wire fall off the rain-drenched tree trunk.

"Duck!" Shogo yelled. The rattling burst through. Right above Shuya and Noriko's heads, the rock wall burst into sparks. Its shards rained down on them.

Crouched, Shogo held the Uzi and shot into the shrubs.

Maybe he was hit or maybe he wasn't, Kazuo (who else could it be now?) didn't return fire. Shogo said, "This way! Hurry!" They ran south along the rock wall away from Kazuo.

Once they reached the area beyond the rock wall where Shogo had been using the bird call, they heard a gun rattle off again. It missed them. They entered the bushes ahead.

There was a crevice in the rock waist deep, less than a meter wide. Covered with dirt and leaves, it continued southward. Shuya didn't know about its existence, but Shogo probably chose their position with this place in mind. It was a naturally formed trench. Shogo urged them on. Shuya and Noriko jumped down. Shogo rattled off his Uzi and followed them. A different rattling followed from behind. A thin tree with roots along the edge of the crevice exploded with a pop right by Shuya's head.

"Run!" Shogo shouted, and they ran down the crevice. Shuya almost tripped over a dry branch lying on the ground, but he managed to regain his footing and followed after Noriko. Behind them, the two guns exchanged shots.

Suddenly Noriko stopped as if she were hit by something. She moaned and crouched over. Shuya, who was turned towards Shogo, quickly ran to Noriko. Did she trip over something?

No. She looked up at Shuya. A cut ran under her left eye and blood gushed down her cheek. Maybe her right hand was cut too then. It was also bloody. The Browning that had been in her hand was on the ground by her feet.

Shuya put his right hand on her shoulder, looked up, and found...a thin, twisted wire stretched out across the crevice, neck-high. It didn't matter where Kazuo had found it (he'd probably unfastened the wire used to secure some object). Kazuo had already anticipated their escape by this route. At Shuya's height the wire would have cut right into his neck. At least this didn't happen to Noriko—but she could have lost her sight.

Shuya was furious. I don't know what Kazuo's about. Shogo had said, "He just chooses as he goes." I don't know if he's abnormal or normal, or a kind of genius or madman, but hurting Noriko, that was just unforgivable. I'm going to kill that motherfucker!

He tucked his CZ75 in front to help Noriko up, picked up the Browning, and then held Noriko's shoulder with the gun in his hand. Noriko staggered but managed to get up.

Shogo caught up as he fired away. He glanced back at the two of them and then—maybe he caught a glance of the wire—clenched his teeth. As he turned around again, Shuya saw beyond him Kazuo Kiriyama in his school coat jump into the crevice.

Shogo yelled, "Duck!" as he fired away. Holding his machine gun, Kazuo quickly ducked behind a curve in the crevice. Shogo's shots tore at the rock along the curve. Dust flew up.

"Run!" Shogo repeated. Shuya held Noriko up and proceeded to run under the wire. He slowed down though, in case of any more wire traps.

Shuya was frustrated. If he could only use both of his arms he could pummel Kazuo with bullets while he held Noriko.

Shogo continued firing away as he stuck close to them from behind. Kazuo also returned gunfire as he approached them.

The crevice that continued for fifty or sixty meters came to an end. Shuya leaped up to the ground before Noriko. He took Noriko's uninjured left hand and pulled her up. Noriko bravely stiffened her face to conceal her pain, but the left half of her face was now covered with blood.

"Don't stop!" Shogo yelled over the gunfire. Shuya pulled Noriko's hand and dashed into the bushes ahead.

Once they came out of the bushes, they found themselves in the front yard of a residential house built against the side of the mountain. It was an old single-story building. There was a white light truck right next to an entrance road in front of the house. For some reason there was a washer and refrigerator, both on their sides, loaded in the light truck. Were they being dumped?

"Get behind the truck!" Shogo's shouted again. Shuya and Noriko stepped onto the rain-drenched soil. Holding each other's hands, they made their way behind the truck.

By the time Shogo followed and slid in, Shuya had Noriko sit down, the Browning in his hand. He caught a glimpse of a figure moving in the shrubs. He shot several times at it. He felt a searing pain through his left shoulder, from the bullet lodged inside it. The pain sizzled, but he had to ignore it.

Shogo reloaded a magazine into his Uzi and handed it over to Shuya. He said, "Shoot away. Hold him back."

Shuya put his Browning down by his feet, took the Uzi, and fired away at the area where Kazuo appeared again.

Kazuo didn't shoot back. As Shuya peeked above the pickup truck rack, Noriko planted herself right next to him. In her hands was the Browning he had put down.

"Are you all right, Noriko?" he asked as he checked for Kazuo's movements in the shrubs.

"I'm okay," Noriko replied.

Shuya glanced beyond Noriko over at Shogo. Shogo opened the door, dove into the driver's seat, and started working on something.

With the sudden revving sound, the truck Shuya and Noriko were leaning against began to vibrate. The revving became a low hum as the water drops on the truck body began trickling with the soft vibration.

Shogo poked his head out. "Come on! We're getting out of here! Noriko, hurry!"

Shogo offered her his hand and helped her into the truck. "Shuya! The front passenger's seat!"

Shogo shouted as he started backing up the truck. He steered the wheel, backed the truck towards Kazuo, and then turned it around. The passenger's seat door was there for Shuya. Noriko opened the door.

The rattling exploded as Shuya reached out his right hand to get in. This time though, it was accompanied by a hammering sound. A hole formed in front in the truck's narrow cabin ceiling and the exiting bullet tore through the windshield from inside right in front of Shogo. Shuya leaned against the truck—he knew where Kazuo was now—pointed the Uzi upward and fired away. The shadow slipped away into the bushes surrounding the houses up in the side of the mountain. Kazuo had made his way up there.

Without a second to lose, Shuya leaped into the passenger's seat. Shogo pulled the car out. The truck slid out onto the unpaved entrance road. The machine gun rattled, shredding the hose of the washer on the rack. It thrashed in the air like a snake, fell off the car, and vanished behind them.

The gunfire ceased.

"Are you all right, Noriko?" Shuya asked.

In between Shuya and Shogo, Noriko tilted her face, covered in red, and nodded. "Yes." But her body was still tense. She still held onto the Browning. Shuya put the Uzi in his right hand between his thighs, pulled out a bandanna from his pocket, and wiped her face. Blood came pouring out of the wound, and her pink flesh showed underneath. A simple operation wasn't enough to remove the scar from this wound. To do this to a girl...

"Damn it," Shuya looked over at Shogo, who steered the wheel. "He already knew where we were a while ago. That's how he knew about our escape route."

But Shogo shook his head, saying, "No." As he quickly shifted gears to weave his way through the winding road, he said, "He couldn't have known for sure. He only figured it out at the very end. Otherwise, he would have shown up before Sakamochi's announcement. We would have come out welcoming him, thinking it was Hiroki, and then he would have easily finished us off. He didn't know where we were, so during the breaks between the bird calls he planted that wire to bide his time. He probably planted that wire in other spots too."

Shuya then thought, I see. That might have been true. To bide his time. But that was what ended up severely injuring Noriko. He said, "Noriko, show me your right hand."

Noriko then finally let go of her gun (its grip was also covered in blood) and gave Shuya her hand. It seemed small and frail, but there was a sharp tear running down between her middle and ring finger. The palm of her hand was covered with a web of blood in the pattern of the textured pistol grip. He surmised, the wire must have cut her face first and then as she fell, it must have torn through her hand she put forward as she fell. The wound might have been much more severe if the gun hadn't been in her hand.

Shuya wanted to wrap a bandanna, but realized he couldn't use his left hand.

Noriko said, "I'm okay. I'll do it." She took the bandanna from Shuya, flapped it, and spread it out, and then wrapped it around her right hand. She folded the edges and tied it up.

Then she held the Browning again.

Beyond the bullet-ridden front windshield the view suddenly opened up. The truck was descending the mountain. Under the sunset, the flat field widened between the mountainous woods.

Shuya realized something urgent and said, "Shogo. We're heading into a forbidden zone—"

"Don't worry. I know what I'm doing." Shogo answered as he looked ahead. "Did you hear? The forbidden zones are B=9 after 7 p.m., E=10 after 9 p.m., and F=4 after 11 p.m. Add those to the map."

Shuya remembered too. He pulled out the worn out map from his pocket, spread it out on his thighs, and marked off the areas while the truck shook.

The truck descended and passed by houses. It entered a road equally wide, but paved this time. The southern mountain was visible beyond the row of fields. On the right was a low hill. On the left approximately two hundred meters away was a residential house (it seemed to be in a forbidden zone). There were two more ahead slightly to its left. And then beyond were scattered houses leading up to the residential area on the island's eastern shore. In front of that region there was the field, now hidden in the shade of the low hill, where they first encountered Kazuo . One more hill over was the school, which was also hidden from view.

Shogo slowed the truck down and continued forward. And now the wide longitudinal road crossing the island was right there in front of them.

They passed through the fields and came onto the road. Shogo turned the wheel and turned it again. He stopped the truck in the middle of the road, its engine idling. Shogo then lunged at the cracked front windshield with his fist and knocked the entire window out onto the front of the truck. The glass made a shattering sound.

"Check the map," Shogo said, his hand back on the steering wheel. Shuya picked up the map again. "According to my memory we should still be able to take this road all the way east. Am I right?"

Shuya checked the map with Noriko. "Yeah, that's right. But F=4 ahead is going to be shut off at 11 p.m."

"That won't matter," Shogo said, his eyes glaring ahead. The black, rain-drenched asphalt stretched out in a straight line. "So this road should be okay right up to the eastern residential area?"

"That's right. We're fine up to the front of the curve."

Shogo nodded in response.

Shuya poked his head out of the window again and looked back. "What about Kazuo?"

Shogo looked at Shuya. "He'll be coming. How could he not? Take a close—" he said when an old, worn out, light-olive minivan suddenly appeared after turning the curve of the mountain road they'd just descended. Shuya immediately realized it was the vehicle parked by the house they had just passed by.

Shogo adjusted the rearview mirror, looked at it, and said, "See?"

It quickly closed in on them, and the moment Shuya confirmed Kazuo was sitting in the driver's seat, a burst of shots came exploding out. Shuya tucked his head back in. The bullets hit the truck with a clanging sound. Shogo shifted gears, and the truck moved out onto the wide road, heading east.

As Shuya leaned out of the window looking back, Kazuo's minivan also got on the same road. Shuya fired his Uzi. Following Kazuo's reflexes, the minivan smoothly moved to the right and dodged the shots.

"Aim good, Shuya."

By then Kazuo's minivan had sped up and caught up to them.

"Shogo! Can't you drive faster!?"

"Calm down," Shogo said and steered the wheel slowly from left to right—probably so Kazuo couldn't aim at the tires. Kazuo began shooting again, and Shuya tucked his head in. It seemed Kazuo had also smashed his windshield so he could have better control of his gun. Shuya leaned out again and fired away at Kazuo's torso. Kazuo steered away and dodged the gunfire. He hardly ducked.

The row of shells popping out of the ejection port suddenly stopped, and the Uzi trigger mechanism made a locking sound. Shuya realized he was out of bullets.

Shogo leaned over Noriko and gave him another magazine. Before Shuya could take it, Kazuo's minivan suddenly came up to them. Shuya pulled out his CZ75 and fired away. Undeterred, Kazuo came at them.

"Damn," Shogo said. His profile broke into a slight grin. "You're dead wrong if you think you can beat me driving."

Shogo suddenly made a sharp turn. He simultaneously pulled on the side brake with his left hand. Shuya was thrust to his side. The truck spun around the entire road like a car in a chase scene.

While the truck spun around, Kazuo's minivan came racing at them. The familiar rattling sound burst at them from the driver's seat. The rearview mirror shattered above Noriko's head.

"Duck!" Shogo yelled. But Shuya was busy firing away at Kazuo with his CZ75.

It was a miracle Kazuo's machine gun bullets missed Shuya. But Shuya's shots also ended up missing Kazuo too. As the truck's front bumper skimmed by the minivan's left frontside, Shuya got a close up view of the eternally frigid eyes of Kazuo Kiriyama.

The tires screeched against the wet surface. The spinning finally halted. By the time it stopped, the hunter and the hunted were reversed. Shogo had managed to dodge the front of Kazuo's minivan, completing a full spin. Kazuo's minivan was in front. Shogo immediately accelerated forward. The engine whirred away with a sudden surge of power, and the pickup lunged forward towards the back of the minivan. Kazuo was turning around.

"Fire away, Shuya! Everything you got!" Shogo yelled.

He didn't have to be told. Shuya squeezed the trigger of his reloaded Uzi with all his might and fired away with the gun on full auto. He knew the scorching, empty shells were bursting out at Noriko, but he couldn't be concerned about that. The minivan's rear windshield burst apart. Along with a popping sound, the rear hatch opened up. Then the right tire was blown out with a popping sound. Shuya was out of bullets, but the minivan was now tottering over to the edge of the road.

Shogo stepped on the gas. He pulled up to the left side of the minivan, swerved the wheel, and smashed the right side of the truck against the minivan.

The blow was hard on them, but it was nothing compared to the damage it did to Kazuo's minivan. At first, it lost control, then it slid to the right side of the road, and flew over its edge. The next moment it landed into the lower field and nosedived to the ground. Cabbage leaves flew up into the air.

Suddenly, it was still.

Shogo stopped the car parallel to the minivan and stepped on the emergency brake. He looked over its roof.

"Give me the gun, Shuya," Shogo said. Shuya gave him the Uzi. Shogo changed the magazine, extended his arm out of the window, pointed the gun at the minivan, and pulled the trigger. Shogo's hand shook vertically. Even from the front passenger's seat Shuya could tell the minivan was getting pummeled with bullets.

Shogo reloaded another magazine and fired away. He inserted another magazine and emptied that one as well. Meanwhile, Noriko was inserting spare bullets into the emptied out magazine with her wounded hand. After she was done, Shogo took that too and fired away. Noriko loaded more magazines. Slightly bent over, Shuya looked at Noriko's hands, then at Shogo's, and finally at the minivan.

They went through this round once, then twice. Because the Uzi was a 9mm weapon, they ended up using the bullets from the same caliber CZ75 and Noriko's Browning too.

The Uzi trigger device indicated the magazine was empty with a locking sound. It was out of bullets. Blue smoke drifted up from the short muzzled Uzi. The narrow cabin was filled with the odor of gunsmoke. How many bullets had Shogo fired? The Uzi Shuya had taken from Yukie's group came with five extra magazines and plenty of spare bullets, but if they were to include the bullets from the CZ75 and the Browning wouldn't the number go up to two hundred and fifty? Or three hundred?

With its left-side front passenger's seat and roof facing them, the minivan was honeycombed. It looked more like a strange beehive in the shape of a car.

The sky was orange now. Shuya couldn't bother to look at it, but judging from the light, he assumed there was a nice sunset in the western sky.

"Did you get him?" Shuya asked. Shogo was about to reply when—

The minivan proceeded to move. It was backing up. It cut across the edge of the field and backed up to the shoulder of the road. Once again, towards the back of their truck.

Shuya was speechless. Not only was the van's engine still functioning, Kazuo was still alive and operating the vehicle. Shogo had wagered everything by emptying their entire bullet supply and yet…Kazuo was still alive!

Beyond the bullet-ridden vehicle, Kazuo's upper body sprung up like a jack-in-the-box. With a machine gun. With the rattling sound, the small window above Noriko's head shattered. Two holes were punctured into the steel board next to it. The truck was a domestic model made of flimsy steel, so Shuya was surprised it had actually remained unscathed this long. This also might have been thanks to the washer and refrigerator lying on the rack. Or maybe, Shogo had loaded them, anticipating this situation.

"Damn it!" Shogo shifted gears and moved the car out. "Shoot, Shuya! Back me up!"

Shuya fired his CZ75 at Kazuo's minivan. Kazuo fired back, the bullets landing right next to Shuya's face as sparks flew from the steel frame of the truck.

Shuya immediately emptied his gun. He changed the magazine and fired. Then he realized, once I shoot this round, I'm out of bullets. We'll only have Noriko's Browning and her extra magazine. That's it.

While he hesitated, Kazuo fired. He heard the rattle. A zinging sound. More sparks this time from the refrigerator on the rack. The small door on the freezer swung open and fell out.

"Shogo! I'm out of bullets!"

Shogo calmly steered the wheel. "His machine gun will be useless too. He doesn't have time to reload it."

Just as Shogo said, single shots came at them now. BLAM, POP. The seat by Noriko's shoulder exploded.

"Noriko! Get down!" Shuya yelled, stuck his arm out of the window, pointed at Kazuo, who now held a gun in one hand, and fired. He was out of bullets. He took the Browning from Noriko's hand. He fired again.

To the left of the pickup, between the houses and the field, was a warehouse burnt to the ground. That must have been what Shogo had been referring to, the building that went up in flames in the late night explosion. Now they had less than two hundred meters before hitting the curve that led to the residential area on the eastern side of the island.

"Hey, Shogo, that's—"

Shogo replied, "I know," and swerved the wheel to the left. The left side of the truck under Shuya's body floated up. But once it regained its balance, the truck leaped onto the unpaved road. It was another road twisting through the fields, heading back up to the northern mountain. Kazuo followed after them in the minivan.

Shuya aimed and fired. Kazuo ducked and fired away. This time the steel board right next to Shogo's head was punctured.

"Shuya! Just keep on shooting until you're out! Don't let him shoot!" Shogo yelled, hunched over the wheel. Shuya noticed the left shoulder of his school coat was torn and bleeding. He'd been hit by Kazuo.

Shuya was about to protest, but he leaned out of the window and fired. Shogo might plan on escaping into the mountain again. If so, then the thing was to make sure Kazuo couldn't shoot. Or by some stroke of luck, maybe I'll end up hitting him—

He fired.

And now the Browning was emptied out, the breechblock held open. He was out of bullets.

They were approaching the mountain. A familiar sight. Strangely enough, there was a farmhouse surrounded by a concrete wall. And a field. A tractor.

Shuya realized this was where they first fought against Kazuo. But now they were on the opposite side.

"Shogo, I'm out of bullets! Are we escaping into the mountain!?"

Shuya could make out Shogo's profile breaking into a slight grin. He replied, "Oh, we still got bullets."

Shuya knit his brows, puzzled.

The truck ran off the entrance road that led to the farmhouse and dashed onto the ridge road. He passed by the side of the tractor. The road ahead became too narrow for the truck.

Shogo didn't seem to care and drove the truck straight ahead. Kazuo came after them, maintaining the same distance behind—only twenty meters. He fired from the driver's seat.

The truck dove into the farm and stopped. The side of the front passenger's seat where Shuya sat now faced Kazuo. Shogo kicked open the door and yelled, "Get out, this way!" He jumped out of the car.

Shuya nudged Noriko, crouched down and followed them. He glanced back. Kazuo's minivan was coming right at them!

There was a blast.

The left front tire of Kazuo's minivan was blown off. It was only ten meters in front of them.

The minivan tottered…and slid along the ridge of the elevated field on the left, and its front went up in the air like a surfboard taking on a large wave. The next moment it rolled over on its roof into the field.

Right before or after the minivan came to a complete halt, a black shadow leaped out. By the time it somersaulted and came to a kneeling position, Shuya could see it was Kazuo. Sparks flew out from his hands with a continuous popping noise. Then there was another blast.

Shuya was still inside the truck as he saw it through the window of the passenger's seat: the sight of Kazuo Kiriyama's body being blown back like an arrow.

Kazuo landed on the field with a thud. He was completely still.

Shuya suddenly recalled the way Kyoichi Motobuchi had

died. His sausage-factory trash-bin stomach. Kazuo was too far away to check the condition of his stomach. Still, given how he was pummeled with shotgun pellets, there was no way he could have been alive.

Then Shuya finally emerged from the truck. He saw Shogo holding that shotgun—the one Shuya had tossed into the field when he was running away from Kazuo—as he rose from behind the truck rack.

"Oh, we still got bullets." Shogo had picked up the shotgun Shuya tossed away yesterday, loaded the shotgun cartridges he still had (he must have only been able to load two shots in that span of time), and fired away...and shot down Kazuo.

"Right at the beginning...," Shogo said slowly, "...he missed us with his surprise attack. So he lost. Because then he had to take on all three of us."

He took a deep breath, put down the shotgun which thumped against the refrigerator on the truck rack, and took out a pack of Wild Sevens from his pocket. He took one out and lit it.

"You're bleeding, Shogo," Noriko said, pointing at his left shoulder.

"Yeah." Shogo glanced at his wound and then grinned. "It's nothing." He exhaled.

Bang. Shogo's body bent over. The Wild Seven cigarette fell from his mouth, leaving a trace of smoke in the air. The stubbly face contorted. His eyes gazed down at Shuya's feet.

Shuya saw Kazuo's raised torso on the lower field, holding a gun in his right hand. He was still alive! But his stomach had been pummeled by the shotgun blast!

Shogo's body slowly caved in. Kazuo quickly pointed his gun at Shuya. Shuya realized that he was, along with Shogo, no longer behind the truck. He had no gun in his hand. No, he had no bullets. It was too late for him to reload the shotgun on the truck rack. It was way too late.

The small muzzle of Kazuo's gun a good ten meters away looked like a giant tunnel. A black hole engulfing everything.

Bang. Shuya instantly closed his eyes. He felt a piercing sensation run through his chest and thought, oh, man, I'm dying.

He opened his eyes.

He wasn't dead.

There was Kazuo in the diagonal orange light of the setting sun, a red dot punctured by his nose. The gun fell from his hand. He immediately fell back and crashed onto the ground.

Shuya slowly turned his head to his left. Noriko was standing, holding the Smith & Wesson .38 caliber revolver with both of her hands.

Wow. So that's what it was. While Shogo loaded the shotgun, Noriko had also loaded the revolver Shuya had tossed aside yesterday with her remaining .38 Special bullets.

Noriko's hands were trembling with the gun.

"Huh." Shogo stood up before Shuya could even help him up.

Shuya nervously asked, "Are you all right?"

Shogo didn't respond. He picked up the shotgun, and as he loaded it with the cartridges in his pocket, he walked toward Kazuo. Exactly two meters in front of him, he pointed the gun at Kazuo's head and pulled the trigger. Kazuo's head flinched only once.

Shogo turned on his heels and came back.

"Are you all right?" Shuya asked him again.

"Yeah, I'm fine."

Shogo walked over to Noriko, gently held her hands, still holding the Smith & Wesson, and lowered them. He quietly said, "He's dead. I'm the one who killed him, not you." Then he looked over at Kazuo. "So he was wearing a vest," he said.

Shuya then finally understood. Kazuo Kiriyama had been wearing a bulletproof vest.

"Shogo," Noriko asked, her voice slightly trembling. "Are you really all right?"

Shogo smiled kindly and nodded. "I'm all right. Thanks, Noriko." Then he took out his pack of cigarettes again. It seemed empty so he looked around and picked up the lit cigarette which had fallen from his mouth, and slowly raised it to his mouth.

Shuya turned around and stared out at the sun setting over the island. It was over. At least this wonderful game was. And now, including Kazuo Kiriyama over there, thirty-nine of their dead classmates were lying sprawled all over the island.

Shuya had that dizzy spell again. Maybe his thoughts were numbed by this hollow feeling. What the hell was this all about?

Faces flashed by one by one. Yoshitoki Kuninobu's face as he shouted, "I'll kill you!" Shinji Mimura's face grinning slightly as Shuya left. Tatsumichi Oki's face as he swung the axe with bloodshot eyes. Hiroki Sugimura who vanished into the dark outside the medical clinic, saying, "I have to see Kayoko Kotohiki," Hirono Shimizu as she ran away from Shuya after shooting down Kaori Minami. The tearful Yukie Utsumi saying, "I just wouldn't know what to do if you died." Yuko Sakaki, who pried Shuya's fingers loose. Then the cold eyes of Kazuo Kiriyama, who'd cornered them until now.

They were all gone. Not just everyone's lives, but so many other things were destroyed.

But it wasn't over yet.

"Shogo," Shuya said. Shogo looked up, shortened cigarette in hand. "We should treat you."

Shogo smiled. "I'm all right. It's nothing. Take care of

Noriko's wounds." Then he said, "I'm going to collect Kazuo's weapons." He walked over to the overturned minivan.

3 students remaining

75

Shogo led the way up the mountain. The weapons he picked out of Kazuo's assortment were tossed into the day pack on his shoulders. He didn't offer them to Noriko or Shuya. It wasn't necessary for the time being.

Shuya followed Shogo as he held Noriko up on his left side. They had cleaned Noriko's cheek wound with water for now and covered it with a row of four band-aids. Shogo said they were better off not stitching it. Shuya cleaned her hand wound and wrapped it again with the bandanna. Shogo had also quickly taken care of his wounds.

It was already getting dim in the mountains, but there was no need to make their way through bushes, so it was relatively easy to climb. The ground strewn with piles of leaf mold was damp from an entire afternoon of rain.

They had covered quite a distance ever since Shogo announced, "We're climbing the mountain," and proceeded forward.

"Shogo," Shuya called. Shogo turned around. "Where are we going?"

Shogo grinned. "We have just a little more to go. Just follow me."

Shuya readjusted his arm on Noriko and followed him.

The peak with the viewing platform where Yukiko Kitano and Yumiko Kusaka were killed and its southern side had become a forbidden zone a long time ago. Shogo stopped right before they entered that area, in the upper mid-region of the mountain. Come to think of it, Shuya thought, a little ways below I saw Hirono Shimizu shoot Kaori Minami.

"This should do it," Shogo said.

The slope and woods ended here, and the area offered a good view. They could see the entire island, now immersed in dim blue after sunset, where the fierce battle between the classmates of Third Year Class B Shiroiwa Junior High School took place. However, the school holding their final enemy, Sakamochi, was hidden by hills.

Shuya took a deep breath. Then he asked, "What's up here anyway? How are we going to escape?"

Shogo smiled without looking at Shuya. Then he said, "Relax. Take a look over there."

Shuya and Noriko looked over where Shogo was pointing.

It was over the southern mountain. Although it was growing dim, they could still make out the ocean, several islands, and beyond, the mainland. Shuya could make out a mist of lights scattered over the mainland. If they were closer, they could have discerned which ones were neon lights and which ones were lights along the shore highway.

Now Shuya also knew that this was Okishima Island in the Takamatsu-shi Bay. There were two others islands, Megijima and Ogijima, forming a vertical row of islands, where Okishima was the one at the far northern tip. Which meant that the small island beyond the southern mountain was Megijima, and beyond that was Ogijima, and beyond that was the mainland—Kagawa Prefecture of Shikoku.

Shogo said, "It's not very familiar to me, but that's your home over there. Shiroiwa-cho must be over there. You won't see it again, so have a good look."

Did he mean they'd never return because they were escaping the country? Still…

Shuya looked back at Shogo. "Don't tell me we came all

the way up here for this."

Shogo snickered. "Hey, what's the rush?" Then he said, "Show me your gun. There's something I need to check."

Noriko handed over her Smith & Wesson to Shogo. He opened up its cylinder and checked it. Shuya thought Noriko had reloaded it after taking that single shot at Kazuo.

Shogo didn't return the gun and instead held it in his right hand. He took a deep breath and said, "Do you remember how I kept on saying I might be doing this just to have a group, and that my intention might be to kill you off in the end?"

Shuya raised his brow. Yes, you said that, but?…

"Yeah, but?…"

"So," Shogo said, "you both lose."

Shogo pointed the Smith & Wesson at them.

3 students remaining

76

Shuya felt a strange expression forming on his face. As if he were grinning and bewildered at the same time. Noriko probably felt the same way.

"What is this?" Shuya said. "It's not such a great time to be joking right now."

"I'm serious," Shogo said and cocked the hammer.

Shuya's grin vanished. His right arm felt Noriko stiffen.

Shogo continued, "You can enjoy the view a little more. I told you, it'd be the last time." His stubbly face broke into a slight grin. It was a sinister grin he'd never shown before.

A crow cawed. Was it flying up above in the darkening evening sky?

Shuya finally spoke. His feelings were out of sync with the

situation, he could only croak out pathetically, "What? What are you talking about?"

"You are so thick," Shogo responded with a shrug. "I'm going to kill you both. I'll be the winner. My second in a row."

Shuya's lips were trembling. No. This can't be.

He stuttered, "Come on…stop it. Then…then you were just acting until now? You…you looked after us. You helped us so many times."

Shogo replied calmly, "You're the ones who helped me. I probably couldn't have killed Kazuo without your help."

"Then…so that story about Keiko was a lie too!?" His words trembled. The more he tried to keep his voice down the louder it became.

"Yep," Shogo answered curtly. "It was true I participated in the Hyogo Prefecture Program last year, and it's true there was a girl named Keiko Onuki. But there was nothing between us. The girl in that photo's my girlfriend, but her name's Kyoka Shimazaki, a totally different person. She's still in Kobe. She's out of her mind….Well, anyway, she insisted I hold onto this photo. I got to say she was a good lay, though."

Shuya took a deep breath. A light early summer breeze blew against his skin, but for some reason it felt chilly. Then he cautiously asked, "But what about that bird call?…"

Shogo had another curt response. "I just happened to find that at the general supply store. I figured it'd be useful. And it proved to be, in the end."

It grew darker and darker.

Shogo continued, "You lost the moment you trusted me," but Shuya still couldn't believe it. That can't be. That just…can't be. Then something occurred to Shuya. This…must be…

Noriko spoke out before Shuya, "Shogo…is this some test

to see whether you can really trust us? Is it because Keiko couldn't trust you?"

Shogo shrugged his shoulders and said, "Unbelievable how you still believe in that fairy tale."

Those were his last words. Shogo held the gun in his hand and slowly pulled the trigger.

Two gunshots rang out as evening descended upon the island.

1 student remaining—GAME OVER—Report from Third Year Class B Shiroiwa Junior High School Program Headquarters Tracking System

77

Shogo Kawada (Male Student No. 5) reclined against the soft sofa on the ship. He was swaying slightly from the rough waves.

The room was fairly spacious for a small patrol ship. The ceiling itself was low, but the room must have been a couple square meters. There was a low table in the middle, and two sofas on each side, with Shogo sitting on the one away from the door.

Because the room was below deck it had no windows, so he couldn't see anything outside, but it must have been past 8:30 p.m. by now. The yellow ceiling lights shined against the glass ashtray. Shogo didn't have any more cigarettes to smoke, though.

Once the forbidden zones were all deactivated after the game was over, Shogo obeyed Sakamochi's announcements and made his way to the school. In front of the school were the bodies of Yoshio Akamatsu and Mayumi Tendo, and inside the classroom, the bodies of Yoshitoki Kuninobu and

Fumiyo Fujiyoshi, all left untouched.

His silver collar was finally detached, and after the shooting for the news segment, he was taken away by soldiers and escorted to the harbor. There were two ships docked there. One for the winner…and the other a transport ship to return the soldiers packed inside the school. Most of the soldiers boarded this ship. Only the trio who were in the classroom during Sakamochi's game instructions joined Sakamochi to board Shogo's ship. And tomorrow the subcontracted clean-up crew would take care of the remaining bodies of the students on the island. The speakers and school computers at the school building would also be dismantled in a matter of days. Of course the software and data for the game had already been removed from the computer. This was the identical procedure taken immediately after the Kobe Second District Junior High School Program came to an end ten months ago.

And now Shogo was waiting here. They were now south of Okishima. The patrol ship was returning directly to Takamatsu Harbor, but the soldiers' transport ship would probably alter its course and head west towards the military base.

The doorknob rotated with a click. The soldier who stood guard (the uncharismatic one called "Nomura") by the door looked in, then moved away. Kinpatsu Sakamochi appeared. He came in with a tray with two teacups and asked, "Did I keep you waiting, Shogo?" as he entered the room. Nomura closed the door.

Sakamochi walked up to him with his short legs. He put the tray on the table and said, "Here. It's tea. Drink all you want." He took out a flat, letter-sized envelope from under his left armpit and sat on the sofa facing Shogo. He tossed the envelope onto his side of the table, then combed back his shoulder-length hair behind his ear.

Shogo glanced down at the envelope indifferently and began speaking while staring at Sakamochi. "What do you want? I wish you'd leave me alone. I'm tired."

"There you go...." Sakamochi brought the cup to his mouth with a grimace. "You should be more polite with adults. I had this student Kato once. He used to give me a hard time, but now that he's grown up, he's quite respectable."

"I'm not one of your pigs."

Sakamochi opened his eyes as if taken aback and then smiled again. "Come, come, Shogo. I wanted to have a nice chat with you."

Shogo slouched against the sofa and folded his legs. He remained quiet as he rested his cheeks in his hands.

"Where should I begin?" Sakamochi put his cup down and rubbed his open hands together. "That's right." His eyes glimmered. "Did you know we have a betting pool for the Program, Shogo?"

Shogo squinted his eyes as if looking at filth. Then he said, "I wouldn't be surprised. You guys are tasteless."

Sakamochi smiled. "I had my money on Kazuo. Twenty thousand yen. With my salary, that's a lot. But thanks to you, I lost."

"Too bad," Shogo said in a tone devoid of sympathy.

Sakamochi smiled again. Then he said, "I explained how I could tell where everyone was with those collars, right?"

The answer was obvious. Shogo didn't respond.

Sakamochi stared at Shogo. "You were with Shuya and Noriko throughout the game, right? Then you betrayed them in the end. That's what it came down to, right?"

"What's wrong with that?" Shogo replied. "There are no restrictions in this wonderful game. Don't make me laugh. You can't criticize me for that."

A broad grin spread over Sakamochi's face. He combed

back his hair, took a sip of tea, and rubbed his hands. He spoke as if he were sharing a secret, "Hey, Shogo. I'm not really supposed to be sharing this with anyone, but I'll tell you the truth. These collars have built-in mics, so we could hear everything the students said during the game. I bet you probably didn't know that."

Shogo, who seemed so indifferent in his responses, finally seemed interested. He knit his brows and pursed his lips. "How the fuck...would I know about that?" he said. "So then you heard everything, how I tricked them."

"Uh huh, that's right." Sakamochi nodded. "But that wasn't very nice, Shogo. Was it. 'Even if we managed to capture Sakamochi, I'm sure as far as the government's concerned he's expendable'? You said that. Being a Program Instructor is a pretty respectable occupation. Not everyone can do it."

Ignoring Sakamochi's complaint, Shogo asked, "Why are you telling me this?"

"Oh, I don't know," Sakamochi replied. "With your wonderful performance I couldn't resist telling you."

"This is bullshit."

Shogo looked away, but Sakamochi pressed more insistently, "A wonderful performance, but..." Shogo looked back at him. Sakamochi continued, "...there's something I don't get."

"What's that?"

"Why didn't you shoot those two right after Kazuo was killed? You could have, right? That's the one thing I just don't get."

"Just as I told them," Shogo, replied without hesitating, "I just thought I'd let them have one last look at their home. A little gift for them before their descent into hell. You may not believe this, but I can be pretty loyal. I mean, thanks to them, I won."

Sakamochi continued smiling and uttered, "Hmmm." Then he raised his cup to his mouth. He sat back on the back of the sofa with the cup in his hand and spoke again, "Hey, Shogo, I got hold of the data on the Kobe Second District Junior High School Program." Then he stared at Shogo. Shogo stared back at him and remained silent. "And as far as I can tell from the data, nothing indicates you had any special relationship with Keiko Onuki."

"Onuki? Like I said I made that up," Shogo interrupted him, but Sakamochi spoke over him and continued, "As—" Shogo shut up.

"As you said, to Shuya Nanahara and Noriko Nakagawa, you saw Onuki twice—the first time only for a moment and then the second time right before you won, when she was already dead. Even according to the taped conversations, you never even once uttered her name. Not once. Do you remember that?"

"How could I? It's like I said—there was nothing between me…and her. You heard me, right?"

"But the thing is, Shogo, the second time around you stopped there for two hours."

"That was just a coincidence. It was a good spot to hide and rest. That's how I was able to remember that name so vividly. I tell you, she died a horrible death."

His grin still glued across his face, Sakamochi nodded, hm hm. "The other thing is…the entire eighteen hours which transpired in this game—which is actually quite fast, maybe the designated area was too small—in any case, you didn't exchange a single word with anyone. I mean, aside from saying things like, 'Stop' or 'I'm not an enemy.' "

"That was just an act too," Shogo interrupted him. "It's so obvious."

Sakamochi smiled, ignoring Shogo's statement. "So I have no idea how you approached this game. You moved around a lot but—"

"It was my first time. I didn't know how to play it smart."

Sakamochi then nodded, hm hm. He held back a grin as if concealing his amusement. He sipped his tea and returned the cup to the table. Then he looked up and said, "By the way...what about that photo? I'd like to look at it, if you don't mind."

"Photo?"

"Come on, you showed it to Nanahara and Nakagawa, right? You said it was a photo of Onuki. Let me see it. It was actually a photo of someone named Shimazaki, right?"

Shogo twisted his mouth. "Why should I show it to you?"

"Come on, just show it to me. I'm your instructor. Please. Come on, please," Sakamochi said and bowed over the table.

Shogo reluctantly reached around and searched his back pocket. He raised his brow and swung his hand back. It was empty.

"It's gone," he said. "I must've dropped it somewhere when we fought Kazuo."

"Dropped it?"

"Uh huh. It's true. I dropped my wallet. Well, I don't need it anyway."

Suddenly, Sakamochi burst out laughing. As he laughed he said, "I get it." He held his stomach, slapped his thighs, and kept on laughing.

Shogo looked perplexed...but then he squinted his eyes. He looked up at the ceiling in the windowless room.

Despite the insulation of the patrol ship's walls, he could hear the faint but definite whirring sound. It was definitely not the sound of the ship's engine.

The sound became louder and louder...and then after a certain point, it receded. Then it was almost entirely gone.

Shogo grimaced.

"Does that trouble you, Shogo?" He stopped laughing. He

still had that creepy smile on his face, though. "That was a helicopter." He reached out for his tea again and emptied his cup. He put the empty cup on the table. "It's heading toward the island where you all fought."

Shogo knit his brows, but this time his reaction seemed to have a different connotation. But Sakamochi didn't care. He arrogantly leaned back on the sofa and changed the subject, "Hey, Shogo. Let's talk about those collars again. Well, you know, they're actually called 'Guadalcanal No. 22.' That doesn't matter. Anyway, weren't you telling Shuya about how they couldn't be dismantled?"

Seeing how Shogo didn't respond, Sakamochi continued, "In fact, your theory was right on the mark. Each unit is equipped with three different systems, so even if one of them has a one percent margin of error, with three systems, only one in a million can break down. In reality, the chances are even slimmer. So, it's just like you said. No one can escape from them. Any attempt to remove it will ignite it, killing its wearer. It's very rare someone actually tries that, though."

Shogo still remained silent.

"The thing is...," Sakamochi then leaned over, "...I just thought I'd get in touch with the Defense Forces weapons lab this time around. And guess what?" He looked at Shogo. "They said it could be deactivated by anyone with a basic knowledge in electronics, using basic transistor parts, the kind you find in a radio. Of course, that's assuming you already know the circuitry inside the device."

Shogo stayed quiet, but as Sakamochi's continued staring at him, he suddenly said in a strange, blank tone of voice as if the thought suddenly occurred to him, "I don't get it. Who could possibly have that information?"

Sakamochi grinned and nodded. He continued, "Yes. Well, anyway, if we were to assume the collar was disabled, then obviously it would transmit a signal informing us of the wearer's death, right? In other words, if there was a student who could remove that collar, then he could survive without a hitch. He'd just have to wait out the game, and once the military leaves the premises he could take his time escaping. That's right, just like you said to Shuya Nanahara. Say the game were to end in the afternoon, then the subcontracted clean-up crew comes the following day. So there's plenty of time in between. Also, this time of year the water isn't too cold to swim in."

Sakamochi gave Shogo an imploring look, but Shogo only responded with a "Huh." Sakamochi leaned back on the sofa. "This is absurd. The collar circuits are supposed to be top secret, right? How could a junior high school kid possibly know about it?"

Sakamochi replied, "He could, though." Shogo looked back at Sakamochi. "See, all of this information, including your records, and the Guadalcanal device, under normal circumstances I wouldn't have looked up any of this stuff. I would have just sat back, impressed by your intelligence. This time though, I was contacted by Dictator Headquarters and the Special Defense Forces before the game began. I mean, on the twentieth."

Shogo stared at Sakamochi.

Sakamochi continued, "They said someone hacked into the government's central operations system in March." He paused. Then he added, "Of course, the hacker thought he managed to leave without a trace. He was incredibly skilled, and although he encountered the administrator while he was hacking, he managed to erase his log-in access before escaping. But…"

Sakamochi paused again. Shogo kept quiet.

"…the government system has tight security. It has a another secret log-in system that records every operation. Of course, they usually don't monitor this system, and the administrator didn't think there was anything abnormal at the time. That's why they took so long to discover it. But they found it. Yes, they did."

Shogo sealed his lips and stared at Sakamochi. But his Adam's apple moved ever so slightly. The movement was hardly discernible.

"Look," Shogo said. "A subcontractor really did tell me about rounding up the corpses. I was having a few drinks at this bar with him. The topic just came up. And the instructor from our last game told us the Program hardly ever ends from just time running out. You can even ask him."

Sakamochi rubbed his right hand under his nose and stared at Shogo. "Why are you telling me this? I didn't even ask you about that."

Shogo's Adam's apple moved again. This time it definitely moved.

Sakamochi then snickered and continued, "So apparently some of the hacked data included information on the Program. In other words, technical specifications on the Guadalcanal collar. Why would someone take such useless information? I mean, what's the point? Even if the hacker were to publicize it, the government would only design a new collar, and that would be the end of that. There's no sign of that for now. But maybe we can assume this much: the intruder was driven to access this information at all cost. Don't you think?"

Shogo didn't respond. Sakamochi sighed and picked up the envelope he'd tossed out. He flipped it over with one hand and pulled out the contents. He placed them side by side in front of Shogo.

There were two photos. They were both black and white and printed on B5 paper. One of them had no contrast at all, so it was hard to tell what it was, but the other one clearly showed a truck and three black dots scattered around it. Given how it was the top of a truck, the three dots were obviously heads.

"You see, right?" Sakamochi said. "That's the three of you just a while ago. Right after you killed Kazuo. Those were taken by satellite. We don't usually do this kind of thing. But I want you to take a closer at this other photo. See? You can't really make out anything, right? But that's actually a photo of the mountain. It was taken when you shot those two. There wasn't enough light, and it's obscure because you're all hidden by the woods. That's right, you can't see it."

He fell silent. The ship swayed a little, but Shogo and Sakamochi stared at each other, completely still.

Then Sakamochi took a deep breath and once again combed back his hair behind his ear. He broke into a smile and spoke in a strangely intimate voice, "Say, Shogo. I've been keeping track of this game from the very beginning. Right? After you shot Shuya Nanahara and Noriko Nakagawa, Nanahara took fifty-four seconds to die, while Nakagawa ended up taking one minute and thirty seconds to die. They should have died instantly if you shot them point blank. So what's this time lag about?"

Shogo was silent, but—whether he was aware of it or not—his cheeks stiffened. He managed to speak out, "It can happen. I'd have thought they died immediately but—"

"Enough." Sakamochi cut him off. He said in an adamant voice, "Let's put an end to this." He looked into Shogo's eyes and nodded as if admonishing him. Then he said, "Shuya Nanahara and Noriko Nakagawa are still on that island. They're still alive, right? They're hiding in the mountain. You're the one who hacked into the government central system. Or one of your friends. You knew how to dismantle that collar. You knew we could monitor your conversations, so you gave us that radio drama performance of shooting those two. Then you removed their collars. Am I right? I didn't say it *was* a wonderful performance. You're still in the middle of that wonderful performance."

Shogo gazed at Sakamochi. He grimaced through clenched teeth.

Sakamochi kept on smiling and continued, "Didn't you give them some messages about meeting spots? And you were supposed to hook up together later, right? Well, you can forget about that. That helicopter that just flew by is going to spray the island with poison gas. It's a composite poison mustard gas developed recently called Greater East Asia Victory No. 2. The guard ships are still over there. Nanahara and Nakagawa are finished."

As he stared at Sakamochi, Shogo dug his fingers into the synthetic leather elbow rest. Sakamochi took another deep breath and sank back into the sofa. He combed back his hair. "We have no precedent for this. Strictly speaking, you're not really the winner. But one of the education committee officials I work for bet a lot of money on you. So I decided to treat this internally. It'll help my career if I help him out...therefore, you'll be the official winner. According to the records, you'll be the killer of those two....Are you satisfied now, Shogo?"

Shogo was utterly stiff, as if he might start shaking any second now. But as Sakamochi raised his brow, Shogo looked away from him and stared down at the floor. "I...don't know what you're talking about...." he said. He nervously opened and then clenched his fist several times. He glanced back at Sakamochi and then anxiously said, "Why bother spraying gas? You're just wasting tax money."

Sakamochi snickered. "We'll soon see whether I am." Then he said, "Oh, that's right." He pulled out a small automatic pistol from under his coat and pointed it at Shogo. Shogo opened his eyes wide. "I've decided to take care of you as an internal matter too. You have dangerous ideas. I think it's against this country's interests if we let someone like you live. Have to toss the rotten apple out of the box. The sooner the better. You arrive DOA due to injuries from the game. How's that? Oh, don't you worry. If you happen to have friends too, we'll hunt them down. We won't have to interrogate you."

Shogo slowly tore his eyes away from the gun and looked at Sakamochi. "You…," he said. He was now baring his teeth. Sakamochi broke into a grin. "Bastard!" Shogo howled in a voice full of indignation, despair, probably mixed in with a dose of fear towards everything incomprehensible. What he wanted to do most was grab Sakamochi by the neck. But the gun restrained him. He could only clench his fists over his thighs.

"Don't you…don't you have any kids? How can you accept this fucked up game?"

"Of course I have kids," Sakamochi replied casually. "You know, I like to have a good time, so we're about to have our third."

Shogo didn't respond to the joke, yelling instead, "Then…how can you accept this? One of your kids might end up in this game in the future! Or…or is it that…kids of high-ranked officials like you are exempted?"

Offended, Sakamochi shook his head. "That's preposterous. How can you say that, Kawada? You read the Program Requirements, right? There are no exceptions. Of course I've done some sneaky things. Using connections to get my kid into a prestigious school. I'm human. But being human also means we have to abide by certain rules…oh, that's right, you weren't able to steal that, huh? The top secret agenda also had information on the Program. I'll tell you now, this country needs the Program. The thing is, it's not an experiment at all. Come on, why do you think we have the local news broadcast the image of the winner? Of course, viewers might feel sorry for him or her, thinking, the poor student probably didn't even want to play the game, but had no choice but to fight the others. In other words, everyone ends up concluding, you can't trust anyone, right? Which would extinguish any hope of uniting and forming a coup d'etat against the government, hm? And so the Republic of Greater East Asia and its ideals will live on for eternity. Naturally everyone has to die equally for the sake of this noble goal. I've passed this wisdom onto my kids. My oldest kid is in the second grade now and she's always saying how she'll sacrifice her life for the Republic."

Shogo's cheeks began to tremble. "You're...insane," he said, "You're out of your mind! How can you be like that?" He was nearly sobbing. "A government is supposed to serve the needs of the people. We shouldn't be slaves to our own system. If you think this country makes sense...then you're insane!"

Sakamochi let him finish. Then he said, "Hey, Kawada. You're still a kid. It looks like you guys had some talks, but I want you to think a little more. This is a marvelous country. It's the most prosperous country in the world. Well, you might not be able to travel abroad much, but its industrial exports are unsurpassed. The government's slogan is telling the truth when it claims our per capita production is the best in the world. The thing is though, this prosperity only comes as a result of unifying the population with a powerful government at the center. A certain degree of control is always necessary. Otherwise...we'll decline into a third-rate country, like the American Empire. You know, right? That country is in turmoil from all kinds of problems like drugs, violence, and homosexuality. They're living off their past glory, but it'll only be a matter of time before they fall apart."

Shogo remained silent. He clenched his teeth. Then he

spoke quietly, "Let me say one thing."

Sakamochi raised his brow. "What? Go ahead."

"You guys might call it prosperity, but…" Shogo's voice sounded tired, but still dignified. "…it'll always be phony. That truth won't change even if you kill me now. You're doomed to be phony. Don't forget…that."

Sakamochi shrugged his shoulders. "Are you done with your speech?" He pointed his gun at him. Shogo tightened his mouth and glared at Sakamochi, ignoring the gun. He seemed ready to face the consequences.

"Later, Kawada." Sakamochi nodded as if to bid him farewell. Then his finger began pulling the trigger when—

BRRRATTA…the tapping, typewriter-like sound pierced through the room.

Sakamochi's finger stopped for a moment. He glanced at the door for a split second…long enough to be distracted. By the time he looked back Shogo was right in front of his face. Even though there was a table in between them, he was only ten centimeters away. He'd moved instantly, like a magician, as if he'd teleported.

The rattling sound continued outside the room.

Shogo's left hand held down the gun in Sakamochi's right hand. Sakamochi froze up and looked up at Shogo's face, now within kissing distance. His long hair wasn't too messy. He didn't try to swing his hand loose from Shogo. He merely looked at Shogo with his mouth closed.

The rattling sound again.

The door opened. "An attack—" Nomura stopped once he grasped the situation and attempted to lift his rifle.

Still holding Sakamochi's right hand down with his left hand, Shogo spun Sakamochi's body around as if dancing a tango. As he turned, he squeezed Sakamochi's index finger on the trigger and began firing away. Three shots pierced Nomura right above his heart. He groaned and collapsed. The rattling sounded louder now, with the door open.

Shogo looked into Sakamochi's eyes again. Their bodies still entwined, he drove his right fist under Sakamochi's chin.

Sakamochi coughed out blood. His eyes stared up at Shogo. The blood spilled from his lips, dripping down to his chin and onto the floor.

"I told you, it was a waste of tax money." Shogo twisted his fist further into Sakamochi's chin. Sakamochi's eyes rolled away from Shogo. Then they slowly rolled upwards.

Shogo moved away from Sakamochi, and Sakamochi crashed onto the sofa. His throat was now exposed. A brown stick poked out of his windpipe like a strange ornament. Closer up, the gold logo, "HB," on its butt-end was visible. This was one of those pencils that everyone, including Shogo and Shuya, had written, "We will kill each other," but Kinpatsu Sakamochi probably had no idea.

After glancing down at Sakamochi he tucked the gun into his belt. He dashed over to Nomura, who was lying face up, and picked up his rifle. He took the extra magazines from his belt and left the room. He opened the two doors down the corridor on the right, but there were only rows of bunk beds. No one was inside.

The rattling was approaching him. A soldier came tumbling down the stairs beyond the narrow corridor. Unarmed except for the gun in his hand—maybe he'd thought he was safe now that the game was over—it was the soldier Kondo, now dead.

Shogo stepped around Kondo's body, entered the staircase, and looked up.

There was Shuya Nanahara (Male Student No. 15) holding an Ingram M10, standing next to Noriko Nakagawa (Female Student No. 15). They both looked down at him. They were soaking wet.

78

"Shogo!"

Seeing that Shogo was safe, Shuya cried in relief. Upon hearing the gunfire besides his shots, he thought they might have been too late.

Shogo ran upstairs with a rifle he'd taken from one of the soldiers.

"So you're all right?"

"Yeah." Shogo nodded. "Sakamochi's dead. Did you get rid of everyone?"

"We got everyone on deck. But we couldn't find that one called Nomura—"

"Then that's everyone. I got rid of Nomura," he said. He passed by them and ran to the bridge where the pilothouse was located.

There was one body lying in the corridor leading to the pilothouse, then two more inside and outside the briefing room under the pilothouse. One of them was the soldier Tahara, the others were the ship's naval crew, but Tahara was the only with a gun, and it was only a pistol. Shuya had blown them away with the Ingram. There were two others lying on deck, the first naval soldiers Shuya killed.

After glancing at Tahara's body, Shogo grabbed the railing that led up to the pilothouse and said, "You were merciless, Shuya."

"Yeah." Shuya nodded. "I was."

Once he was up in the pilothouse, there were two more of Shuya's victims, crew members sprawled in the corner. In the dark window were several holes formed either from stray bullets or shots that had torn through the crew members.

The ship passed an island lit up with residential lights (probably Megijima). Shuya wondered whether the gunfire could be heard over there or even further into the sea around them. Well, it wasn't that uncommon to hear sudden gunfire in this country, so he wasn't too worried.

Shogo looked straight ahead. Shuya and Noriko looked in the same direction and saw what looked like a gravel carrier approaching them on their right. Shogo held the steering wheel and shifted the bar next to it methodically.

"I hope you didn't catch a cold," Shogo asked.

"I'm fine."

"And you, Noriko?"

"I'm okay too." Noriko nodded.

Shogo squinted ahead as he said, "I'm sorry. I did the easy work this time." The gravel carrier was approaching.

"That's not true," Shuya responded as his eyes shuttled between Shogo's hands and the ship ahead of them. "I wasn't in any condition to take on Sakamochi. He was armed. You were the right man."

As he kept watch, the carrier loomed larger and larger. But…they managed to skim past each other. The carrier's lights receded.

"Phew." Shogo took a deep breath and then let go of the steering wheel. He began pressing the intricate rows of buttons on the nautical instruments. He gazed at the panel for a while, and after seeing one of the diodes go out, he took the radio transmitter. A voice came through the speaker, "This is the Bisan Seto Inland Sea Traffic Advisory Service Center." That's what it sounded like.

Shogo responded, "This is Defense Patrol Ship DM 245-3568. We need you to confirm our location."

"DM 245-3568, we cannot confirm. Are you having trouble?"

"Our DPS navigation device seems to be broken. We will stop the boat for an hour or so to repair the device. Could you notify the other ships?"

"Yes. We need your present location."

Shogo read off the display on the nautical instrument. Then he ended the transmission.

He was only buying time to move the ship somewhere. Shogo steered the wheel now and made a sharp left turn. Shuya felt the ship rock from the wide turn.

As he cautiously handled the wheel Shogo said, "That bastard Sakamochi realized what was going on. I'm glad I had you guys get on board."

Shuya nodded. Water dripped down from his bangs.

He was right. After Shogo had shot his gun twice into the air, he pressed his fingers against his mouth, signaling Shuya and Noriko, who were both blinking, to stay quiet. He took his map out of his pocket and scribbled on the backside. The note was obscured in the dim light, but they managed to read it. Then Shogo removed their collars. All he used was a wire attached to a transistor—which he had for some reason—a knife, and small screwdriver. And then Shogo took out a simple ladder made of bamboo and rope from his day pack. He scribbled more on the map, "Sneak into the ship they put me on. It'll be nighttime, so you'll be fine. Make your way to the harbor by beach. There'll be a chain tied to the anchor. Tie the rope ladder to it and hold on. Once the anchor comes up, and the ship starts moving, climb up to the deck and hide behind the life preservers on the ship's stern. Then attack when the time's right."

Of course...it was no easy feat holding onto this flimsy rope ladder as the ship sped up, stirred up waves, and dragged them through the sea. It was also hard to reach the deck less than half a meter above the top of the ladder. Without his left arm, Shuya just couldn't do what should have been an easy task. But Noriko managed to lift herself up there despite her wounded hand, then offered a hand to Shuya. Noriko's strength took Shuya by surprise. In any case...they managed to do it.

"But…," Shuya said, "…I wish you'd told us about this earlier."

Shogo returned the wheel to the right and coyly shrugged his shoulders.

"It would have made our actions less natural. Sorry, though."

He let go of the wheel. The black sea spread out in front of them. For the time being, there was no sign of any ship approaching. Shogo then began checking several of the ship's meters.

"It's amazing," Noriko said. "You managed to hack into the government computer system."

"Yeah, really," Shuya agreed. "You were lying about being computer illiterate."

His gaze still fixed ahead, Shogo grinned. "Well, they found out anyway. Anyway, it all ended up working out."

Shogo seemed satisfied with the meter readings and moved away. He walked up to one of the soldiers on the floor. Wondering what he was doing, Shuya and Noriko looked on as Shogo went through his pockets.

"Damn," he said, "So even the Defense Forces aren't smoking now."

He was looking for cigarettes.

He did manage to extract a crumpled pack of Buster from the other soldier's breast pocket. The pack was covered in blood, but he casually pulled out a cigarette, put it in his mouth, and lit it up. He leaned against the side of the helm, and as he squinted his eyes, he exhaled contentedly.

As she watched him Noriko said, "If our group was too large…we wouldn't have been able to escape like this."

Shogo nodded. "That's true. And it had to be at night. But there's no point in going over that. We're alive. Isn't that enough?"

Shuya nodded. "That's right."

"Why don't you two go take a shower," Shogo said, "It's in front of the stairs. It's tiny, but it should have hot water.

You can just steal the soldiers' clothes."

Shuya nodded and put the Ingram down onto the low desk by the wall. He clutched Noriko's shoulder. "Come on, Noriko. You go first. Wouldn't want you to get sick again."

Noriko nodded. They were about to head towards the stairs when Shogo stopped them. "Shuya," he said, "wait, hold on." He rubbed out his cigarette against the bottom of the helm. "First I'll show you how to steer this ship."

Shuya raised his brow. He figured that Shogo would take care of guiding the ship. Come to think of it, Shogo probably wanted to take a shower too. Shuya and Noriko would have to steer the ship then.

Shuya nodded again and returned to the helm with Noriko.

Shogo took another deep breath and lightly tapped on the wheel. "I'm steering the ship manually right now. It's less confusing than having it on auto-pilot. Now this…" Shogo indicated the lever by the helm. "It's like an accelerator and brake. Tilting it forward increases the speed and backwards slows it down. Simple, huh? And over here…" Shogo pointed at the round meter installed right above the wheel. The thin needle was tilted leftward. It was surrounded with numbers and letters indicating directions. "This is a gyro compass. It gives our direction. You see that ocean map?"

Shogo indicated the route they were taking to weave their way through the islands and reach the mainland Honshu from their current position east of Megijima Island. They would be best off, he said, landing on some hidden beach in Okayama Prefecture. Then he provided simple instructions for the radar and depth gauge.

He touched his chin. "That's about it for your crash course. That's enough to steer this thing. Now, you always steer right of an oncoming ship. And the other thing is that you can't stop immediately. As you approach the shore you have to slow down well in advance. Got that?"

Shuya raised his brow again. He wondered, why is he advising me about docking too? He continued to nod, though.

Shogo added, "The notes I gave you guys. Do you still have them? It actually has your contact information."

"Yeah...we have them. But...you're coming with us, right? Right?"

Shogo didn't respond immediately to Shuya's question. He took out one of the cigarettes he'd stuffed inside his pocket, put it in his mouth, and lit his lighter. It lit up...but right then Shuya noticed something strange. Shogo's hand holding the lighter was trembling.

Noriko seemed to have noticed too. Her eyes were wide open.

"Shogo—"

"You guys asked me...," Shogo said over Shuya's words, his cigarette dangling from his mouth. His trembling hand tossed the lighter by the helm. He continued, "...to come with you to the U.S." He removed the cigarette from his mouth with his shaking hand and exhaled. "I thought it over. But..." He stopped and put his cigarette in his mouth. He removed it, then he blew out smoke. "It looks like I won't need to answer that anymore."

Suddenly, Shogo's body slid down. His head slumped forward as he fell on his knees.

79

"Shogo!"

Shuya ran over to Shogo and grabbed his right arm and held him up. Noriko also ran over to him and held his left arm from the other side.

Emptied of strength, Shogo's body felt heavy. That was

when Shuya finally realized how Shogo's back was soaked. There was a tiny hole right below his neck. It was Kazuo's shot. The one Kazuo fired at him. Shogo claimed it was nothing. Why...why didn't he treat it immediately!? Or did he know it was fatal? Or...did he delay it so Shuya and Noriko could get aboard?

In their arms, Shogo's body slowly gave way, and he slumped down on his butt.

"I'm sleepy. Let me sleep," he said.

"No, no, no, no!" Shuya screamed. "We'll take you to the nearest hospital!"

"Don't be ridiculous," Shogo laughed and like the two soldiers sprawled in the corner of the room, he lay down on his side.

"Please." Shuya knelt down and touched Shogo's shoulder. "Please get up."

"Shogo." Noriko was crying.

"Noriko!" Shuya scolded her. Noriko looked over at Shuya. "Don't cry! Shogo can't die!"

"Shuya. Don't get angry with her over nothing," Shogo kindly admonished him, "You have to be kind to your girl." Then he added. "Besides, sorry, but I'm going."

Shogo's face became increasingly pale. In contrast, the scar above his left brow was dark red now like a centipede.

"Shogo..."

"I-I-I'm still not sure...," Shogo said. His head began to tremble. But he continued moving his lips. "...whether I'm going to join you. B-b-but I-I w-want to th-thank you guys."

Shuya shook his head over and over. He stared at Shogo. He couldn't say anything.

Shogo raised his trembling right hand. "G-g-goodbye."

Shuya held his hand.

"N-N-Noriko, you too."

Holding back her tears, Noriko held Shogo's hand.

Shuya now realized Shogo was dying. No, he had already known, but now he was accepting it. What else could he do? He tried to come up with something to say. He knew what it was.

"Shogo."

Shogo's eyes drowsily shifted over from Noriko to Shuya.

"I'll tear this fucking country down for you! I'll tear it down, goddamn it!"

Shogo grinned. His hand fell from Noriko's hand onto his chest. Noriko followed his hand, and squeezed it.

Shogo closed his eyes. He seemed to be grinning again. Then he said, "I-I-I-I-I told you, Sh-Sh-Sh-Shuya. Y-y-you d-don't h-have to d-d-do th-th-that. F-f-forget about i-i-it. You t-t-two sh-sh-should just try t-to l-l-live, p-p-please. I-i-just like w-w-we d-did here, t-t-trust each other. A-a-all right?"

Shogo said this much and took a long, deep breath. His eyes remained shut.

"That's what I want," he declared.

That was it. Shogo stopped breathing. The dim yellow light falling from the ceiling of the pilothouse shined against his pale face. He seemed at ease.

"Shogo!" Shuya yelled. He still had more to say. "You'll see Keiko! You'll be happy with her! You're—"

It was too late. Shogo couldn't hear anything anymore. But his face just looked so damned peaceful.

"Damn it." Shuya's lips trembled along with his words. "Damn it."

Holding Shogo's hands, Noriko was crying.

Shuya also put his hand on Shogo's thick hand. A thought occurred to him. He searched through Shogo's pockets and found it...the red bird call. He pressed it into Shogo's right hand and closed his hands over it so he could hold it. Shuya then finally burst into tears.

Epilogue

UMEDA, OSAKA

In the bustling crowd at the Umeda-Osaka train terminal, each pedestrian busy for whatever reason, Shuya Nanahara (Male Student No. 15, Third Year Class B, Shiroiwa Junior High School) heard the announcement, "We have this report on the recent murder of a Program Instructor in Kagawa Prefecture," as he was stepping off one of the pair of escalators that ran along the station's wide stairways. He gently squeezed Noriko Nakagawa's (Female Student No. 15, same school) shoulder with his right hand and stopped.

On the giant TV screen as high as the escalator, there was a large, closeup image of a reporter in his fifties, his hair parted in a 7:3 ratio.

Shuya and Noriko walked up to the screen together. It was Monday, past 6 p.m., so there were students and salarymen in business suits waiting around the area. Shuya and Noriko were no longer wearing their school uniforms. Shuya wore a pair of jeans, a print shirt, and a denim jacket. Noriko also wore jeans along with a dark-green polo shirt and a light-gray windbreaker on top. (They did however keep their sneakers, washing them after the game before they wore them again.) Shuya's neck was bandaged, but it was hidden by the jacket collar, and Noriko's left cheek was covered with a large bandage, but it was obscured by her black leather baseball cap that she kept pulled low over her eyes. She still dragged her right leg, but it wasn't so conspicuous anymore. Since his left arm was still paralyzed, Shuya shifted the bag strap against his left shoulder with his right hand.

Shogo's notes indicated the name of a doctor and his address in the city of Kobe. A small clinic in the back streets of the city, probably similar to the one Shogo's father ran. The doctor who still seemed to be in his twenties warmly welcomed them and treated their wounds.

"Shogo's father was a senior of my dad's in medical school. I owe a lot to that man too, though," the doctor said. He seemed to be well-connected, and the following day, that is, yesterday, he arranged their escape from the country. "Shogo had me hold onto some money just in case of an emergency. We'll use that." They would first take a fishing boat from a small fishing village in Wakayama Prefecture into the Pacific Ocean, and then transfer to another boat in the Democratic Nation of the Korean Peninsula. "You won't have any problems getting from Korea to America. It'll be the transfer from that first boat that's going to be hard." The doctor voiced his concern, but Shuya and Noriko really had no other choice.

Noriko called home before they left the doctor's house today. She first called a close friend from another class, having her relay a message to her family to call the doctor's house from a payphone. It was a precaution against wiretapping. Shuya left Noriko alone for a while, but he could hear Noriko's sobbing from the hall where the phone was. Shuya himself didn't contact the Charity House. He thanked Ms. Anno and bade her goodbye in his heart. He did the same with Kazumi Shintani.

The reporter continued, "Due to the Defense Forces helicopter's dispersal of poison gas over Kagawa Prefecture's Okishima Island, where this Program was held, the inspection of the site was delayed. However two days after the incident, the inspection was finally held this afternoon. We now know two students are missing."

The image changed. A zoom-lens camera from sea captured police officials and soldiers inspecting the island where Shuya and the others had fought for their lives. There were piles of corpses. For a split second, Shuya managed to make out two bodies. There were Yukie Utsumi and Yoshitoki Kuninobu, on the edge of a black pile of school coats and sailor suits, facing the camera. Despite the dispersal of poison gas, their faces managed to stay unharmed because they had died indoors. Shuya clenched his right fist.

"The missing students are Shuya Nanahara and Noriko Nakagawa, third-year students of Shiroiwa Junior High School in Kagawa Prefecture." The screen now displayed large closeup photos side by side. They were the same photos used for their student I.D. cards. Shuya shifted his eyes, but no one in the crowd staring at the screen seemed to notice them.

An image of an empty coast right beside a mountain appeared. As the camera zoomed in, a small military-colored patrol ship which had run ashore appeared, and was now being examined by police officials and soldiers on the beach. This segment was shot immediately after the incident became known, so it was less recent.

"On the early morning of the twenty-fourth, the Kagawa Prefecture Program Instructor Sakamochi's patrol ship was found on the shores of Ushimado-cho in Okayama Prefecture. Instructor Sakamochi and nine Special Defense Forces soldiers, including Private Tokihiko Tahara were discovered along with the Program's winner, Shogo Kawada." Sakamochi's closeup photo appeared. He had long hair. "Suspecting there was a conflict, the police and Defense Forces officials proceeded to investigate. Authorities now believe the two missing students from today's report may provide the crucial link to the incident. They are currently searching..."

The reporter continued, but Shuya was too preoccupied with the following to listen.

It was a short clip subtitled, "Winner Shogo Kawada—Found Dead." Under normal circumstances, they would have only shown a generic subtitle, "Male Student Winner," and the short segment would have only been broadcast on the Kagawa Prefecture local news. Shuya and Noriko watched the news at the Kobe doctor's house several times, but they only showed Shogo's photo. This was the first time they saw this clip.

Held between the soldiers, Shogo stared into the camera. Then—

At the end of the clip, which lasted approximately ten seconds, he grinned and raised his right fist with his thumb pointing up.

The crowd staring at the screen sounded dismayed. They probably thought Shogo was proud about his victory.

But of course that wasn't it at all, Shuya thought as he watched the screen return to the image of the reporter.

Was it a message to him and Noriko? Did he already know he was going to die when he stood in front of the government camera? Or was it just a display of his unique sense of irony?

I'll never know. Just as Shogo once said.

Then Shuya and Noriko's closeup photos were displayed again.

"Any sightings should be reported to..."

"Let's go Noriko. We have to hurry," Shuya whispered. He took her left hand with his right hand. They turned away from the screen and began walking.

"Shogo told me...," Noriko said as they walked, holding hands, "before you came back...when you were with Yukie's group, he told me something."

Shuya tilted his head and looked at Noriko.

Noriko looked up at Shuya. Her eyes covered by the brim of her hat were moist. "He said he was glad to have such good friends."

Shuya looked up and nodded. He just nodded.

They let a group of six or seven students pass by, and then they started walking again. Shuya said, "Noriko. We'll always be together. I promised Shogo."

Noriko seemed to be nodding.

"For now we escape...but some day I'm going to tear this country down. I'm still keeping the promise I made to Shogo. I want to tear it down for Shogo, for you, for Yoshitoki, for everyone. Will you help me when the time comes?"

Noriko squeezed Shuya's hand and replied assertively, "Of course, I will."

They departed from the crowd. They stood in front of a ticket dispenser. Noriko looked up at the display above the ticket machine, took out some change, and counted it out. Then she stood in line in front of the ticket machine to buy their tickets.

Shuya stood still, waiting for Noriko's turn to come. It came immediately. She put the coins into the coin slot.

Shuya casually looked over to his left.

He squinted his eyes. There was the entrance to the station concourse, and he could make out the Osaka highrise district, just beyond the road where taxis and cars were passing each other. A tall, uniformed man emerged from this background, heading straight towards them. He skillfully dodged the flow of pedestrians and made his way toward Shuya.

It was a policeman's uniform. There was a gold peach insignia shining at the center of his cap.

With his right hand Shuya slowly reached for the Beretta M92F tucked in the back of his jeans as he looked for an escape route. There was a road at the entrance opposite the policeman. If they could get there, they could grab a cab—

Shuya whispered to Noriko, who returned with their tickets, "Forget about the train, Noriko."

Noriko understood. She quickly turned and opened her eyes wide after seeing the policeman.

"That way," Shuya said. The policeman came

running at them.

"We have to run, Noriko! Run as fast as you can!" he said. As they dashed out, Shuya thought, hey, doesn't that sound familiar.

He glanced behind him. The police officer held out his gun. Shuya pulled out his Beretta. The officer shot immediately. BANG BANG. Two sweeping shots, but luckily no one in the crowd, including Shuya and Noriko, was hit. There were cries though, as some fell to the ground for cover, while others having no idea where the gunfire came from scattered in random directions. The officer, his gun down, ran toward them again, but then crashed into a fat woman carrying groceries, and clumsily fell. The woman fell too, and her bag of vegetables for dinner tumbled and slid on the floor.

That was all Shuya saw. He was looking ahead now.

As he ran next to Noriko, a thought suddenly occurred to him. The screaming, their hasty footsteps, and the officer warning them to stop all receded as his mind was occupied with this thought.

It might have been inappropriate. And besides...he'd ripped it off. Oh, man.

But still he thought this:

Together Noriko we'll live with the sadness. I'll love you with all the madness in my soul. Someday girl I don't know when we're gonna get to that place. Where we really want to go and we'll walk in the sun. But till then tramps like us baby we were born to run.

The screaming and yelling swelled back, returning with the sound of Noriko's heavy breathing and his heart thumping.

We're still on the run. That's for sure.

Right on. This time we're on.

And we won't stop till we win.

Now, once again, "2 students remaining."
But of course they're part of you now.

ABOUT THE AUTHOR

Koushun Takami was born in 1969 in Amagasaki near Osaka and grew up in Kagawa Prefecture of Shikoku, where he currently resides. After graduating from Osaka University with a degree in literature, he dropped out of Nihon University's liberal arts correspondence-course program. From 1991 to 1996 he worked for the prefectural news company *Shikoku Shinbun*, reporting on various fields, including politics, police reports, and economics. Although he has an English teaching certificate, he has yet to visit the United States.

Battle Royale, completed after Takami left the news company, was rejected in the final round of a literary competition sponsored by a major publisher due to the critical controversy it provoked among jury members. With its publication in Japan in 1999, though, *Battle Royale* received widespread support, particularly from young readers, and became a bestseller. In 2000, *Battle Royale* was serialized as a comic and made into a feature film.

Mr. Takami is currently working on his second novel.

ABOUT THE TRANSLATOR

Yuji Oniki is a writer and translator.

01
02
03
04
05
06
07
A
B
C
D
E
F
G
H
I
J
Exposed Rocks
Small Shinto Shrine
Northern Mount
(Viewing Pla
Hill
House with Well
Farmhouse
House with
Concrete Wa
Hill
Sch
Farm Coo
Southern Mountain Peak
Hill
Sandy Beach
Reef
0
0.5
1 km